ARKANSAS DUCK HUNTER'S ALMANAC

To Buzz Roberts

Good Hunting!

2/12/98

2/12/98

RICHARD E. BISHOP
'61

ARKANSAS DUCK HUNTER'S ALMANAC

STEVE BOWMAN AND STEVE WRIGHT

OZARK DELTA PRESS, PUBLISHER

For Casey, John and Melissa, may they grow to know what their fathers love about ducks and swamps.

First printing January 1998.

Printed in the United States of America by magnaIV, Little Rock, Ark.

Layout and design by Walker Creative Inc., Fayetteville, Ark.

Cover photo by Steve Bowman.

Arkansas duck stamps courtesy Larry Grisham, Grisham's Art, Jonesboro, Ark.

Bishop/Queeny Christmas cards courtesy Carl Hunter and Richard E. Bishop, LTD., Ambler, Penn.

Claypool's Reservoir, pages 2-3, photo by George Purvis, circa 1950, near Weiner.

Inside photos by Steve Bowman and Steve Wright, except where otherwise noted.

Library of Congress Catalog Card Number: 97-92574

ISBN 0-9638832-2-4

Ozark Delta Press Inc.
P.O. Box 4653
Fayetteville, AR 72702-4653
501-582-4696

READ THIS FIRST

First of all, an apology is in order. When we began this project two years ago, we thought we had a grasp of the rich duck hunting tradition in Arkansas. In reality, we were as green as the timber that has made Arkansas duck hunting famous. Therefore, this is the first in what we hope will be a series of books on the subject. Its culmination will be a definitive history of Arkansas duck hunting. This book barely skims the surface. Our apologies are directed toward the people who have played a significant role in Arkansas duck hunting, but lack of time or space prevented their inclusion here. As we have researched this book, one story has led to another and another and another. The stories of people like Wayne and Rick Hampton and J.I. Seay at Stuttgart deserve to be included here and will be in the future. Consider this a starting point.

We also realize this first book will spark some interest from people previously unaware of our project. We encourage you to call us or write us. An important generation of duck hunters is dying day-by-day. Our ultimate goal is to record as much history as possible so future generations can fully appreciate the great tradition of Arkansas duck hunting.

ACKNOWLEDGEMENTS

The driving force behind this publication was the number of people who were willing to help. At the top of that list are Biff Morgan of Little Rock and David Perdue of Pine Bluff. As Morgan said more than once, "I'm having more fun doing this than you are." Keep in mind that, in the name of research, we got to duck hunt in all areas of Arkansas during the 1996-97 season. So we've had more than our share of fun. But Morgan and Perdue never tired of helping us any way they could. Their contributions show up here in the form of photographs, stories and deep background. As their wives will attest, they've got duck fever worse than most.

Arkansas Game and Fish Commission director Steve N. Wilson and Game and Fish Foundation director Steve Smith encouraged us to take on this project, and they were always available to share knowledge and advice.

This book would not have been possible without an Arkansas Game and Fish Commission payback grant presented to Steve Wright, which allowed him to devote most of his time to this project in 1997. A special thank you to the members of the Commission who approved it — Bill Bridgforth, Kirk Dupps, Rick Evans, Jim Hinkle, Marion McCollum, Dr. James Moore Jr. and Witt Stephens Jr.

The following people also played important roles in this book:

— Bob Lutgen and Wally Hall, for allowing the use of photographs and articles previously published in the *Arkansas Democrat-Gazette*. Others at the *Democrat-Gazette* who have helped make this book possible include Estel Jeffery, Rick McFarland, Matt Jones and Glen Chase.

— Billy Jeter of Pine Bluff, for introducing us to Morgan and Perdue, among others, and for constant encouragement.

— Tim Walker at Walker Creative Inc. in Fayetteville, who has survived working on another project with Steve Wright. The first was *Ozark Trout Tales*. Walker was again reminded of the horrors of working with Wright, and again emerged with a sense of humor bent, but not broken. Thanks also to Daniel Bertalotto, Scott Mattson and Neil Shipley for their fine work at Walker Creative.

— Tom Ewart of TE Photography in Fayetteville, who spent weeks scanning maps and photographs. He did amazing work in making some worn old photos printable again.

— George Purvis of Little Rock, Steve Bowman's longtime Sunday school teacher and mentor, whose place in Arkansas hunting and fishing has helped shape its history. His photographs and experiences were vital.

— Mark Blackwood in Fayetteville, who did everything from hunting ducks to reading copy. Most importantly, he provided more encouragement to Wright and support for this project than anyone will ever know, including him.

ACKNOWLEDGEMENTS

— Tim Ernst in Fayetteville, the man behind the Ozark Highlands Trail and an accomplished photographer and self-publisher, who is always there with advice and assistance on everything from computers to barcodes.

— All the people at the Arkansas Game and Fish Commission, from biologists to secretaries, who answered questions and pointed us in the right direction.

— Barry "Kingpin" Thomas, Mike Suchan, Grant Tennille, Clay Henry and especially Jim "The Midnight Rider" Harris, all of whom spent time reading and editing copy and now know more about duck hunting than they ever wanted to know.

— Stephanie Meehan at EdiType Business Services in Fayetteville, who proofread, made copies, coordinated corrections and also knows more about duck hunting than she cares to.

— Bill Brewer of Paragould for use of Buffalo Island photos and a collection of *Arkansas Game and Fish* magazines.

— Drew Baker of Maumelle, for providing the "Mother Duck," a 24-foot recreational vehicle that has made two tours of Arkansas duck hunting areas with Baker at the wheel.

— Barry McFarland of Hornersville, Mo., a gold mine of information on Big Lake and duck call making, who provided some great old photos in addition to his knowledge.

— Marion, J.W. and Bud McCollum and Pat Johnston in Stuttgart, for historical perspective and direction in the Rice and Duck Capital of the World.

— Kim, Roger, John and Mike Ward of War Eagle Boats for their hospitality in south Arkansas.

— Michael Dabrishus, director of the University of Arkansas Library special collections in Fayetteville, who went out of his way to help with old maps and photos; and Eric Gorder, of UA computer services, who scanned those materials.

— The staff at the Arkansas History Commission, who led two blind hogs to many acorns of duck hunting history.

— Roy Hunter in Pine Bluff and Jim Rebbe in St. Louis. They provided enough information on Edgar Queeny and Wingmead to do another book.

— Carl Hunter in Little Rock, who became a good friend in the course of providing invaluable information about almost everything in the Arkansas outdoors.

— Frank C. Bellrose in Havana, Ill., who has devoted a lifetime to waterfowl research. He never tired of answering our questions about ducks in Arkansas.

— Tom Barre in Pocahontas has compiled a huge file of Arkansas duck hunting history and willingly shared it for use here.

— Barbara Ekenseair in Little Rock for typing and moral support.

— Ginnie Wright in Fayetteville for patience, patience, patience.

— As we traveled the state, we called on many old friends for help, and they often introduced us to people who have now become friends in the course of sharing a love of Arkansas duck hunting. Those friends, old and new, include: in Batesville, Blair Arnold, Donald Coleman and Rocky Willmuth; in El Dorado, Danny Layne; in Helena, Blanche Lambert Lincoln; in Hope, Bill Butler, Mary Ann Butler, Kenneth Paddie, Wendell Light and Charlie Walker; in Marion, Lawson Anderson, Fred Swan Sr. and Fred Swan Jr.; in Nashville, Johnny Wilson; in Newport, Kaneaster Hodges Jr.; in Slovak, Jeryl Jones and Frankie Lisko; in Memphis, Dr. Wayne Capooth, Billy Hughes, Scott Liles and Terry McFarland.

About the Authors

Steve Bowman has been outdoor editor of the *Arkansas Democrat-Gazette* since 1988. His freelance work has appeared in *Southern Outdoors, Bassmaster* and *Arkansas Sportsman*. Bowman was born in Jonesboro, graduated from Ouachita Baptist University and lives in Little Rock.

Steve Wright previously wrote and published *Ozark Trout Tales, A Fishing Guide for the White River System*. He worked as a sports writer for the *Northwest Arkansas Times, Arkansas Gazette, Arkansas Democrat* and *Arkansas Democrat-Gazette* before concentrating on outdoors writing. He was the outdoors editor of the *Northwest Arkansas Times* for six years. His freelance outdoors writing has appeared in *Outdoor Life, Trout* and *Fishing World* magazines and the *Arkansas-Democrat Gazette*. Wright was born in Batesville, graduated from the University of Arkansas and lives in Fayetteville.

TABLE OF CONTENTS

Page 16

Page 39

Page 52

Acknowledgements **7**
Foreword **14**

CHAPTER 1
Mallard Mecca

The epicenter of duck hunting in America **17**
Timeline — Arkansas duck hunting **18**
Nature set the perfect table for ducks **21**
Rice a bonanza for ducks, hunters **24**
Public cried out for land to hunt ducks **26**
Water critical element for the future **29**
A gallery of old duck hunters **30-33**
Portraits of a duck hunter's best friend **34-35**
Presidential duck hunting **36-37**

CHAPTER 2
St. Francis River

The Great Swamp **39**
Timeline — The history of Big Lake **40**
Few people injured in New Madrid quakes **41**
Beckhart made a living from Big Lake **42**
The battle over Big Lake **44**
Rules of the Big Lake Shooting Club **47**
Taming the Great Swamp **48**
McFarland carries on tradition of duck call-making **49**
Big Lake produced World War I hero **50**
Horner recalls days of market hunting **51**
Blinds still standing tall **53**
Big Lake WMA **55**
Blankenship grew up hunting ducks on Big Lake **55**
Railroads key to exploring swamp **56**
The Buffalo Island Hunting and Fishing Club **57**
De shootinest gent'man **58**
St. Francis Sunken Lands WMA **59**
Baiting common practice at early clubs **59**
History of the Warrior Hunting Club **60**

TABLE OF CONTENTS

Page 73

CHAPTER 3
Black River

Where the Delta meets the Ozarks **63**
Timeline — A history of Black River **64**
Coleman recalls Black River forest **66**
New era brings new attitude toward game laws **68**
Dave Donaldson/Black River WMA **69**
Donaldson counted millions of ducks **70**
Shirey Bay-Rainey Brake big timber stands tall **73**
Shirey Bay-Rainey Brake WMA **74**
Grammer calls on years of experience **75**
Getting the best results from steel shot **78**

Page 80

CHAPTER 4
Weiner

Duck Capital II **81**
Timeline — Poinsett County **82**
Craft land continues to contribute **83**
Waterfowl wonderland on live TV **84**
Purvis has observed changing times **88**
Ruesewald wouldn't leave Swan Pond **90**
Earl Buss/Bayou DeView WMA **93**
State duck stamp a story of success **94**
Pickle was pure Arkansas backwoods **96**

Page 107

CHAPTER 5
Cache River

Save the Cache **99**
Timeline — Battle for the Cache River **100**
River bends hold key to Black Swamp **100**
Rex Hancock/Black Swamp WMA **101**
Cache River site of landmark battle **102**
Old cypress trees are like old people **106**
Be prepared to fight your way in here **108**
Dagmar WMA **109**
Learning how to change duck tunes **110**
Cache River NWR **111**

TABLE OF CONTENTS

CHAPTER 6

Stuttgart

Rice and Duck Capital of the World **113**
Timeline — History of Stuttgart **114**
History of World's Championship Duck Calling Contest . . . **116**
The music and mania of duck calling **118**
Major development in calling ducks **120**
Johnston is first lady of duck calling **122**
Richenback duck calls are rich in tone **123**
The birth of commercial duck hunting **126**
Green-tree reservoirs began on Grand Prairie **128**
Queeny's place on Grand Prairie fit for a king **130**
Prairie Wings continues to raise funds for ducks **132**
Bishop always welcome at Wingmead **134**
Pulitzers brought attention to Stuttgart **136**
Rollie Remmel is King Duck in Arkansas **138**

CHAPTER 7

White River

An inland sea **141**
Timeline — The White River **142**
Boat ride from hell usually worth it **143**
Henry Gray/Hurricane Lake WMA **143**
Bald Knob NWR **144**
Deer stand duck hunt opens some eyes **145**
White duck had big following in Hurricane **146**
Meacham killed ducks to save rice crop **148**
Wilcox Lake known round the world **152**
White River NWR **155**
Flight ducks are late season bonanza **157**
Leading ducks into decoys on a string **160**
A White River cabin boat trip in 1892 . . . . **163**

Page 121

Page 136

Page 145

TABLE OF CONTENTS

Page 172

CHAPTER 8

Bayou Meto

The Scatters 173
Timeline — History of Bayou Meto 174
Bayou Meto WMA 175
Bryant always willing to share The Scatters 178
Halowell Reservoir changes with time 181
Tent Camp preserves traditions of the past 183
LaCotts has ducks thick as gnats in a swill pail 187

Page 190

CHAPTER 9

Arkansas River Valley

Central Flyway turn lane 191
Timeline — Arkansas River Valley 191
Galla Creek WMA 192
Keeping up with ducks in the corridor 193
Nimrod WMA 194
Harris Brake WMA 195
Cold conditions make hunting hot 196
Enjoying the beauty of Petit Jean 198
Petit Jean WMA 199
Big river ducks drawn to little magnets 200
Bell Slough WMA 201
Ed Gordon/Point Remove WMA 201
Food, shelter keeps ducks lingering 202
The treasured jewelry of duck hunting 204

Page 206

CHAPTER 10

South Arkansas

From the Mississippi to the Red 207
Timeline — South Arkansas 208
Swamp holds a devilish attraction 209
Seven Devils WMA 210
The 8:30 a.m. flight will arrive on time 211
Cut-Off Creek WMA 212
Where the Delta meets the piney woods 213
Overflow NWR 214

TABLE OF CONTENTS

Felsenthal NWR **214**
A mixing pot of migrating ducks **215**
Beryl Anthony/Lower Ouachita WMA **216**
Bois D'Arc among best WMAs **217**
Bois D'Arc WMA **218**
A way station for Red River ducks **219**
Sulphur River WMA **220**
Pond Creek NWR **220**
Arkansas' ultimate step back in time **221**

Appendix
Arkansas duck seasons, 1915 through 1997 . . . . **224**
Duck migration corridors **226**
Mallard migration corridors **227**
A collection of Arkansas duck calls **228**
World's Championship Duck Calling Contest, 1936-97 . . . . **248**
Arkansas land in North American Waterfowl Plan **251**

Bibliography **252**
Index **253**
Resources **255**

List of Maps
Natural divisions of Arkansas **20**
Arkansas' major rivers and streams **22**
Great Swamp, 1838 . . . . **38**
Black River, 1955 AGFC **79**
White River, Batesville to Clarendon, 1955 AGFC **147**
Early railroad map, 1884 . . . . **162**
New Map of Arkansas, 1836 steamboat routes **170**
Lower Arkansas, White rivers, 1955 AGFC **189**
Southwest Arkansas, 1955 AGFC **222**

Page 214

Page 222

Page 228

Foreword

THE RELIGION KNOWN AS DUCK HUNTING IN ARKANSAS

The flashlight confirmed Greg Brown's fear. A sawbriar was stuck in the cornea of his left eye, near the middle of the pupil. In the predawn darkness of Bayou Meto, as he was thrashing his way through knee-deep water and thick brush, he never saw the sticker-covered vine as it whipped into his eye.

Jimmy Barnett volunteered to become the "instant ophthalmologist." As Brown kept his eyelids pulled apart, two other duck hunters shined flashlights on the triangular thorn that had pierced a soft contact lens before lodging in his cornea. Barnett pulled the tweezers from his Swiss Army knife. With a steady hand, he plucked out the thorn. Brown never considered leaving Bayou Meto. The eye pain and the loss of a contact lens didn't prevent him from killing the first two mallards he shot at that morning.

■ Donald Coleman's black Labrador retriever, Buster, had already fetched more than a dozen dead and crippled ducks. But it was suddenly apparent that Buster wasn't feeling so well. After one more long retrieve and with no dry ground in sight, Buster let loose a stream of diarrhea, while bowed up in Coleman's johnboat. Coleman, seated at the boat's stern, expressed disgust, but not anger. Even after the dog coated the stock of his master's Benelli shotgun, Coleman didn't get mad. While holding the barrel of the unloaded gun, he swished it clean in the water beside the boat. Both man and dog continued to hunt that morning.

■ The three hunters started scrambling when they realized their johnboat had come loose from the bungee cord that held it to the ladder of their blind. The steady breeze blowing from behind the blind — the same breeze that had helped put ducks fluttering into the decoys in front of them that morning — was now pushing their boat away. The duck blind was on a tiny island of flooded timber in the overflow of Black River. It stood six feet over the surface of 10-foot-deep water.

While standing at the top of the wooden ladder leading to the blind, I leaned hard on a willow limb that bent down to the boat, momentarily halting its escape. But the branch wanted to pop back up to its natural position, so I leaned harder. With a loud crack, the limb snapped, and I took a December swan dive into Black River. But at least I had found the solution to our problem of retrieving the boat — backstroke, in neoprene waders and Columbia quad parka. Billy Shelton, Donald Coleman and I needed one more duck each to fill our limits. I insisted we stay until we'd done that, and I shivered until we did.

Shelton called the secretary at his dental office that day to report he would be late for his first appointment, saying, "We had a boating accident." As he ended the cellular phone call, he looked at me and said, "Well, it was an accident, and it did involve a boat."

One helluva lot of suffering goes on during duck season in Arkansas. But until spending the entire 1996-97 season traveling the state, I didn't realize the depth of the pain. The three incidents described previously occurred during that season.

Arkansas weather alone can be insufferable. One Friday morning in January we swatted mosquitoes and watched for cottonmouth snakes during a hunt near Carlisle. A week later, we broke inch-thick ice to reach a flooded timber hunting spot in the Felsenthal National Wildlife Refuge, near the Louisiana border. A few weeks before, we dodged a tornado at Jackson Point along the Mississippi River.

All this was done in the name of research. Steve Bowman and I were determined to experience the highs and lows of Arkansas duck hunting in as many different places as possible. The mosquitoes, briars, ice, wet clothes, high winds and sick dogs are among the highs of the sport. They serve as bookmarks in the chapters of duck seasons we compile in our lives. A duck hunter knows few lows when the season is open.

It's the non-hunting friends, family and particularly spouses of duck hunters who experience the lows. Spouses may claim that duck hunting season in Arkansas puts them through more pain than can be imagined by any eye-poked, winter-swimming, dog-crapped-on duck hunter.

"Duck hunting is a disease," my own

mother said, when first told of the plans for this book. The tone in her voice and the disgust in her pronunciation of "dis-ease" were the unmistakable sounds of a woman who has been married to a duck hunter. That man was my father. Duck hunting didn't cause their divorce, but let's just say it didn't help their marriage.

"It's madness," another woman said. "I've never seen otherwise intelligent, frugal men throw so much money at so little opportunity."

If you look at the 30- to 60-day seasons and three- to six-duck daily bag limits of recent years, that may seem like "so little opportunity." Compared with Arkansas' fishing season that stays open all year long and the archery deer hunting season that lasts five months, the chance to hunt ducks comes and goes as quickly as a Grand Prairie thunderstorm. And that's just the point. Duck season in Arkansas has the intensity of a major storm. Some would say tornado.

The season is short enough that hunters can build up vacation time and sick leave in order to hunt ducks every day possible. I know one man who, for over two decades, quit his job every year as duck season started and found a new job after the season ended. There are many more like him. This is how one man described his good fortune in being laid-off his job and drawing unemployment through an entire duck season: "It was like getting paid to guide yourself."

Time of year adds to this intensity. Duck season falls within the Thanksgiving-Christmas-New Year's framework when many of us overindulge. We do this while promising to change and "act right" as soon as the calendar flips. Duck hunters generally make their New Year's resolutions near the end of January, when the hunting season ends, rather than on New Year's Day.

In a story for *Sports Afield* magazine, entitled "The Way Home," Thomas McGuane noted how our lives today are "extremely thin on ceremony, religious ceremony, family ceremony." He wrote of how the "indoctrination of one generation by another is at best a paltry matter."

Killing your first duck is a religious ceremony in Arkansas. If you've forgotten that day, you can bet your father hasn't. It's during duck hunts, and particularly at private duck clubs, where young boys first see how their fathers move among other men. Not how they act at work or at church or at home being "dad," but how they really are. And it's during that "little opportunity" of duck season, when young boys learn to move comfortably among older men.

If you doubt that duck hunting is one of the last bastions of ceremony and the rites of manhood in Arkansas, turn to Chapter 8 and read how the men at Tent Camp worship duck season.

Rollie Remmel poured coffee for his three companions as they sat in a duck blind near Carlisle one morning.

"My wife once told me there's nothing women do together that has the camaraderie of a duck hunt," said Remmel.

It's within that camaraderie where you ultimately find the essence of duck hunting. Rob Reiner's 1986 movie *Stand By Me* opens with a scene from a treehouse where four 12-year-old boys are smoking cigarettes, playing cards and telling dirty jokes. The movie's themes of friendship and manhood are woven through a one-day trip to the woods in search of a body.

The movie is a flashback to the youth of a character played as an adult by Richard Dreyfuss. The story ends with Dreyfuss, a writer, typing these words into his computer: "I never had any friends later on like the ones I had when I was twelve. Jesus, does anyone?"

Yes, duck hunters do have friends like that. For one short season each year, they get to enjoy everything that made them happy as kids — tromping through mud puddles; camping out; smoking, cussing and telling dirty jokes in the treehouse — all done with a dog at their side, ever eager for the next adventure.

Duck hunting is the fountain of youth in Arkansas. Amen.

— Steve Wright
December 1997

Mallard Mecca

ARKANSAS HAS BEEN CALLED THE EPICENTER OF DUCK HUNTING IN AMERICA, AND FOR GOOD REASON

"Of all I had seen America it (Arkansas) was the one which pleased me most; ...I shall never forget the happy days I passed there, where many a true heart beats under a coarse frock or leather hunting-shirt."

Friederich Gerstacker, 1854
"Wild Sports of the Far West"

Dallas Cowboys owner Jerry Jones says that his duck hunting club near Stuttgart is where he made the final decision to select UCLA quarterback Troy Aikman with the Cowboys' No. 1 pick in the 1989 NFL draft.

When General John J. Pershing announced America's greatest heroes of World War I, the fourth name on the list was Herman Davis of Manila. Davis was known as a duck hunter and fisherman; he had never mentioned any of his war experiences before Pershing's announcement. It's said Davis recounted his World War I heroics only twice; both times were to close friends while in duck blinds on Big Lake.

◄ More mallard ducks winter in Arkansas than any place else in the world, although they aren't usually as concentrated as in this 1950s photo from Claypool's Reservoir.

Arkansas' reputation as the duck hunting capital is built on flooded green timber.

It's difficult to separate duck hunting from anything connected with Arkansas.

The first humans to set foot in Arkansas were duck hunters. Archeological studies of Paleo-Indian mounds near Big Lake in the state's northeast corner revealed more bones from mallards than any other bird.

Duck hunting remains just as important for today's Arkansas residents, too. In 1997, when *The Wall Street Journal* published a story about how duck hunting was the prestigious business trip of the '90s, naturally part of its focus had to be on Arkansas and Stuttgart, the "Rice and Duck Capital of the World."

As you will see in the following chapters, the entire story of Arkansas — geography, history, business, agriculture, socio-economics and politics — can be told through duck hunting,

That story begins with the landscape. Arkansas has within its borders 8 million acres of the 24 million-acre Mississippi River Alluvial Plain, which is better known as the Delta. No other state has more Delta land.

In terms of drainage area, the Mississippi is the third-largest river in the world. At one time, the huge floodplain that stretches from Cairo, Ill., to the Gulf of Mexico was one vast bottomland hardwood forest that absorbed the rages of the river.

While the early white settlers generally found these dark, mosquito-infested swamps uninhabitable, hunters and anglers have been visiting them for more than 200 years. Louisiana now carries the official slogan "Sportsman's Paradise," but in the 19th century, that term was often

used to describe all of the timbered bottomlands in the Delta.

Black bears that roamed the bottoms gave Arkansas its first state slogan, "The Bear State," and its early reputation as a place to hunt. It was big game, like bears, that attracted those hunters, who took advantage of the thick waterfowl flocks whenever they needed fresh meat. German writer Friederich Gerstacker tromped through the swamps in the mid 1800s and wrote of his adventures in a book published under the English title *Wild Sports in the Far West.* Gerstacker wrote that he enjoyed the people in Arkansas because they were true hunters, unlike some he met in other states who were already showing the effects of living too close to too many people.

Of course, the same traits that Gerstacker enjoyed were the ones that helped give Arkansas its reputation as a place where the typical man was "sort of a professional hunter who fought for fun and drank by instinct," as the *Arkansas Historical Quarterly* once described it.

The native black bear population was decimated by the early 1900s. The era of market hunting remained in full swing for another decade, but most everyone had noticed the reduced populations of all species of game and fish.

During this time Arkansas got its first national wildlife refuge, and it was duck hunting that led to it. In 1915, only 10 years after President Theodore Roosevelt had begun the concept of "game sanctuaries," President Woodrow Wilson settled a long feud over market hunting of ducks by declaring Big Lake one of the first inland game refuges in the U.S.

It's been said that Arkansas isn't the end of the world, but you can see it from there. While that wasn't intended as a compliment, if you understand Arkansas' hunting and fishing heritage, you can take it that way. Arkansas has always been a jumping-off place for hunters and anglers. In a world that is rapidly running out of "end of the world" real estate, Arkansas still has some of the wild places that have been attracting visitors, like ducks and hunters, for more than a thousand years.

(Above) Duck hunters continue to flock to Arkansas, as they have for hundreds of years. (Right) Arkansas has been called "the heart of the ancestral mallard wintering ground," and continues to attract ducks even though much of the original bottomlands have been cleared for agriculture.

Being at the end of the world does have its advantages. As duck hunter Rex Hancock pointed out in his fight to save the Cache River, "Other states have experienced the ruin resulting from channelization. Arkansas should profit from their mistakes."

Thanks to people like Hancock, Arkansas can still call itself "The Natural

Arkansas Duck Hunting — A Timeline

600 — 800 A.D.	1751	1820	1900	1915
Paleo-Indians make use of the abundant waterfowl, especially mallard ducks, as indicated by the Zebree archeological site at Big Lake near Blytheville.	French explorer Jean Bernard Bossu travels the Arkansas River and notes "game of all kinds is plentiful...wood pigeons, swans, geese, bustards, ducks of all kinds, teals, divers, snipes, water hens...and other birds not known in Europe."	Naturalist John James Audubon explores the Arkansas River and records 50 species of birds, including green-winged teal, pintails and mallards.	Big Lake Shooting Club forms. Although there are no federal or state regulations concerning daily bag limits, Big Lake Shooting Club rules limit members to 100 ducks per day.	Big Lake is declared a national wildlife refuge, Arkansas' first, by President Woodrow Wilson. This action also ends a 15-year feud between market hunters and members of the Big Lake Shooting Club.

State." The remaining natural bottomlands along the Cache River, Bayou DeView and White River are now recognized as "wetlands of international importance." But if ducks didn't winter in Arkansas in the huge numbers they do, there's no doubt those wetlands would no longer exist.

The Arkansas Delta has been described by esteemed Illinois waterfowl biologist Frank Bellrose as "the heart of the ancestral mallard wintering ground." Bellrose, who may have flown more aerial waterfowl surveys than any other man on earth, helped count the 1.1 million mallards here during a typical winter in the 1970s.

All through the up-and-down cycles of duck populations in recent decades, Arkansas has remained the place most closely associated with hunting mallards. From George Wilcox's lake along the White River, which was featured in newspapers around the world in the 1930s, to Wallace Claypool's reservoir, which was showcased on live television in 1956, the thousands of ducks in Arkansas have attracted national attention. And in the years since the first duck calling contest in 1936, Stuttgart has earned its billing as the "Rice and Duck Capital of the World."

Only when you fully understand this duck hunting heritage do you realize how it has become a part of everything in Arkansas.

John Gierach once wrote, "Creeps and idiots cannot conceal themselves for long on a fishing trip." The same can be said for a duck hunting trip.

"There's probably more business done in duck blinds in Arkansas than people would ever believe," said Tommy Hillman, a farmer, avid sportsman and chairman of the board of Riceland Foods Inc. "To build a strong business base, you need to really know who you're doing business with.

"When you hear someone in Arkansas say, 'I wouldn't share a duck blind with him,' that's all you need to know."

Arkansas remains a place where you can get cathead biscuits, sausage gravy and hot coffee in a country store at 4 a.m., so a duck hunter can carry a full stomach of that near-nuclear fuel to the flooded timber on a cold January day.

It's a place where you can drag yourself into a motel office wearing mud-caked camouflage clothes, stare at the clerk with a pair of eyeballs that look like two cherries in a glass of buttermilk and glance back to check on your dog sitting in the passenger seat of the pickup truck — all without causing alarm. Instead of the motel clerk turning on a "No Vacancy" sign as you approach the desk, he'll smile and ask, "Did you get your limit today?"

Arkansas is a place where duck hunting is just as important now as it always has been.

Arkansas Duck Hunting — A Timeline

1936	1956	1972	1990	1997
Thomas Walsh of Greenville, Miss., uses his natural voice and hands, in lieu of a duck call, to win first place and a $6.60 hunting coat in the first "National Duck Calling Contest" at Stuttgart.	On Dec. 23, NBC's "Wide Wide World" features live coverage of a duck hunt at Wallace Claypool's Wild Acres Farm, near Weiner, where 300,000 ducks have congregated on the reservoir.	In July, U.S. Army Corps of Engineers' draglines begin operating round-the-clock channelizing the Cache River, and Rex Hancock of Stuttgart helps organize the Citizens Committee to Save the Cache River Basin.	Ramsar Convention names the lower White River-Cache River-Bayou DeView floodplain a "Wetland of International Importance." It joins the Everglades and Okefenokee Swamp among only eight U.S. areas so designated.	*The Wall Street Journal* notes that duck hunting has become "the prestigious business trip of the '90s, right up there with golf," in a Jan. 10 story that features Wildlife Farms near Stuttgart.

NATURAL DIVISIONS OF ARKANSAS

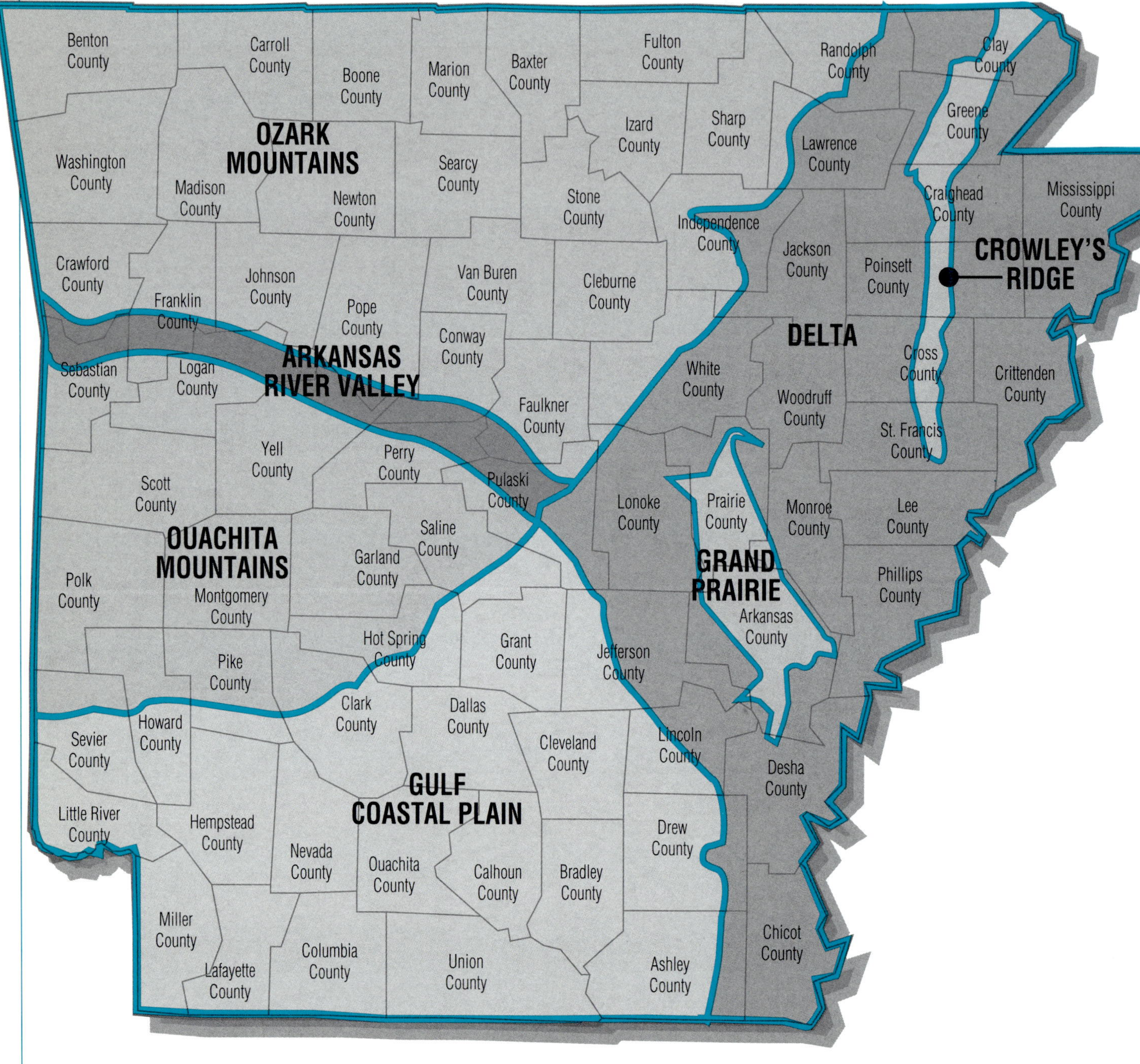

Matt Jones

A mallard hen, sitting quietly in flooded timber, becomes alarmed and quickly lifts off the water, leaving a splash in her path.

Nature set the perfect table for mallards

Mississippi River Alluvial Plain widest between Little Rock and Memphis

When you travel Interstate 40 between Little Rock and Memphis, you are crossing the widest section of the Delta. Combine that with the state's relatively mild winters and you have the reasons Arkansas attracts so many ducks.

The Delta is more correctly called the Mississippi River Alluvial Plain. At one time its 24.2 million acres were covered in forest, from Cairo, Ill., south past New Orleans. This represented the largest forested wetland complex in the U.S., until the draining and ditching began.

Seven states are included in the Delta, but Arkansas contains by far the most Delta land — over 8 million acres.

All North American waterfowl species migrate from breeding grounds in northern states and Canada through four flyways in the U.S. (See migration maps, Appendix.) From east to west, the flyways are Atlantic, Mississippi, Central and Pacific.

The Mississippi Flyway is known as the mallard flyway. In the chart on Page 23, you'll notice that only three of the top 10 mallard harvest states are outside the Mississippi Flyway — California, Washington and Oregon. The 14 states of the Mississippi Flyway accounted for 50% of the annual mallard harvest, based on figures from 1991-95. (The

The Grand Prairie and Crowley's Ridge are regions within the Delta. Both are results of ancient paths taken by the Mississippi, Arkansas and Ohio rivers.

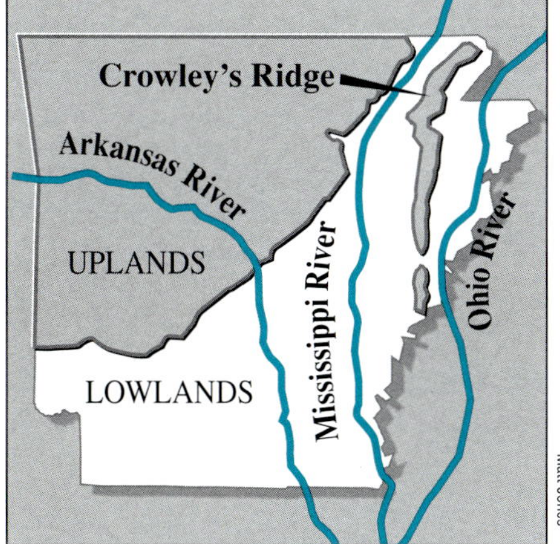

During the Pleistocene Age, which began 1.6 million years ago, the Mississippi River flowed west of Crowley's Ridge.

Mississippi Flyway could also be called the duck hunter's flyway, as it accounted for 44% of the U.S. duck stamp buyers in 1991-95.)

The Mississippi River ranks as the world's third largest in terms of the amount of land it drains (41% of the 48 contiguous states) and annual flow. The Mississippi Flyway follows this vast drainage area, which is often described as a funnel — wide at the top, narrowing to a spout. The Delta represents the spout of the funnel. There lies Arkansas, with the most Delta land in this bottleneck of waterfowl.

Arkansas annually leads the nation in mallard harvest. The state average was estimated at 380,020 mallards killed each season from 1991-95, according to the U.S. Fish and Wildlife Service. That's almost double second-place California's 204,940 average over the same period.

Sixty-five percent of the ducks killed in Arkansas each season are mallards, with gadwalls and wood ducks a distant second and third. That is the basis for this Arkansas expression: "If it ain't got a green head, it ain't a duck."

"Almost 1,500,000 mallards find their winter home in this Delta country, particularly in Arkansas, where 1,100,000 congregate," wrote waterfowl biologist Frank C. Bellrose in *Ducks, Geese and Swans of North America*.

The Delta is a land shaped by rivers, particularly the Mississippi, but also the Ohio and Arkansas rivers. During the Pleistocene Age, which began 1.6 million years ago, the Mississippi River ran west of Crowley's Ridge and the Ohio followed the present-day path of the Mississippi. The narrow band of Crowley's Ridge — 150 miles long and up to five miles wide — represents the only area in the Arkansas Delta that wasn't eroded by these two great rivers.

Arkansas' Grand Prairie region of the Delta was formed from alluvial soils deposited by the Mississippi and Arkansas rivers.

As these dominant streams changed courses in the Delta, like unmanned firehoses, they deposited a deep base of rich soil and created the paths for the smaller streams that flow through the Delta today, like the St. Francis, Black, lower White, Cache, L'Anguille and

Arkansas' Major Rivers and Streams

Matt Jones

Bayou DeView.

In this complex connection of wetlands, dabbling ducks, like mallards, could always find a perfect dinner table set somewhere in the Arkansas Delta. Unlike diving ducks, dabblers (also called puddle ducks) don't submerge their bodies to feed. Only food in shallow water is available to them, at a maximum depth of about 18 inches, as they tip up their tails and extend their necks underwater to feed.

A half-inch of rain in one section of this flat alluvial plain starts a chain reaction that sets new dinner tables along countless rivers and bayous.

Before man's impact on the Delta, ducks fed primarily on acorns, moist-soil plant seeds and invertebrates in the flooded bottomland hardwood forest.

"The forests then were probably a lot different than what most people think," said Arkansas Game and Fish Commission assistant director Scott Yaich, a former AGFC chief waterfowl biologist. "If you look at the food value of flooded oak forests, it just doesn't fit. They were probably more open then. The big trees were more likely to blow down, creating openings in the canopy. These openings were the original moist-soil areas, where ducks could feed on millet and smartweed."

Mississippi Flyway mallards are mostly responsible for the development of the duck call. Because they evolved in this wetland hardwood forest, mallards depended on audio cues to lead them to the openings where other ducks were feeding.

This is the essence of duck hunting in Arkansas, where you can stand beside a tree in flooded timber, blow a duck call, kick some water and bring mallards fluttering down through the branches. Although Arkansas offers all types of duck hunting, including lakes, big rivers, flooded agricultural fields, dead-timber reservoirs and even baitfish ponds, the state's reputation is built on flooded timber. It remains the big attraction for out-of-state hunters, who have so little opportunity to experience it elsewhere.

Arkansas' Delta today, however, in no way resembles the hardwood-covered bottoms of 100 years ago. By 1985, only 875,000 acres of the state's forested wetlands remained, a loss of 89%. No inland state has lost more wetland acres than Arkansas.

Mallards, the most adaptable of all waterfowl species, continue to adapt to the changing Delta. The have learned to feed on the soybeans, corn, milo and, most importantly, rice that are grown on the cultivated land that replaced the forested wetlands.

"Agricultural fields can provide tremendous waterfowl habitat," Yaich said. "But a 100 percent rice diet doesn't have nearly the food value of a 100 percent natural diet. Crops like rice provide the calories to get by, but moist-soil plants are like vitamins for ducks."

The one thing that hasn't changed is this complex system of rivers and bayous that offers everything a duck wants.

MALLARD HARVEST
PER SEASON

1. Arkansas	**380,200**
2. California	204,940
3. Washington	176,200
4. Minnesota	173,500
5. Louisiana	161,940
6. Wisconsin	130,060
7. Illinois	122,980
8. Michigan	118,480
9. Oregon	102,820
10. Mississippi	102,380

ALL-DUCK HARVEST
PER SEASON

1. Louisiana	919,220
2. California	849,100
3. Arkansas	**583,400**
4. Minnesota	568,080
5. Texas	478,460
6. Wisconsin	317,820
7. Washington	297,880
8. Michigan	260,460
9. Oregon	225,920
10. Illinois	222,500

U.S. Fish & Wildlife Service estimates, 1991-95

"It's a perfect table setting for ducks," said Tim Moser, a former AGFC waterfowl biologist. "When there's two inches of water in a soybean field, there's four inches of water in bottomland hardwoods and six inches of water in a rice field.

"Everything is there — different foods at different water levels. That's especially important for invertebrates, which hatch at different water levels. The variety gives you a whole lot of different microhabitats."

Finally, one often-overlooked factor makes a significant contribution to Arkansas duck hunting. In reality, ducks don't fit so neatly into the Atlantic, Mississippi, Central and Pacific flyway corridors under which they are managed.

"If it ain't got a green head, it ain't a duck."

Arkansas is considered the heart of the Mississippi Flyway wintering grounds, as it should be. Many mallards that winter here, however, migrate down the Central Flyway before hanging a left turn at either the Arkansas River or the Red River. The Arkansas River has always served as a migration corridor for birds and animals. If you refer to the migration maps in the Appendix, you'll see the significance of mallard migration in the Red River valley, where a miniature version of the Delta exists in southwest Arkansas.

You must look at the big picture; that may be migrating waterfowl's most important lesson for man. State, flyway and national boundaries can't contain them. Any discussion of wintering ducks in Arkansas isn't complete without considering their birthplace. Increasingly, Arkansas mallards come from Canada. Banding data from 1961-75 showed that U.S. prairies produced 16 percent of Arkansas' wintering mallards. Data from 1975-84 showed that figure had dropped to 11%. Within Canada, southwestern Saskatchewan produces 25 percent of Arkansas mallards.

Rice a bonanza for ducks and hunters

Crop symbolizes the continuing evolution of duck hunting, habitat in Arkansas

It's only appropriate that W. H. Fuller of Carlisle was on a hunting trip to the Louisiana coast in 1896 when the rice fields there captured his attention.

Fuller had moved to Arkansas from Nebraska. He was using a well and a windmill at Carlisle to irrigate oats and corn. When he saw Louisiana's rice fields, Fuller thought the Grand Prairie region of Arkansas would be the perfect place for rice. He talked to Louisiana rice farmers and brought some seed back to Arkansas after his hunting trip.

When he discussed his rice plans with others in Carlisle, Fuller was called a "crank" and "a little off balance," according to the *Arkansas Historical Quarterly*.

His first experiment with a three-acre field was encouraging enough to send him back to Louisiana for more lessons on growing rice. Fuller returned five years later. He persuaded people in Carlisle and Hazen to put up a $1,000 reward if he could produce an average yield of 35 bushels on a 70-acre field.

In the winter of 1903, a 154-foot well was dug to irrigate the crop. A steam engine pump provided him 400 to 500 gallons of water per minute. In 1904, Fuller earned his reward and forever changed the Grand Prairie of Arkansas and duck hunting.

Fuller more than doubled the required 35 bushels, averaging just over 74 bushels per acre. Suddenly, the man previously mocked as a crank had created widespread interest over the cheap land in this section of the Delta. Rice was grown in Arkansas County for the first time in 1906. By 1908, the St. Louis Southwestern Railway Co., better known as the Cotton Belt, had published a booklet entitled "Arkansas Rice: Its Growth and Possibilities," encouraging people about the bonanza awaiting them in the Grand Prairie.

In those early years of rice farming, harvest season conflicted with the arrival of wintering waterfowl. Farmers frantically fought to protect a year's work that was piled in shocks to dry. Left unmolested, the great flocks of ducks could wipe out a rice field in one night.

But with the development of combines and quicker growing rice varieties, ducks began to complement the work of rice farmers.

The ultimate complement was Verne Tindall's 450-acre reservoir built just a few miles outside Stuttgart. Tindall wanted to store water that could be used to irrigate his rice fields and alleviate some of the cost of pumping underground water. In 1926, he started building a short levee around some timber-covered acreage that was otherwise worthless to him. Water from the rice fields was pumped into the shallow reservoir before harvest in 1927.

"The first few years it seemed as if all the ducks in the country tried to get into it," Tindall once told the Stuttgart *Daily Leader*.

Ducks were the unexpected by-prod-

In 1996, Arkansas farmers planted 1.18 million acres in rice. Arkansas County led with 108,000 acres; Poinsett County was second with 103,000. Arkansas and Poinsett rank first and third in duck harvest density.

uct of rice reservoirs. Thus, Tindall, like Fuller, had left a significant mark on the Grand Prairie of Arkansas. Soon individuals were building reservoirs just for commercial duck hunting.

Once people realized standing water killed the timber in these reservoirs after about seven years, they developed green-tree reservoirs on the Grand Prairie. Hardwood timberlands were flooded only to attract waterfowl; the water was drained as soon as hunting season ended, and the trees continued to grow.

It's important to recognize the evolution of duck hunting in Arkansas as influenced by rice.

"For mallards, the basic objective is to winter as far north as they can find food and water," said Scott Yaich, Arkansas Game and Fish Commission assistant director.

While the state has long been the primary wintering ground for mallards in the Mississippi Flyway, ducks have seen a drastic change in the scenery here.

"It is not too lyrical, I hope, to say that the Stuttgart region has become one of the wonders of America," wrote Ralph Coghlan of the St. Louis *Post-Dispatch* in 1949.

The key words there are "has become." It's entirely proper that Stuttgart bills itself as the "Rice and Duck Capital of the World." Without one, there would not be the other, at least not in amounts to claim "capital of the world."

In 1996, Arkansas produced 42 percent of the U.S. rice crop. The two leading counties in the state were Arkansas, which includes Stuttgart, with 108,000 acres harvested, and Poinsett, which includes the town of Weiner, with 103,000 acres harvested. It's no coincidence that those two counties also rank first and third, respectively, in duck harvest per square mile in the state, according to the AGFC.

In all the great U.S. rice-growing regions, you'll find ducks. California, Louisiana, Texas, Mississippi and Missouri, in that order, follow Arkansas in rice production, and all are ranked among the leaders in mallard and all-duck harvest. Although there is little grain left in the fields by the time ducks arrive now, rice producers have realized the benefits of managing the land for wintering waterfowl.

Rice grows as both a symbol of the marshy terrain that naturally attracts ducks and a sign of what man can do to enhance waterfowl habitat.

Rice also serves to remind us of how little control state and federal agencies ultimately have over wildlife. Although Arkansas does have extraordinary public land duck hunting, the AGFC manages less than one percent of the state's 53,000 square miles. Over 90 percent of Arkansas is privately owned.

Farming trends in the Delta will always carry the greatest influence in terms of providing habitat for wintering waterfowl. Ducks don't "cotton" to cotton, the crop that once dominated the Delta. Rice and ducks happen to be a

(Above) A mallard drake and hen swim through a rice field. (Right) When steel pit blinds are sunk, rice fields produce revenue for farmers during duck season.

Public cried out for land to hunt ducks

Holder, AGFC were able to purchase large areas when land was cheap

Do you buy public land only when you have the funds to manage it? Or do you buy all the land you can afford, then worry later about managing it properly?

That's the dilemma the Arkansas Game and Fish Commission faced after World War II. It was a time when land was cheap. Few people saw the change that was coming, when heavy machinery would make land-clearing quick, and growing soybeans would make it highly profitable.

Before 1950, most of the land acquired by the AGFC cost less than $10 an acre. By 1970, the average price for public hunting land was $73 an acre. The price jumped to $140 an acre in 1972 and $225 in 1974.

Fortunately for everyone who duck hunts on public ground in Arkansas, one man had the foresight to make land acquisition the priority. Trusten Holder served as the AGFC's federal aid coordinator from 1940 to 1969.

"Trusten Holder said don't worry about developing it, just buy all the land you can get," said Carl Hunter, who retired as an assistant director of the AGFC in 1986.

It was under Holder's direction that the AGFC laid the foundation for its public lands treasury, beginning with the 34,000-acre Bayou Meto Wildlife Management Area and including other jewels like 23,000-acre Black River WMA, 11,000-acre Shirey Bay-Rainey Brake WMA and 18,000-acre Hurricane Lake WMA.

"The public hunting opportunities are just tremendous compared to most states," said Scott Yaich, the AGFC's assistant director. "Arkansas bought land when there was no money to manage it. So now it has these huge blocks.

"Most other states have these postage stamp-sized pieces, where you have to draw for blinds and things like that. Duck hunters in Arkansas don't realize how bad the conditions are in some other states."

Duck hunters in Arkansas did, however, realize how bad the conditions were in this state at one time, and they deserve some of the credit for urging the AGFC to buy land.

In the 1940s, ducks were hunted in all of the places they are hunted now. But the practice was hindered by several factors. The most pressing was that any land open for public hunting was at the mercy of Mother Nature and sufficient rainfall. There were no levees, gates or water control structures to capture rainwater because no public land was managed for waterfowl. Areas flooded, but often the flooding of the overflow bottoms in the river valleys came long after the season ended.

An aerial view of 34,000-acre Bayou Meto Wildlife Management Area, the AGFC's first public land purchase, shows how sharply it contrasts with the agricultural lands around it.

The majority of the duck hunting took place on private clubs that had leased rice farmers' reservoirs or flooded some of the bottoms by artificial means.

Along Two Prairie Bayou, Mill Bayou and Bayou LaGrue, there was a solid row of private duck clubs, where members and guests usually had excellent hunting. But if you didn't have access to those clubs, you barely had a place to get your boots wet. That situation forced the AGFC to face the problem of providing suitable hunting grounds for the general public.

After promising to remedy this situation, the AGFC leased the 22,000-acre Singer Tract, located on the east side of the White River near Crockett's Bluff.

"Would you believe what the duck hunters found when they tried to hunt in this area?" Holder said. "They found that the only place in the entire 22,000 acres that was any good for duck hunting prior to the arrival of a general overflow was a place called Round Pond. And Round Pond was not available to the public because it had been specifically excluded from the lease and was being operated as a private club."

The broken promise created more of an outcry for the AGFC to do something, Holder said.

Coinciding with increased public demands were changes in the federal aid program, which allowed Arkansas' annual allocation to jump from $31,387 in 1946 to $131,821 in 1947, Holder said. Using 25% state funds to get 75% federal matching funds, the AGFC had about $175,000 to work with. But federal rules stated the money had to be used for game restoration.

"Trying to generate support for habitat preservation in the late 1940s was a hopeless task. Business and political leaders, like those of the preceding 150 years, were still trying to eliminate the woodlands and the lowlands."

"Providing people with a place to slaughter ducks was not considered to be a bona fide game restoration activity," Holder said.

Fortunately, the AGFC convinced the U.S. Fish and Wildlife Service that game restoration benefits through the preservation of valuable wildlife habitat would outweigh the loss of wildlife from the legal harvest of ducks. Holder noted there was a critical need to preserve carefully-selected areas of valuable habitat. Without the habitat there would be no game.

"But trying to generate support for habitat preservation in the late 1940s was a hopeless task," Holder said. "Business and political leaders, like those of the preceding 150 years, were still trying to eliminate the woodlands and the lowlands. Purchase of land was too contrary to the false thinking that prevailed about wildlife conservation."

The AGFC's objective was to identify the best land available and buy as much of it as possible. The first purchase of the Wabbaseka Scatters (Bayou Meto WMA), spearheaded by Holder, proved to be invaluable.

It is, by any comparison, the best and most used public duck hunting ground in the country. While the AGFC can be lauded for acquiring Bayou Meto, the commission of the 1940s wasn't concerned with doing it the right way, according to Holder.

Holder was in charge of locating parcels of land and acquiring options to buy land for the purpose of duck hunting. Most of the land had previously belonged to the state, but it had been sold about four years earlier. If action had been taken a few years before, the entire area could have been acquired on much easier terms.

Holder didn't get a break in acquiring the land until a man entered the AGFC office one day and told him he had 6,500 acres he wanted to sell, all of it in the Wabbaseka Scatters. The price was set at $10 an acre, with a 10-year reservation on the timber and half the minerals. Holder agreed to try to get the commission to buy it. A few days later, the same man returned with an offer to sell an additional 6,000 acres under the same terms.

"I thought at the time that the Lord had sent this man to me," Holder recalled in his book, *A Tiny Bit of Americana*. "I certainly didn't claim to have the least vestige of an inside track on such matters, but I have heard that

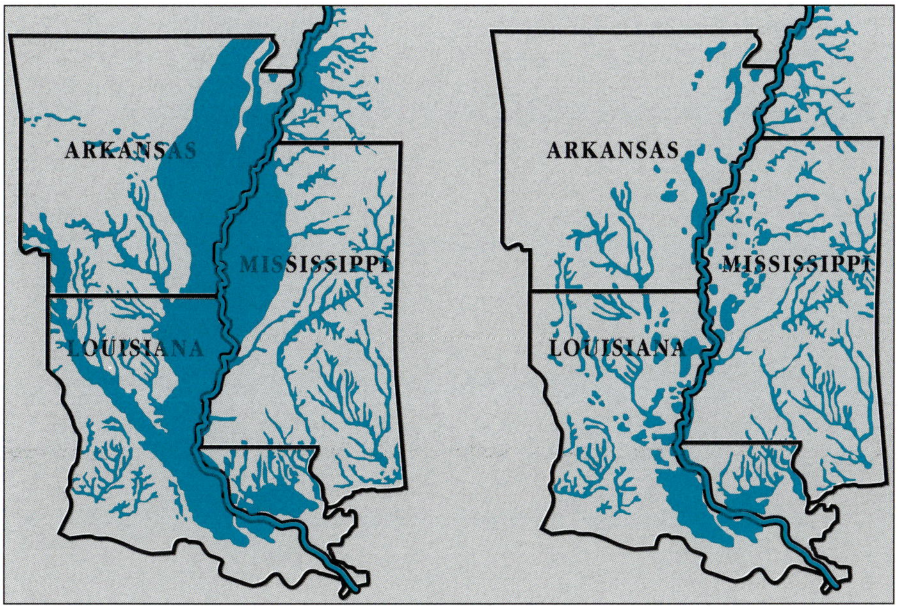

Courtesy U.S. Fish and Wildlife Service

The chart on the left represents the original extent of the bottomland hardwood forest in the lower Mississippi River valley. The chart on the right shows what was left by 1982.

(Above) Mark Bishop and his father killed this pair of wood duck drakes in Bayou Meto. In the Mississippi Flyway from 1961 through '96, wood ducks were second to mallards in total harvest 31 seasons. Recently gadwalls have moved into the No. 2 spot.

ARKANSAS DUCK SPECIES

HARVEST PER SEASON

Species	Total	%
1. Mallard	380,200	65.2
2. Gadwall	68,980	11.8
3. Wood duck	44,740	7.7
4. Green-wing teal	37,040	6.3
5. Shoveler	14,440	2.5
6. Wigeon	11,720	2.0
7. Ringneck	9,040	1.5
8. Pintail	6,980	1.2
9. Blue-wing teal	4,280	.7
10. Lesser scaup	4,180	.7
11. Black duck	1,000	.2
12. Redhead	640	.1

U.S. Fish & Wildlife Service estimates, 1991-95

the Lord acts in mysterious ways, and for all I know He might have done it."

Holder began working on approval from the USFWS to use federal aid to help purchase the land for the AGFC. With the ball rolling, Holder tried to obtain the necessary appraisals. While working on those, he acquired an option to buy an additional 2,200 acres, known as Buckingham Flats, for $7 an acre. During that process, he had the occasion to visit with Brooks Henslee, the owner of the 6,500-acre tract the AGFC was attempting to buy.

"I had made no effort to talk to the owners and left it in the hands of the man who had come in to see me about selling the land, whom I assumed was the agent of the landowners," Holder said.

When Holder met with Henslee, he informed him that he had just acquired an option for buying Buckingham Flats at $7 an acre, and that it was every bit as good as Henslee's land. Thinking that Henslee was behind the $10 option on his land, Holder asked him to accept $7 instead.

"I fully expected him to answer that he would not," Holder said.

But Henslee agreed to the $7 offer. Henslee then told Holder that he doubted they would actually buy it for $7 because he was suspicious of the AGFC's acceptance of his original verbal agreement to sell the land at $6 an acre.

"Up to that moment, it never occurred to me that other commission representatives had had anything whatsoever to do with the land negotiations," Holder said. "I knew then that the real intent of the proposed purchase was a raid on the treasury by a few who were in authority."

According to Holder, a few commissioners and the director of the AGFC at the time intended to buy the land at $10 an acre and keep the additional $4 an acre, while taking credit for providing an excellent place to duck hunt.

But Holder was able to complete a successful end run by going back to the landowners and getting options to buy the land at $7 an acre, cutting out the crooked middle men.

Activity like that was believed to be common during the early years of the AGFC, Holder said. It didn't last long, and the AGFC mounted its biggest effort to acquire more land.

Next came Big Lake, Black River and Dagmar WMAs. Those areas are all in the eastern half of the state. Even in the 1940s, the AGFC recognized that other parts of the state were in need of duck hunting land. Purchases were made in the Petit Jean area in Yell County and Bois D'Arc in Hempstead County.

While these first acquisitions have proven to offer excellent duck hunting, a few that might have been just as good got away.

At first it seemed the Pond Creek bottoms in Sevier County would be on that list. The AGFC wanted the land, but the lumber company that owned it refused to sell. As it turned out, most of the timber in the bottoms was destroyed by the impoundment of Lake Millwood.

Through lengthy negotiations the AGFC did gain Cut-Off Creek and Hurricane Lake WMAs. Those were big successes, Holder said.

The biggest heartbreak was Raft Creek bottoms in White and Prairie counties, according to Holder. The area was at the top of the acquisition list for the AGFC because it is one of the first along the White River to flood when the river leaves its banks.

Holder said at one time the entire Raft Creek bottoms — more than 15,000 acres — could have been purchased for $25 an acre. In addition, another prime tract of land to the northwest of Raft Creek could have been purchased for $15 an acre. But both tracts were lost "due to a lack of action by the commission," Holder said.

The Raft Creek bottoms were cleared of timber in the late 1960s to make way for agricultural fields. The area still floods and often fills with ducks today. But the open water makes hunting them difficult at times.

Since the initial push to purchase land, the AGFC has continually made land acquisitions a priority. But with each passing year, the general rule is that smaller and smaller parcels will come with larger and larger price tags. Without the framework of large areas that Holder helped the AGFC build, many Arkansas public land duck hunters would still be singing the blues.

Water key to the future of Arkansas

Water table critical in the Delta; management crucial for attracting ducks

Nothing symbolizes the changes on the horizon for Arkansas' Delta like the critical level of the water underneath it.

In 1995, wells pumped an average of 5.46 billion gallons of water a day from the Alluvial Aquifer, which underlies most of the Delta. The aquifer dropped more than 15 feet in some areas during a six-year period in the early 1990s. By 1997, it had reached a critical level that would require tighter and tighter restrictions on the use of its water.

The method by which this problem is handled could be the next important chapter in Arkansas' duck hunting history.

"All up and down the eastern side of Arkansas, the duck population depends on the availability of water during the winter," said Tommy Hillman, a farmer and duck hunter, who became chairman of the board of Riceland Foods Inc. in 1993. "How we manage that resource of water will dictate how future generations will enjoy Arkansas duck hunting."

Rice farmers have noticed the lowering of the underground water table since shortly after rice came to the Delta in the early 1900s. The increasing costs of digging wells and pumping water are why so many large, shallow reservoirs have been built on the Grand Prairie. Since Verne Tindall built that first 450-acre reservoir outside Stuttgart in 1927, ducks and duck hunters have enjoyed the extra benefits of this farming practice.

With no more large underground aquifers to tap for irrigation, developing more surface water sources is a must. Arkansas receives more than 50 inches of rainfall each year. Various ways of capturing the runoff from that rainfall are being explored.

Big irrigation projects that would tap into the White and Arkansas rivers through a series of canals are also being studied. Before any of the big projects are funded, they will have to meet requirements for fish, wildlife and water quality.

But the bottom line is this — anything that adds surface water to the Delta will also benefit waterfowl.

The North American Waterfowl Management Plan, signed by the U.S. and Canada in 1986, seeks to provide habitat for waterfowl populations of the 1970s (62 million breeding ducks and a fall flight of 100 million). In Arkansas, the goal is to provide adequate habitat for 2.9 million migrating and wintering ducks and 263,000 geese during years of normal precipitation. Water management is the key to achieving that goal.

Arkansas is already ahead of most states in managing water for ducks. One study showed that of the 400,000 acres of private land managed for wintering waterfowl in the Delta, over 200,000 were in Arkansas.

During the land-clearing craze that soybeans created, many stories were told about how ducks came back to the same spot in a flooded field that had been flooded timber the season before.

The obvious lesson in those examples is that water, more than any other natural resource, is the key to attracting waterfowl. And water will be the most important factor in the future of duck hunting in Arkansas.

(Above) The Arkansas duck hunting tradition of blowing a call and kicking water in flooded timber depends upon an abundance of water. (Below) Many private clubs, like Circle T shown here, have the ability to flood the woods with water from a reservoir.

Photo courtesy Joy Dickey Cook

Photo courtesy Biff Morgan

(Above) Written on this 1929 photo are the results of this hunt, which took place near DeWitt. With their heads surrounded by "120 ducks, 96 quails, 3 geese, 2 squirrels" are, top row, from left, Major League Baseball Hall of Fame catcher Bill Dickey, N. Terrell, Gus Dickey, bottom row, John Matthews and Sam Byrd.

(Left) Around 1925, this group of Stuttgart businessmen posed in front of the Arkmo Lumber Company with 200 ducks. The hunters are, from left, Hugh Kyler, Henry Schilling, Earl Wright, W.J. Lancaster, Elmer DeRosier (kneeling in front), an unidentified doctor from Oklahoma, E.J. Hoolihan and Harold Robbins.

Photo courtesy Lane Arkansas

(Above) Lane Arkansas Co. in Stuttgart, under its president J.I. Seay, drilled the wells that allowed rice farming to thrive in the Grand Prairie. Seay was an avid duck hunter and conservationist. Lane Arkansas clients and employees were often treated to excellent hunting. The unidentified men standing in front of the Layne Arkansas building with their gun barrels facing them would have flunked a hunter safety course, but their hunt obviously was a success.

(Right) The presence of the ox and the native grass on the Grand Prairie would date this photo to the early 1900s. These men employed a hunting technique in which a domestic animal is used to provide a "moving blind." By staying in step with the ox, which didn't frighten the ducks, the men were able to get within shooting range.

Photo courtesy David Perdue

Photo courtesy Johnny Riley

Photo courtesy Joe Cook Jr.

(Above) From left, baseball pitcher Elwin Charles "Preacher" Roe, Johnny Riley, Ben Powell, J.B. McCune, Hubert Chancey and J.C. Keyes were photographed after a successful hunt near Weiner circa 1950. Roe was born in Viola and raised in Ash Flat. He led the National League in strikeouts in 1945 as a member of the Pittsburgh Pirates; he pitched from 1948 through 1954 for the Brooklyn Dodgers.

(Left) The Alpha Studio in Pine Bluff provided the setting for this 1930s photograph of Joe Borecky, Leonard Cook and A.L. "Arnie" Kliner, who were all Cotton Belt Railway employees in Pine Bluff. Notice that Kliner is wearing the badge-type hunting license of that day over his left breast pocket. Neckties and leggings, like those worn by Cook, are also things of the past in the Arkansas duck woods.

Photo courtesy Joy Dickey Cook

(Above) Major League Baseball Hall of Fame catcher Bill Dickey, second from left, is one of the hunters shown in this photo that includes, from left, Ed Smith of Jackson, Miss., left, and Gus Dickey, right. Gus and Bill were brothers. Bill signed with the New York Yankees in 1928, about the time this photo was taken. He played 16 seasons for the Yankees, participated in eight World Series and compiled a lifetime batting average of .313. Dickey's professional career also included a stint as Yankees' manager (1946) and as an actor (in *Pride of the Yankees,* he portrayed himself). Obviously, he liked to shoot ducks, too.

Photo courtesy Joe Cook Jr.

(Right) Dick Brewer, Albert Lyle and John Ed Cook went to Logue Studio in Pine Bluff for this 1938 photograph documenting a successful duck hunt in the Wabbaseka Scatters.

Photo courtesy Arkansas Game and Fish Commission

Duck hunting isn't duck hunting without man's best friend. (Above) Wallace H. Claypool was always accompanied by his Labrador retriever, George, when he hunted in the flooded timber surrounding Claypool's Reservoir near Weiner.
(Left) Sometimes a dog has to make do with whatever's available for a dry perch in flooded timber.

Opposite page:
(Top left and middle left) Jeryl Jones rewards his dog after a job well done.
(Top right) Bud gives the appropriate glance toward his master, Phil Madison, after several shotguns fired and no ducks fell.
(Bottom left, bottom middle) Terry Jerry's black Lab, Rebel, anxiously awaits the next chance to retrieve a duck.
(Bottom right) Jeff DeVazier of El Dorado trains Chesapeake Bay retrievers, like his Bayou Meto boat companion.

Photo courtesy Kaneaster Hodges Jr.

Former President Jimmy Carter has made several visits to Arkansas' duck country with close friend and Newport resident Kaneaster Hodges Jr. In his book, *An Outdoor Journal*, Carter described a hunt in Leonard Sitzer's woods near Weiner. (Above) It was after a hunt in Sitzer's woods when this photo was taken. The hunters, from left, are as follows: Allen Turner from Chicago; John Peel from St. Louis; Carter; Frank Moore from Washington, D.C., a congressional liaison; Dave Whitlock, (kneeling) Arkansas' best-known fly fisherman and the illustrator of Carter's book; Dr. Buck Rusher from Jonesboro; Hodges; Sitzer; and Red, a Chesapeake Bay retriever.
(Right) Carter also has hunted at Claypool's Reservoir near Weiner. He posed for a photo in front of the clubhouse fireplace with, from left, Johnny Riley and Hal Turner.

Photo courtesy Johnny Riley

Photo courtesy Marion Hartz

(Above) Former President George Bush came to Stuttgart to hunt with members of the Hartz family in Dec. 1994. Seated to Bush's left in the front of the boat is former Arkansas Congressman John Paul Hammerschmidt. Marion Hartz is behind Hammerschmidt and Chesley Pruet is seated to Hartz' right. Doug Hartz and his dog, Maggie, are standing beside the boat. The unidentified man standing to the left is a Secret Service agent.

(Right) President Bill Clinton included a duck hunting trip in a 1994 visit to his home state. Advisor and fellow Arkansan Bruce Lindsey, middle, and Bobby Robinson, right, of Cotton Plant, were among those who accompanied Clinton.

Photo courtesy Rick McFarland/Arkansas Democrat-Gazette

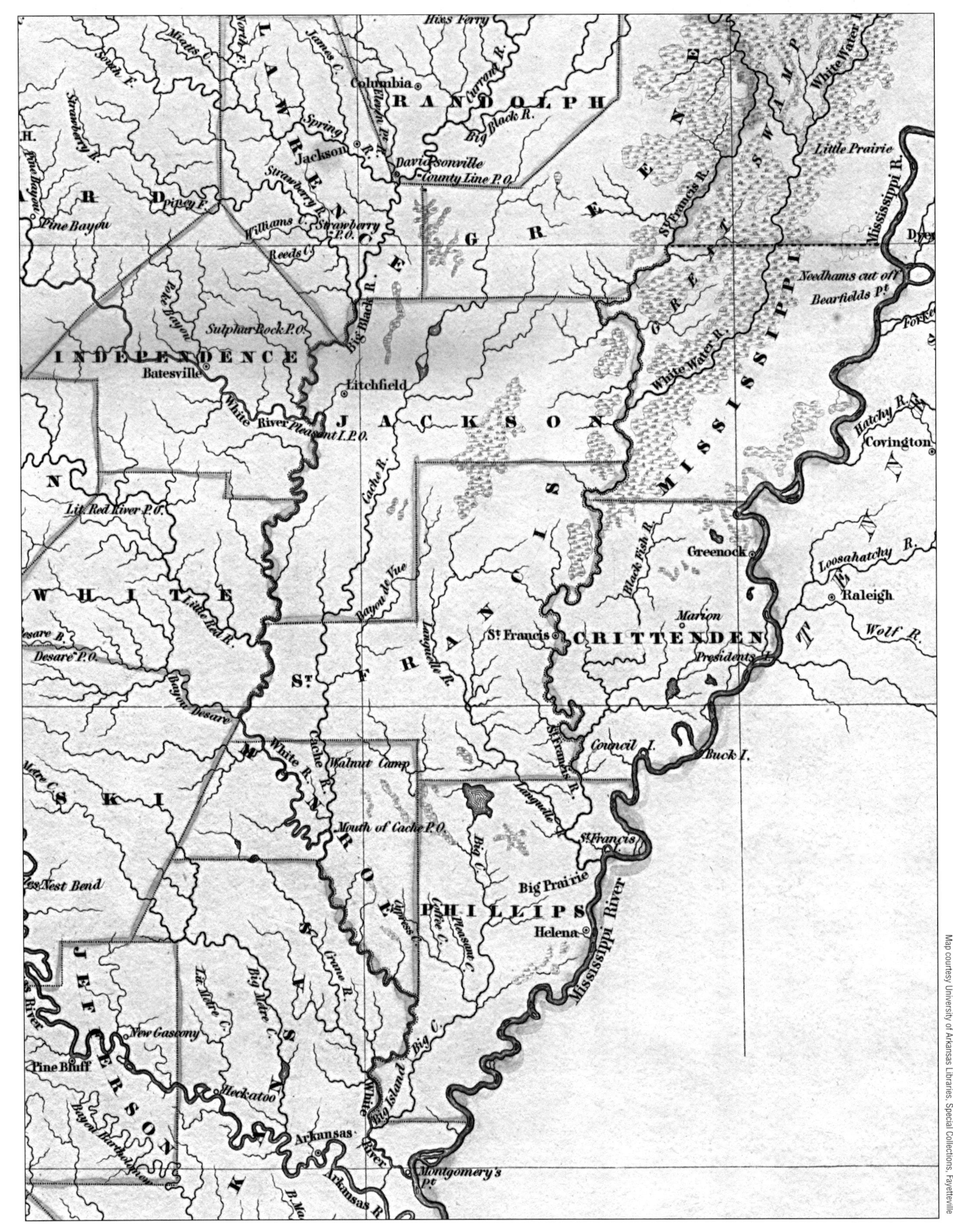

Map courtesy University of Arkansas Libraries, Special Collections, Fayetteville

The Great Swamp

MARKET HUNTERS, SPORTSMEN PUT IT ON THE MAP NEAR TURN OF THE CENTURY

No place stands above the Great Swamp in the history of Arkansas duck hunting. During the past century it has been the focal point for everything, good and bad, concerning waterfowl hunting in the state. Ducks by the million, a widespread reputation for great hunting, duck call-making tradition, market hunting slaughter, human bloodshed over hunting rights, over-cut forests and channelized streams — it's all taken place in the Great Swamp. Only remnants of swamp remain.

The Ozark escarpment marks the western boundary of this vast bottomland that was created by the meanderings of the Mississippi and Ohio rivers. These two great rivers now converge at the northern tip of the Great Swamp. But at one time during the past 1.6 million years of the Earth's history (Pleistocene Period), they flowed as parallel streams through this area, with the Mississippi River located west of Crowley's Ridge and the Ohio to the east. That geological period laid the foundation for the bottleneck of the Mississippi Flyway.

◀ As this 1838 map shows, "Great Swamp" wasn't just a colloquial term for the swamps and sunken lands of the St. Francis Basin.

James T. Beckhart came to the Great Swamp in the late 1800s because of its abundance of fish and game.

Man's dependence on migratory waterfowl here can be traced to the earliest inhabitants. The Zebree archeological site at Big Lake was a home for Paleo-Indians. Among the deposits that have been dated to about A.D. 600-800 are 813 bird bone fragments. Of those, 585 were from waterfowl, and the greatest single species found was, of course, the mallard (174 fragments).

In more recent times, writers such as Friederich Gerstacker in the 19th century and Nash Buckingham in the 20th, left us more detailed pictures of the Great Swamp.

"The swamp is covered by the most wonderful, luxuriant primeval forest one could imagine in all the earth," wrote Gerstacker. His book, *Wild Sports in the Far West*, described Gerstacker's wanderings through the Arkansas wilderness from 1837 to 1843.

Buckingham used a similar phrase, "primeval jungle," in writing about the "gorgeous gameland of the lush St. Francis Basin."

For most people, "uninhabitable" was the word most often associated with this mosquito-infested, malaria-ridden swamp. Of course, it was precisely that characteristic that made this a sportsman's paradise. By 1900, man had tamed most of the U.S. The glory days of big game hunting out West had already peaked. But Mother Nature kept the Great Swamp free from man as long as possible, as noted in this excerpt from an 1893 Missouri Pacific Railway

Photo courtesy Special Collections Division, University of Arkansas Libraries, Fayetteville

In the 1800s, steamboats brought sportsmen up the St. Francis River from its mouth at the Mississippi River near Helena. This photograph was taken in 1885.

booklet entitled "Ideal Hunting and Fishing Grounds":

"...Centuries have passed since powder and lead first superseded the Indian's arrow in its destructive work among the deer and bears of the great Southwest, and in this interval the bison herds of the plains have been literally annihilated, and the wildest recesses of the Rocky Mountains penetrated in search of game; but still the brakes of the Southern Swamps guard their denizens as jealously as in the past — a vast and inexhaustible reservoir replenishing from its abundance the game supply of a thinly inhabited region two hundred miles in width and reaching from Southern Missouri to the waters of the Mexican Gulf."

The Great Swamp was so thinly inhabited that no accurate death count exists from one of the great seismological events of the time, the New Madrid earthquakes of 1811-12.

The quakes only enhanced what was already paradise for waterfowl. Depressions created by the earthquake formed Big Lake and the St. Francis Sunken Lands in Arkansas and Reelfoot Lake in Tennessee.

Steamboats first presented access for sportsmen into the canebrakes and cypress sloughs of the St. Francis River basin. The hunting party pictured above came from Cincinnati — down the Ohio and Mississippi rivers — to reach the famous hunting grounds of the Great

History of the Great Swamp — A Timeline

1811-12	1858	1887	1890	1900
The New Madrid earthquakes cause depressions that create Big Lake and St. Francis Sunken Lands in Arkansas and Reelfoot Lake in Tennessee.	Memphis *Commercial Appeal* reports that Lake Wapanocca is swarming with thousands of ducks. Memphis hunters fire three shotguns at one time and kill 27 ducks.	Wapanocca Outing Club begins organizing. Its membership will eventually include legendary outdoor writer Nash Buckingham. The club buys 6,500 acres for 50 cents an acre, all of which is covered in forest, except for the lake.	James Beckhart, a market hunter and guide, begins making duck calls at Buck's Point on Big Lake, where he lives with his family on a houseboat.	Big Lake Shooting Club forms. Although there are no federal or state regulations concerning daily bag limits, Big Lake Shooting Club rules limit members to 100 ducks per day.

Swamp.

When Nash Buckingham first began accompanying his father to the Wapanocca Outing Club in 1890, no bridge existed across the Mississippi River at Memphis. Train cars were loaded on transport steamers for the river crossing, then put back on the rails in Arkansas.

Timber industry demands directed rail lines to the edges of this massive stand of bottomland hardwoods and provided convenient jumping off points for sportsmen. Wapanocca Outing Club, Buffalo Island Hunting and Fishing Club, Big Lake Shooting Club, Hatchie Coon Club — all were located along railroad lines.

This era is known as the "Golden Age of Waterfowling." Clubs often set bag limits — the Big Lake Shooting Club allowed each member no more than 100 ducks per day — but the first federal daily bag limit (25) wouldn't come until 1918.

However, the Golden Age of Waterfowling was short-lived. Far down the list of destruction caused by the Mississippi River flood of 1927 was the fact that much of Wapanocca Lake's natural vegetation washed away. It marked the beginning of a steady decline in waterfowl use there.

Much of the Great Swamp would never be the same after 1927. The Flood Control Act of 1928 began a period of levee building, ditch digging and agricultural development that carved the Great Swamp into tiny pieces.

Mallards continue to funnel into this narrowing of the Mississippi Flyway, but today they see only islands of flooded bottomland timber in a sea of furrowed fields.

Few people injured, duck habitat enhanced during violence of New Madrid earthquakes

They created two of America's most famous duck hunting holes and are considered, as a whole, one of the most significant seismological events in modern time, yet the New Madrid earthquakes will always be somewhat of a mystery.

In a sense, the series of earthquakes from Dec. 1811 through Feb. 1812 was one massive duck habitat improvement project. In the *World Almanac*'s list of major earthquakes, which dates back to A.D. 526, only the New Madrid event has no number of estimated deaths.

One study indicated that only one person could be definitely confirmed as having died on land during the series of quakes: "...that one was a woman who ran until exhausted and died of fright." Other unconfirmed reports said that several people drowned during the upheavals in the Mississippi River.

If there were such a thing as the perfect place for an earthquake, the sparsely inhabited Great Swamp along the Mississippi River in the early 1800s was it. Falling chimneys posed the biggest danger to what few people lived here.

It's been said the Mississippi River flowed backward as the water rushed to fill depressions left by the quakes. Two of the biggest depressions became Reelfoot Lake in western Tennessee and Big Lake in northeast Arkansas, which would soon be major gathering points for sportsmen, market hunters and duck call makers. A section of the St. Francis River also was affected. A 1904 account describes Lake St. Francis and the Hatchie Coon Sunk Lands as a 40-mile-long lake averaging a half-mile in width. Modern geological studies have located an earthquake-related depression and uplift in the St. Francis River channel that probably created the lake.

The series of tremors that shook this area beginning in 1811 is now estimated to have included at least three "great earthquakes," with a magnitude greater than 8.0 on the Richter scale, plus hundreds of lesser tremors.

One eyewitness account included the following: "The morning of December 15, 1811, was cloudy and a dense fog prevailed, and toward nightfall the heavens showed signs of distress. On the following morning, the 16th, about 5 o'clock a.m., we felt the shock of an earthquake, accompanied by a rumbling noise resembling the distant firing of a cannon, which was followed in a few minutes by the complete saturation of the atmosphere with sulphurous vapor. The moon was shining brilliantly, but the sulphurous vapor caused the earth to be wrapped in absolute darkness. The wailing inhabitants, the stampede of the fowls and beasts, the noise of falling timber, the roaring of the Mississippi, the current of which was retrograde for a few minutes — formed a scene too appalling to conceive of."

The New Madrid Seismic Zone remains a source of anxiety today. Another event of this magnitude would be catastrophic for many cities and towns, which have sprawled since the Great Swamp was conquered.

History of the Great Swamp — A Timeline

1910
Game warden E.V. Visart estimates that 5,000 ducks per day are being killed at Big Lake and shipped out of state, in violation of state and federal laws. Wild ducks bring 50 cents each and are commonly served in restaurants.

1915
Big Lake is declared a national wildlife refuge, Arkansas' first, by President Woodrow Wilson. This action also ends a 15-year feud between market hunters and members of the Big Lake Shooting Club.

1947
Drainage projects in the Lower St. Francis River Basin, which began in 1930, now include 685,000 acres — 89 percent of the land in the lower river basin.

1985
Only 11 percent (875,000 acres) of Arkansas' original 8 million acres of wetlands remains. No other state in the Mississippi River Alluvial Plain has lost a greater percentage of its wetlands than Arkansas.

1988
A James Beckhart-made Big Lake style duck call, originally priced at $5 around 1900, sells for $4,290 at the Callmakers and Collectors Association of America convention.

Beckhart made a living from Big Lake

Duck call-making craftsmanship provided another source of revenue

The boxes that held James T. Beckhart's duck calls were stamped "The Famous Big Lake Duck Call." Beckhart had no way of knowing how prophetic that slogan would become. At the turn of the century, when a typical day's wage was a dollar, making and selling duck calls helped Beckhart support his family.

He sold the fancy hand-checkered calls for $5 and the plain ones for $2.50. Big city "sportsmen" took them home after hunting trips to Big Lake as mementos of their excursions into the "Great Swamp."

Today, Beckhart's calls are among the most valuable to collectors. One Beckhart call brought $4,290 in 1988. Undoubtedly a good Beckhart would be worth twice that much today, but seldom do these calls change hands anymore.

James Tillman Beckhart (pronounced "BECK-hart") was born on Valentine's Day, 1864, in Warsaw, Ind. He moved his wife, Anna, and daughter, Bertha Clare, from Pennsylvania to St. Louis in 1887. They took a riverboat from there to Osceola. The abundance of game and fish gradually lured Beckhart up the St. Francis and Little rivers until he stopped at Big Lake.

The Beckhart family settled in a houseboat at Buck's Point on Big Lake, where they formed the typical commercial enterprise of this area. (Buck's Point, once a landing on the lake, is now the town of Buckeye.)

Soon after the railroads brought access to Big Lake, and its wealth of fish and game, local bank records indicate more income was produced from the lake than from surrounding farm land.

Beckhart often took a large wooden boat to one of the local landings, like Hornersville, Mo. He'd pick up the "sports," who had taken the train from St. Louis, Chicago, Memphis or Kansas City, and bring them back to his houseboat. Over the years, he put down pilings around the once free-floating houseboat and added extra rooms for more guests.

A houseboat on Big Lake provided both home and workplace for Beckhart (standing next to his daughter, at left) and family.

Photo courtesy Barry McFarland

Five Beckhart duck calls. Note far right example with shotgun and duck carved on panels.

Duck season at this time was defined by a simple phrase. Hunters in Arkansas shot ducks "from when they came, until when they left" — in other words, from late fall until early spring.

The sportsmen might stay any length of time on Beckhart's houseboat — from a few days to a few weeks to a few months — enjoying duck hunting that would never again be matched and savoring the home-cooked meals of Beckhart's wife, Anna.

Beckhart had plenty to keep him busy — hunting and fishing for market, guiding hunters and building boats. But living on a houseboat limited any other distractions. This lifestyle left Beckhart plenty of time to carve his wooden duck calls, which were then soaked for hours in hot linseed oil to make them waterproof.

Beckhart made his first calls around 1890. They were such a success that he converted a sewing machine into a lathe. This simple machine would help him form the basic shape of a duck call. Then he added the extras by hand, like checkering and images of ducks, dogs, turtles, alligators and guns.

With ducks as thick as mosquitoes, live decoys common and backwoodsmen like Beckhart serving as guides, rare was the time a visiting sportsman actually needed to blow a duck call to ensure a successful hunt. Beckhart's calls were effective. They were usually made of walnut, although he did use some cedar. They almost always held a German silver reed, which provided a relatively quiet and consistent sound for that era.

With hundreds of thousands of mallards wintering in the Great Swamp, all it took was a hint of duck talk to bring them within gun range. Beckhart's duck calls could easily accomplish that. But, again, the visiting hunters had little reason to learn to blow one of these calls. They bought Beckhart's craftsmanship because of what it symbolized: the best duck hunt of their lives.

That's part of the value of Beckhart's calls today. They represent the best of both craftsmanship and hunting opportunity in the sport.

Beckhart was only 58 years old when he died, on November 11, 1922. Failing health attributed to high blood pressure had limited his hunting and fishing for several years. With those options out, Beckhart relied more and more on making duck calls for income. By 1915 he was working at call-making full time.

After his death, Beckhart's widow sold the walnut blocks and call-making utensils to Claude Stone of nearby Hornersville. The legend of "The Famous Big Lake Duck Call" was established. Stone was already making a Beckhart-style call when he bought Beckhart's wood and tools.

With Big Lake as the background, Stone would build on the legend.

Documents from court case provide look back at era of market hunting

(Editor's note: James Beckhart was one of the defendants in a legal battle with the Big Lake Shooting Club that began in 1903. The following deposition was taken from Major William Herman Ray at Manila on Oct. 31, 1904. Ray identified himself as a merchant who had run a 38-foot paddle wheel boat powered by a gasoline engine on Big Lake.)

Q: What streams have you navigated your boat upon?

Ray: St. Francis and Little River.

Q: As to the Katy Ray Opening in Big Lake, I would ask have you ever run your boat there?

Ray: A number of times; yes sir; a number of times. That was my regular run when I was allowed — before the game law became so strenuous in Mississippi County. I bought ducks and fish and I would always make old Uncle George's Camp about a half a mile above the head of Dry Cypress; I made that a number of times, the Morrell Camp, and then this gap in here where Donovan was camped.

Q: When you would come down into Big Lake from the north, going into this country near Butterfly Camp with your boat, what course would you take?

Ray: Well, when I was in the game business I had stations on the west side. For instance at Tim's Point I had an ice box that I kept stocked with ice; at Feather Point I had an ice box that I kept stocked, and at the Gar Hole the same thing. As I went down I would go this run. I came right through Lick Ladder Drag Over, and through what is known as Catfish Chute, and a due southwest course or a little west of south rather, to this Long John Island, and then a straight course as I could steer to Sand Slough, but mind you as I would come down I would pick up the game and replenish my ice boxes; then after going to the Gar Hole I would go back up the same run to Hog Island, then I would turn northeast, leaving Cottonseed, run up here to the Katy Ray Gap, under Katy Ray, provided I didn't have any business up in here at Morrell's Camp. I didn't buy many ducks from that party, because they had a steady buyer and would not leave him."

Photo courtesy Barry McFarland

James Beckhart used a push-pole to maneuver his wooden boat. The Big Lake Shooting Club boat docks are visible behind him.

The battle over Big Lake

Blood shed, clubhouses burned in long fight over hunting rights

"Club Warden Shot The Twelfth Time" read one headline in the *Arkansas Gazette*. "Big Lake Clubhouse To Be Fireproof; Col. Joseph H. Acklen Will Fight To The End" read another in the Memphis *Commercial Appeal*. Still another declared, "Quiet at Big Lake; Pinkertons Are There, However, And Further Trouble Expected."

Big Lake made big news at the beginning of the 20th century in a battle over hunting rights — specifically, duck hunting rights. And the uproar finally reached the White House.

More importantly, the battle at Big Lake represents the time when market hunting and the rampant slaughter of waterfowl peaked. International treaties and federal regulations, especially from 1916 on, increasingly attempted to halt the waterfowl population crash that was the result of this era.

By the late 1800s, dwindling supplies of game and fish were being addressed by the Arkansas legislature. Various hunting and fishing laws were passed and repealed with little effect. For instance, one 1899 law declared it illegal to discharge firearms after sundown with the intent of killing, injuring or frightening any aquatic fowl in Mississippi, Crittenden, Cross, Poinsett and St. Francis counties. Fines of $25 to $50 could be levied against violators.

Modern technology finally was overwhelming the swamps. Railroads brought in sportsmen and market hunters. More importantly, when combined with another modern convenience, ice-making equipment, the rails created new avenues for shipping game and fish to the major cities.

In 1873, New York City's Fulton Market posted these prices: Swans, $2; wild geese, 75 cents; canvasbacks, $1 a pair; mallards, 75 cents a pair; teal, 50 cents a pair; wild turkey, 15 cents a pound; and deer legs, 11 cents, saddles (tenderloin), 18 cents, and haunches, 20 cents.

Although sportsmen began noticing reduced numbers of waterfowl, it was difficult to mount any kind of conservation effort, simply because ducks and geese remained relatively abundant.

Consider this turn-of-the-century letter to *Forest and Stream* magazine from a St. Louis man: "No; wild ducks are not all dead yet, not if we may judge from the vast multitudes to be seen in the swamps of the sunk land of Missouri and Arkansas.

"In October of 1894 a party of four from this city, and four from Cincinnati, shot over one thousand ducks in one week, and, from the hordes still seen, it did not look as if any were missing. To the average amateur, the piles of ducks would have looked like three times the quantity, as nine-tenths of them were choice mallards. Nor were these all the ducks shot in this quiet and celebrated spot that week. Five market hunters were in there all the time, and in this particular week averaged from 80 to 140 ducks per day each.

"A netter was also at work, who made a shipment of twenty barrels of mallards at one time. Again, to the average amateur, or even to the semi-professional, this may sound fishy. If the receipts of the steamboat which brought the ducks to this market will be proof, they can be produced. The netter made no more shipments, for the natives forced him out of the country with Winchesters."

As noted in the *Arkansas Gazette* story on this page, ducks were bringing about 50 cents each in 1910. Common laborers were paid only a few dollars a day then. A 1909 *Gazette* advertisement for M.M. Cohn Co. listed Hart, Shaffner & Marx men's suits on sale for $16.75 (regular $20 to $25) and shoes for $1 a pair. Obviously, if you could kill 100 ducks a day, you were making good money.

The Big Lake Shooting Club attempted to end that lifestyle for market hunters in 1901. The group of wealthy men, mostly from Memphis and Nashville, included no Arkansas residents. The shooting club organized during the summer of 1900. A deed was executed on July 2, 1901, between the Chicago Mill and Lumber Company and the Paepcke-Leicht Lumber Company, both based in Illinois, and the Big Lake Shooting Club. For the sum of $5, the club purchased the rights to a 10-foot strip of land around Big Lake, and claimed control of the waters within it by riparian rights. The property was to be used only as a game and fish preserve by the Big Lake Shooting Club. The two lumber companies retained rights to the timber.

In short, the Big Lake Shooting Club was attempting to lock out the market hunters, including James Beckhart. The battle would last for almost 15 years. It first moved to the courthouse in 1903, with the market hunters contending that Big Lake was a navigable part of Little River and thus not subject to ownership.

APPALLING TRAFFIC IN DUCK SLAUGHTER

Wholesale Shipment of Game in Big Lake District by Evading Laws Described by Game Warden

Arkansas Gazette, December 15, 1910

"I do not think that there is any place in the United States where more ducks are being killed by market hunters and shipped out of a state than at Big Lake, the scene of the burning of the clubhouse several weeks ago," said State Game Warden E.V. Visart yesterday afternoon when asked about reports of the wholesale slaughter and shipping of ducks from that place.

According to Mr. Visart, 5,000 ducks are killed every day on this lake and about 150 barrels of game daily are shipped out of the state from this point.

When asked further about the slaughter and why the hunters could ship this game out when the laws of Arkansas prohibited this practice, Mr. Visart said: "It will only be a matter of a short time until ducks will be exterminated in that county. To give you an idea of the enormity of the slaughter, if all the ducks that are killed in one week by market hunters who infest this territory were to fly in one drove and in a straight line, they would stretch to Hot Springs and half way back to Little Rock. This is a comparison simply to show you what it means in numbers.

"In regard to barrel shipments, there are on an average of 75 ducks to the barrel, so if 150 barrels were shipped in a day this would mean 11,250 ducks. These ducks bring, retail, about 50 cents each, on an average, which means about $5,625 worth of ducks sold out of Arkansas by men who do not pay one cent license to the state for the right to hunt here.

"The reason of these men being allowed to ship these ducks is simply this: The members of the Big Lake Club succeeded in having a law passed which allowed them to carry a certain amount of ducks out of the state. Nearly all of the Big Lake members are prominent men from other states and after their hunting trips to Big Lake they wished to carry some of their game home with them. They established a bag limit and have lived up to it, for all of them are true sportsmen.

"In order that they might have the right to hunt on the lake and to keep the market hunters from slaughtering the ducks these Big Lake members purchased a strip of ground around the entire lake, which would prevent outsiders from hunting, on account of the trespass laws. This was done simply to protect the club, but had little effect.

"Injunctions then were asked from the court to prevent the market hunters from shooting on the lake, but had just as little effect, for the shooting goes on unhindered. Now another thing about this law up there. It not only affects that district, but the entire state. Game is shipped from all parts of the state to that district, where it is then shipped out of state. This is an easy way to evade the law. Unless some action is taken to stop these market hunters one of the best duck stands in the United States will be gone."

According to Mr. Visart, the conditions around Big Lake are very much the same as the Reelfoot Lake affair in Tennessee. These market hunters on Big Lake consider that they have the right to hunt there and to kill as many ducks as they please. Theirs, they think, is an inherent right which no law can dispute. The passing of the law allowing the shipment of game from that district has aided them, Mr. Visart says. The buying of the strip of land around the lake by the Big Lake members has made them all the more determined, Mr. Visart also says.

It is stated that a movement is now on foot to have the club deed its property to the United States government as a national game preserve. This would result in its being policed by federal rangers and the ducks protected.

The Big Lake Shooting Club won initial victories in court but paid a heavy price. Its 20-room, $8,000 clubhouse burned to the ground in July 1904. A bigger and better clubhouse was built in its place; fire destroyed it, the boat docks and boats in 1910, at an estimated loss of $50,000.

After that, Col. Joseph H. Acklen, the Big Lake Shooting Club member who led the fight against the market hunters, declared he would rebuild the clubhouse better than before and use concrete and steel to make it fireproof, if necessary. Acklen also made a visit to the governor's office in Little Rock. Newspaper stories the next day reported that Governor Donaghey might "order the Blytheville company of the state troops to the scene."

A third clubhouse was built, but not of concrete and steel. It included a large dining room, reception rooms and 24 bedrooms, each with a private bath. The Big Lake Shooting Club hired six Pinkerton men to guard the area.

The burned clubhouses were just one indication of the violence that resulted from this confrontation. In the initial court case — Frank G. Fite and J.H. Acklen, Trustees, et al., vs. W.H. Harrison, et al. — Acklen testified that Harrison told him, "the market hunters intended to take eighty-five cents of Winchester rifle shells (the price of a box at Manila) and settle the whole matter." Acklen claimed Harrison told him that Big Lake Shooting Club members and their paddlers would be shot if they went on the lake. After making his threats, Harrison "then pulled a flask of whiskey out of his pocket, took a drink and left," according to Acklen.

Those threats weren't just talk. As the the accompanying newspaper articles indicate, club caretakers and watchmen were the targets of several shooting incidents.

Although Acklen was determined to win this war, it became apparent that local market hunters would never abide by the various court orders. They believed they had God-given rights to hunt and fish on Big Lake.

In 1913 when President Woodrow Wilson took office, he appointed Acklen to the office of Chief Game Inspector of the United States. It was a new position under the Department of Agriculture that headed up the United States game wardens. With federal power on the club's side, more legal battles were won against the market hunters. But the violence continued.

By the next year Acklen realized the animosity would continue against the club. Wanting to stop market hunting and protect the waterfowl, he convinced President Wilson to make the area a game preserve. In 1915 Wilson signed an Executive Order that created Big Lake Reserve and made it unlawful for any person to hunt, trap, capture, disturb or kill any bird of any kind within the reservation.

Interestingly, the period from 1900 until 1916 is considered the time when waterfowl populations first became endangered. It coincides almost exactly with the years of the Big Lake battle.

Around the U.S., more effective ammunition and automatic shotguns increased the efficiency of market hunters, in particular, but also sport hunters.

Declaring Big Lake a federal refuge didn't completely stop the slaughter of ducks there. However, it signaled — as did the 1916 international treaty on migratory birds — that the problem had been recognized and efforts would be made to do something about it.

QUIET AT BIG LAKE

Pinkertons Are There, However, And Further Trouble Expected

The Commercial Appeal, Nov. 12, 1911

JONESBORO — From reports received in this city today there is peace and quietude at Big Lake, but an outbreak at any time will cause no surprise, from the fact that there are now a number of Pinkerton men and much ammunition there ready to be used in case the hunters should make an assault upon the club members at any time.

A trunk belonging to one of the club members came in here today, riddled with shot, but it was impossible to ascertain at what time the shots were fired into the trunk. The supposition is that this occurred when the night watchman, Lees, was shot. From parties who came here today, it is learned that the club members will be ready to defend themselves if an assault is made.

Lees, the wounded man, who was shot by the unknown men at the clubhouse, has improved sufficiently to enable him to return to the clubhouse this afternoon. If the club members are attacked again, a bloody battle is expected.

CLUB WARDEN SHOT THE TWELFTH TIME

Walter Gleabes, 45, Ambushed Near Blytheville, May Die From Bullet Wound

Arkansas Gazette, March 1, 1915

BLYTHEVILLE — Walter Gleabes, 45, deputy United States marshal and warden for the estate of the Big Lake Shooting Club, last night was shot from ambush the twelfth time. A bullet from a .38-caliber gun passed through his left lung. It is thought he will die. Gleabes was shot as he passed from the rear door of the clubhouse on the preserve. Bloodhounds were rushed to the scene, but the assailant took a boat and escaped down the lake.

The shooting is the result of a feud that it is alleged exists between residents of the section and the owners of the club, who are not residents of the state. All of the shootings, it is said, have been the result of attacks upon Gleabes because he was employed by the club and had made arrests of trespassers for violations of the club's hunting rules.

RULES OF THE BIG LAKE SHOOTING CLUB

(Editor's note: The Big Lake Shooting Club was formed in 1900. Its rules and by-laws were entered as evidence in W.H. Harrison, et al., vs. Frank G. Fite, et al. in 1903.)

The purposes of this club are to afford opportunity to its members for healthful recreation and relaxation from business cares and pursuits, and to cultivate gentlemanly intercourse and pleasant social relations.

Rules of the Executive Committee

1. No one is entitled to the privileges of the clubhouse or permitted to use the boats belonging to the club, except members and their guests.
2. Guests going to the club on the evening train will be allowed to shoot the whole of the next day only, but will be permitted to remain at the club house that night.
3. The season for shooting ducks shall open and close at the discretion of the Executive Committee.
4. Fishing season for families and guests shall be from March 25 till the opening of the fall season for shooting.
5. No member or guest shall kill more than one hundred ducks in any one day.
6. No member or guest shall carry more than two guns on the lake, and under no circumstances shall he carry or shoot a rifle on the lake.
7. No member shall be permitted to use individual property of any other member of the club, except by written permission of said member.
8. A member while at the clubhouse shall pay to the keeper for his meals $2 per day — that is to say, for every day he shall pay for three meals, whether he eats them or not. The price of meals for guests shall be the same as for members.
9. After arrival of train preceding time of going on the lake, members, guests, and visitors shall choose: First, for paddler; second, for stand; and the lowest number drawn shall have first choice. Paddlers shall not be paid more than the following amounts for their work:
From daylight to noon — $1.50;
From daylight until night — $2.00;
For two men shooting in the same boat all day — $2.50;
For two men shooting in the same boat half day — $2.00;
and only two men shall go in the same boat when absolutely necessary on account of scarcity of paddlers. It is the duty of paddler to clean the gun and draw the game of his employer on returning to the clubhouse.

No member or guest shall kill more than one hundred ducks in any one day.

10. A list of the regular paddlers at the lake shall be posted at the clubhouse. In choosing paddlers, members and guests shall be required to exhaust the regular list before any outside paddlers are employed. After exhausting the regular list, members and guests may employ any person available to paddle for them, provided they have not been excluded from the club grounds.
11. No member or guest shall employ or send either his paddler or an extra man on or about the lake for the purpose of routing up the ducks or making them fly.
12. Paddlers are prohibited from carrying or using a gun on the lake, except to kill crippled birds.
13. No paddler or other employee shall be allowed to shoot game on the grounds of the club.
14. Dogs shall not be allowed in the clubhouse sleeping or dining rooms.
15. Members and guests must not leave the clubhouse to go upon the lake before daylight, and must not shoot in the evening when the flash of the gun can be seen.
16. Any member who shall shoot on the grounds or lake on Sunday, or use the premises of the club in bringing in game killed on Sunday, shall, for the first offense, be fined $10, and for the second offense be dismissed from the club.
17. Anyone who shall kill a songbird, other than gamebird, on the club grounds, shall be fined $5.
18. Members and guests shall not enter the carpeted rooms of the club house with dirty boots on.
19. The keeper of the clubhouse shall keep the same clean and in good order at all times: see that fires are made promptly, keep clean linen on the beds, and clean towels in their proper places.
20. Any member violating any of the foregoing rules shall be reported by the keeper to the President of the club. Should the keeper fail to report any violations of these rules which may come under his observation, he shall be fined $5 for each offense, said fine to be deducted from his monthly wages.
21. The game warden shall have general supervision of all employees of the club, keep a close supervision over the lake and grounds, call attention to any violations of club rules, and report same to the Secretary.
22. The penalty for the violation of any of the above rules shall be fixed by the Executive Committee after an investigation.
23. If a paddler does not report, and is not ready for duty at the proper time for going on the lake, he shall not be allowed to go out with any member or guest that day.
24. Members or guests who do not intend to go shooting on the day for which paddlers and stands are to be drawn shall not be permitted to draw for paddlers or stands. If a member or guest, after drawing a paddler or stand, concludes not go shooting that day, such paddler or stand shall be drawn for again by those who have not secured a paddler or stand, as the case may be. A violation of this rule shall be punished by fine in the discretion of the Executive Committee.

Taming the Great Swamp

More dirt moved in draining 'Swampeast Missouri' than at Panama Canal

It was no exaggeration to label this convergence of big rivers and Ozark streams the "Great Swamp." In fact, it's difficult to exaggerate when describing: 1) an area that has been compared with Egypt's Nile Valley for soil fertility; and 2) an engineering feat bigger than the Panama Canal.

In Missouri's bootheel and Arkansas' northeast corner, a flat bottomland stretches more than 100 miles, east of the Ozark foothills. To the north, the Ohio River flows into the Mississippi. Ozark streams, like the St. Francis River and Little River, meet here, too. This was paradise for wintering ducks, where the wide funnel of the Mississippi Flyway starts to constrict. That's why Big Lake concentrated market hunters, too.

But hunters enjoyed the Great Swamp on their terms. In winter, nature shielded them from the full assault of malaria-carrying mosquitoes. And, as visitors, they weren't affected by the frequent flood waters of the Mississippi River. For all those people other than duck hunters, the Great Swamp was hell. However, in one of the great engineering feats of mankind, the Great Swamp was transformed into the Great Plantation.

Missouri's Little River Drainage District serves as the prime example of what would take place throughout the Delta lands of Arkansas, Tennessee, Mississippi and Louisiana. Little River is the largest drainage district in the United States. While its legal boundaries cover 540,000 acres, from Cape Girardeau to the Missouri-Arkansas line, more than 1.2 million acres are drained through a series of man-made ditches, canals and levees.

Before this massive engineering pro-

Dredge boats worked their way through the Great Swamp, leaving straight lines of drainage ditches behind them.

ject, the state's bootheel area was often called "Swampeast Missouri." Less than 10 percent was free of water year-round. The thick forest of massive cypress, gum, hickory and oak trees, some nearly 30 feet in circumference, attracted the timber industry in the late 1800s. Railroads were built to accommodate timbermen. The rails served sportsmen and market hunters as well, allowing them access to the Great Swamp.

Once the trees were cut, the need to drain the Great Swamp increased. The lush forests indicated the richness of the soil beneath them.

The 1910 Bureau of Labor Statistics report compared this area with the Nile Valley. It stated: "The inexhaustible supply and fertility of the Egyptian soil is no greater than the alluvial depositions of Missouri because both have been formed in identically the same manner and possess practically the same properties."

But the Great Swamp was so vast and flat that only a massive project could transform it into farm land. From 1914 through 1928, more than 1 million cubic yards of dirt were moved in constructing 957 miles of ditches and 304 miles of levees. That total exceeds the amount of earth moved in constructing the Panama Canal.

Where only 10 percent of the land was farmable before, 96 percent was dry now. And, as predicted, the fertile soil began producing bumper crops of cotton, corn, soybeans, grain sorghum and rice.

Little River Drainage District represents the largest example of numerous similar projects taking place in the Delta at this time, especially in Arkansas.

About one-third of Arkansas lies in the Mississippi River Alluvial Plain, better known as the Delta. This region includes 8 million acres of wetlands at one time. Most of those acres were covered in bottomland hardwoods, especially the red oak species.

From 1960 to 1970, an average of 150,000 acres of Delta timberland was cleared per year. By 1985, only 11 percent (875,000 acres) of Arkansas' wetlands remained. No other state in the Mississippi Alluvial Plain has lost a greater percentage of its wetlands than has Arkansas.

Photo courtesy Barry McFarland

McFarland carrying on Big Lake tradition of duck call-making that began with Beckhart

Beginner's luck played no part in 1993 when Barry McFarland's first entry took top prize in the "fancy" division of the Call Makers and Collectors Association of America show. No one else on earth has McFarland's connections to the turn-of-the-century creators of the "Big Lake style" duck call.

McFarland lives in Hornersville, Mo., which was the jumping off point for sportsmen coming from cities like St. Louis and Chicago to hunt Big Lake. It was on a houseboat in Big Lake where J.T. Beckhart made his duck calls. Beckhart's hand-checkered calls are now among the most highly sought collectables.

Claude Stone shared many traits with Beckhart, especially the enjoyment of hunting and fishing around Big Lake. Stone could make a duck call, too. In fact, he was making a "Big Lake style" call when Beckhart died in 1922. Stone bought the checkering tools and remaining walnut blocks from Beckhart's widow. At one time, he made enough calls to supply the York Arms Co., a mail-order sporting goods store in Memphis.

Claude Stone died in 1973, but not before handing down the call-making tradition to his sons. As a youngster, McFarland hunted often with Claude's son Joe. He admits missing many days of school in order to attend his outdoor "classroom." Stone showed him how to blow a duck call and, after his eyesight began to fail, taught McFarland how to do the hand-checkering that makes these calls unique.

Joe Stone died in the early 1990s at the age of 76. By then McFarland was turning out a few of his own calls. McFarland has become a collector of old duck calls and a student of Big Lake history.

Big Lake style duck calls, also referred to as "St. Francis River style" calls, feature four panels on the barrel. The early calls were usually large, giving the call-maker more space to display his craftsmanship. Often only three panels were checkered and the fourth was left open for initials or carvings, like the rifle shown on McFarland's call above.

Photo courtesy Barry McFarland

Barry McFarland makes 10 duck calls a year, like the one shown here. They sell for about $500 each. He strictly follows the Big Lake style, including a German silver reed.

Most Big Lake style calls were made from walnut. Early call-makers usually kept a pot of linseed oil near the stove. Soaking the finished calls in warm linseed oil made them waterproof.

McFarland owns an oil and gas distributorship in Hornersville. He doesn't rely on call-making for income.

He follows the old traditions, making most of his calls from walnut and soaking them in linseed oil for up to four weeks. Occasionally he uses cedar, as Beckhart did.

McFarland carves about 10 calls a year. They usually sell for around $500.

But McFarland's pleasure comes from his sense of history and the role he's playing as one of the few remaining disciples of the original Big Lake duck call-makers.

Big Lake produced World War I hero

Manila's Herman Davis listed fourth among Gen. Pershing's top 100

"The ducks and geese, flying southward in autumn from the cold northland, were the targets that trained the woodsman in the fine qualities of marksmanship which probably saved a company of Americans in France from annihilation."

— George M. Moreland, "Herman Davis: An Arkansas Immortal," Memphis Commercial Appeal, Aug. 8, 1926.

When General John J. Pershing announced the 100 greatest heroes of World War I, the fourth name from the top of the list was Private Herman Davis of Manila. Davis' friends were shocked.

They knew Davis as an excellent hunter and fisherman who had never ventured far from his beloved Big Lake except for an 11-month Army tour of duty. Reportedly, Davis missed the call when his draft notice arrived because he was hunting and fishing on Little River.

When he returned from the war, he seemed unchanged. Davis didn't talk about his experiences in the battlefields of France. A friend helped him find a job with a Big Lake hunting club. It was back to business as usual — hunting and fishing.

Davis was said to assume that he'd simply done what any other soldier would have. The military did not then have the public relations machine in place to inform newspapers about their hometown heroes.

Only when General Pershing issued the list did anyone discover that Davis was Arkansas' greatest World War I hero. At the urging of friends, Davis finally showed them his medals. They were again shocked when he pulled them from an old fishing tackle box.

Two statements ultimately define Arkansas' greatest World War I hero:

1) Davis kept some of the most treasured medals of military service next to his prized fishing lures;

2) Only two times did Davis discuss his war exploits, and both were with close friends in duck blinds on Big Lake.

It has been written that Davis wiped out a German machine gun nest "with a coolness he might have displayed when aiming at a flock of mallards flying southward over his beautiful valley home in Arkansas."

Only two times did Davis discuss his war exploits, and both were with close friends in duck blinds on Big Lake.

Whatever his actual style and frame of mind, Davis earned the Distinguished Service Cross for his actions at Molleville Farm, near Verdun, France, on Oct. 10, 1918. The citation described his actions as follows:

"On duty as a company runner, he was accompanying the left assault platoon of his company during the advance through the woods, when it was fired on by an enemy machine gun. As soon as the gun opened fire, the members of the platoon scattered and attempted to flank the gun, but Private Davis pushed on ahead, being the first to reach the nest, attacked it single handed, and killed the four enemy gunners. His gallant act enabled his platoon to continue the advance."

With his duties as a runner or scout, Davis worked ahead of his company and often encountered the enemy. Other instances of his bravery have been reported, including killing 11 Germans, one by one, as they emerged from a dugout. Another instance helped confirm the legend of his shooting ability. Along front line trenches, German soldiers could be seen about 1,000 yards away, moving as if they were out of rifle range.

Davis reportedly said, "Why that's just good shootin' distance," then proceeded to kill five Germans before the others took cover.

Davis' exploits may have grown with time, but there is little doubt he was an excellent marksman.

As George Moreland wrote in the Memphis *Commercial Appeal*, in 1926: "Even before his government pinned upon his breast the badge of sharpshooter he had known he could shoot. A woodsman from birth — a son of the swamp section of Arkansas — he had learned to shoot straight in early boyhood."

If Davis' heroics did grow with time, it wasn't because of anything Davis said.

In an *Arkansas Historical Quarterly* article, "Herman Davis: Forgotten Hero," which appeared in 1955, Margaret Smith Ross chronicled Davis' life from his birth on January 3, 1888, at Big Lake Island to his death on January 5, 1923, at a Memphis hospital. Ross reported that Davis never wore his medals in public, but his wife did wear them occasionally during public functions she attended with Davis.

And it was Ross who found no evidence of Davis recounting his war experiences, except for the two times in duck blinds on Big Lake.

In addition to the Distinguished Service Cross from the U.S. government, the French government awarded Davis the Croix de Guerre with palm, a gilt star for the Croix de Guerre and the Medaille Militaire, which Moreland termed "the highest military decoration in the world."

Poison gas that Davis encountered during the war reportedly contributed to the tuberculosis that killed him just two days after his 35th birthday.

However, Davis' presence remains prominent near Big Lake. A granite monument honoring him stands in Manila, just off Highway 18, at Herman Davis Memorial Park.

Horner recalls days of market hunting

'I've seen times when you just got tired of shooting. You quit.'

Like many people living around Big Lake in the 1920s and 30s, Jess Horner relied on it for everything from putting food on the table to money in his pocket. He remembers selling thousands of ducks "in the rough" for 35 to 40 cents each. If there was anything to hunt, trap or fish around Big Lake, Jess Horner pursued it.

"In the 1920s, I bought my first car, a Ford," said Horner, who celebrated his 90th birthday in August 1997. "I paid $500 in cash for it. All of that money was made from trapping and hunting on Big Lake."

When asked about the most ducks he ever killed in a single day on Big Lake, Horner replied, "About a hundred, I guess. You could only carry so much ammunition.

"I've seen the times when you just got tired of shooting. You quit. You just didn't want any more."

The good old days of Big Lake are long gone, but not forgotten. Horner was one of a half-dozen men who guided "sports" from St. Louis, Kansas City, Memphis and Chicago, where Big Lake's hunting reputation had spread.

"We had the ducks coming in so thick one time, they were coming in from all directions," Horner laughed. "I remember one guy stood up and said, 'Oh, hell, they're shitting on us.'"

Horner said the early laws concerning duck hunting were pretty much ignored.

"We didn't pay too much attention to the legal season, but the ducks didn't come down until it got cold," he said.

Even after Big Lake was declared a wildlife refuge, the hunters came.

"I don't remember even seeing a game warden for years," he said. "Everybody considered that a free place to go."

One time Horner did find a note in a shotgun shell hull that he'd left at a favorite Big Lake hunting hole the day before. The note was from the game warden, and it read: "Jess, you'd better quit hunting here, or I'm going to have to do something about it."

The use of live decoys was prohibited in 1935. Until that time, live decoys were common in Arkansas, and a Little Rock company made neck collars and leg bands for live decoys.

Horner was born in Manila. His father, Joe, captained steamboats that ran from Hornersville, Mo., to Marked Tree.

Jess remembers James Beckhart and Ed St. Mary, two of the best-known makers of Big Lake style duck calls. He bought calls at St. Mary's house in Manila. He finds it difficult to comprehend their value to collectors today.

"That was the caller I used, a St. Mary," Horner said. "You could buy a caller for a dollar. They got up to two dollars. I sold one for $500. Somebody paid me $500 for one of my last St. Mary callers, and it wasn't even complete."

Horner started duck hunting in the age of live decoys. He usually kept about four dozen around the farm all year. During duck season, they stayed in a pen near the Big Lake shoreline at Tim's Point.

"Before you knew it, the ducks were trained," Horner said. "You'd put a collar on the hens and just leave the drakes free. Three or four hens was all you'd ever have. When you finished hunting, you'd pick up the hens with their anchors and put them in the boat. Then you'd tap on the boat with a paddle and here'd come the drakes. They'd jump in the boat and ride all the way to shore. As you got to shore, they'd fly and go to the pen, where they'd wait on me to feed them."

After live decoys were banned in 1935, duck hunters had to rely more on their calling ability. Horner and the hunters of that era gained special insight for calling ducks because they were around so much waterfowl, both wild game and tame decoys. And they had never depended exclusively on live decoys to attract ducks. Horner's father taught him to blow a duck call.

"A lot of people don't understand duck calling," Horner said. "They think you're supposed to say, 'quack, quack, quack.' That's not it.

"You're not trying to sound like one duck, you're trying to sound like a lot of ducks. You're trying to make noise like the woods are full of ducks. And that takes a little know-how."

Jess and another frequent hunting companion, Bud Wilson, were known as two of the better duck callers on Big Lake.

"Our two callers were poison," Horner said with a smile. "We could take the ducks away from anybody."

But Horner claims nobody could blow a duck call on Big Lake as well as Henry Ashabranner.

"I've always said he could make a duck stop and back up to get in the hole," Horner said laughing.

With ducks in hand, Russell Leggett of Gosnell wades in front of the 21-foot-tall blind that he has hunted from for several years.

Blinds still standing tall

Big Lake WMA unique in continuing to permit blinds on public land

The blind was a formidable presence in the dark. It stood more than 20 feet tall. With ragged edges and a solid middle it looked more like a huge stump than a small house sitting in the middle of an oak and cypress forest.

The fact that it sat in the middle of the Arkansas Game and Fish Commission's Big Lake Wildlife Management Area makes it an anomaly when it comes to duck hunting in the public hunting grounds of this state. Big Lake is one of two WMAs where hunters are allowed to build structures for the purpose of duck hunting.

Morris Jarrett of Blytheville leads a group of hunters through part of the network of ditches found in Big Lake WMA.

That luxury is often a sore spot among duck hunters at other WMAs, where blinds are strictly forbidden.

The problem is big enough that legislators from southeast Arkansas attempted to pass a law in 1995 that would forbid the building of blinds on public land. The attempt never got off the ground, but hard feelings still remain.

From a hunting standpoint, Big Lake WMA is recognized as one of the state's premier duck shooting grounds. Most hunters don't realize this area provides the background for some of the state's richest hunting history.

Its location in the extreme northeast corner allows it to hide from the attention other WMAs closer to populated cities receive. There are few hunters who travel from outside the immediate area to hunt here; as a result there is very little guide activity.

Given the reputation of Stuttgart, most hunters would not guess that this is where organized duck hunting first began in Arkansas.

The area known as Big Lake was formed by the New Madrid earthquake of 1811-12. On territorial maps it was referred to as the "Great Swamp." Those names, Big Lake and Great Swamp,

Jarrett and a black Labrador retriever look to the sky for ducks. No hunting is allowed in adjacent Big Lake National Wildlife Refuge, and that helps hold ducks near Big Lake WMA.

leave the impression that Big Lake is an expansive swamp, like those in Louisiana and Florida.

But Big Lake WMA is comprised mostly of flooded oak and cypress trees. It looks like the traditional flooded bottomlands of Bayou Meto and Wattensaw.

Today Big Lake refers to two public areas here. The 11,038-acre Big Lake National Wildlife Refuge became the first federal refuge established in the state in 1915. Duck hunting is not allowed in the refuge, and it serves as a rest area for thousands of migrating ducks. The 11,447-acre Big Lake WMA was purchased by the AGFC in 1951. Together they comprise one of the largest wetland areas remaining in northeast Arkansas.

Traditions that die hard, combined with a lack of people, are why blinds are still a part of this area.

"We don't have the large number of people who come here to hunt," said Russell Leggett of Gosnell. "This is more of a community hunting area, and we don't have the hunter conflict problems that other areas have."

The blinds are built and shared by local hunters. They know the blinds are property of the state and, as such, operate under a first-come, first-served basis.

"It works that way, and has for as long as I can remember," Leggett said. "Everybody honors everybody else. You won't find that anywhere else."

While the blinds are often the center of a discussion on Big Lake by those who do not hunt here, it is the history of hunting that sets this area apart.

Morris Jarrett of Blytheville has hunted Big Lake WMA for the past two decades. He called the 1996-97 season "the slowest I can remember."

But Jarrett knows if tradition holds, the good hunting will return. The Great Swamp has been drained for agriculture since Big Lake's heyday at the turn of the century. But its location in the funnel of the Mississippi Flyway assures that as long as there are ducks, they will fly close enough to hear a duck call from Big Lake.

History draws interesting parallels between old and new here, too. It's fitting that the present controversy over permanent blinds would occur at the same place where market hunters and sporting club owners battled almost a century ago.

Local hunters are willing to fight for what they have today, but this is a simple shouting match compared with the gunfire and bloodshed in the early 1900s.

In 1994, when the first attempts at outlawing blinds in Big Lake were made, a public meeting was held in Paragould. According to Jarrett, more than 500 duck hunters showed up to fight the measure.

"If there was ever going to be a lynching around here, that is what it would be about," Jarrett said.

And unlike the hunters during the early part of the century, those who hunt the area get along.

"We just don't have very many problems," said Brent Farmer of Manila, who manages the area for the AGFC. "I believe you can go to almost any blind, and, if there is room, they will invite you to go hunting with them."

While most of the hunting takes place in blinds, water levels often are ideal for wade hunting. However, a boat is required to get across the grid of ditches in the area.

Getting lost in Big Lake WMA would

Before shooting time, Leggett (left) and Jarrett cook breakfast on a gas stove in the blind.

be difficult. Before the AGFC purchased the land, a series of ditches was dug within the timber. Every half mile a ditch runs east and west. All the ditches hook up to a main ditch that runs through the area from north to south. The ditches ensure that even during the driest of falls, Big Lake has some water for duck hunting.

Hunting from a blind can be done by asking for an invitation at the boat ramp or asking local hunters where abandoned blinds sites are located.

Jarrett and Leggett share a blind that is 18 feet long by six feet wide. The floor is 13 feet off the ground. Boats are placed under the floor, and hunters climb a ladder to the top level to shoot. That top level includes a gas stove, where eggs, bacon and biscuits are cooked each morning before shooting time.

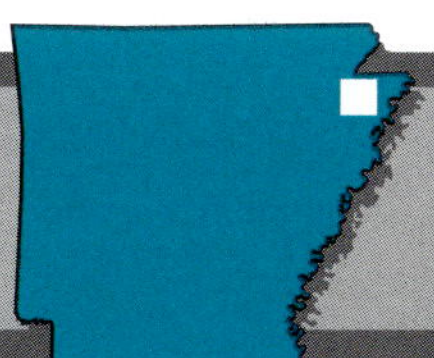

BIG LAKE WMA

Acres: 11,447
First land purchase: 1951
Location: Between Manila and Blytheville in Mississippi County, just south of the Missouri bootheel. The south boundary is only 1.5 miles from Arkansas Highway 18; the north boundary is formed by the Missouri line.
Topo maps (7.5 series, U.S. Geological Survey): Half Moon, Dell.

Big Lake Wildlife Management Area forms the eastern half of one of the last remaining large tracts of bottomland hardwood timber in northeast Arkansas. And it contains all of the public duck hunting land in this area. Big Lake National Wildlife Refuge, 11,038 acres adjacent to the west, doesn't allow waterfowl hunting.

Much of Big Lake WMA, which is managed by the Arkansas Game and Fish Commission, is flooded for waterfowl hunting each fall and winter. A series of drainage ditches forms a grid that allows hunters easy access to the flooded timber. This is one of only two WMAs where permanent blinds are allowed.

Mallard Lake, a 300-acre AGFC-built lake, forms the southern tip of the WMA. A state record 16-pound, 4-ounce largemouth bass was caught here in 1976. The lower lake serves as a waterfowl rest area during the hunting seasons.

Blankenship grew up hunting ducks on Big Lake

If you've hunted at Big Lake Wildlife Management Area, you've heard some of the names: Yellow Duck, Hay Opening, Lighthouse, Yoke, Upper Stake, Middle Stake, Lower Stake, Goose Opening, Grassy, Honey Hole, Big Alek and Little Alek. Those are just a few names of duck hunting holes at Big Lake WMA.

"These are all holes that were hunted after they made the refuge," said Koehler Blankenship, referring to the adjoining Big Lake National Wildlife Refuge, which is closed to waterfowl hunting. "These were low spots, before they started flooding this area."

Blankenship farms land near Dell that adjoins Big Lake WMA. He represents the third generation of his family to enjoy the lowlands of the Great Swamp.

"I first started hunting Honey Hole with my mother," Blankenship said. "My dad didn't think I was old enough to go with him yet. My mother was one of the best duck pickers ever. It took the feathers from 30 duck breasts to stuff a pillow. We started keeping up with how many pillows she had made from ducks I killed at Honey Hole. When my dad realized that, he decided I could start going with him."

Blankenship grew up hearing the stories about how his grandfather, John August Koehler, would stay in the swamps of Big Lake all winter, coming home only for Thanksgiving and Christmas. He passed the winter this way from 1880 to 1890.

"They would pole boats from place to place and set up hunting camp," Blankenship said. "They'd have to move from time to time because the smell of all the animal carcasses would get so bad."

True to his blood, Blankenship spent weeks at a time hunting this area during his high school years. He describes Big Lake as if it were his living room. He knows the names of all the old duck hunting holes in the refuge, too: Big Green, Little Green, Butterfly, Katy Ray, Stumpy and Cottonseed. There's a story behind every name.

"A boat loaded with cottonseed sank right there in Big Lake," said Blankenship, explaining one of the names, and, at the same time, showing how the old duck hunting stories of Big Lake have stayed alive.

Photo courtesy Bill Brewer

Railroads provided easy access to the clubhouse of the Buffalo Island Hunting and Fishing Club, located on the St. Francis River.

Railroads key to exploring swamp

'One hundred-fifty pounds of baggage, including guns and dogs, carried free'

In 1858, the Memphis and Little Rock Railroad began operating trains between Hopefield on the Mississippi River and Madison on the St. Francis River. Over the next 40 years, parallel iron rails would crisscross the Delta.

Many of the short-line routes to the swamps were built initially for timber harvest. They dead-ended in the middle of nowhere, which is exactly where hunters and anglers wanted to be. Railroads into the Great Swamp in the late 1800s were equivalent to float planes into Alaskan wilderness almost a century later.

Railroad employees knew how to get to the best hunting and fishing spots. Sportsmen, especially the more well-to-do adventurers, learned to rely on railroad workers for information.

Eager to sell tickets to anyone, the rail lines catered to sportsmen. Flatcars could be loaded with boats and gear. Ice blocks were carried in; game and fish were hauled out.

In 1893, the Missouri Pacific Railway offered a 60-page pamphlet devoted strictly to hunting and fishing opportunities along its "Iron Mountain Route" from southeast Missouri through eastern Arkansas into Louisiana.

In the back of the brochure, under the headlines, "Important Information" and "Hunter's Rates and Special Cars" it stated: "The Iron Mountain Route have (sic) arranged for special rates for hunters in parties of three or more, to the more important points in Missouri, Arkansas and Louisiana. Tickets are good for thirty days, and stopovers are allowed at pleasure. One hundred-fifty pounds of baggage, including guns and dogs, carried free of charge.

"Hunting cars, having sleeping accommodations for any number up to thirty, with cook, cooking utensils and full equipment, can be chartered by parties, and may be sidetracked at any point desired."

As the best places were discovered, "outing clubs" and "shooting clubs" formed and clubhouses were constructed. The photograph, at right, of the Buffalo Island Hunting and Fishing Club perfectly illustrates the concept. Step off the train and you were at the club's headquarters. Step into a boat and you were on your way to the clubhouse.

Many of the best-known clubs of the late 1800s, such as Wapanocca Outing Club and Oak Donic Outing Club, had clubhouses just off the tracks. Hatchie Coon was a railroad stop, and the Hatchie Coon Outing Club could be reached by hand-car.

Big game hunting, for black bear and deer, received most of the attention in these railroad pamphlets. But no aspect of Arkansas outdoors tradition is linked more closely with the railroads than duck hunting.

The number of duck call-makers who worked for railroads highlights that point. From Henry Kenward of Jonesboro, maker of the "New Bechhart" call in the early 1900s to Chick Major of Stuttgart, who took duck call-making to a new level before his death in 1974, numerous Arkansas call-makers have been associated with the railroad. Kenward worked as an engineer for the Cotton Belt line from 1885 to 1925. Major drove a truck for a railroad agency.

The Big Lake Shooting Club, which engaged in a 15-year battle with local market hunters, also was tied to the railroad. Most of its members were wealthy; they included lawyers, doctors and even horse-racing-track owners. None lived in Arkansas. Most resided in Nashville and Memphis, but some lived as far away as Chicago and Pittsburgh.

The rails made Big Lake accessible to them. They would ride in private cars to Big Lake, where the cars were side-tracked until the sportsmen were ready to return home. Before the clubhouse was built and between clubhouse fires, the private cars served as lodging, too.

That basic concept continues today. The railroads are no longer necessary. But private clubs that construct a common clubhouse are numerous. And private railroad cars exist today in the form of camper-trailers and recreational vehicles that are "sidetracked" around the clubhouse during duck season.

Photo courtesy Bill Brewer

Buffalo Island Hunting and Fishing Club

(Editor's note: This is an excerpt from a Missouri Pacific Railroad pamphlet, published in the late 1890s.)

Bertig, Arkansas, is located about ten miles east of Paragould, on the St. Francis River. The principal manufacturing concerns of Bertig are the Smeltzly Lumber Company, Penrod & Wood saw mill, and the American Hardwood Lumber Company.

These are large concerns, giving employment to a great number of men, and their annual shipments over the Paragould Southeastern amount to many millions of feet.

But to prospectors, and especially the devotees of the rod and gun, the leading attractions at Bertig are the splendid clubhouses. These clubhouses are built partly extending into the river, and you step from their broad verandas into your boat and go in any direction you may choose in quest of game and fish. The Buffalo Island Hunting and Fishing Club, with S. Virgilio as manager, is a home for the weary traveler from whatever direction he may come. Mr. Virgilio caters to the wants of his guests with all the skill of a connoisseur, being an experienced hotel and club house manager. The officers of this club are C.S. Wheeler, president, Equitable Building, St. Louis, Mo., and John H. Holmes, secretary, 506 Columbia Building, St. Louis, Mo. The rates to club members are $1.00 per day, which includes boats, board and lodging, and to non-members, $2.00 per day.

The membership fee is fixed at the nominal sum of $2.50 per year. The membership certificates expire on the first day of each year, and membership is open to all persons of good standing. This clubhouse is situated about one-half mile from Seneca Slough, which affords the best duck shooting from the first of September until the first of March. It is a mile and a half to Badwell's Lake, which can be reached by hand car. This lake is about 20 miles long, with an average width of half a mile, with water from two and a half feet to twenty feet deep. This body of water is celebrated for its fine fly and minnow fishing.

Fifteen miles below Bertig is another clubhouse, under the same management, and is located, it is said, on the finest duck shooting waters in the United States. Mr. Virgilio furnishes boats and guides to his guests and transports them to the lower boathouse, where they are admitted on the same membership. When we state, upon the authority of hundreds of sportsmen, who have tried it, that the average day's catch in these waters is from 40 to 125 bass per day, we are warranted in saying that this is the sportsman's paradise, and that the followers of Sir Isaac Walton can here find everything to gratify their most fastidious dreams.

Buckingham's famous shotgun, 'Bo Whoop,' disappeared in Arkansas

Nash Buckingham's Burt Becker-made 12-gauge magnum double-barrel shotgun remains the best-known gun in waterfowling history, even though the original version disappeared in 1948.

Buckingham acquired the gun in 1926 and nicknamed it "Bo Whoop," because of the sound it made when he fired it.

"...you could always recognize its roar. It made a *whoom*, more like a cannon," wrote Buckingham's friend Berry Brooks, as noted in *The Best of Nash Buckingham*, by George Bird Evans.

The gun weighed 10 pounds and had 32-inch over-bored barrels. Each barrel patterned at better than 90 percent in a 30-inch circle at 40 yards. Buckingham's marksmanship was legendary, especially for making long-range kills on ducks and geese.

On Dec. 1, 1948, Buckingham hunted at the Section 16 Club near Clarendon. Two game wardens arrived just as Buckingham was getting a ride back to town with a man named Clifford Green. The wardens checked licenses and ducks, but the main business at hand was for one warden to get a look at "Bo Whoop." The gun was laid on the fender of Green's car.

Buckingham realized "Bo Whoop" was missing before he got back to Clarendon. Retracing their route from the Section 16 Club didn't produce the gun. Buckingham's name and "Built by Burt Becker" were engraved on the distinctive double-barrel.

Word of the lost gun spread quickly. Local game wardens, police and hunters joined in the search. At least two people reported seeing the gun still lying on Green's car fender near the town of Roe. Ads were placed with local newspapers and radio stations, but Buckingham never saw the gun again.

"It's fully insured, but I'll never get another friend like that gun," Buckingham wrote in a letter.

An admirer later commissioned Becker to craft another gun for Buckingham. There is continued speculation that someone somewhere must have the original "Bo Whoop."

De shootinest gent'man

Buckingham loved Arkansas' wild duck places

Many a duck hunter has relived the glory days of waterfowling through the writings of Nash Buckingham. But Arkansas hunters have an edge when it comes to appreciating Buckingham's work.

From Wapanocca, just a few miles west of his Memphis residence, to Maddox Bay on the White River, Buckingham hunted many of the best-known duck holes in Arkansas. Though the times have changed, a special frame of reference still exists for those who know this state.

"The night air, sharpened by frost on the rice paddies, is raucous with duck calls being tested," Buckingham wrote in *Blood Lines*, describing the night before the 1937 season opener in DeWitt. "Pretty much every youngster, field hand and outdoor businessman-hunter in that whole region can do pretty well on a duck whistle. Why not? The rice-region boy babies — and some of the girls — cut their teeth, not on rattles, but on wooden or hard-rubber duck calls."

If you know Arkansas, as Buckingham certainly did, you know that's not much of an overstatement, even today.

Buckingham's father, Miles, owned memberships in two clubs when Nash was growing up. One was in Mississippi, the Beaver Dam Ducking Club, located three miles south of Tunica. The other was, of course, Wapanocca. (Buckingham, by the way, always spelled Wapanocca with one "c." This text will stick with the two "c" version used at the national wildlife refuge today.)

Buckingham wrote that he shot his first Arkansas duck — a mallard drake on Thanksgiving Day at Wapanocca in 1890 — at the age of 10.

As an adult, he would become a member of the Lakeside Club, south of West Memphis, and the Section 16 Club near Clarendon. Buckingham hunted with Edgar Queeny on Mill Bayou, near DeWitt, and on Peckerwood Lake, where Queeny would establish Wingmead Farms. It was those early years at Beaver Dam and Wapanocca, however, that laid the foundation for one of the South's most important men in waterfowling.

Photo courtesy Derrydale Press

Nash Buckingham

Buckingham was a natural athlete who lettered in football, baseball and track & field at the University of Tennessee and also distinguished himself as an amateur boxer. That athletic ability carried over into his handling of a shotgun, where he was noted for everything from trap to pigeon to quail shooting. But the stories of his long-range duck shooting stand above all other tales about his marksmanship.

In the introduction of Buckingham's book *Hallowed Years*, Col. H.P. Sheldon describes watching Nash shoot from a nearby blind one morning in Arkansas. Buckingham killed his limit of 15 ducks and used only 17 shells. Sheldon estimated that none of the targets was closer than 50 yards.

Buckingham's best-known book probably is *De Shootinest Gent'man*.

Other titles include *Ole Miss'*, *Game Bag*, *Blood Lines*, *Mark Right* and *Tattered Coat*. They are collections of stories, many of which were first published in the leading outdoor magazines of the time, including *Field & Stream*, *Sports Afield*, *Outdoors*, *The American Field* and *Recreation*.

His articles carried a great deal of practical how-to. But the outdoor magazines hadn't begun to lean on how-to nearly so heavily as they do today. A good story was still the top priority then. Modern readers may wince at much of the black dialect Buckingham used. But his work leaves you with a portrait of the true Southern gentleman.

The most important element of Buckingham's work, however, was his sense of conservation. Born in 1880, Buckingham hunted through the end of the Golden Age of Waterfowling. It gave him a special perspective when waterfowl numbers started to crash.

"Comin' Twenty-One" in *Hallowed Years* may be the single best story to read if you want to discover the essence of Buckingham. It recounts a Washington's Birthday hunt — Feb. 22, 1901. The date alone tells an incredible story. Since the federal government began setting waterfowl seasons in 1918, the latest hunting date has been Jan. 31.

Buckingham would turn 21 years old in May 1901. This hunt was his last at Wapanocca under his father's membership privileges. Upon reaching 21, full membership was required.

Buckingham recounts how he and Judge George Gilham decided to concentrate on drake pintails that day. Wapanocca club rules set bag limits at 50 ducks per day, although there were no state or federal bag limits at this time. After "shooing" countless mallards, gadwalls, teal, shovelers and scaup from their decoys, Buckingham and Gilham finished with 92 pintail drakes and eight mallard drakes. A warm south wind the next day sent the ducks north.

Nash Buckingham started preaching and teaching waterfowl conversation long before it became a popular cause. He spoke with his actions as well. Buckingham served four years as executive secretary of Wild Fowlers, a national conservation organization based in Washington, D.C., dedicated to restoring duck and goose populations.

Nash Buckingham died quietly in his sleep on March 10, 1971, at the age of 90.

ST. FRANCIS SUNKEN LANDS

Acres: 25,425
First purchase: 1957
Location: Located near Marked Tree, Trumann, and Jonesboro in Craighead, Greene and Poinsett counties.
Topo maps (7.5 series, U.S. Geological Survey): Paragould East, Dixie, Lake City, Marked Tree, Hatchie Coon.

Strung out for approximately 30 miles along the St. Francis River bottoms, the St. Francis Sunken Lands WMA can be reached off several state highways from south of Paragould almost to Marked Tree. A major portion of the area is located near Trumann in northern Poinsett county. Primary access during duck season is by boat on the river.

The Sunken Lands were created by the New Madrid earthquakes of 1811-12. Of Arkansas areas in the North American Waterfowl Management Plan, the St. Francis River Management Unit has the highest percentage of land in agriculture and is among the lowest in surface water.

Before all the drainage projects, the St. Francis River was more important than the Cache and White rivers for wintering ducks. When water conditions are good, the public land here continues to provide excellent duck hunting.

Besides waterfowl, the area offers some good squirrel and deer hunting in the bottomland hardwoods. Camping is in designated areas only.

Early clubs considered baiting with corn standard practice

They were described as "the most rigid shooting regulations in the history of wildfowling" when Biological Survey chief J.N. "Ding" Darling announced them in 1935.

Along with a 30-day duck season and a reduced bag limit of 10 ducks per day, the new regulations included a ban on live decoys and prohibited shooting over baited water or land.

For duck call-makers, this signaled a boom period. As the art of calling ducks became better appreciated, hunters longed for their live decoys less and less.

Baiting, however, didn't fade away. Private clubs had baited heavily before the prohibition as a way to retain large numbers of ducks on their waters. Many of these clubs also set and adhered to daily bag limits before they were imposed by the federal government. But baiting also led to some massive duck slaughters by greedy hunters, thus the ban.

In 1928, "A Red Letter Day at Waponoca," by W.L. Moore appeared in *Sportsman's Digest* magazine. Moore mentioned how mallards prefer the shallow lake as it "allows them to feed off the bottom without having to dive for the corn that is daily thrown out near the blinds, or shooting stands. The club has fed with corn for several years, though up to this year there was plenty of natural feed in the lake."

Moore wrote that baiters threw out about 25 bushels of shelled corn a day, and stated: "Feeding the ducks and providing them with the big rest lake, where they are never disturbed, holds them in this locality from the time the first flight comes South in October till they go north in the spring and there are always thousands of ducks on the lake..."

The Wapanocca Outing Club members were considered first-class sportsmen. Many of the club's rules were more strict than federal regulations. Feeding ducks was considered a conservation practice as long as it didn't involve over-harvest.

Even today, defining the thin line between providing food for wildfowl and hunting over bait remains controversial.

(Editor's note: In the early 1960s, there were approximately 350 private duck hunting clubs in Arkansas, according to a survey by the Arkansas Game and Fish Commission. To fully appreciate duck hunting in this state, you must understand the role these clubs have played in so many people's lives. In the chapters that follow, the stories of several clubs are chronicled. Jimason Daggett's letter, which appears below, details the history of Warrior Hunting Club and provides the background for the formation of a typical private duck hunting club in Arkansas.)

January 18, 1994

Mr. West Higginbotham
Marianna, Arkansas

Dear West,

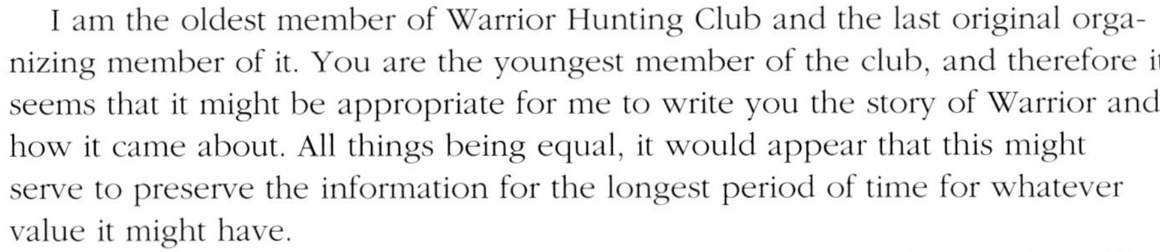

I am the oldest member of Warrior Hunting Club and the last original organizing member of it. You are the youngest member of the club, and therefore it seems that it might be appropriate for me to write you the story of Warrior and how it came about. All things being equal, it would appear that this might serve to preserve the information for the longest period of time for whatever value it might have.

I organized Mallard Ponds Hunting Club, which was one of the earliest (if not the earliest) hunting clubs in this area. It's located about two miles from Fisher. Fisher is north of Hickory Ridge. It was a most successful venture. In those days there were countless numbers of ducks, and the area owned by Mallard Ponds was right in the middle of the grand prairie and thus in the middle of the ducks.

One day I took my Uncle Dag (M.D. Daggett — the druggist) and Dr. W.S. Crawford (a local physician) to Mallard Ponds as my hunting guests. The federal limit was fifteen but the club had a club limit of twelve and we killed our limit in a matter of fifteen or twenty minutes. We waded out of the woods and were standing on the levee looking at the ducks milling around by the thousands with Dr. Crawford commenting that he never saw anything like that in his life. I responded that we had the potential for the same type club in Lee County. My law office then was on the second floor of the Daggett Drug Store building and Dr. Crawford's office was right across the hall. The next day Dr. Crawford appeared in my office and asked me to repeat to him what I had said about a potential club in Lee County. I told him that the area in Warrior Bottoms in the southwest corner of Lee County and southwest of Aubrey was located squarely between the lower White River area and Big Creek — both well known duck habitats. He then wanted to know who owned it and could it be purchased and for what amount. I told him that I was handling the liquidation of the Greenbriar Drainage District, owned much of it and that I was confident that I could block up an area between 1,200 and 1,400 acres and that I thought H. P. Thompson owned the biggest area of it. He was a man in the logging business and he had recently stripped the land of all merchantable timber. I felt we could acquire the land for not in excess of $5 per acre. Dr. Crawford told me to buy it and assured me that he would provide the funds for me to do so. In reliance upon these instructions I acquired title to the property and subsequently created Warrior Hunting Club.

It originally had thirty-six members and we paid $200 each for our membership. The area is a natural saucer with the Greenbriar Drainage District Canal running from north to south along the west perimeter of our lands. All we had to do to impound the water was to stop up the holes in the spoil bank along the drainage canal and this we did. Originally we had no well but very shortly (I think in the year 1943) we sank the original well and we acquired an old diesel engine from A. C. Mahan that he had formerly employed in the operation of the ice plant here in Marianna. That was before the days of electric ice boxes or refrigerators and when they came into being the ice plant vanished.

Obviously this one well was not sufficient, but it was the best we could do with what we had. Sometime thereafter we put down another well on the west side in the immediate vicinity of where it is now located.

I believe the first year we shot Warrior was in 1943, and I was in the United States Navy. We built the little two-room house on the north end of the club with the idea of having a caretaker there to provide us a "warm-up shack" for there were no roads to Warrior. When the winter weather turned bad you either walked or rode a horse and wagon. The "turn around" road came into being many years later. We used to walk from what we knew as the Homer Thompson Road (which is the road that goes south from the county road down to the Bennett lands) across the open field into the woods and down into Warrior. It was no simple task.

An interesting story is the sale of the timber. I believe our original deeds were acquired in December of 1942. Thereafter we put down two wells and built two reservoirs, one of which we have subsequently drained and converted into a rice field. In 1982 the state and federal foresters advised us that our oak timber was dying, would all be gone within four to five years and that we should cut it immediately. I then advertised for bids with all of the lumber companies operating in the area. I reserved the right to reject all bids and the Hammond Lumber Company in Little Rock made the highest bid of $250,000, which I rejected. I called and talked to Mr. Hammond and told him that we had $7,000 in "expenses," and that if he would increase his bid to $257,000.00 we'd sell him the timber as marked. We had Larry Lewis mark each tree that we were selling so that there would be no wrongful cutting of small timber. Mr. Hammond agreed to this, and the sale was consummated. Thus we paid approximately $7,000 for the land. We now have 200 acres in cultivation with two very, very large rice wells, we have approximately 1,000 to 1,500 feet of underground irrigation pipe and we "don't owe nobody nothing." Needless to say I'm rather proud of what this "older generation" has accomplished with Warrior.

It is a commonplace occurrence "now-a-days" to hear the politicians and economists bewail the fact that we are mortgaging the souls of our grandchildren by the economic policies which we have set into motion. Certainly far too many of these allegations are true and the fiscal responsibility of our people and government is in a deplorable state. However, I like to think occasionally that some of the things we've done are not all bad, and while acknowledging that Warrior Hunting Club is but a fly speck on the universe, nevertheless it has provided, and will hereafter provide, many pleasant interludes for us and ours. The design and purpose of Warrior's "founding fathers" was indeed to create a place where fine young sportsmen such as you represent will find entertainment rather than having to resort to the pool halls and local taverns. A sound argument can be made that our goal has been to a very large extent accomplished.

I have enjoyed my hunting associations with all of you. My best personal regards.

Yours very truly,

Jimason J. Daggett

Where the Delta meets the Ozarks

BLACK RIVER BOTTOMLANDS FORM WATERFOWL CORRIDOR BETWEEN OZARKS, CROWLEY'S RIDGE

An aerial view when the Black River's bottomlands are overflowed explains everything a duck hunter needs to know about this area. As you look north, from its confluence with the White River at Jacksonport, Black River appears to be one vast lake.

And it's easy to see why ducks would flock to this western edge of the Delta. The Arkansas Game and Fish Commission noticed that 50 years ago. When the AGFC made the purchase of duck hunting land a top priority in the late 1940s, the Black River area in Clay, Greene and Randolph counties ranked third on the list, behind only Bayou Meto and Big Lake.

In fact, that view of the Black River bottoms 50 years ago would have been even more convincing for a duck hunter.

"It was a wilderness," said Jim Barnett, a Batesville resident whose family has owned a few thousand acres of Black River bottomland since the early 1900s. "I flew over it in December 1947. I wish I had a picture of that. There was about a 10-mile-wide band of timber from the mouth of Black River all the way to Missouri."

◄ The decoys are set as a hunter awaits shooting time on an oxbow lake near Black River.

Three mallard drakes find refuge in the flooded timber of Black River WMA.

At that time, the Black River bottoms still retained the characteristics that originally attracted wintering ducks to the Arkansas Delta.

"When the bottoms were all in woods, you could count on Black River being flooded in the fall and staying up until spring," Barnett said.

These high water periods provided the only opportunities to cut some big timber out of what was an almost impenetrable forest.

"They'd cut cypress trees during the overflows and float them out," Barnett said. "You'd see stumps eight or 10 feet high after the water receded. But that was the only way to do it, because there were just no passable roads in the bottoms then."

Though much of those forested bottoms now have been cut and cleared, Black River isn't scarred as badly as its sister stream, the St. Francis River. The two Ozark waterways are only about 15 miles apart when they enter Arkansas' northeast corner in Clay County. The distance between the two increases from there, as Black River flows at a western angle toward the edge of the Ozarks.

The town of Black Rock in Lawrence County presents a dramatic view of "the escarpment," as some local residents call it. When you cross the Highway 63 bridge there, it's obvious you've gone from the Delta bottomlands to the Ozark hills. While the St. Francis was assaulted by drainage projects from both sides,

The Gibson & Taylor Mill Camp as it appeared in 1898, when the town of Lockhart thrived as sawmill and steamboat landing on Black River.

the Ozarks shielded the Black River on the western edge of its bottomland.

That's an important feature for duck hunters, too. AGFC waterfowl biologists have determined that more ducks per square mile are killed in the western Arkansas River Valley than any other region in Arkansas. That sounds unbelievable until you realize it's a combination of two factors: 1) lots of ducks flying through that west-to-east corridor from the Central Flyway to the Mississippi Flyway; and 2) very little duck habitat once you get away from the immediate river area.

Black River represents another version of those factors — the blocking effect of the Ozarks to the west and bottomland spreading out all the way to the Cache River and Crowley's Ridge on the east. This was the Mississippi River channel almost two million years ago, when it flowed west of Crowley's Ridge.

The north-south corridor between the Ozarks and Crowley's Ridge helps explain why the AGFC ranks Clay and Randolph among the top 10 Arkansas counties in terms of duck harvest per square mile. (As with the western Arkansas River Valley region, the mountainous section of Randolph County is factored out of this formula.)

Only the Cache/Lower White River area attracts a higher density of ducks per square mile than the Black River/Middle White River unit, according to AGFC figures in the North American Waterfowl Plan.

Today you have to go north into the Missouri Ozarks to see how the river itself once appeared. Some claim there is no clearer stream in the Ozarks than the upper reaches of the Black River, which remains a popular float stream in Missouri. (It's been said that Black River got its name from aquatic vegetation, which made the water appear dark.)

The timber that lined the Black River bottoms was more than man could cope with until the late 1800s. The St. Louis, Iron Mountain and Southern Railroad had extended into Arkansas by 1872. Tracks

BLACK RIVER — A TIMELINE

1.6 million years ago	1815	1831	1854	1872
During the Pleistocene Period, the Mississippi River flows between the western side of Crowley's Ridge and the eastern edge of the Ozarks, laying the foundation for the Black River bottomlands.	The first post office in the Arkansas Territory is established at Davidsonville on the Black River, where a steamboat landing operates until 1829.	Congress appropriates $15,000 for improvements on the Military Road from Jackson in Lawrence County (through Davidsonville) to Washington in Hempstead County. Later this would be known as the Southwest Trail.	Jacksonport, a thriving port at the confluence of the Black and White rivers, becomes the Jackson County seat.	St. Louis, Iron Mountain and Southern Railway route crosses Black River between Corning and Knobel and runs parallel to the river down to Newport.

crossed the Black River between Corning and Knobel. Crosscut saws and axes were the tools of timber harvest. Oxen teams pulled the logs from the forest. Timber harvest was spurred by the railroad.

Around 1890, the Henry Quallmalz Lumber and Manufacturing Company bought a sawmill at Brookings near the Black River in Clay County. As the forest was cleared, cotton was planted in its place. The Quallmalz Company holdings eventually included 27,000 acres and five cotton gins, but the once-booming sawmill town of Brookings died when the Quallmalz Company failed after World War I.

You must see the thick woods of the AGFC's Dave Donaldson/Black River and Shirey Bay-Rainey Brake wildlife management areas to appreciate what the Black River bottoms once looked like. Much of the 21,150-acre Dave Donaldson/Black River WMA is made up of land formerly owned by Quallmalz.

Black River, top, flows into White River at Jacksonport, which once was a thriving river town at the mouth of Black River.

That timber clearing period of the early 1900s was only a fraction of what would take place beginning in the 1950s when the potential for growing soybeans was discovered.

Black River — A Timeline

1890
The Henry Quallmalz Lumber and Manufacturing Company organizes at Brookings and expands to include 27,000 acres of land and five cotton gins.

1951
As part of a commitment to buy land for duck hunting, the Arkansas Game and Fish Commission makes its first purchase in the 21,000-acre Black River Wildlife Management Area near Brookings.

1954
In another major step toward providing public land for duck hunting, the AGFC buys 10,000 acres near Black River, and names it Shirey Bay-Rainey Brake WMA.

1960
As demands for soybeans increase, bottomland hardwoods begin to fall at an unprecedented pace. During this decade, 1.4 million acres of Arkansas Delta land will be cleared, including thousands of acres along Black River.

1970
The AGFC votes to name a new 525-acre reservoir Lake Ashbaugh. It is located near Brookings, along the southern edge of Black River WMA, and now serves as a waterfowl rest area.

Coleman recalls Black River forest

Bottomland wasn't worth much during time when timber was your enemy

One Black River bottoms red oak tree in particular stands out in Ewell Ray Coleman's memory. A scaffolding eight feet tall was built around it, just so Coleman and his crew could reach a place where a six-foot crosscut saw could be used on it.

"Even then, we had to take a handle off one end of the saw before we got through it," Coleman said.

The Black River bottomlands once were covered with massive trees like that. Coleman is an authority on the subject. He estimates that he cleared 10,000 acres of them.

"I will never forget the morning I started clearing," said Coleman. "My father throwed a fit with a hole in it. This land had never been farmed before. He said, 'You're crazy. It won't work. You can't farm it, it's too wet.' He was about half right."

But Ewell Ray Coleman beat the elements more times than not, and became a successful farmer and businessman because of it. His son, Donald, and his grandsons enjoy duck hunting along Black River now. Ewell Ray doesn't regret all the timber clearing he did. He worked too hard and achieved success in an area where few folks made a living to feel that way. But hindsight has convinced him that he would do it differently if he had the chance.

"I can look back now and say I'd be better off today if I hadn't cleared all that land," Coleman said. "All I've done is work my butt off all my life. I wish I'd just managed to protect the environment more. If we'd managed it like the Indians, we'd be so much better off. We've wasted more than this country is worth, and I'm part of that."

It's easy to agree with Coleman now. But following a life lived along the Black River from the beginning of the 20th century allows you to understand how he got to this point. Timber was your enemy. Hardwood lumber wasn't nearly so valuable then.

"The canopy was so high and thick and the trees so big that you could run a horse at full speed through these bot-

Oxen teams carried logs through the thick canopy of the Black River bottoms near the town of Lockhart in 1911.

toms," Coleman said. "It was open."

Coleman was born near the town of Cord in 1925. Lockhart was an active sawmill camp and steamboat landing on Black River then. Coleman's parents bought a general store in Dowdy, and his mother served as postmaster for 38 years until the Dowdy Post Office was closed in the mid 1970s. Lockhart is no more, but you can still find Cord and Dowdy on the map in the northeast corner of Independence County.

Clearing much land at all just wasn't feasible in those days. Everybody had a small field for feeding livestock, and that was about it. There weren't many options for making a living.

"A few wealthy people had cattle and hogs they'd run in the bottoms," Coleman said. "Cutting timber paid a dollar a day. The rest of the people living here made whiskey.

"One time in Cord there were not enough people to put out a fire because they were all in jail at Batesville for making whiskey."

It wasn't unusual for the Black River bottoms to overflow in late autumn and remain that way until late spring. Cutting the timber off it seemed to be the only use for the land.

"I bought my first 490 acres of land in 1943 for $12.50 an acre," Coleman said. "At that time, this was all in woods."

Coleman operated a sawmill for the next 10 years. But that barely made a mark in the bottoms. Everything was cut for lumber and crossties. Crossties paid the best money, from $1 to $1.25 each.

"Back then, there was a standing bid. You could buy the land, timber and all, for $15 to $20 an acre. I'd buy the timber and let them have the land back for $5. Nobody thought that land was worth anything."

Coleman began clearing land to farm it in 1953. The thick canopy and huge logs in the Black River bottoms made an already difficult task even tougher.

"I've seen pin oak flats where you couldn't put all the timber on the ground at one time," Coleman said. "You had to haul some out, then come back and cut some more."

Coleman claims to have put the first bulldozer into the west side of the Black River bottoms. Once the bulldozer went to work, clearing land took on a whole new perspective. Portable stump saws cut the trees at ground level, and the dozer pushed all but the best logs into piles for burning. The stumps were left in the ground to rot.

"We could cut an acre a day," Coleman said. "That was a good day's work. By about 1955, I had a D-8 with a cutting blade. That was the biggest dozer Caterpillar made then. I could clear 10 acres a day.

"By 1960, I had nine bulldozers working at one time, cutting and piling and burning. It was awful the stuff we wasted. We burned what would be considered good timber today."

Coleman cleared his last 1,000 acres in 1963. Of the 10,000 total, most was done in those last five years, thanks to the increased efficiency provided by bulldozers.

Soybeans hit the Delta big time in the 1960s. With their short growing season and tolerance for moist soils, soybeans could be planted in areas that no one had considered farming before.

"I never lost a crop," Coleman said. "I never failed to plant, and I never failed to harvest."

Many acres of Black River bottomland were cleared for "free." Contractors, like Coleman, would clear the land in exchange for the right to farm it the next five years.

"We would cut it, clear it and plant it in the same year," Coleman said.

Coleman hired Lane Arkansas Co. to drill a well for rice irrigation around 1954. At one time, he was farming soybeans and rice on 5,000 acres of prime Black River bottomland that he had cleared.

Again, perspective is important. What sounds like an easy business decision now — whether or not to plant fertile Delta soil in soybeans — was a huge gamble then. It hadn't been done before. Some had gone broke trying.

"Now, if all that land was covered in timber, it would probably be worth 10 times more than the cleared land is now," Coleman said.

Duck hunters seeking a place for a private club will pay much more for timbered bottomland than it is worth for planting soybeans. In Coleman's lifetime, the roles have reversed.

'The miracle bean' fueled Delta clearing

From 1960 to 1970, 1.4 million acres of Arkansas Delta hardwoods were cut to make room for "the miracle bean" — soybeans.

"It was the crop that enticed you to clear," said Ewell Ray Coleman, who cleared 10,000 acres of Black River bottomland.

The combination of high prices, a short growing season and tolerance for moist soils put soybeans on 5.2 million acres of Arkansas ground by 1979. In comparison, when cotton was king in the South, Arkansas cotton acreage peaked at 3.5 million in 1930.

The rapid rise of soybeans ranks among the great success stories in U.S. agriculture. Soybean cultivation in China can be traced to the beginning of recorded history. An intensive U.S. research effort that began in the 1930s resulted in new soybean varieties featuring higher yields and oil content. Average seasonal prices per bushel jumped from $2.80 in 1966 to $6.96 in 1974.

Soybeans are used in making everything from plastics to paints. Most soybeans, however, are processed for the oil, which is used in margarine, shortening and other food products.

While the soybean was an agricultural success story, it wasn't good news for wetlands and duck habitat. In the book, *Disappearing Wetlands in Eastern Arkansas*, Trusten Holder recounts how one east Arkansas duck club sold its 320 acres after the season ended one year; before the next season opened, every tree had been cleared and 320 acres of soybeans harvested.

Mallard ducks, particularly, have adapted to the changing Delta landscape. But of the major food crops planted, soybeans have the least food value for waterfowl. Ducks can't assimilate soybeans efficiently.

In a comparison of natural wetland habitat and harvested croplands, these figures indicate the number of ducks that can be adequately fed per day on one acre:

1) moist-soil seeds*	1,380
2) corn	970
3) milo	849
4) rice	750
4) soybeans	121

* Includes smartweeds, wild millets, etc., which grow naturally in wetlands.

New era brings a new attitude

Willie would like to forget his days of ignoring game law regulations

Bobby Joe Willie (left) calls ducks while pulling a decoy jerk string in Black River WMA.

Bobby Joe Willie doesn't like to talk about it. He claims he doesn't remember the year it happened, or how many duck hunting violations were involved.

"I'd rather just forget about it," Willie said at the end of a morning's hunt in Black River Wildlife Management Area.

The questions were unexpected. An hour earlier, he had finished the day's hunt after spending six hours calling in flocks of ducks, first to waiting hunters, then to cameras.

During the day, he had shot twice at flying ducks. It was 1994 and the mallard limit was two.

Once that was done, the rest was fun. He didn't think about violating the law and didn't want to be reminded of the time he got caught when his resolve wasn't quite as strong.

"I always said if I got caught, I'd take what's coming and that would be the end of it," Willie said.

But it's not the end of it. He receives constant reminders from hunting partners, who don't mind sending a barbed message that he was the one who got caught, although in the past they may have been as guilty.

Willie is one of several hundred duck hunters in the state who have been caught by wildlife officers in the act of violating game laws. He is one of the few who has served jail time for activities that were once considered just another part of the hunting season.

Today, he watches over those in his hunting party like a stern commandant, waiting for someone to step out of line.

"People around here say (hunting with Willie) is just like hunting with a federal game warden," Willie said proudly.

It wasn't always like that.

In his outlaw days, Willie would go from daylight until dark, double-dipping, triple-dipping and more.

"Everyone did it, two or three times a day," Willie said. "We didn't consider that violating. There wasn't any enforcement, and we knew we weren't going to get caught."

But when federal marshals showed up at his door, after two years of unknowingly guiding federal wildlife officers and violating game laws, he received a wake-up call.

"There wasn't any enforcement, and we knew we weren't going to get caught."

It was a call that has since changed his impression of duck hunting in Arkansas.

Willie's outlaw story is like so many. He grew up in a time when people had a double-edged respect for those who could kill a lot of ducks. He may not have been the guy you wanted your daughter to bring home, but no one would turn down a chance to go duck-hunting with him.

"I ain't proud of it," Willie said.

That's just the way it was, although Willie says that much of his reputation was blown out of proportion. After a short course in jail time and three years probation, "I learned (that reputation) ain't that big of a deal," Willie said.

Although his current reputation includes being a known convicted violator, Willie believes it has been one of the best things that ever happened to him.

Willie's probation was easier than most. At the time of his arrest, a significant portion of his income came from guiding duck hunters. A federal magistrate allowed Willie to continue guiding, although he was unable to take a gun.

"The judge gave me a break, and I wasn't going to let him down," Willie said.

His conviction also sent messages to others. Willie does most of his duck hunting in the Dave Donaldson/Black River Wildlife Management Area. It is in duck country, but it doesn't receive the attention from enforcement officers like counties in the southeast section of the state.

"With the exception of taking those federal game wardens, I've only been checked once in the duck woods," Willie said. "If we were going to get caught it would be on the river or at the

Willie says he doesn't care if he never kills another duck; he enjoys watching them work in the Black River bottoms.

parking lot. If we could get past those, which we always did, we had it made. People knew that. But after I got caught, it helped a bunch up here. There's people who still (violate), but it's nothing like it used to be."

And it gets better every day. Like most duck hunters who grew up in Willie's day, he has seen a change take place throughout the duck-hunting community. People no longer respect the game hog, or the guy who had the ability to kill a lot of ducks.

The change is evident even in the young duck hunters' attitudes, many of whom think killing a hen is an abomination and killing over the limit is a hanging offense. For those who still ignore the rules, Willie has some simple advice.

"I think the guys who violate just to violate should go without a gun, and see if they get a kick out of it," Willie said. "If it's just the killing, then they should kill them out of a pen.

"I've told a bunch of people since then, if I don't ever kill another duck, that's OK; I've killed my share. I would rather watch the dog work, and I like watching the ducks work."

DAVE DONALDSON/ BLACK RIVER WMA

Acres: 21,150
First purchase: 1951
Location: Near Pocahontas and Corning in Randolph and Clay counties
Topo maps (7.5 series, U.S. Geological Survey): Pocahontas, Reyno, and Peach Orchard.

Black River is the state's second largest wildlife management area, but due to the fact that in wet years it can provide as much as 18,000 acres of flooded shooting, Black River could easily be described as providing the most duck hunting.

Bayou Meto, the largest WMA with 33,832, only floods about 12,000 acres in a wet year.

Black River is surrounded by 17 miles of levees, stop-log dams and other water-control structures, making it possible to flood 7,000 to 8,000 acres even in dry years.

Access to the Black River Wildlife Management Area is off U.S. Highway 67 and State Highway 90, northeast of Pocahontas and south of Corning.

Roads and walk-in access are at a minimum. Most of the hunting is done by boat. This area is unique in that AGFC regulations allow hunters to leave decoys out overnight. But holes with decoys in them are open to any hunter who goes there.

In addition to the normally excellent duck hunting, the squirrel and deer hunting are generally good. Parking areas and boat launching ramps are located at Brookings, Hubble Bridge, and near Reyno on the boundaries of the area.

Fishing for catfish and bass is generally good in both the Black and Little River. Also, the 17-acre Lake Hubble offers good fishing and receives high use during the warmer months.

Lake Ashbaugh, a 525-acre reservoir located on the southern edge of the area, is a rest area, and its large expanse of open water often accommodates thousands of waterfowl.

There are no camping areas on Black River WMA, but the AGFC allows a vehicle to park for up to two weeks in any of these access locations: Brookings Access off Highway 280 north of Delaplaine, Hubble Bridge Access off Highway 280 east of Brookings, the Datto Access off of Highway 67 south of Reyno and WMA headquarters southwest of Peach Orchard.

Donaldson counted millions of ducks

'Mr. Duck' in Arkansas became expert in compiling aerial survey numbers

When the Arkansas Game and Fish Commission publishes statistics indicating that 100,000 or 200,000 ducks are in one area of the state or another, skepticism often results.

For the average duck hunter, who has seen a few mallard-filled rice fields and flooded pin oak flats, the question is obvious: How in the world can you accurately count 100,000 ducks?

Add up the number of wings and divide by two, is the punch line of an old joke.

But Arkansas aerial waterfowl surveys aren't a joke, and the late Dave Donaldson is a big reason why. Nationwide mid-winter aerial inventories began shortly after World War II to aid in understanding the distribution and habitat of waterfowl. Donaldson was hired by the AGFC in 1946 after earning a master's degree in wildlife management at Texas A&M. He flew his first survey that year, with U.S. Fish and Wildlife Service personnel. After the AGFC bought its first airplane in 1954, Donaldson flew every mid-winter inventory in Arkansas until he retired in 1977.

There have always been questions about the accuracy of these inventories. They are published as estimates, not bird-by-bird counts. There are some years when weather conditions don't allow accurate counts. But with experienced biologists doing the counting, these surveys have proven to be accurate and provide valuable management information.

Donaldson took pride in his accuracy. To test it, Donaldson once flew with Frank Bellrose, the Illinois waterfowl expert who was considered to have flown more aerial surveys than anyone else at that time. They shielded their notes from each other. After counting more than one million mallards in Arkansas, their estimates were within 10,000 of each other's.

Donaldson and AGFC biologist Carl Hunter gained invaluable experience in performing aerial surveys in the 1950s, during a three-year, federally-funded study of the Mississippi Flyway. Each state in the flyway was asked to compile waterfowl numbers every two weeks. The schedules were coordinated so each state compiled duck numbers on the same days of the week.

"It was a lot of fun," said Hunter. "We flew the entire state every two weeks, fall and winter. We gathered some excellent data on when and where the ducks went at different times of the year, throughout the flyway."

Occasionally, Hunter and Donaldson checked their estimates against actual counts made from aerial photographs of huge concentrations, like at Peckerwood

Waterfowl biologists learn to make quick and accurate counts of ducks from the air.

Lake or Claypool's Reservoir.

"We were getting within 10 percent accuracy on our estimates," Hunter said.

The basic method of counting any concentration of ducks is to start with small fractions of the group and build up. By learning to recognize groups as small as 10, 50 and 100, the biologists can break down any size group and arrive at an accurate measurement.

"All the biologists working that Mississippi Flyway study got to be very accurate," Hunter said. "If we'd had a big movement of ducks in the state, we would call around. The Missouri biologists might say they were down 200,000 ducks that week, and our counts would show we were up about 200,000."

In his decades of canvassing Arkansas' duck habitat, Donaldson learned where they would be under different weather conditions.

"If there is no big overflow and if everything is frozen up, then the ducks will be on the eastern side of the White River Refuge," Donaldson wrote in an article for the AGFC magazine in 1971. "During the 1971 survey there was a general freeze-up and all of the ducks had moved to the flowing water of the Cache-White River bottoms in the Clarendon-Augusta area."

From the air to the ground, Dave Donaldson was considered the duck expert in Arkansas, and he earned a national reputation for his knowledge of mallard habits.

"Dave Donaldson was Mr. Duck in Arkansas," said Hunter.

Donaldson, who lived in Paragould, did everything from banding ducks in the Canadian prairies to devising the water system for flooding the Black River Wildlife Management Area, which now carries his name.

Within the time he served as the AGFC's waterfowl biologist, from 1950-77, Donaldson also became recognized as an important member of the Mississippi Flyway Council Technical Section. In 1975, the Arkansas Wildlife Federation named him "Conservationist of the Year" for "the business of trying to preserve habitat over a quarter of a century, and he has kept at it, which — in view of severe obstacles — is something of a record."

All-season decoy rule rooted in tradition

No one knows exactly when it started or when it will end. But on Black River, Big Lake and St. Francis Sunken Lands wildlife management areas, hunters are allowed to keep their decoys out for the duration of the season. More correctly, hunters on Big Lake and the Sunken Lands are allowed to have blinds too.

"It's been like that for as long as I can remember," said Steve N. Wilson, director of the Arkansas Game and Fish Commission. "They've always been able to do it and they've never been made to change."

One theory is that the areas were heavily used by old market hunters and trappers who lived on houseboats prior to the AGFC buying the land. After the purchase, AGFC personnel spent considerable effort in trying to move the hunters and their boats off commission property. A concession in the forced move might have been that decoys could stay out all season.

Today, if the locals have their way, the practice will continue.

In 1995, the AGFC considered changing the regulations for those areas, to make them pick up their decoys each day. That rule would be similar to the rest of the WMAs. But a public outcry from northeast Arkansas forced the AGFC to reconsider.

"There were more people who showed up at the public meeting on that issue than any issue I had ever seen," said Bill Brewer of Paragould, a commissioner from 1984 to 1991. "That includes the meetings when we tried to ban dogs in northwest Arkansas."

Wilson estimated the crowd at 650 or more, all saying that these remote WMAs didn't have the problems of those in central Arkansas.

"Their point was if it's not broke, don't try to fix it," Brewer said. "And most of them couldn't see how removing decoys was going to solve any problems."

Brewer, who hunts Black River WMA, said the areas are not as accessible as other WMAs and traditionally they have had low duck hunter use. Brewer said the system works well on the areas, as long as sportsmanship is honored.

"Years ago we made hunters pick up their decoys," Brewer said. "They said, all right, we'll get faster boats. Then we limited the size of the boats. They said, all right, we'll just get there earlier. Then we put limits on the times they could go in. It all boils down to sportsmanship and doing the right thing."

Shirey Bay-Rainey Brake stands tall

Big timber in WMA remnant of entire Black River bottoms before clearing

It's a foggy, rainy morning in Shirey Bay-Rainey Brake Wildlife Management Area. Hunters slip into the grayness, following a road erased by rising water. Huge willow oaks and red oaks stand on either side, the bark wet and black. Drops of water and acorns, heavy from the rain, plop loudly all around.

But the plopping of water is not easy to hear. More important sounds are coming from all around. Mallards are calling in the distance, looking for a place to light.

Agricultural fields border the timber of Shirey Bay-Rainey Brake WMA.

From the hunters' perspective, the submerged road will do nicely. The opening above is perfect to allow wood ducks and mallards to use the road as a runway and landing strip.

After walking less than 400 yards, the hunters ease up to tree trunks in an attempt to conceal themselves. It is 8 a.m., two hours past the time most duck hunters enter the woods, but it is not too late.

It is their first time in Shirey Bay-Rainey Brake; the area is unfamiliar. But there are some things that are always the same in flooded timber. Blackened silhouettes of timber, sporadic booms and overhead chuckles of passing ducks, for instance. But entering unfamiliar ground on a day like this is best done once natural light is available to show the way.

Hopeful hunters are standing next to trees and kicking water, comfortable with the unfamiliar woods. If they close their eyes and forget they are just a few miles from the gateway to the Ozarks, it is easy to imagine that they are in Bayou Meto, or another flooded timber area in the Delta region.

They are testing an idea that works in most public shooting grounds, which is if you stay until 9:30 a.m., you will have less competition from other hunters.

While they wait, limits of mallards

Even in dry years, Lake Charles provides water to flood timber in Shirey Bay-Rainey Brake.

flutter overhead, and wood ducks buzz and bomb the flooded road. Listening, they find there are good callers, bad callers, sky busters and hen shooters in Shirey Bay-Rainey Brake. Some things never change on public shooting ground.

By 10 o'clock, there is no calling or shooting, and mallards start responding to calling more positively. They work easier, and drop through the trees, despite the lack of decoys.

In every favorite duck hunting hole, there is a memory that separates it from the usual. Shirey Bay-Rainey Brake is no different. Hunters watching the skies for passing ducks hear a feeding chuckle to the right and see a big mallard hen swimming between the trees.

Behind her was a solid stream of hens and drakes, coming from who knows where and going to the same place. The hen was like the head of a huge snake, leading a body of ducks that ranged from four-ducks-wide to as many as a dozen. Judging by the length of time it took for them to pass, the train of ducks had to be at least a quarter of a mile long.

It actually was longer, if you counted the second train of ducks that was coming. Because there was a break between the duck trains, singles and doubles were pitching in and joining the group.

After 15 minutes of watching, it seemed a wise time for each hunter to kill a greenhead from the ducks flying in. It only took a few more minutes to finish the limits.

On the walk out, the source of the train of ducks was found. The hunters' positions were on the edge of the WMA's rest area, where ducks had spent the morning piling in and escaping the shooting of the other hunters.

By mid-morning, as the remainder of the WMA had quieted, the ducks took the cue and began leaving the rest area. The fact they did it in almost single-file fashion added an interesting twist to duck behavior.

The lead hen was the boss and her movements were imitated by the other ducks. In one case, she made the mistake of swimming into a brushtop, and she had to stop and pick her way through. When she stopped, the followers had a delayed reaction, creating a Keystone Cop routine of duck bills bumping into duck tails. The graceful beauty of ducks in flight was lost in a moment of comic relief.

Shirey Bay-Rainey Brake is a traditional flooded timber area located northwest of Jonesboro on the Black River. Its approximately 10,000 acres of bottomland timber were once just a small part of a wide band of timbered land running down the Black River.

The other timber in this area was cleared during the soybean craze of the 1960s and 1970s. Along with the Black River WMA, located several miles upstream, these are basically the last hold-outs of wooded wetland habitat in the Black River basin.

And like the White River in the southeast region, which, when flooded, is the key to holding ducks in that part of the state, the Black River is the key to duck hunting for those in the northeast.

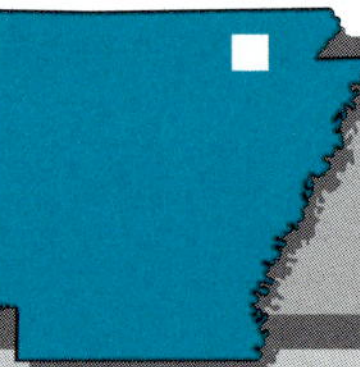

SHIREY BAY-RAINEY BRAKE WMA

Acres: 10,711
First purchase: 1954
Location: Near Lynn in Lawrence County.
Topo maps (7.5 series, U.S. Geological Survey): Eaton, Strangers Home.

Shirey Bay-Rainey Brake Wildlife Management Area is generally bounded on the west by State Highway 361, which provides the best access to the area. The area is about 10 airline miles southwest of Walnut Ridge.

Managed primarily for waterfowl, about 4,000 acres of the management area are flooded with water from Lake Charles, just north of the area, by a series of levees, pipes and stop-log structures. Normally, the area provides some excellent duck hunting.

In addition to the duck hunting, there is good deer, squirrel, and swamp rabbit hunting in the bottomland hardwoods. About 500-600 acres of upland habitat provide some good quail and rabbit hunting.

There is only one all-weather road on the Rainey Brake side and two all-weather roads on the Shirey Bay side. Camping is permitted in a few designated areas.

Black River, which separates the 3,000-acre Shirey Bay part of the area from the Rainey Brake part, provides excellent fishing for catfish, bass, bream and crappie. Hill's Slough, a 12-mile long body of water on the western edge of the area, and Horseshoe Lake — near the center of the management area — also provide some good fishing.

Grammer calls on years of experience

Direction of the wind, number of other hunters determine duck-calling styles

By knowing when to hook ducks with a comeback call, Grammer controls their flight pattern.

Lilly Mae Grammer was visiting with a friend in Batesville one day in 1965. Duck season bag limits and hunting days had been shrinking. That year the mallard limit dropped to an all-time low of one per day. Most everyone in Batesville knew how much Lilly Mae's husband, Norman, enjoyed duck hunting. But a one-mallard-a-day limit seemed hardly worth the effort.

"Is Norman going to duck hunt this season?" the friend asked.

Lilly Mae quickly responded, "Norman would keep duck hunting even if you had to go two days to kill one mallard."

Said long-time friend Robert A. "Lit" Craig, "Norman Grammer is the quintessential duck hunter. He has killed more ducks than anyone in Batesville."

Grammer's dental office always closed on Wednesdays and Saturdays, which afforded him more hunting and fishing time than most people. And from the time he began his dental practice in Batesville until he retired in 1984, the office never opened during duck season until 1 p.m. All mornings were reserved for duck hunting.

"I hunted a little at least four or five days a week," Grammer said. "I never would hunt in the rain. It wasn't all that good, and it was so darn miserable."

When the Arkansas Game and Fish Commission purchased the Shirey Bay-Rainey Brake Wildlife Management Area in 1954, it became one of Grammer's favorite hunting places. The shrinking availability of duck hunting on privately owned land had created a demand for public areas.

"It got to where you darn near had to have a place of your own," Grammer said.

He hunted some on the Ruesewald farm at Swan Pond near Weiner, where blinds were rented for the day. The AGFC was just beginning to purchase public land for duck hunting.

Most long-time duck hunters in northeast Arkansas refer to the Shirey Bay-Rainey Brake area simply as Lynn, the name of the small town closest to the WMA in Lawrence County.

"When Lynn opened it was just super," Grammer said. "You didn't need a boat or anything on the north end. You'd just go strolling through those woods blowing and shooting. We'd kill a limit of squirrels every time we went duck hunting."

Grammer describes the acorn crop in those early years as "thick enough to skate on."

It was from observing so many ducks in various places along the Black and White rivers near Batesville that Grammer developed his calling theory. It's based

Two hunters use a johnboat to motor through the flooded timber of the Turkey Hill Hunting Club in the Black River bottoms.

around the concept of a decoy spread representing an airport landing strip.

"An airplane goes downwind, hooks and turns into the airport," Grammer said. "A duck does the same thing, if you'll just be the controller."

The most crucial notes in controlling duck flight patterns are those of the comeback call. Grammer describes it as, "One high note, then right down the scale, the first one just as loud as you can blow it.

"Except for real high ducks, I don't have any use for the hail call. If ducks are paying any attention to you, all you need is the comeback call."

But most important of all is knowing when to use it and when not to use it.

"The only reason to call, other than just making duck noise, is when they are upwind and downwind," Grammer said. "I'm talking about ducks that are listening to you. Most people won't let ducks go downwind far enough. They get anxious and they hook them a little quick."

Rather than constantly calling ducks, which can result in tighter and tighter circular flight patterns over the decoys, Grammer attempts to keep them working back and forth with the wind. Let them fly downwind, then hook them back. Again, remember the airport landing strip. If you avoid calling when the ducks are flying crosswind, you've got a better chance of getting them to land in your decoy spread like you want them to — directly into the wind.

"If you're constantly calling and getting them in these little tight circles or calling them as they fly across the wind, they'll land off to the side of your decoys or sometimes they'll just hover and look," Grammer said.

Either scenario is bad, especially the second one. The more time ducks spend circling directly over your decoys, the longer they have to look for signs of trouble below. It's difficult for many hunters to be hidden well enough and hold still long enough to escape 40 or 50 sets of duck eyes when they hover over a decoy spread.

"They'll see something," Grammer said. "Maybe it doesn't scare the hell out of them, but it bothers them."

After he has hooked a flock of ducks with a comeback call, duck noise is all that's required. It helps to have more than one caller. The second-most important set of notes, according to Grammer, is one he refers to as the "grass feed call." Others call it the "contented call."

It's four notes, right down the scale — quack, quack, quack, quack.

"You'll hear ducks all over the woods doing it, if there's nothing bothering them," Grammer said.

"If ducks are around close, you just want a lot of duck racket."

Remember to use the comeback call strictly as its name would imply — when you want ducks to come back in your direction.

"I hear lots of people who can call and sound like a duck, but they don't understand wind," Grammer said. "They don't know when to hook a duck so it will come right in."

There is, however, a time to blow the comeback call when ducks are flying crosswind, according to Grammer. When in the flooded timber of crowded public hunting areas, there are days you have to take what you can get. If you wait for ducks to come fluttering into the decoys, you may go home without firing a shot.

"You've got to have some tricks in public shooting areas," Grammer said. "When you call ducks crosswind they'll come across you about as low as they're going to get."

When ducks won't light in flooded timber because of all the commotion around them, you can use this method to get a sporting shot.

"I've shot many a duck that way on public ground," Grammer said.

Grammer refers to it as "sky-busting."

But it's far from the out-of-range duck shooting on public land that carries the same label and cripples so many ducks.

Crowding from other hunters is a common problem on public land, too. You might be working a group of ducks, when, as they swing around for another pass at your decoy spread, they are shot at by other hunters. Grammer has one simple solution: Pick up your decoys and move.

"You've got a lot of shooters, not hunters, on public ground, and they are going to shoot. When they start shooting on your swing, you go right straight through them and get on the other side."

"You've got a lot of shooters, not hunters, on public ground, and they are going to shoot," Grammer said. "When they start shooting on your swing, you go right straight through them and get on the other side. Then you've got them. I've done it a helluva lot."

Some people recommend a softer-sounding duck call for flooded timber. Grammer disagrees. He blows a Yentzen Sure Shot double-reed call.

"I like one that will knock the acorns off the trees," Grammer said. "It just seems to work for me. If you're right, the ducks don't seem to care how loud you are."

Grammer's duck-calling theories have been honed through years of experience. The man who would continue duck hunting if you had to go two days to kill one mallard hasn't missed many days of Arkansas' duck seasons over the past six decades.

"It's just fascinating to watch ducks, especially if they are working to a call," Grammer said. "It seems like it gives you some control."

Names of Craig, Grammer mentioned whenever duck stories told in Batesville

At the scene of the duck hunting accident, Robert A. "Lit" Craig assumed the leadership role in applying first-aid. As a dentist, he represented the next best thing to a physician. The hunter, a Batesville resident and friend of Craig's, had shot off the index finger on his left hand. The accident occurred as the man hurried to shoot at incoming ducks and mishandled his shotgun.

Craig applied bandages to the wound. Another hunter in their group volunteered to drive the victim to the hospital. The injured man asked Craig to accompany them.

"I've done about all I can do for you," Craig replied. "And besides, I haven't got my limit yet."

While his bleeding but bandaged friend was driven to the hospital, Lit Craig stayed in the Black River bottoms and killed a limit of ducks that morning.

That story has been retold hundreds of times around Batesville. It usually evokes belly laughs from fellow duck hunters and puzzled looks from those who have never participated in the sport, those who have no idea what an addiction duck hunting can be.

When they start telling duck hunting stories in Batesville, invariably the names of Craig and fellow-dentist Norman Grammer are mentioned.

"They've taught a hundred or more people how to hunt and enjoy life," said Mike Jones, a Batesville building contractor who grew up hunting with both men and married Craig's daughter Carol.

Arkansas Game and Fish Commission director Steve Wilson was influenced by both men, too.

"Norman Grammer took me on my first duck hunt," Wilson said. "I'll never forget it. I was about 13 or 14. We went to Shirey Bay-Rainey Brake, or Lynn, as they called it then. I wore a pair of his old waders, and they just swallowed me.

"Lit Craig took me to Lynn, too, plus some wild places way back in the Black River bottoms."

A teenager in Batesville didn't need a father to take him duck hunting. Grammer and Craig didn't hunt together often, but they were always going. And anyone who wanted to join them was welcome.

Cellular phones, better maintained roads, more posted land and improved four-wheel-drive vehicles have taken much of the adventure out of duck hunting trips into the bottomlands of the Black and White rivers. Batesville's location on the edge of the Ozarks made it a jumping-off-point for duck hunters. The tradition here is chasing ducks, no matter where they go.

"I remember many times when I'd have given a hundred dollars for another three feet of winch cable," said Grammer, in reference to the hazards of travel in the bottoms.

Part of the reason Grammer and Craig educated so many younger hunters was that, over the years, fewer and fewer of their contemporaries wanted to risk the inevitable catastrophes.

"The messes you can get into," said Jim Barnett, one contemporary who did enjoy these adventures with Craig. "But we went into some great places. That was the challenge, to find places nobody else knew about or could get to."

Craig's secret weapon for doing that was a canoe and a bicycle wheel carriage. This combination allowed him to hop through a series of oxbow lakes or a partially flooded section of the bottoms. The carriage laid in the middle of the canoe. When Craig and his hunting partner reached dry ground, they took out the carriage, put the canoe on it and rolled the rig until they hit water again.

One of Craig's all-time favorite duck hunts took place in Hurricane Lake Wildlife Management Area, shortly after the AGFC purchased the land along the White River south of Augusta. There were few roads in the WMA then. A two-hour canoe-and-roll took Craig and Barnett down Glaise Creek, across Big Hurricane Lake and into Willow Pond, where they were the only hunters.

"About as soon as we had the decoys out, we'd shot our limits," Craig said.

Getting there often was half the fun, and he always enjoyed wallowing in the bottoms.

"I thought there was a certain romance to them," Craig said. "The river bottoms have always fascinated me."

Getting the best results from steel shot

Combining lessons of the past, new technology produces optimum efficiency

Combine something old with something new and duck hunters can achieve maximum results from a shotgun in the age of steel (non-toxic) shot. That's the formula used by John Clouse at Ballistic Specialties in Batesville.

"With steel shot, it's more critical to get the maximum performance from your shotgun," said Clouse, a long-time hunter and sporting clays competitor, who founded the company. "It takes a little experimentation, but you can make steel perform well."

Clouse recommends that duck hunters begin by taking a few lessons from past masters, then become familiar with some of the basic science and technology of modern ballistics.

Nash Buckingham, one of the all-time best long-range duck shooters, died in 1971; steel or non-toxic shot wouldn't be required for all waterfowl hunters in the U.S. until 1990. But the principles Buckingham learned in firing countless rounds at passing ducks can still be applied today. They are summed up in one sentence: Never send a boy to do a man's work.

Buckingham's famous "Bo Whoop" 12-gauge double-barrel shotgun weighed 10 pounds and featured a pair of 32-inch full-choked barrels. The bore measured .750 inches in both. Although bore diameters will vary slightly in different models and makes, the standard figures are .729 for 12-gauge and .775 for 10-gauge. Buckingham shot what was essentially an 11-gauge gun. A strong conservationist, he ridiculed the idea that banning gauges larger than 10 helped waterfowl.

The introduction of steel shot has many of today's shotgun performance experts echoing Buckingham's thoughts. In some other countries, particularly Scotland, waterfowlers favor 8-gauge guns for long-range goose hunting, and they drop down to the 10-gauge for geese and ducks over decoys.

Because steel is lighter, larger shot sizes are required when attempting to match the killing power of lead. Because steel is harder than lead, its path down a shotgun barrel is more complex, especially in larger shot sizes.

Choke	Constriction
Extra Full	.040
Full	.035
Light Full	.030
Improved Modified	.025
Modified	.020
Light Modified	.015
Improved Cylinder	.010
Skeet	.005
Cylinder	.000

For 12-gauge shotguns, general terms, like "full" and "improved cylinder," translate to the amount of constriction in the choke (shown in thousandths of an inch) as listed.

Getting the most from a shotgun shell offers another opportunity to read Buckingham for advice. A hunting companion of Buckingham's noted that he exclusively favored the three-inch Winchester Super X load of 1 3/8 oz. of Lubaloy No. 4 shot for waterfowl, "never that silly 1 7/8ths load." Speed, not number of pellets, was the critical factor for Buckingham.

Steel shot's lighter weight makes speed an even more important component today. It doesn't matter how many pellets there are in a shell, if they don't arrive at the target with any killing power. Hand-loaders have long recognized the benefits of speed in steel shot. Only recently have the major manufacturers begun marketing faster steel loads — with a muzzle velocity of at least 1,400 feet per second.

"Velocity is the key to steel shot," said Keith Anderson, who has managed Ballistic Specialties since its beginning in 1994.

A fast-moving load of hard steel shot benefits from the smoothest exit possible down a shotgun barrel. That's where Ballistic Specialties comes in, Anderson says. Their custom modifications, like lengthened forcing cones, custom-fitted choke tubes, porting and back-boring can maximize the performance of any shotgun, especially those shooting steel.

The biggest market for Ballistic Specialties is in competitive shooting — sporting clays, skeet and trap. Just as pro golf has spurred the development of products that benefit the weekend amateur, hunters are discovering the advantages of high-performance shotguns.

"Target shooters and turkey hunters realize how important it is to pattern a gun," Anderson said. "Steel shot is doing that, too, for duck hunters."

Von Clouse, John's father, was an Arkansas champion skeet shooter. Both Clouses and Anderson enjoy hunting everything from ducks to wild turkeys. With the Clouses' Batesville Tool and Die Co. as the foundation, they have applied the modern technology and high standards required in the tool and die business to their passions for high-performance shotguns.

In addition to better patterns, Arkansas duck hunters can benefit from the versatility gained from custom-made screw-in choke tubes. Carrying at least a couple of different choke tubes allows hunters to adjust in going from flooded timber to rice fields to big rivers and lakes.

Because steel shot patterns tighter than lead, modified and improved cylinder chokes are standard for steel. But those terms mean different things to different manufacturers. Shotgunners can gauge their needs better by becoming familiar with the exact amount of choke constriction, which is measured in thousands of an inch.

Anderson recommends three basic choke tubes for the duck hunter — .005, .015 and .025. If asked to pick a fourth, he would choose a cylinder bore of .000 rather than a tighter choke. Anderson doesn't recommend anything tighter than .030 for steel shot in a 12-gauge shotgun.

This 1955 Arkansas Game and Fish Commission map shows Black River, from the Missouri line to its confluence with the White River near Jacksonport.

RANDOLPH
SHARP
LAWRENCE
GREENE
INDEPENDENCE
CRAIGHEAD
JACKSON
POINSETT
CROSS
CORNING
HARDY
POCAHONTAS
POWHATAN
WALNUT RIDGE
EVENING SHADE
PARAGOULD
JONESBORO
LAKE CITY
BATESVILLE
NEWPORT
HARRISBURG
AUGUSTA
WYNNE
62
63
67
64
Warm Fk.
English Cr.
Big Cr.
Gut Cr.
Mill Cr.
Dry Cr.
Mud Cr.
Tenn. Cr.
Creek
Peoples Lake
Little Black River
Victory L.
Big Taylor
Corning L.
McGuire L.
Wool Fork Lake
Long L.
Pointer Lake
Knobel Lake
Peachtree L.
Liggett L.
Murphy L.
Shoemaker L.
Gas Plant
Allan Lake
Schnabaum L.
Little Black R.
CURRENT
Fourche
BLACK
Martins Cr.
Janes Cr.
Wells Cr.
SPRING RIVER
POINT
ELEVEN
Rock Cr.
Winebaugh Lake
Old River Lake
Brosnaham Lake
Wilson Lake
Straight Lake
Clear Lake
Hurricane Cr.
Big Cr.
Portia Bay
Swan Pond
Horner Bay
Flat Cr.
Water Cr.
Julian Lake
Mill Cr.
Reeds Cr.
Meadows Park Lake
Sedrick Lake
Tucker Bay
Running
Brushy L.
Shirey Bay
Old River L.
Big
CREEK
Lick Pond Slough
West Cache Ditch
E. Cache Ditch
Simp Wilson L.
Horseshoe L.
Curia Creek
Bay Lake
Round Lake
Straight Lake
Lee Lake
New Old River Lake
Craighead Forest L.
CACHE
VILLAGE
Elgin L.
Otter L.
Dota Cr.
2-Mile Cr.
Curia L.
Dota L.
Otter L.
Willow Ditch
Johnson Lake
Mink L.
Jacksonport Lake
Jack Creek
Point Old Riv. Lake
Gamble L.
Burgin L.
Pagett Sl.
Wall L.
Newport Lake
Brewer Lake
Departe
Whitstein L.
Eagle L.
Drummond Lake
Watson Lake
Clear Lake
Olyphant Horseshoe Lake
Newton Lake
Big Horseshoe Lake
Pickett Lake
Little Horseshoe L.
Bear Lake
Big Bay Ditch
W. Outside Ditch
W. Inside
E. Inside
Lake No. 1
Lake No. 2
Bradford L.
Little L.
White Lake
Arm L.
Lake No. 1
Lake No. 2
Horseshoe L.
DE VIEW
Straight Sl.
TYRONZA
Taylor Bay
Bacon L.
Walker L.
Murphy L.
Eagle L.
Clear L.
Green Tom L.
Brushy Cr.
St. Francis Bay
Barnes L.
Wolf L.
Big Blue L.
Horseshoe L.
Moon L.
Little
Overflow Creek
Big Mingo Cr.
Little Hur. L.
Big Hurricane
Shafer Lake
Old River L.

Duck Capital II

WEINER, POINSETT COUNTY HAVE DUCKS AND HISTORY TO MATCH ANY AREA OF THE STATE

With its location between Bayou DeView and Claypool's Reservoir, the small Poinsett County town of Weiner (pop. 655) can make a valid claim for some sort of "Duck Capital" title.

And you could argue that Poinsett County deserves such a place. The impressive list of duck-attracting waters that flow through it includes the St. Francis River to the east, the L'Anguille River down the middle and Bayou DeView to the west. There's even a short section of the Cache River in Poinsett County's northwest corner.

Duck hunters have been coming to this area for over 150 years. German adventurer Friederich Gerstacker traveled through the swamps here in 1839 and wrote about the lush sportsman's paradise. The Osceola Ducking Club, also known as the Oak Donic Club, was founded along the St. Francis River in 1882 and may be the oldest private club in Arkansas. Hood Lake, along Bayou DeView north of Weiner, was attracting duck hunters a century ago.

◀ Ducks were herded in front of NBC television cameras stationed around Claypool's Reservoir on Dec. 23, 1956.

Photo courtesy George Purvis

George Leach of Weiner was pictured on a postcard after a Hood Lake duck hunt circa 1900.

Farming families around Weiner, like the Ruesewalds and the Crafts and the Sitzers, have extended the traditions of duck hunting to the present. When former President Jimmy Carter wrote his book *An Outdoor Journal*, it included a story about duck hunting with Leonard Sitzer.

And, of course, Wallace Claypool's Wild Acres was the best-known duck hunting place in America at one time. It became that in 1956, when "Wide Wide World" television show host Dave Garroway said, in introducing the final segment of the program on Dec. 23, "If we're lucky, you'll be able to see, for the first time on live television, a quarter-of-a-million ducks."

For the next seven-and-a-half minutes, television screens across America

Photo courtesy George Purvis

One mallard hen stretches her wings as other ducks rest on Claypool's Reservoir.

were filled with ducks from Claypool's. The story captured within the footage told of how Claypool was taking a boy on his first duck hunt.

"A good day for a boy growing to be a man, among the rice fields of Weiner, Arkansas," said Garroway as he closed the show.

The Arkansas town most closely identified with duck hunting is Stuttgart. But Weiner, too, is famous for ducks and rice.

Poinsett County ranks second only to Arkansas County in the state's rice production. Rice was experimentally planted in the Weiner Hotel garden in 1906. By the 1920s, rice had become so important that Weiner began hosting an annual "Rice Festival."

There has long been a debate between Stuttgart and Weiner as to which one has the best duck hunting. Claypool enjoyed fanning the flames of that rivalry, when he was holding 300,000 ducks or more on Wild Acres.

In figures compiled by the Arkansas Game and Fish Commission for the North American Waterfowl Management Plan, Poinsett County ranked third in the state for duck harvest density, 56.2 per square mile. Arkansas County was first at 73.9. Poinsett County doesn't have as much public land or as many commercial operations to accommodate the number of hunters that travel to the Stuttgart area every duck season.

And in recent years, as the number of duck hunters has increased and the number of places to hunt decreased, folks in the Weiner area have tended to be a little more tight-lipped about their duck hunting.

POINSETT COUNTY — A TIMELINE

1811-12	1839	1874	1881	1882
New Madrid earthquakes cause depressions that create Big Lake and St. Francis Sunken Lands, which extend along the eastern side of Poinsett County.	German writer Friederich Gerstacker, author of *Wild Sports in the Far West*, begins extensive travels along the L'Anguille River, St. Francis River and Bayou DeView in Poinsett County.	A post named West Prairie is established after a small group of families settles at what is now the town of Weiner.	Construction of the St. Louis Southwestern "Cotton Belt" Railroad begins. The station is named Weiner, in honor of a railroad official.	Osceola Ducking Club is established along St. Francis River in Poinsett County. It is also known as the Oak Donic Club. In 1898, it would merge with the Hatchie Coon Hunting and Fishing Club.

Craft land continues to contribute

Flooded timber near Bayou DeView major source of conservation funds

A waterfowl exhibit at Arkansas State University honors the late W. L. Craft of Weiner. Many of the ducks and geese mounted in the display were killed by members of the Craft family while hunting on the land that W. L. purchased when he moved to Arkansas from Alabama in 1943.

Since the Craft family has owned it, the 700 or so acres of flooded timber near W. L.'s old homestead have been the setting for some of Arkansas' best-documented duck hunts. Nationally-recognized wildlife artists like Dave Maass, Ken Carlson and Jack Cowan have used their experiences here to paint flooded timber hunting scenes. Arkansas' 1997-98 duck stamp "Bayou DeView Green Timber Mallards" was inspired by these woods. And former President Jimmy Carter described a duck hunt here in a story entitled "Arkansas Rain, Ice, and Ducks" in his book *An Outdoor Journal.*

Darrell Craft recalls being about six years old when his grandfather, W. L., took him on the first of many duck hunts. Naturally, they went to the woods behind W. L.'s house.

"Grandpa never did shoot a lot," Darrell said. "He usually just watched. In the evening, after everybody was in from duck hunting, we'd get back in the boat and go through the woods. If he found a duck dead in the water, he would pick it up, open its bill and smell to see if it was still good. If it was, we took it home. He didn't want anything to go to waste. If you killed it, you ate it."

The late W. L. Craft, standing directly behind his grandson, Darrell, in this 1950s photo, continues to be a force in conservation.

If possible, it would be interesting to tally the number of dollars raised for waterfowl habitat and conservation from these woods. Through wildlife art, duck stamps and cash contributions to organizations like Ducks Unlimited, Craft's land has been a gold mine for waterfowl.

Leonard Sitzer married W. L.'s daughter, Katherine, in 1948. He helped W. L. build the first levees for controlling water in the hardwood timber.

Leonard and Katherine Sitzer are both life sponsors of Ducks Unlimited. Leonard can't remember how many years he worked with the local DU chapter, somewhere between 30 and 40, he estimates.

Leonard Sitzer called the ducks during former President Carter's visits.

"Leonard Sitzer is the best I've ever seen at landing a big bunch of ducks," said Kaneaster Hodges Jr. of Newport, who introduced Carter to the extraordinary duck hunting here.

And as close as Sitzer calls them, you darn well better be able to tell the difference between a mallard drake and a hen. Killing a hen costs you a $50 donation to Ducks Unlimited.

"We hold court in the duck woods," Hodges said. "Justice is swift and sure."

Sitzer was born near Weiner in 1918. His father farmed rice when it first began to boom in Poinsett County. Except during a tour of duty in World War II, Sitzer has had a hand in growing rice all his life. He served on the Riceland Foods board of directors for 33 years.

Sitzer has lived through an era when a man like W. L. Craft could come to Poinsett County and buy around 5,000 acres for one dollar an acre. He has seen Claypool's Reservoir hold almost all the ducks in northeast Arkansas because no one else held any water. And he has witnessed many ups and downs for ducks.

"I think we've got things going in the right direction now," Sitzer said. "Around here, more people are interested in holding water. Ducks Unlimited has helped get other countries involved, like Canada and Mexico. I think it's only going to get better."

W. L. Craft died in 1957, but his legacy continues to be a force in waterfowl conservation.

POINSETT COUNTY — A TIMELINE

1884	1906	1941	1956	1958
O. K. "Pop" Pickle born near Jonesboro. He would begin making duck calls and guiding hunters at Hood Lake and Brown's Lakes in the early 1900s.	J. G. Probst plants rice in the Weiner Hotel garden. The healthy crop marks the beginning of an agricultural trend that will put Poinsett County second only to Arkansas County in rice production.	Wallace H. Claypool buys 3,500 acres west of Weiner and constructs a 1,386-acre reservoir for waterfowl.	On Dec. 23, NBC's "Wide Wide World" features live coverage of a duck hunt at Wallace Claypool's Wild Acres Farm, where 300,000 ducks have congregated on the reservoir.	The Arkansas Game and Fish Commission purchases the 4,400-acre Bayou DeView Wildlife Management Area. It is later named in honor of Earl Buss, a Weiner native and one of the WMA's first managers.

Waterfowl wonderland on live TV

'Wide Wide World' showcased 300,000 ducks on Claypool's Reservoir

As much as Wallace Claypool loved the idea and wanted it to happen, his initial reaction to the idea of televising a duck hunt from his Wild Acres reservoir in 1956 came in one definitive word: "Impossible!"

Earlier that year, George Purvis, the Arkansas Game and Fish Commission's information specialist, had successfully orchestrated a 10-minute live telecast featuring catfishing on the White River at Batesville. NBC's "Wide Wide World," hosted by Dave Garroway, had enjoyed that segment so much they asked the AGFC for another suggestion. Education director Tom Mull mentioned a duck hunt.

Live television had entered a popular era, and Garroway's show was a big part of it. With an audience of four million households, "Wide Wide World" offered the chance to tout Arkansas duck hunting like nothing else before it.

"My job was to have 300,000 ducks in front of the cameras at exactly 3:14 p.m., Central Standard Time, on December 23rd," said Purvis.

In almost 30 years of hosting the AGFC's Arkansas Outdoors television show, Purvis would experience many production nightmares. But none matched this one in 1956.

"It is still amazing to this day that we were able to pull it off," Purvis said.

"The big question in the minds of the producers of the 'Wide Wide World' program was, 'Could we get 300,000 wild ducks, mostly mallards, concentrated at a certain place at a definite prearranged time?'"

There were many hurdles. Initially he dealt with how to hide TV cameras, crews, control trucks and the necessary workmen and equipment and how to get electricity and telephone lines two miles to the woods.

"The complexity of producing a major TV program outside of a studio is not properly appreciated by most viewers," Purvis wrote in the spring 1976 edition of the *Arkansas Game and Fish* magazine. "To start with, the only way to get to the spot selected was over two miles of muddy woods roads where only tractors had gone before.

"The cameras would be two miles from the nearest power line or telephone. This meant using power generators placed far enough back in the woods so as not to disturb the wary ducks. Six telephone circuits were needed to send the audio part of the program to New York.

"Even after stringing two miles of wire there was just one circuit from Wild Acres to Jonesboro, 20 miles away. So a radio loop was installed at the barn. This was a two-way radio relay to cover the 20-mile gap."

Then came concealing the working portion of the broadcast. Camouflaged blinds were built for television cameras and operators, one of which was 40 feet up a hickory tree. An additional blind was built for the remote control truck.

The video would go from the camera to the control truck via the cable, then to an 80-foot relay tower 1,000 feet back in the woods, then 35 miles to another relay tower, then 40 miles to a third tower before being sent to Memphis. There it was transmitted 1,200 miles to New York where the audio and video were combined to be broadcast live.

With the electronics in place, the only thing left was to make sure that at an exact prearranged time there would be ducks in front of the cameras — over a quarter-of-a-million ducks. Even in today's broadcast world of traveling satellites and remote control video cameras, that is some feat.

Purvis was familiar with the reservoir where the filming would take place. He knew that the ducks were reluctant to leave the sanctuary even when disturbed in one part of it.

"I had learned that by leaving one area undisturbed in the vicinity of the

Photos courtesy George Purvis

One television camera filmed from this blind, erected 40 feet up in a hickory tree.

On Dec. 23, 1956, NBC television viewers from coast to coast experienced scenes like this one from Claypool's Reservoir.

picture blind, then driving ducks with boats on open water and using beaters around the edge of the reservoir, that the ducks concentrated in front of the blind," Purvis said. "I thought we could do it again and at a definite time."

To make sure, the day before the broadcast, Purvis and a group of wildlife officers rehearsed with the ducks. Using several boats and about 30 beaters, a full-scale drive was conducted to push the ducks into the area before the cameras. It worked, but the drive took more than an hour and a half.

Regardless, Purvis felt things were in place after weeks of frantic preparations.

Not surprisingly, prior to the broadcast, the New York producers wanted a rehearsal. Purvis would not go along, fearing it would spook the ducks away.

"Originally the Arkansas duck hunting segment was to be eight minutes," Purvis said. "When they saw no ducks, the New York directors decided to limit our part to four minutes."

It looked like weeks of preparation would boil down to four minutes of air time. At 1:30 p.m., Purvis set the drive in motion for the broadcast.

"The ducks began to swim and fly into the staging area by the thousands," Purvis said. "New York was watching over the closed circuits. By 3 o'clock there were 40 acres of ducks in front of the cameras. The directors in New York became enthusiastic and started trimming time off of the other segments of the show and giving it back to Arkansas.

"I could see Claypool sitting in his blind nervously stroking his great blond Lab retriever, George. I knew the thoughts that must have been racing through his mind: 'Just the glimpse of a face, one loud noise, or even a crook of a finger might frighten the ducks away. The whole show would be ruined.'

"All of us were praying that everything would click."

But it would not be a true Arkansas duck hunt without something going wrong. At 3:10, two wildlife officers who were supposed to keep sightseers away decided to get a look. When they crested the levee, most of the ducks flew or swam out of range of the cameras.

"My heart almost stopped beating," Purvis said.

They had four minutes to put the ducks back in place. They managed.

"At 3:14 the program director in New York pushed a button and four million viewers were looking on. Not another duck could be put on the screen," Purvis said. "It was perfect."

To add to the excitement, a rocket holding three blocks of TNT was fired over the ducks and exploded in mid air.

"Then there was another explosion as 300,000 ducks leaped into the air," Purvis said.

With the ducks flying, Claypool and Lynn Parsons, a 12-year old with his new shotgun, stepped out of a blind. Claypool called the ducks in, six shots were fired and Claypool's dog was shown retrieving ducks. New York was begging for more.

"But the ducks had flown away," Purvis said.

Garroway closed the seven-and-a-half-minute segment saying, "Now if you will brush the duck feathers off your sofa, we will go on with the rest of the program."

The impossible had been achieved.

"A lot of people saw it all over the country," Purvis said. "It kind of put Arkansas duck hunting on the map."

Photo courtesy George Purvis

Wallace Claypool enjoyed entertaining guests at Wild Acres. This group included German rocket scientist Werner Von Braun (second from right). Of the others shown here, identified are: Snowden Boyle (far left), Bayard Boyle (third from left), Toof Brown (white jacket), Wallace Claypool (third from right), Sally Claypool (kneeling) and dogs (left to right) Ike, Rip and George.

Reservoir frustrated many hunters

Claypool's Wild Acres demonstrated need for more waterfowl rest areas

Particularly during dry-weather duck hunting seasons, Wallace Claypool wasn't a popular man with other hunters in the Weiner area. As ducks piled into the largest reservoir in Poinsett County and discovered almost no hunting pressure, they seldom left.

Memphis *Commercial Appeal* outdoor writer Henry Reynolds expressed the frustrations of hundreds of other hunters in a column on January 15, 1957:

"Don't get me wrong. Wallace Claypool, the head master of a half million ducks at Wild Acres Farm near Weiner, Ark., is a nice fellow. He could be nicer if he flushed these ducks during the latter part of each season.

"I've broken bread with Claypool and have no personal feud with him. I don't think he is doing the sportsmen of Arkansas right by allowing that many birds to sit on his rest pond as the season wanes.

"Claypool is doing a fine thing in attracting and holding the ducks in Northeast Arkansas during the early part of the season. I have said that before and say it again. But to hold them all year is another thing."

Reynolds pointed out that it took only two weeks for all the ducks to return to Claypool's Reservoir after a TNT charge rousted them for the "Wide Wide World" television cameras.

At the same time that Claypool's Reservoir was holding 300,000 ducks near Weiner, Edgar Queeny's Wingmead estate was attracting similar numbers at Peckerwood Lake near Stuttgart.

"When one or two men control more than three-fourths of the entire duck population of a state as large as Arkansas, thousands of others are bound to get hurt a little," Reynolds concluded.

Carl Hunter was managing Wingmead Farms for Queeny then. Hunter worked as a biologist for the Arkansas Game and Fish Commission when Queeny hired him, and he would retire as assistant director of the AGFC in 1986. Between AGFC stints, he supervised Wingmead for 20 years. Hunter got a special view of how ducks reacted to hunting pressure at Wingmead.

"When the shooting started, the ducks would go to the rest areas," Hunter said. "But as soon as the season closed, there wasn't a duck on Peckerwood Lake. There was nothing to keep them. There wasn't any food for them."

The AGFC was just beginning to address a lack of public duck hunting land. During a dry year, especially, there simply weren't many other large rest areas for waterfowl besides Claypool's and Queeny's. That has changed dramatically since then. Dry hunting seasons will still concentrate ducks on reservoirs and fields where water can be managed. But there are enough of those now that Claypool's Reservoir and Peckerwood Lake don't attract such a high percentage of the state's ducks.

George Purvis began working for the AGFC in 1951. The huge numbers of ducks brought him to Claypool's Reservoir for the first time in 1955. In his job with the AGFC's information and education division, Purvis came to capture Claypool's ducks on film.

"I shot about 400 or 500 feet of film," Purvis recalled. "When I showed it to him, he just fell out. He said, 'I've got to have a copy of that. When can you come back? Where do you want me to build you a blind?' He bent over backward to do anything I wanted to do.

"We hunted together in the mornings and we'd shoot pictures in the afternoons. We'd do it two or three times a week."

Claypool could hunt areas of his 3,500-acre farm and 1,400-acre reservoir without spooking the vast majority of ducks from the rest area. A man with a spoon and a tin pan would make enough noise to raise some of the ducks off the reservoir, and Claypool would call them into nearby flooded timber.

"Claypool's philosophy was to wait until everybody else in that county got through shooting," Purvis recalled. "He'd get out there an hour after sunup, shoot his four (the limit then) and get out."

By the time Claypool had stirred his ducks a bit, many other hunters had gone home, complaining all the while about Claypool hoarding the ducks.

Claypool's neighbor down the road, Fritz Ruesewald, never begrudged Claypool's actions. It was on a visit to the Ruesewald farm that Claypool discovered how good the duck hunting was in this area. Ruesewald family members had operated a small commercial hunting business on their Swan Pond Road farm for many years. After Claypool built his reservoir, the Ruesewalds' hunting remained consistently good.

"If he hadn't been there, we wouldn't have had near as many ducks here," said Ruesewald.

The pictures Purvis took at Claypool's began appearing in newspapers all over the country. In 1956, publicity about Claypool's Reservoir peaked. It began with a picture in *Sports Illustrated* magazine — the January 9 issue with Boston Celtics guard Bob Cousy on the cover — and ended with the "Wide Wide World" television show in December.

All the publicity about the ducks that rafted up at Claypool's Reservoir tends to overshadow the man himself. W. H. Claypool appreciated everything about duck hunting — from the ducks to the dogs to the calls.

In 1915, Claypool began a career in car sales as manager of the Memphis Motor Car Company. In 1922, with partner Hugh Jetton, he organized the highly-successful Bluff City Buick Company. Claypool served as a director of the Memphis Chamber of Commerce and was one of the founders of the Memphis Bank and Trust Company.

Claypool's business success allowed him time to concentrate on his duck hunting hobby. In 1940 Claypool won the World's Championship Duck Calling Contest in Stuttgart. In 1941 he bought 3,500 acres near Weiner and constructed the soon-to-be-legendary reservoir.

George, the blond Labrador retriever that appeared in the "Wide Wide World" show, was another indication of Claypool's love for waterfowling. Claypool appreciated the work of a well-trained retriever. His second wife, Sally, was an excellent dog trainer. Claypool enjoyed showing hunting guests how he could drop his wallet and George would always be able to find it for him.

Claypool was 81 years old when he sold his reservoir to friends from Memphis. One of Purvis' enlarged photographs hangs on the wall at the clubhouse at Claypool's Reservoir today. On the matting around the picture, Claypool wrote: "To my friends and successors, Bayard Boyle, Snowden Boyle, Toof Brown and Norfleet Turner, I entrust the fulfillment of my life's work, Wild Acres and its ducks. Weiner, Arkansas, July 1966 — W. H. Claypool."

Wallace and Sally Claypool continued to live at the farm until shortly before his death in 1973 at age 87.

Riley has been stomping around these grounds since grade school days

In some ways, nothing has changed over the last 60 years for Johnny Riley. As a boy he rode a horse to the Hoot Owl Schoolhouse through the woods near Claypool's Reservoir.

"I've fished here all my life," said Riley.

Riley has managed the reservoir since 1966, when W. H. Claypool sold the property to his Memphis friends — Bayard Boyle, Snowden Boyle, Toof Brown and Norfleet Turner. Riley wasn't looking for work, but he found a perfect job.

Riley had enjoyed a string of successful business ventures that allowed him to concentrate on hunting and fishing at the age of 35. He met Snowden Boyle on a deer hunting trip, and Boyle talked Riley into managing the place.

"You'd think I owned it instead of them," Riley said of the current owners and their families. "That's how they have treated me."

Claypool would certainly approve. The reservoir he built continues to attract big numbers of ducks.

"We'll still hold a quarter-of-a-million ducks a lot of times on this lake," Riley said.

Rice and milo are planted in fields around the reservoir, then flooded for the ducks in November. Six hundred acres of green timber are flooded, too. Riley has helped erect 300 wood duck boxes on the property. A resident flock of Canada geese can usually be seen from the clubhouse.

A 300-acre rest area never gets hunted. The four members can hunt only on Wednesdays, Saturdays and Sundays, and only in the mornings. Each member and Riley are allowed a maximum of three guests. In other words, the ducks probably didn't notice when Claypool left; hunting pressure continues to be light.

But many local residents did notice when Claypool left, and they tried to hunt here.

"When I first came they had five men trying to keep people run out of this place," Riley said. "One Sunday I put 27 people in jail.

"Anybody I caught in here, I would either whip their ass or put them in jail. After that gets around, you don't have many problems."

Purvis has observed changing times

Duck hunters need to remember how quail hunting was once the king

Med Donaldson was a game warden in the days when game laws were ignored. One winter day, Donaldson was sitting in a diner in northeast Arkansas. A duck hunter walked through the doors carrying a sack full of mallards and dumped them on the counter.

Donaldson watched as the owner and the sack-toting hunter haggled over the price of mallards. They finally settled on a price of 25 cents per duck. It was a clear-cut violation of state and federal game laws. Donaldson walked to the counter placed both of the men under arrest, grabbed the sack of mallards and marched the men through the doors toward the courthouse.

It was a short walk, and it was a waste of time. The judge dismissed the case due to lack of evidence.

George Purvis often tells that story in explaining the changes he has witnessed on the Arkansas hunting and fishing scene. The difference in attitude among duck hunters, wildlife officers and judges is just one of the many aspects of change that Purvis has seen during the past 50 years.

Purvis is best known as the stately gentleman who for more than 40 years brought the Arkansas outdoors to the television sets in his weekly "Arkansas Sportsman" show. In the course of the directing the Arkansas Game and Fish Commission's Information and Education Division and putting together the television show, Purvis got a first-hand look at the changing face of Arkansas duck hunting.

"Through the years, duck hunting has taken the place of quail hunting," Purvis said. "It's a faddish type thing, but it's addictive. There was a time when you weren't anything if you didn't have a bunch of dogs and you didn't go quail hunting. But the quail are gone."

Purvis said it's important for duck hunters to understand that and not let history repeat itself. He points out that right after the Civil War, the big thing was fox hunting.

"During Reconstruction days, those who had a little money started turning the hounds out," Purvis said. "It became a status symbol, based on how many hounds you had."

But fox hunting lost its allure as deer populations started taking hold and fox populations declined. Few Arkansas fox hunters today understand the romance and traditions of the sport.

As fox hunting faded, quail came on the scene. The state was rural, and the habitat suited quail. Quail hunting soon became the popular sport. The birds' decline is directly attributed to the destruction of habitat, most of it at the hands of modernization.

There have been times when Purvis felt like the duck would follow the path of the fox and quail.

One of those was in the 1960s when duck populations fell to extreme lows.

"I was convinced we would never go back to a long season and four mallards a day," Purvis said. "But I was wrong."

The duck seems to be withstanding the test of time. It's the sport of hunting that still remains to be tested. Purvis believes the largest threat facing duck hunting is anti-hunters.

"Look at what has happened in England and Australia," Purvis said of the two countries where strong anti-hunting groups have virtually wiped out the sport. "If it happens there, it will someday happen here, especially if we don't take care of what we have."

The bright side is that so many people are taking care of duck hunting. Unlike the times when fox and quail hunting were at the top of the game, this is an age where information is quick and easy to attain from variety of sources.

As a result, today's duck hunters are more educated and more dedicated.

Helping them get to that point were many men who left an indelible mark on Arkansas' duck hunting. According to

George Purvis has seen wildlife enforcement become increasingly important and high-tech, including the use of helicopters.

George Purvis served as AGFC information chief and hosted the television show "Arkansas Sportsman" for many years.

Purvis, a few of the most profound were, as follows:

■ Wallace Claypool, owner of the famous Claypool Reservoir. Claypool and Purvis were best friends brought together by their love of duck hunting.

Claypool's mark was his work on refining the process of attracting and holding ducks in one area. It was so successful that Claypool's Reservoir boosted the state's reputation as duck hunting paradise when it was featured on the "Wide, Wide World" television show.

■ Edgar Queeny, author of *Prairie Wings*, creator of Wingmead and long-time president of the Monsanto Corporation. Queeny's *Prairie Wings* book and video are still popular today. At the time of its release, the video was unprecedented in its quality, showing the flight characteristics of the mallard, and introducing Arkansas duck hunting to a new crowd.

■ The McCollum family, led by Otis McCollum, who developed green-tree reservoirs around Stuttgart and helped create the reputation of great duck hunting in Arkansas. Other noted members of the family are Lloyd and Marion McCollum, who served as AGFC commissioners, and Thad McCollum, who was instrumental in starting the World's Championship Duck Calling Contest.

■ Rollie Remmel, Purvis' best friend, who was the first state director of Ducks Unlimited. Remmel's tireless fund raising and cheerleading for ducks has shaped a conservation ethic among hunters all over the state.

■ Trusten Holder, the AGFC's federal aid coordinator, who orchestrated the purchases of large tracts of land including Bayou Meto, Black River, Hurricane and Dagmar wildlife management areas.

"People thought Trusten was crazy," Purvis said. "At that time, there was a lot of land available. They assumed it would always be like that. But with the purchase of the land, the Arkansas Game and Fish Commission moved out way ahead of other agencies."

■ Rex Hancock, the Stuttgart dentist, who latched onto the Cache River channelization project like a pit bull and didn't let go until the Corps of Engineers stopped channelizing.

Hancock's work brought new attention to the shrinking wetlands of east Arkansas, and helped make conservationists out of duck hunters.

Purvis said there are many more, but the different veins of work of each of the men set standards that are still being followed today.

They have helped from a hunting standpoint, too. When Purvis began working with the Arkansas Game and Fish Commission, duck hunting was relegated to three areas of the state, Stuttgart, Weiner and Black River.

"You really didn't hear much about duck hunting down south or in some of the places you hear about now," Purvis said. "It's spreading out. Rice is being grown all over. We used to think you had to have a hardpan (soil), like that around Stuttgart to grow rice. But they are growing it everywhere."

Too, large wooded tracts like Overflow, Felsenthal and others are managed and water levels are manipulated to attract ducks to areas that before depended solely on Mother Nature.

"We have a situation that is better suited for the hunter than ever before," Purvis said. "I have always believed that a hunter can find the best duck hunting there is with a little sweat. That's even more true today, because there's so much more of it out there."

Point system caused headaches for hunters, and law enforcement

Why would a duck hunter keep a dead mallard hen tucked close to his body? Why would wildlife enforcement officers carry thermometers to determine the body temperatures of dead ducks?

The answer is, the point system. For 14 seasons, from 1974-75 through 1987-88, the daily bag limit of ducks in Arkansas was determined by a point system. Following federal guidelines, some states operated under the point system even longer.

The point system was designed to give greater protection to the species and sexes that needed it most. For example, mallard hens and wood ducks were among those assigned 90-point values during most of Arkansas' years under this system. A daily bag limit was 100 points.

The regulation stated: "The daily bag limit is reached when the points of the last bird taken, added to the sum of the point values of the other birds already taken during that day, reaches or exceeds 100 points."

That meant if you killed either a mallard hen or a wood duck first, you could kill only one more duck that day. It could be a 15-point gadwall or green-wing teal, a 35-point mallard drake or another 90-point duck. As long as you hadn't reached 100 points, you could keep hunting.

(The point values changed during the 14 seasons under the point system. At one time, mallard drakes were 25 points and gadwalls were 10.)

When the order in which the ducks were killed made all the difference between shooting two ducks and being done for the day, or shooting several more before limiting out, the temptations were more than many hunters could handle. One cold hen (90 pts.) and two warm drakes (70 pts.) gave a wildlife officer circumstantial evidence to write you a ticket for being over the limit. So a hunter trying to cheat the system would keep the hen as warm as possible. Wildlife officers used thermometers to add evidence to their cases.

In the last few years of the point system, some of that temptation was eliminated when hens were given 100-point values.

Ruesewald wouldn't leave Swan Pond

Even an offer from Claypool wasn't enough to make him move

"...When a German finally has managed to make a plot of ground arable and has built a house on it, it is extraordinarily difficult to uproot him again. Indeed, you would have to offer him an unusually high price to persuade him to sell."

Friederich Gerstacker,
"In the Arkansas Backwoods"

Fritz Ruesewald, at age 93, demonstrated that he could still blow a duck call. Ruesewald was well-known for his ability to "shoot the high duck" while guiding hunters at Swan Pond.

W. H. Claypool thought he'd made an offer that couldn't be refused. Two friends of Claypool's had discovered the fabulous duck hunting at Swan Pond on the Ruesewald family farm near Weiner. They had brought Claypool back with them, to show him just how good the hunting was.

"How long have the ducks been using the place like that?" Claypool asked Fritz Ruesewald, after another extraordinary hunt.

"Since Moses was a child, I think," replied Ruesewald.

"How much do you want for this place?" Claypool said.

"You don't have enough money," replied Ruesewald.

"You don't understand," said Claypool, who had made himself wealthy with an automobile dealership in Memphis. "How much do you want for this place?"

"No, you don't understand," Ruesewald said. "You don't have enough money."

Claypool finally got the message; no one had enough money to buy the Ruesewald farm. It simply wasn't for sale. So Claypool sought advice from Fritz on the next best thing — a place like the Ruesewald farm. Fritz directed him to some Poinsett County land just three miles down the road.

"You can buy it for a song, and sing the song yourself," Ruesewald told him.

Ruesewald pointed Claypool in the direction of what would become Wild Acres, more commonly known simply as Claypool's. With the live television pictures on Dave Garroway's "Wide Wide Word" in 1956, Claypool's would become the most famous duck hunting hole in Arkansas.

In Fritz Ruesewald's small brick house a black-and-white photograph hangs inside a kitchen cabinet door. It's one of those famous photos showing a cloud of ducks over Claypool's Reservoir. It's signed by W.H. Claypool.

"I was his bosom friend until the day he died," Ruesewald said. "I could go over there and hunt any time I wanted."

But there was rarely a day when Ruesewald didn't have plenty of ducks closer to home.

Born October 28, 1903, in O'Fallon, Mo., Fred Leo "Fritz" Ruesewald was just a few weeks past his 93rd birthday when he took some time to reflect on a life filled with family, farming and duck hunting. Wearing a blue Ducks Unlimited sweatshirt, Ruesewald donned one of the hats that Jimmy Reel gave him decades ago, then obliged a request to blow a few notes on a duck call.

"My daughter, the nun, she's so neat," Ruesewald said. "She threw my Jimmy Reel hats in the washing machine once.

"That's one time a nun got a cussing."

Reel is best known around Eagle Lake, Texas. He was a founder of the Rice Belt Ducks Unlimited chapter there. He died in 1976, but a goose hunting camp at Eagle Lake still bears his name.

"I helped raise Jimmy Reel," Ruesewald said. "For two years I carried a quart of milk every morning and every night to the Reels' house."

Reel learned to hunt waterfowl at his father's hunting camp on nearby Hood Lake before moving to Texas. Weiner has produced an unusual number of well-known waterfowl hunters, and Ruesewald has hunted with most of them.

Fritz Ruesewald quit hunting ducks around 1986. Failing eyesight and a frail body wouldn't allow it.

"I'd still like to stick that shotgun up a mallard's ass and pull the trigger," said Ruesewald with a smile on his face and a gleam in his eye, his left eye.

On New Year's Eve, when Ruesewald was 20 years old, he had planned a date with his wife to be, Rosa Lee Gallagher. But measles had spread through the Ruesewald household, and Fritz was forced to stay home. With nothing else to do, Fritz decided to make a big firecracker, right there in the house. He began pouring the gunpowder from old 16-gauge shotgun shells into a section of shotgun barrel, which had been cut off and sealed at one end.

"I used the powder from 15 black-powder shells," Ruesewald said.

Then he took pages from a Sears and Roebuck catalog, wadded them up and started tamping them down into the barrel with a ramrod and a hammer.

"My dad looked over at me, and said, 'Fritz, you're going to blow your fool head off.'"

Fourteen window panes shattered in the Ruesewald home when the gunpowder ignited. Except for the blood running down it, Fritz Ruesewald's face was solid black.

"My dad yelled, 'Fritz, Fritz, Fritz, you'll never see again.' I said, 'I can see you,'" Ruesewald recalled.

Ruesewald lost the vision in his right eye. The greatest inconvenience that caused was forcing him to shoot ducks off his left shoulder instead of his right.

"I got to where I could shoot better than men with two eyes," Ruesewald smiled.

Although Arkansas is famous for duck hunting in flooded timber, where the mallards come fluttering down in your face, Ruesewald never enjoyed it. He has out-lived most of his hunting buddies around Weiner. But there are some left, and all confirm that Ruesewald was known for shooting the high duck.

"Don't sell that man short," said George Leach, who was born in Weiner in 1919 and delivered the first mail route here in 1941. "Fritz Ruesewald was the best duck shot I've ever seen in my life."

Ruesewald's favorite gun was a 12-gauge magnum Winchester pump known as the "heavy duck gun." It had a 32-inch barrel and a full choke.

In the late 1930s, Ruesewald started charging hunters to use his blind. The rate for up to three men was $2.50 per day, plus shotgun shells for Fritz.

"On a windy day, I used No. 2 shot in three-inch magnum shells; no wind, No. 4s," Ruesewald said. "If anybody brought No. 6s, I'd send them to town to get more shells."

You can understand how commercial duck hunting became a tradition in the Arkansas Delta. Once the land was cleared, a man like Fritz could duck hunt every day during the winter, when there was no farming to do. At the same time, he was putting meat on the table and a few dollars in his pocket. It was the easiest money a farmer could make.

Ruesewald's parents, Joseph and Theresa, were living near St. Louis when they married.

"My mother had left Germany saying she didn't want to raise boys for cannon fodder," Ruesewald said.

Like many other German immigrants in that area, they moved to northeast Arkansas at the urging of a St. Louis real estate agent, who was also of German descent. He helped his clients keep the faith — donating the land to set up a Catholic church in Weiner and a Lutheran church in nearby Waldenburg. But that was as much help as he could give in terms of clearing the swampland he'd sold them.

"When we moved here, I was five or six years old," said Ruesewald. "This place was just like the Indians left it. There were woods from here to Weiner.

German POWs helped Ruesewald family harvest rice crop

The Ruesewald family faced a dilemma. With World War II drawing almost all the manpower in America, it would be nearly impossible to harvest a rice crop with only the three Ruesewald brothers left on the farm.

There was one other source of labor. Between 1942 and 1947, thousands of German prisoners of war were housed in over 20 camps around Arkansas. The sites included Harrisburg, located just 10 miles from Weiner.

"We couldn't get any hired hands to harvest the rice," Fritz Ruesewald remembered. "We were told we could get some help, but they were German prisoners, Hitler's boys. I said, 'Well, we've got to have some help.' They sent over nine men the next day.

"My brothers, Joe and Bill, were afraid of them. I looked at them with a smile on my face and said, "Guten Morgen (good morning)."

As the children of German immigrants, the Ruesewald boys grew up speaking German around the house, even after they moved to Arkansas.

"I couldn't speak English worth a darn," Ruesewald. "I was a little German boy."

He had retained enough German to communicate well with the POWs. An armed guard accompanied them. One day after lunch, the guard went to the Ruesewald barn and took a long nap. When the guard woke up, he came from the barn with a worried look on his face. He thought someone had stolen most of his bullets.

"Those prisoners were sitting on rice shocks, eating cakes and apples for lunch," Ruesewald said. "They got to laughing. They realized he had lost his bullets. One of them told me, 'Fritz, you don't need a gun. Where in the hell would we go from here?'"

The bullets were found in the barn, where they had fallen from the guard's pockets.

"I really enjoyed those prisoners," said Ruesewald. "They were just people, like you and I. But they were sad. They knew when the war was over they had no place to go home to."

It wasn't Swan Pond then, it was Swamp Pond. There was lots of malaria and cottonmouths. And there were ducks by the blue million."

Shotguns blasting throughout the night are Ruesewald's earliest recollections of duck hunting.

"Men from Chicago and St. Louis and Jonesboro would come down here when the moon was right," he said. "They would shoot all night long. A man with a wagon would pick up the ducks and take them to the train depot. They'd pack them in barrels with ice and excelsior."

Weiner was a stop on the Cotton Belt railroad line that ran from St. Louis to Texarkana. It brought the Ruesewald family to Weiner and provided the chief form of in-town entertainment.

"A passenger train came every morning and every evening," Ruesewald said. "One way we amused ourselves was to walk to the train station and see who got off."

Joseph and Theresa Ruesewald had 10 children. Their home was centered around a love of music and strong Catholic faith. As a youngster, Fritz learned to play the harmonica — a German-made Hohner, of course — and the mouth harp.

Those talents helped Ruesewald master a duck call. He lived in the heart of Arkansas' hand-made duck call region, and he collected a few over the years. But Ruesewald, like many every-day duck hunters, favored the small black hard-rubber P.S. Olt call. A "meat call" is the term often used to describe those like the Olt. That was a high compliment during the time Ruesewald was growing up, then raising five kids of his own.

"The only groceries you needed in those days were coffee, flour, sugar, salt and pepper," Ruesewald said. "We lived like kings. We sang and prayed. We thought we were happy."

This was a time when finding enough food for your family was the primary focus of each day. For about half the year, ducks helped solve that problem.

"We hunted them from when they came until when they left," Ruesewald said.

Ruesewald's home offers a view of duck hunting unlike any other. From the living room window, you can look out over Swan Pond and the agricultural fields that were once thick woods. This land was cleared the hard way — with crosscut saws and chopping axes.

Before the trees were cleared, it was flooded timber with a floor of pin oak acorns that attracted ducks. The acorns were plentiful enough to fatten the free-ranging hogs the Ruesewald family kept.

Anything that cut into their food supply, whether it was wolves killing hogs, hawks killing chickens or bald eagles killing ducks, was also fair game for Fritz Ruesewald.

"If you raised chickens, which we did, you had to keep them up at night or the hawks would get them," Ruesewald said. "I like eating chickens too much to let the hawks eat them."

At one time, the Arkansas hunting license carried a message encouraging hunters to kill hawks and owls. Ruesewald claims to have killed a bald eagle that had a 10-foot wingspan.

"My blind was in the middle of a field," he said. "All the weed seeds would bank up in front of my blind. There would be five- or six-thousand ducks feeding on that weed seed. One time, about two weeks after the season was out, I saw this big bird eating something."

Ruesewald soon realized it was a bald eagle feeding on ducks. He watched it dive into a raft of ducks, then carry its prey back to a tree. When the eagle left the tree to go hunting again, Ruesewald crept to a good shooting position and waited until it returned.

"It came back with another duck," Ruesewald said. "It lit on that limb and it ripped into the duck with its beak. I'll never forget that big ol' golden eye. It was the meanest looking bastard I've ever seen."

A close viewing of the big eagle left Ruesewald wanting more firepower. When the bird flew off to hunt again, Ruesewald crawled away with his shotgun and No. 4 shells. He was waiting with a .22-caliber rifle when the eagle returned.

"I put the scope right at his pulley bone and pulled the trigger," Ruesewald said.

He knew bald eagles were protected, but the eagle had violated the basic logic that helped a man feed his family.

"I could out-run all the game wardens," he said. "They were all big fat guys in those days."

Ruesewald showed the eagle to a friend, and said, "It's an American bald eagle. Our patriotic bird. If a game warden catches me, they'll throw me so far back in jail they'll have to shoot the beans to me."

Mallards, pintails and teal, especially blue-wings, are Ruesewald's favorites among the waterfowl. He calls a specklebelly "the best goose on the wing." Those preferences are based on taste.

"It doesn't matter how pretty they are," said Ruesewald. "It only matters when I get it in the skillet and eat the hind leg."

Sister Rosalie Ruesewald lives in Fort Smith, Arkansas, where she teaches at St. Scholastica Academy. In looking back now, she realizes how little money her parents had to manage a household.

"We really were poor, but we didn't think of it that way," she said. "We were happy."

She remembers her father practically living in a duck blind when the season was open. She recalls being amazed when men would come all the way from Memphis, St. Louis and Chicago to duck hunt with her father. And she remembers enjoying the taste of duck.

"That's what we ate during duck season," Rosalie said.

In the spring of 1952, a tornado touched down near Weiner. Rosalie told of how her mother took one daughter to the safest section of the house and tried to talk Fritz into coming with them.

"If it's going to get us, it's going to get us," said Fritz, refusing to leave the comfort of his bed.

The tornado took the roof off the house. Fritz' bed collapsed and a brick from the house hit him in the nose. But he didn't move.

Fritz smiled as his daughter retold the story. He looked out the living room window at Swan Pond.

"My heart and soul is still down there," Ruesewald said. "I've had a wonderful life. It was rough and tough as hell sometimes. But I've lived next to the best duck pond in the world."

It's important to beat the crowds in order to get the best holes in a popular AGFC wildlife management area like Bayou DeView.

EARL BUSS/BAYOU DeVIEW WMA

Acres: 4,435
First purchase: 1958
Location: Near Weiner in Poinsett County.
Topo maps (7.5 series, U.S. Geological Survey): Weiner, Risher.

Bayou DeView Wildlife Management Area is located in the middle of what many sportsmen consider to be the greatest duck hunting area in Arkansas. The area lies along Bayou DeView from State Highway 14 to just north of State Highway 214. The area can be reached by county roads west out of Weiner on State Highway 39 or off State Highways 14 and 214.

Getting to Bayou DeView first is often a prerequisite for hunting this small area. Bayou DeView WMA is almost seven square miles of acreage, but small when compared to traditional public duck hunting areas in the Delta.

Comparatively speaking, it is to Jonesboro hunters what Harris Brake is to hunters in Little Rock — a quick, close area that can produce a limit of ducks if the pressure isn't too heavy.

The bottomland hardwoods of Bayou DeView are surrounded by acres and acres of prime duck food — rice, soybeans and other grain crops — making this WMA excellent for duck hunting. The area is flooded each fall by trapped rainfall.

There are no developed camping areas on the WMA.

The WMA features various hardwood trees — pin oak flats mixed with stands of nuttall and post oaks.

AGFC waterfowl reports consistently state that there are few ducks on Bayou DeView. That is often true. But Bayou DeView is surrounded by private duck hunting clubs, including Claypool's Reservoir to the east, which hold a tremendous number of ducks that make periodic flights over the area.

Bayou DeView WMA is separated into three areas: the Martin Impoundment, which is 1,200 acres of naturally flooded timber; the Thompson Impoundment, 2,000 acres of pumped area; and the Oliver tract, 1,400 acres of naturally flooding bottomland.

According to Robert Zachary, AGFC district biologist, the keys to having good duck hunting in the area are having enough water in the St. Francis and Cache river bottoms, as well as having fields and surrounding areas flooded. Combined, these areas hold ducks for most of that region.

Lake Hogue also helps attract ducks to Bayou DeView WMA. This 340-acre AGFC-built lake serves as a waterfowl rest area during duck season.

The WMA's namesake, Earl Buss, was a Weiner native and one of the first area managers.

State duck stamp a story of success

Grisham's vision has grabbed attention of nation's top waterfowl artists

Larry Grisham's vision of Arkansas waterfowl hunting occupies a place in every duck hunter's pocket. It presents itself in pictures of mallards cupping into Bayou Meto, wood ducks swimming through Hurricane Lake and Canada geese sailing over Lodge Corner. These Arkansas waterfowl scenes appear every season on a 1 1/2- by 1-inch stamp.

A $7 Arkansas duck stamp is required of everyone who hunts waterfowl in the state, along with an Arkansas Game and Fish Commission hunting license.

To some the Arkansas duck stamp simply allows them to hunt waterfowl. To the AGFC it serves as a vital source of income for waterfowl programs. To others the duck stamp represents a work of art.

For Grisham, the stamp reflects an aspect of Arkansas that sets it apart from every other state. That's one reason it's so important to him. Grisham has worked closely with the AGFC since the state stamp program began in 1981.

"For many people, duck hunting in Arkansas is like playing golf at Augusta National," Grisham said. "Hunting ducks in Arkansas' flooded timber is something you name-drop. We have people all over the country who want Arkansas duck stamps."

The popularity of the stamp has made it one of the most visible images of Arkansas duck hunting.

"On a per capita basis, the Arkansas state duck stamp raises more money than any other state," Grisham said. "In volume, we sell more stamps than any state with the exception of Texas."

Arkansas stamp sales reached an all-time high of approximately 68,000 in 1996-97.

Larry Grisham of Jonesboro calls ducks from flooded timber near Bayou DeView.

Part of that demand results from Grisham's insistence on picking the top waterfowl artists in the U.S. to create the Arkansas stamp. The state series began in 1981 with Lee LeBlanc's "Bayou Meto Mallards." Since then, Arkansas duck stamp artists have included the top names in the field, like David Maass and Maynard Reece.

"Those are household names for collectors," Grisham said. "And they have built a standard where every artist wants to paint the Arkansas stamp. It is a feather in his cap.

"Collectors and hunters want our stamp because of that reputation and the fact we have kept a high standard in the artists who paint our prints."

After the first stamp, Grisham began

a close relationship with the AGFC in which he picks the artist and handles sales of the prints. The combination of the stamp and the accompanying prints produced just over $5.5 million through the 1996-97 season. All of that money has been used in acquiring waterfowl habitat and funding waterfowl research.

But there's one other big reason the Arkansas stamp has been so successful. All the credit here goes to Mother Nature, for providing Arkansas with legendary duck hunting, plus a near-monopoly on flooded timber duck hunting. Some Arkansans have grown accustomed to seeing mallards flutter down through the trees. They need only share that experience with an out-of-state hunter to be reminded of how special it is.

"People don't believe it when they see how close the ducks get," Grisham said. "They just can't believe it."

Since the days of Audubon, waterfowlers have loved scenes of ducks and duck hunting that can only be captured on canvas. Photographs and videos fail to relay a moment's mood, color and action like the work an artist can lay down with a brush. As a result, paintings of ducks in natural scenes are common in duck hunters' homes, more than in any other hunting sport.

A waterfowl artist's ability to recreate a scene stands particularly tall when flooded timber is the backdrop. The Arkansas duck stamp has given hunters the opportunity to enjoy images they might not experience otherwise.

"So much of it is someone seeing a print of mallards cupping into a flooded timber stand, and they think, 'Man, wouldn't I like to be standing right there behind that tree right now,'" Grisham said. "It allows someone for a moment to feel like they are really there."

This has proved to be especially compelling to those who live outside of the state.

"The scenes sell Arkansas duck hunting," Grisham said. "It's a nice image of the state."

And it's an image that Grisham never fails to appreciate. He doesn't miss many mornings in the flooded timber near Bayou DeView during duck season. Grisham, who lives in Jonesboro, follows the philosophy of his friend in Weiner, Leonard Sitzer, who says that you should go duck hunting every day of the season so you don't miss any of the good days. And they are all good days as far as Grisham is concerned.

"I don't even go to Razorback basketball games until duck season is over," said Grisham, who played for the University of Arkansas basketball team that won a Southwest Conference championship and qualified for the NCAA tournament in 1958.

"There is nowhere else I'd rather be. Business just takes a back seat to duck hunting. Most people around here just mark off the mornings to go hunting."

Grisham still appreciates the many scenes from Arkansas' flooded timber that hunters often experience here for the first time.

Pickle was pure Arkansas backwoods

'I first saw the light of this world through the cracks of a pole shack'

He killed rabbits and ducks with a slingshot, exploded bumble bees off a honeysuckle bush in his front yard with a .22 pistol and once felled a goose from high in the sky with a 30-30 rifle.

O. K. "Pop" Pickle played the mandolin and harmonica, whittled some of the most highly-prized duck calls ever made and may have had a hand in the "liquor game" during Prohibition days.

Pickle also was known as a storyteller second to none, when guiding "sports" at his camp on Hood Lake and at Brown's Fishing and Hunting Club in the 1930s. It's no wonder that when Pickle left his hometown of Otwell for California in 1939 he would be recognized as an entertainer and eventually land a few small parts in movies, basically just being himself.

Tom Barre of Pocahontas collects duck calls. After finding a few Pickle calls and doing some initial research about their maker, he became fascinated with Pickle's life story.

"Pop Pickle is Arkansas duck callmaking, calling and hunting at its best," said Barre, whose research provided most of the information for this story. "He is an interesting chapter to add to our proud hunting tradition."

Pop Pickle was a true "angel of the swampland" and a pure Arkansas backwoodsman.

"No, I was not born with a silver spoon in my mouth, far from it," Pickle once wrote. "I first saw the light of this world through the cracks of a pole shack."

Born near Jonesboro in 1884, Pickle never knew who his father was. His mother left him for members of her family to raise. Despite that bleak start, a series of physically demanding jobs around sawmills, cotton gins and grist mills, and burying two wives who died from the flu, Pickle never lost his zest for life. He had little formal schooling, but he could read and write. In later years, Pickle would record his recollections of those early years, some in story form.

Photo courtesy Tom Barre

O. K. "Pop" Pickle

"At an early age my greatest ambition was to become a hunter as carefree and, if possible, as successful as any Indian that ever roamed the hills and swamps of Arkansas," Pickle wrote in a story entitled "The Game Trails of the Forest."

"My ancestors must have had a strain of Robin Hood blood in them, for when civilization began to crowd them down in Mississippi, they threw a gourd of water on the fire, called the dogs, and headed for Arkansas where they could have elbow room...therefore, I, you might say, was dropped into this world in the middle of a thicket down in the Wonder State before it was crisscrossed by railroads and highways...and the highways that I wished to learn most about were the game trails of the forest."

Pickle spent those early years tromping through the swamps. He lived off the land — hunting, trapping and fishing — as many did in that day.

Pickle fathered six children. After his second wife died in 1924, he accepted the added burden of raising them alone. It required every bit of the work ethic and ability to improvise that he had honed while practically raising himself. The extra couple of dollars that a handcarved duck call provided were vital household income.

Pickle's calls reveal his mastery of making do with whatever he had. He may have been influenced by James

Photo courtesy Tom Barre

Pickle killed this mountain lion in California with a .22-caliber target pistol. He sent the picture to a friend in Arkansas, after Pickle began work as predator hunter.

Beckhart at Big Lake. Pickle's calls are of the Big Lake or St. Francis River style, with four checkered panels and a German silver reed.

In his early calls, the reeds are held in place with a small wooden wedge, in the Reelfoot style. This style caused problems for anyone who had to take the call apart, especially on a hunt in flooded timber. The reed and wedge were loose when the insert was pulled from the barrel, and could easily drop into the water.

Pickle began adding a metal clip to hold the reed in place. The clip fit into a slit cut in the insert, and the reed wouldn't slip out. Cutting and bending small sections of Prince Albert tobacco cans provided the materials for the clip.

Such a practical innovation had to come from a man who spent considerable time using a duck call. Pickle was considered the best duck-caller in a region of good callers.

"He could call ducks away from anybody," — that was Pickle's reputation. In the 1930s, he blew a duck call for the audience of a Paragould radio station. Pickle's ability to entertain became more widely recognized and led to many other radio sessions. With all of his backwoods skills and love for telling stories, Pickle was a natural entertainer.

In 1939, at the age of 55, Pickle traveled to California to visit a couple of his children living there. He competed in the "World Champion Bird Calling Contest" at the Treasure Island World's Fair and took second place. In the process, he amused the crowd by playing "The Star Spangled Banner" on his duck call.

"At an early age my greatest ambition was to become a hunter as carefree and, if possible, as successful as any Indian that ever roamed the hills and swamps of Arkansas."

Pickle stayed in California in the San Francisco area. Two years later, he was employed as a predator hunter in the Sacramento River valley. It was there that he killed a 110-pound mountain lion with a .22-caliber target pistol. Apparently he was about to move back to Arkansas before landing that job. In a letter back to a friend in Jonesboro, Pickle wrote:

"I thought when I left Arkansas that my time as a mossback was over, but after spending eight months in the city of San Francisco (and believe me I saw that burg as well as I had ever seen Jonesboro) I became so disgusted with all that make-believe stuff and was just about in the notion to head back to God's country when I got the opportunity to go up to the Central Valley Reclamation area."

He settled in Petaluma, where a son, Kay, and daughter, Virginia, lived. Kay was an entertainer and musician. Pop began playing the mandolin in his son's band.

In another letter to a friend in Arkansas, Pickle wrote: "I have been here almost two years now and am known for 50 miles up and down Sacramento Canyon as Old Pop Pickle and when you see my picture you will have no cause to wonder why I am called Pop."

Pickle had grown a long, white, Buffalo Bill-style goatee. Pickle continued to make duck calls in California. He won the California duck calling championship once.

It was during this period when he appeared in some minor movie roles as a sharpshooter and rodeo announcer.

As one more sign of the ever-present kid in him, Pickle submitted some of his stories under the pen name "A. Gherkin."

In 1965, at the age of 81, Pop Pickle died in Petaluma. He was cremated and his ashes were returned to Otwell Cemetery.

"Pop Pickle was a page from the past," wrote one Petaluma journalist after Pickle's death. "He kept up with the present and had a tremendous enthusiasm about the future. He had that once-in-a-lifetime quality that made him unforgettable."

Pickle passed along the woodworking skills and call-making tradition to his son, Leonard. Born in 1910, Leonard lived in Otwell until he died in 1985. Like his father's, Leonard Pickle's duck calls are highly sought by collectors.

Photo courtesy Tom Barre

Pop Pickle's duck calls are examples of the Big Lake or St. Francis River style, with four panels — three checkered and one left plain, where the owner's initials or some other form of personalization could be added. The miniature call is an example of Pickle's sense of humor.

Save the Cache

DUCK HUNTERS, PARTICULARLY ONE, PLAYED CRUCIAL ROLE IN LANDMARK CONSERVATION BATTLE

The quality of the duck hunting along the Cache River is no secret. In the battle that began in the 1970s to stop a U.S. Army Corps of Engineers channelization project, all the facts and figures came out. They were best summed up by Dave Donaldson, who had served as the Arkansas Game and Fish Commission's waterfowl biologist since 1950.

"When we get an overflow on the Cache, that's where most of our birds go," said Donaldson, in a 1973 court testimony.

Thankfully, that remains true today. Led by Stuttgart dentist Rex Hancock, the efforts to save the Cache River and Bayou DeView from a 232-mile channelization project have never seemed more important than they do now.

"The damage done by dredging is easy to see," said Kaneaster Hodges Jr. of Newport. "You can't kill a duck on the Cache River north of Grubbs (Jackson County)."

The altered sections of the Cache at both its headwaters near Grubbs and its confluence with the White River near Clarendon serve as reminders of what could have happened to it and Bayou DeView.

◄ A Corps of Engineers channelization project threatened these cypress trees and many more like it along the Cache River.

Photo courtesy George Purvis

Photo courtesy Joe Coogan

The Cache River bottoms are considered one the world's most important wintering grounds for mallard ducks.

Instead they remain key components of the most important wintering area for mallards in the Mississippi Flyway. The Cache forms the northern section of "The Big Woods of Arkansas" — a 550,000-acre study area for The Nature Conservancy that represents the best — and the last — example of the bottomland ecosystem that once included seven states and 24 million acres of the Mississippi River Alluvial Plain. The Big Woods extends south to Catfish Point on the Mississippi River.

Monroe County, which includes the confluence of the Cache and White rivers, has the second-highest duck harvest rate in the state. According to figures compiled by the Arkansas Game and Fish Commission, 62.0 ducks per square mile were killed here from 1970-79, topped only by Arkansas County's average of 73.9.

The Cache River-Bayou DeView 100-year floodplain forms a long strip of natural wetland bordered by agricultural land that connects with the White River National Wildlife Refuge. This nearly 500,000-acre area was 26 percent wetlands, 28 percent rice fields and 38 percent soybean fields in the late 1980s, according to AGFC data.

It fulfills all the diverse needs of wintering ducks, when water is available. But water is the key. Remember Donaldson's words: "When we get an overflow on the Cache, that's where most of our birds go."

And remember, too, that the main reason for channelizing the Cache was so it would seldom, if ever, overflow its banks again.

River bends hold key to Black Swamp

Ducks may start funneling in at any moment along Cache River

The bend in the river looked ominous in the early morning light. It seemed much smaller than it was, with tall tupelo cypress trees reaching up into the dark sky.

The gray and black bark of the trees against the sky's backdrop made it feel like the trees were closing in. A slight breeze waved their branches, which seemed to be playing a game of tag with the stars. This could be the setting for a Stephen King novel.

On this day, however, a constant buzz from outboard motors traveling up and down the river and spotlights dancing through the trees remind you that you're not the only human in the dark stretch of water along the Cache River known as the Black Swamp.

"When you fly over it, it looks like someone has spray-painted it black," said David Cassinelli of North Little Rock, who has hunted the swamp for almost three decades, and is one of the fortunate few to own timbered land within the Black Swamp area.

It is a black spot in the terrain that acts as a magnet to passing ducks. On clear days, flocks of mallards, so far up they look like grains of pepper sprinkled across the sky, fall with wings cupped to the natural attractions of bends in the river.

Hunters lucky enough to see their descent are often awestruck that something so far away can drop so fast to a decoy-filled hole and touch down so gracefully.

Mallards often pour into Black Swamp at mid-morning, after feeding in the fields nearby.

Shooting is good on clear days, and this was one of them. Flocks of mallards numbering as many as 100 birds decoyed to the bends with little coaxing. Out of four limits from this group, two of the birds carried bands, adding an exceptional memory to an area some consider a perfect duck hunting hole.

The fact that the hunt took place in a bend in the river was not lost on the small group of duck hunters waiting for first light and flocks of mallards to visit.

In 1970, the Cache River, which provides a large portion of winter habitat for mallards that migrate through the state, was slated for a landmark project that would have straightened the river and destroyed the way hunters enjoy duck hunting in Arkansas today.

The Cache River Drainage Project proposed to channelize 232 miles of river basin along the Cache River and Bayou DeView — removing the river bends and all the trees along their banks. But the late Rex Hancock, a dentist from Stuttgart, saw the importance of

Battle for the Cache River — A Timeline

1938	1970	1972	1973	1974
U.S. Army Corps of Engineers begins studying the Cache River channelization project.	Congress allocates $60 million to channelize 232 miles of the Cache River and Bayou DeView in Monroe, Woodruff, Jackson, Cross, Poinsett, Craighead, Lawrence, Greene and Clay counties — from Clarendon to the Missouri line.	In July, U.S. Army Corps of Engineers' draglines begin operating round-the-clock channelizing the Cache River, and Rex Hancock helps organize the Citizens Committee to Save the Cache River Basin.	After four miles of Cache River channelization is complete, a federal appeals court decision brings Corps of Engineers work to a halt. *Outdoor Life* magazine names Rex Hancock its Conservationist of the Year.	A new 1,200-page Corps of Engineers environmental impact statement replaces the original 12-page document and claims there is "no indication that the project will have significant or even measurable impacts upon mallard populations."

the Cache River. He knew it was a vital resource, not only to Arkansas duck hunters, but waterfowl populations on an international level.

Hancock continually preached, "If they drain this basin, you can hang up the Mississippi Flyway."

"If you could get everyone to hunt like that — have more patience — then duck hunting would be just as good in all the public lands."

His efforts eventually paid off, and the project was stopped, although approximately seven miles of the river had already succumbed to drag lines that channelized it. No Arkansas Game and Fish Commission wildlife management area is more appropriately named than the Rex Hancock/Black Swamp WMA.

A unique aspect of the Black Swamp is the variety of hunting available. It offers a change of pace for hunting ducks next to cypress trees and ironwood bushes. The cypress are as old as the river itself.

The most popular spots to hunt in this region aren't hugged up against trees, kicking water, but rather sitting in boats in river bends of the muddy Cache.

If you are lucky, you may get a chance to hunt in one of the huge blinds that have been erected on private land along the Cache. Most are outfitted with stoves and heaters; some have makeshift bathrooms.

Ducks were flocking to these bends in the Cache River long before man threw out a spread of decoys. The closeness of the river bends would make a newcomer think that hunters are packed in too tightly to do any good.

"Not really," Tom Denniston of North Little Rock said. "Most of the duck hunters here are the old-timers. They've been doing it for years, and there isn't a whole lot of sky busting."

Denniston said the average duck hunter in the swamp will wait to get ducks fluttering over decoys before shooting, which makes it better for everyone.

"If you could get everyone to hunt like that — have more patience — then duck hunting would be just as good in all of the public lands," Denniston said.

Beside the river bends, there are other opportunities as well. Oak flats that are similar to hunts in most WMAs can be found, and ducks decoy to them well. Small, cypress-lined sloughs that dissect ridges and humps through the swamp offer exceptional hunting for wood ducks and mallards, too.

Black Swamp also features classic river basin hunting, in which ducks are attracted more by the resting opportunities than anything else. The area is surrounded by agricultural fields that are filled by the backwaters of the river. Ducks feed there, and in mid-morning huge flocks fly into the swamp to rest.

"At times you can sit here and look at nothing but blue sky for an hour or more," Cassinelli said. "And then just like that, they can be filling the skies and funneling in."

Often times those daily migrations don't occur until mid-morning or later. Many hunters stick with it to the bitter end. The public area closes to hunting at noon.

"At any moment, it can just happen," Cassinelli said.

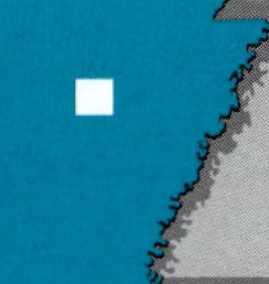

REX HANCOCK/ BLACK SWAMP WMA

Acres: 6,284
First purchase: 1971
Location: Near Cotton Plant in Woodruff County
Topo Maps: (7.5 series, U.S. Geological Survey) Cotton Plant, Gregory.

The only public access into Black Swamp is by a graded county road leading east out of Gregory on State Highway 33. There are no developed camping areas at Black Swamp, but camping is permitted on the two parking areas.

Black Swamp is split in the middle by the Cache River, which furnishes access by boat when the area is flooded during the waterfowl season.

Hardwoods, such as cypress, tupelo, oak and hickory, provide home and food for squirrels, deer and waterfowl. The WMA is located in some of the best duck hunting territory in the U.S.

A memorial to Rex Hancock marks the place where his ashes were buried in the Black Swamp.

BATTLE FOR THE CACHE RIVER — A TIMELINE

1977
Cache River project funding is authorized in Congress and three more miles of the river are channelized before the Environmental Protection Agency halts the work.

1978
A government task force concludes the Cache River channelization project is the "single most damaging project to waterfowl in the nation today" and federal funding ends.

1980
Plans for the Cache River National Wildlife Refuge are announced by the U.S. Fish and Wildlife Service.

1986
Rex Hancock dies at the age of 63 from cancer, shortly after learning that $3.1 million from duck stamp funds will be used to purchase land for the Cache River National Wildlife Refuge.

1990
Ramsar Convention names the lower White River-Cache River-Bayou DeView floodplain a "Wetland of International Importance." It joins the Everglades and Okefenokee Swamp among only eight U.S. areas so designated.

"Can you imagine this ditch running all the way to Missouri?" said Rex Hancock after seeing the first four miles of channelization.

Cache River site of landmark battle

Rex Hancock led the charge after Corps began dredging in July 1972

The U.S. Army Corps of Engineers crossed the line in July 1972. That's when the draglines and bulldozers began carving up the Cache River. It might as well have been Dec. 7, 1941, for Dr. Rex Hancock of Stuttgart. His Pearl Harbor had suffered a devastating sneak attack.

While everyone else awaited an appeals court decision on the Cache River-Bayou DeView Channelization Project, the Corps of Engineers did as it pleased. A contractor operated for 12 days, around the clock, before anyone else found out about the dredging at the mouth of the Cache near Clarendon.

When it was discovered, the Corps defied orders to cease from Governor Dale Bumpers. The ditching continued 24 hours a day for the next eight months as four miles of the Cache were channelized.

It's generally agreed there have been two great conservation battles in Arkansas — the first, over the Buffalo River in the Ozarks; the second, over the Cache River in the Delta.

Hancock served as field general in the battle for the Cache. Describing this conservation fight in war terms isn't much of an exaggeration. At one point, Gov. Bumpers threatened to call out the National Guard to stop the dredging.

Nothing short of an enemy troop invasion could have roused the emotions that fueled Hancock. That's how strongly he felt about duck hunting and the Arkansas legacy he wanted his children to enjoy.

"I want to make it emphatically clear that I have no monetary or material gain from leading this battle," Hancock wrote in a letter sent to everyone who expressed interest in helping save the Cache. "I am just a concerned sportsman, conservationist, taxpayer. I am the father of five children and had always assumed that the same recreational opportunities would be available to them that have been to me. However, as I write this letter to you my faith in the ability of our Country and State to preserve these opportunities is being severely shaken."

There are some in Arkansas who think every duck hunter here should be required to pay tribute to Rex Hancock at the start of each season, just like buying a hunting license and a duck stamp. They believe the core of Arkansas' wintering duck habitat was one man away from being cut out and washed down a ditch by the U.S. Army Corps of Engineers.

Plans for channelizing the Cache River were studied as early as 1938. One plan was approved in 1950. But it wasn't funded until 1970, when newly-elected Congressman Bill Alexander, who had campaigned in the Delta on this issue, combined forces with Senator John McClellan.

The Cache River-Bayou DeView project was going to be one of the biggest channelization efforts in U.S. Army Corps of Engineers history: 232 miles — 140 on the Cache River, north from its confluence with the White River; 75 on Bayou DeView, the Cache's major tributary; and the rest on smaller tributaries. The initial price tag was $64 million.

Hancock termed it "an outrageous project and an insult to God's planning of the earth." He claimed only big landowners in the area would benefit, noting many had bought this unwanted land for as little as a dollar an acre, by paying the delinquent taxes on it. Meanwhile, the majority of U.S. taxpayers would pay for the project, pay for the subsidies that kept other farmland uncultivated and, most importantly, lose some of the finest winter habitat for mallards left in the world.

Channelization of a stream involves dredging and straightening the channel and clearing the banks of vegetation. The process of dredging and ditching an area once known as the "Great Swamp" was almost complete by 1970. The original 24 million acres of bottomland hardwood forests in the Mississippi River Alluvial Plain had been reduced to less than five million acres. Over 75 percent of the Cache River basin's 1.2 million acres of bottomland hardwoods were gone by 1970. A few people began to realize that the benefits of creating so much fertile agricultural land in the Delta had peaked.

"Other states have experienced the ruin resulting from channelization," Hancock said. "Arkansas should profit from their mistakes."

As the Cache drainage plan got closer to reality, Texarkana lawyer Richard Arnold filed suit to stop it. Arnold had been hired by environmental groups because of his success in attacking the environmental impact statement (EIS) of another Corps project. The original EIS justifying the Cache drainage project was only 12 pages.

In May 1972, U.S. District Judge J. Smith Henley ruled the EIS was adequate. Arnold took his case to the Eighth Circuit Court of Appeals in St. Louis. While awaiting a decision from this court, in July 1972, the Corps began dredging.

Both Tom Pugh, chairman of the Arkansas Game and Fish Commission, and Gov. Bumpers pleaded for the Corps to stop. But the draglines kept operating around the clock.

"This is absolute unjustifiable arrogance," Hancock wrote, after agreeing to become president of the Citizens Committee to Save the Cache.

Rex Hancock wasn't a newcomer to environmental battles. Born in Laddonia, Missouri, in 1923, Hancock had always enjoyed hunting and fishing. His dental office on Stuttgart's Main Street included a grizzly bear mount, a small one. The Hancock family's den held the big grizzly — 11 feet tall, mounted upright. Various waterfowl and fish mounts adorned the walls.

In 1958, Hancock noticed Arkansas wasn't represented in the whitetail deer records of the Boone & Crockett Club. He knew that wasn't an accurate portrait of the state. He trained to become an official scorer for Boone & Crockett, and by 1964 Arkansas had over 70 entries in the whitetail record book, more than any other state.

In the early 1960s, Hancock was talking to a long-time commercial fisherman, when the subject of Bayou Meto came up.

"Hell, Rex, the fishing's no good," the man said. "You don't catch anything, and when you do it smells like creosote. There's not any cranes (great blue herons), there's not any turtles. It's dead."

Bob Apple recalled Rex's conversation with the fisherman.

"Rex cut his teeth on that Bayou Meto deal," said Apple, who worked 20 years as the National Wildlife Federation's South-Central Region Executive. "He started checking it out. He put minnows in water from Bayou Meto, and they'd live for only about 35 or 40 seconds."

Hancock soon traced a severe pollution problem to dioxin originating from a chemical plant in Jacksonville.

After it was discovered that the Corps was dredging the Cache River, eight people met in a room at the Coachman's Inn in Little Rock to form the Citizens Committee to Save the Cache. They were: Nesbit Bowers, Lee Bowers, Jane Stern and David Perdue, all of Pine Bluff; Tom Foti and Pratt Remmel of Little Rock; Bay Fitzhugh of Augusta; and Hancock.

"Rex was elected president, and that's all it took (to save the Cache)," recalled Perdue.

Photo courtesy Jan Gregory

From left, Dale Bumpers, Rex Hancock and Bob Apple share one of the lighter moments of the Cache River battle, which Bumpers calls the beginning of his environmental education.

Bellrose remembers Hancock as one of all-time greats in conservation

Frank Bellrose crossed paths with Rex Hancock in Chicago's O'Hare airport once. He immediately noticed that $20 bills were sticking out of every pocket in Hancock's suit.

"Rex, you're in danger of getting mugged," Bellrose said.

Hancock was returning to Arkansas after speaking to a Michigan group about saving the Cache River. His speech, evidently, had helped raise funds for the cause.

Bellrose is often called the dean of waterfowl research. He began working for the Illinois Natural History Survey in 1938. He had helped band over 100,000 ducks in Illinois, and he knew the value of the Cache River when the battle began.

"We had band recovery data over 10 years and so many of the bands were recovered from the Cache and Bayou DeView areas," Bellrose said. "That told us how important it was as a wintering area."

Knowing the reputation Bellrose had among waterfowl experts, Hancock recruited him into the fight for the Cache. It's an experience Bellrose will always treasure. He remembers attending a meeting with Hancock when the Corps of Engineers offered a compromise plan. It would have put ditches around the main river channel and pumped water into the wetlands to keep them alive.

"Maybe we better accept it, Rex," Bellrose suggested.

"Hell no, we won't compromise with those bastards," replied Hancock.

And that was Hancock in a nutshell.

In a letter to Hancock's widow, Jan, shortly after Rex's death in 1986, Bellrose wrote: "Rex was one of the all-time greats in conservation. I've never known anyone who had his dedication, courage and tenacity. I gave up hope a number of times on the Cache drainage project and thought that all was lost. But not Rex! He always found a way to overcome the many road blocks."

Time has not altered that opinion.

"I think of him every once in awhile and tears come to my eyes," Bellrose said. "He sacrificed so much to save the Cache."

Courtesy George Fisher

Arkansas Gazette editorial cartoonist George Fisher was an important force in educating the public about the Cache project, according to Bumpers. This particular cartoon was used as the letterhead for the Citizens Committee to Save the Cache.

Thus began a legendary high-energy high-wire act. Story after story is told of how Hancock left patients in his dental chair for long periods as he took phone calls from anyone interested in helping save the Cache. Time of day and time zones meant nothing as Hancock spread the word.

"With Rex it was Cache, Cache, Cache," said Apple.

Hancock was never one to hide his emotions, and he often expressed them in graphic language.

"He could cuss like a sailor and did most of the time," laughed Apple.

Hancock cast seeds that sprouted into favorable publicity. *Outdoor Life* magazine in February 1973 featured a story entitled "Black Day for Mallards," and more and more newspapers covered the story.

Bumpers, who would move from the Governor's office in 1974 to the first of four terms in the U.S. Senate, calls the Cache River battle "really the beginning of the environmental education of Dale Bumpers." Public opinion favored channelization.

"I lost a lot of friends over that issue," Bumpers said. "More people were for channelization than were against it. But the environmentalists were persistent."

Bumpers credits the editorial cartoons of George Fisher and the editorial stance of the *Arkansas Gazette* for helping educate the public and build opposition to channelization. And, like everyone else, Bumpers singles out Hancock as the man who wouldn't let the Cache River go away.

Ducks made the Cache River battle more than just an Arkansas controversy. As duck hunters and environmentalists in the 13 other Mississippi Flyway states began realizing what was at stake — destruction of the best wintering habitat for mallards in the world — they joined in. Minnesota was the first state to add its name to the lawsuit against the Corps, followed by Iowa, Illinois, Ohio, Kentucky, Wisconsin, North Dakota, South Dakota and Louisiana.

In 1973, the federal court in St. Louis ruled on the appeal and ordered the Corps to stop dredging. Four miles of the Cache had been channelized in seven months.

Hancock's efforts were recognized by *Outdoor Life* magazine in 1973, when it named him Conservationist of the Year

The Corps compiled a new environmental impact statement, replacing the 12-page document with 1,200 pages, in 1974. It concluded there was "no indication that the project will have significant or even measurable impacts upon mallard populations."

The document was approved in court, and funding was authorized for channelization to resume in 1977. Various compromises and amounts of mitigation land, ranging from 30,000 to 70,000 acres, had been offered by the Corps, but Hancock insisted — no compromises.

The Environmental Protection Agency stopped the project after three more miles of the Cache were channelized. In 1978, a government task force concluded the Cache drainage project was the "single most damaging project to waterfowl in the nation today," and Congress cut all funding.

In 1980, plans for the Cache River National Wildlife Refuge were announced by the U.S. Fish and Wildlife Service. The USFWS revealed in 1986 that $3.1 million in federal duck stamp funds would be used to buy land for the Cache River refuge. By this time, Rex Hancock was a very sick man.

"He never told anybody," said Apple. "He kept telling me that he was having trouble with his hip. I knew that wasn't the problem."

Rex Hancock succumbed to pancreatic cancer on July 8, 1986, at the age of 63.

"...we have witnessed part of the life and times of one of America's truly great and effective conservationists..."

The Arkansas Game and Fish Commission had named the Black Swamp Wildlife Management Area in Hancock's honor before he died. Hancock's body was cremated and his ashes buried in the Black Swamp, where a monument honors him today.

"Rex Hancock singlehandedly raised more money and did more in general for conservation than anyone else in Arkansas," said AGFC director Steve Wilson, after Hancock's death. "Without Rex, we never would have been able to save the Cache and successfully create a refuge there. We will miss him dearly."

David Perdue of Pine Bluff was among the original eight that met to form the Save the Cache committee. Perdue, an avid duck hunter and guide for many years at Circle T Club, worked with Hancock for two decades on environmental issues. Wrote Perdue:

"There are many words that might be used to describe Rex Hancock — tough, persistent, dogged, uncompromising, energetic, fighter, visionary, environmentalist. All of these and many more might fit him but, in my opinion, we have witnessed part of the life and times of one of America's truly great and effective conservationists, one whose efforts will be appreciated even more by generations to come."

Cache River recognized among wetlands of international importance

In 1970 there was enough public support and federal funding to drain the life out of the Cache River bottomlands.

Exactly two decades later, the area gained recognition as "Wetlands of International Importance" by the Ramsar Convention, an intergovernmental treaty signed by 49 countries that provides the framework for protection of the world's most significant wetlands.

The area recognized by the Ramsar Convention includes the lower White River, Cache River and Bayou DeView floodplain. At that time, only seven other sites in the United States had received this designation. The list included Florida's Everglades and Georgia's Okefenokee Swamp.

"It's a significant day for conservation in Arkansas," said Nancy DeLamar, director of the Arkansas field office of The Nature Conservancy, at the news conference announcing the designation on July 25, 1990. "It gives international recognition to what people in Arkansas have known all along — Arkansas holds ecological treasures of global significance."

The Cache River serves as a prime example of how public opinion about swamps has taken a U-turn. From being abhorred as breeding grounds for mosquitoes, malaria and cottonmouth snakes, wetlands are now recognized for their beauty, biodiversity and ability to function as kidneys for the earth.

Duck hunters, of course, have always had a special appreciation for swamps. It was a duck hunter, Rex Hancock, who brought passion, determination and leadership to the fight to save the Cache River and Bayou DeView from channelization.

Now the Rex Hancock/Black Swamp Wildlife Management Area along the Cache River not only serves as a prime wintering place for ducks, but also the model for a better understanding of wetlands.

In 1987 the Black Swamp area was selected by the Corps of Engineers Waterway Experiment Station for a long-term study. It will develop and evaluate techniques to determine more precisely how wetlands function.

Photo courtesy Dave Stahle

Old cypress trees are like old people

One-thousand-year-old swamp residents still around to tell their stories

It's best not done from a speeding car. But if you can find a way to take a long look, a view north from the Highway 70 bridge over Bayou DeView, between Brinkley and Brasfield, offers a trip back in time. A 1,000-year trip back in time.

The trip is in the trees, the bald cypress trees.

"It's a spectacular view," said University of Arkansas professor Dave Stahle. "The southern end of Bayou DeView represents the largest stand of ancient bald cypress that we know of in the entire lower Mississippi River valley."

These cypress trees are part of the Dagmar Wildlife Management Area. Stahle heads the tree-ring laboratory of the geography department on the UA's Fayetteville campus. By taking pencil-thin samples with a special coring instrument, Stahle (pronounced "stay-lee") can read the annual growth rings and determine the age of any tree.

"We have found some that are a thousand years old," said Stahle, who directs the UA's tree-ring laboratory. "Most of them are 800 years old. I wouldn't doubt there are some trees older than 1,000 years. We've only cored a tiny fraction of them. These are the oldest trees we know of in Arkansas."

Bald cypress trees represent the dominant landscape feature of the swamps. Many a duck hunter has leaned against the broad base of a cypress tree, waiting for ducks to cup into a decoy spread. From the leaves that turn a blend of rust and gold in the fall to the knobby knees, nothing says swamp like cypress.

Lumbermen were also attracted to cypress trees. Although their location in the swamps made them difficult to harvest, most of the old-growth cypress trees were cut. The even-grained, water-resistant wood was too valuable to be left standing.

That's why this stand at the southern edge of Bayou DeView, less than five miles from its confluence with the Cache River, is so special.

"A lot of the real old cypress wasn't cut because it was low grade timber," said Stahle, noting the number of trees you'll see in any cypress stand that have a hollow core. "They can live for centuries being completely hollow."

That trait has created some of the myths of the swamp. One of the most common is the tale of an old logger who began cutting down what he thought to be a solid cypress tree. As he felled the tree, a 400-pound black bear came out of its hollow core and ate the logger. According to the legend, the bear had entered the tree to hibernate when it was a cub. The bear grew so much it couldn't get out the following spring. It lived off the fish and game of the swamp that also explored the cypress opening during seasonal changes in the water level.

"That's a recurring tale you always hear in cypress swamps," Stahle said. "Sometimes it's a giant alligator snapping turtle instead of a bear."

The true stories told by these ancient cypress trees interest Stahle more than the myths. Revealing a tree's age represents only a fraction of the information held in the rings. By precisely measuring the differences in growth rates contained within the annual rings of a tree's core, Stahle can determine past weather patterns.

Using bald cypress and post oak trees, Stahle and fellow UA dendrochronologist Malcolm Cleaveland were able

The cypress trees near Bayou DeView's confluence with the Cache River represent the best stand of ancient cypress in the region.

Photo by Graham Hawks; courtesy Dave Stahle

By taking a pencil-thin sample, Dave Stahle can read the rings of a tree without harming it.

to estimate the annual water levels of the White River at Clarendon from 1700 to 1980. Using the U.S. Army Corps of Engineers records at Clarendon from 1900 to present, they established a baseline for interpreting yearly growth in the two moisture-sensitive tree species.

"Old trees are like old people," Stahle said. "They are still around to tell their stories of what it was like in the past. We need to know where we've been in order to get perspective on where we're going."

What kind of perspective does this work give to a duck hunter? Other than North America's total duck numbers, nothing determines annual hunting conditions in Arkansas more than the water level of the White River.

Stahle and Cleaveland found that wet and dry years tend to run in cycles. For example, a year of high water levels is more likely to be followed by another year of high water than it is by a drought. The Clarendon gauge shows and tree rings confirm three consecutive years of low water levels in 1900-02, 1954-56 and 1963-65, and high levels in 1927-29, 1949-51 and 1973-75.

One period of 27 consecutive years without surplus runoff was discovered in this 280-year glance back in time.

Cypress knees' function somewhat of a mystery, but Stahle has theory

The exact function of the knees that distinguish cypress trees hasn't been determined. The most common theory explains the knobs poking from the water at the base of a cypress tree as aerating organisms.

Another theory places the role of the knees in stability. Cypress trees have one long main root. The knees fanned out around its trunk give a cypress tree a wider base in the soft mud of a swamp.

The first theory has been proven false. But University of Arkansas professor Dave Stahle thinks it may be closer to the truth than the second theory.

"Cypress trees have two types of roots," Stahle said. "In addition to the deep and heavy main root system, they also have a system of fine feeder roots that lies near the surface of the water or saturated soil.

"Dissolved oxygen stratifies in the water near the surface, too. I think the knees function to allow this fibrous root system to spread out away from the trunk. The knees help the tree increase the surface area of its roots in well-oxygenated areas."

Stahle says cypress trees are one of the most important species for studying climate history because of their long lives. By reading the differences in a tree's annual growth rings, Stahle can determine weather patterns of the past. By taking core samples of the cypress trees at Tennessee's Reelfoot Lake, Stahle found proof of the New Madrid earthquakes of 1811-12.

"The tree rings showed a huge growth spurt following the formation of that lake," he said.

Other characteristics of the cypress trees at Reelfoot indicate changes caused by the earthquakes. Trees that once lined a river suddenly had roots in the bottom of a lake.

"The old knees were no good; they couldn't grow to the surface," Stahle said. "The surviving trees grew a new 'hanging buttress' and associated fine root system, which sprouted from the flooded mid-stem just below the new water level of Reelfoot Lake."

This new fibrous root system was much smaller than the previous system, and the tree canopies shrunk as a result.

Be prepared to fight your way in here

Dagmar Wildlife Management Area provides rough country ducks love

Dagmar Wildlife Management Area is one of the last places a duck hunter wants to walk without a clue or a compass. You have to fight your way in. It is rugged land, thick with tangles and winding sloughs. To get to good duck hunting, be prepared to work.

Dagmar's 7,920 acres don't flood as much as most of the wildlife management areas used for duck hunting. Its elevation is higher than that of Hurricane WMA and the White River National Wildlife Refuge, located above and below Dagmar on the White River.

Because of that, Dagmar is one of those WMAs that is easily overlooked by the throngs of duck hunters that leave Little Rock every morning. But its location in the flyway periodically makes it one of the best duck-holding spots in the state.

Dagmar is at its best when the White River rises to the point that much of Hurricane WMA and the White River NWR are too deep for dabbling ducks, like mallards, to feed. Dagmar and the Cache River shine during those conditions. Water floods new ground, and all of the ruggedness of Dagmar provides perfect refuge for thousands of mallards filtering down the White River.

Most of Dagmar WMA lies between the Cache River and Bayou DeView. Bayou DeView flows through four miles of it, and the White River is close enough to help in flooding and channeling ducks to the flooded timber.

Those three waterways are major corridors for waterfowl in the Mississippi Flyway. And unlike much of the public lands found in the eastern side of the state, this area represents some of the few remaining examples of the natural Delta streams that once dominated the entire Mississippi River alluvial plain.

It remains in its natural state for the very reason ducks like to come there — fluctuating water levels. Man avoided this ground because it was too low and too swampy.

By the time the federal government got into the flood control business after the great flood of 1927, the surrounding land was quickly cleared and put into farmland. The rest, like Dagmar, was heavily logged. By the 1930s forest land could be bought at bargain prices.

That didn't change much into the 1950s, when the AGFC began buying up as much bottomland forest as possible.

Currently Dagmar is 7,920 acres, put together in four acquisitions for about $200,000.

The primary duck hunting area is an 800-acre tract that floods by gravity flow as the White River gets high, then the Cache River overflows and backs down Robe Bayou. The entire area is susceptible to flooding when the White River gauge reads 28 feet. At that level, the AGFC shuts the Dagmar entrance gates to all vehicles.

And that's also when ducks flood in. Because of the lack of access, many hunters claim this is the best of times for Dagmar.

Boats provide the best way to get into this WMA then, and the fight it takes to boat through the heavy brush leaves much of the interior of Dagmar open for use.

"Dagmar is one of those places where pressure doesn't normally run ducks out," said George Cochran, a regular at Dagmar when river levels are high. "Ducks can always find a place to hide and rest. Plus, it can be so hard to boat through, and since many hunters won't hunt far from their boats, it's almost wide open.

"If you are willing to get a compass and walk, you can have the best hunting possible."

That was the case during a two-week period in 1996 when perfect water levels coincided with a freeze-up in area fields. Pressure was heavy, but the ducks stayed in the area until the weather warmed and the water started dropping.

"It was crazy," said Tim Burnley of Brinkley. One morning there were more than 70 vehicles parked at the front gate of Dagmar, according to Burnley. Additional hunters were accessing the area through Bayou DeView and other points.

One hunter was able to kill his limit each day in an area so close to Interstate 40 that the roar of passing vehicles prevented him from hearing the shotguns of other hunters in Dagmar.

Although the hunting was good then, Jim Sullivan, a wildlife biologist with the AGFC, said the hunting has been much better. In the early 1990s, Dagmar hunting was limited to Tuesdays, Thursdays and Saturdays only.

Dagmar is known for thick cover, which provides refuge for waterfowl, like this gadwall.

DAGMAR WMA

Acres: 7,920
First purchase: 1952
Location: Near Brinkley in Monroe County.
Topo maps (7.5 series, U.S. Geological Survey): DeValls Bluff SE, DeValls Bluff NE.

Access to Dagmar WMA is off U.S. Highway 70, about six miles west of Brinkley, and half-a-mile mile west of the Bayou DeView bridge. There is no access off Interstate 40, which crosses the wildlife management area.

When there is adequate rainfall, much of Dagmar is flooded in the winter for ducks. The hunting is in green timber, primarily for wood ducks and mallards.

Many locals believe the area doesn't get good until the White River is high enough to close the road leading into the WMA. That is when Dagmar is considered best.

But even in times of lower water, knowledgeable hunters can find flocks of birds that provide adequate shooting.

In addition to ducks, there is good squirrel, rabbit and deer hunting.

Crappie, bream and bass abound in Big and Little Robe bayous and Hickson Lake. There are also six major areas for camping.

Hunters and fishermen are cautioned that during rainy periods, or when the area is flooded for ducks, many roads will be impassable or closed to prevent damage by vehicles.

Local hunters complained about losing four hunting days per week, and the AGFC opened the area for the whole week.

"Since that time the quality of the hunting has really gone down," Sullivan said.

Dagmar has a brighter future. Land in the Cache River National Wildlife Refuge is being acquired at such a rate that boundaries are often confusing. But every protected acre in the Cache River basin adds more to the attraction of Dagmar.

Learning how to change duck tunes

Crawford says key is varying routine, especially when luring call-shy ducks

Most Arkansas duck hunters know how to blow a duck call. But many don't know when and how to use specific calls to their advantage, according to Trey Crawford, a world champion duck caller.

Crawford, who is from North Little Rock, is recognized as one of the top competition callers in the country. He won the World Championship at Stuttgart in 1976, '86 and '93. While calling in competition and calling for ducks vary greatly, Crawford is an expert at both.

"One thing I've noticed is most hunters — especially in Arkansas, where the average duck hunter's pacifier was replaced with a duck call at an early age — have little trouble making the right sounds and the right rhythm," Crawford said. "Where most of them have trouble is knowing when to blow, and what notes to blow at the right time."

Crawford's contention is that mallards, as wild creatures, respond differently every day to calling, and hunters need to recognize when they need to change their approach to be more successful.

"A lot of people have success calling ducks with their particular style," Crawford said. "They may be aggressive or even timid with their calls, and during the course of the season, they will call in ducks.

"But if they stick to the same routine on a daily basis, they are hurting their chances at calling ducks effectively day in and day out.

"You have to read the ducks, and change with them on a daily basis."

Crawford offers an example of an opening morning duck hunter. His calls are the basic hail call, or a string of quacks that gets the ducks' attention. On opening day, that may be all that is needed, since the ducks have been under very little calling or shooting pressure.

"A week later when the guy goes back to the duck woods, that same series of quacks may not be enough," Crawford said. "Sometimes you have to talk the ducks into wanting to land, but the average duck hunter sticks to what was working last week. If the ducks don't come in, they just say they are call-shy."

Trey Crawford of North Little Rock has won three world championship duck calling titles.

Ducks definitely get "call-shy," Crawford said. A lot of that shyness comes from the caller, who isn't convincing the ducks there is a lonesome hen waiting on the water or a smorgasbord of acorns under the water.

"It doesn't take long for ducks to get wise to the same basic series of quacks and then a gunshot," Crawford said. "That makes them call-shy. When they hear the same sounds coming from every opening in the woods, then, you bet, they will equate that with danger. The trick is to sound more like ducks on the water, while still getting their attention, and not just calling the same routines that everyone else is calling."

Kaneaster Hodges Jr. of Newport has hunted with Crawford many times. And he has become a believer in Crawford's theory.

"Trey Crawford imposes his will on a duck," Hodges said. "I think that ability to change each day is the key."

By just listening to real ducks on the water, you can learn a lot, Crawford says. Memorize the sounds they make and try to duplicate them.

Crawford also believes in putting movement in a decoy spread, with a jerk-string tied to several of the blocks.

"Late in the year, a jerk string can call in more ducks to the water than anything, if you get their interest up with your calls," Crawford said.

Crawford has the confidence to be more aggressive than most duck callers, but he says that many hunters may not feel confident enough to keep blowing.

"I like blowing a duck call; that is what I do," Crawford said. "But you can get the same message across without being as aggressive as I am. You have to choose that approach for yourself.

"The key, however, is getting that message across in a way that draws a response from the ducks."

Photo courtesy Joe Coogan

Trey Crawford believes that watching the ducks' reactions to calls will make you more effective in luring call-shy ducks.

CACHE RIVER NATIONAL WILDLIFE REFUGE

Acres: 39,000
First purchase: 1986
Maps: The group "Friends of Felsenthal" offers a Cache River NWR boundary map, $11.25 by mail or $10 at the refuge office: Cache River Refuge, Rt. 2, Box 126T, Augusta, AR 72006.

Most refuges are one continuous block of land, but the Cache River National Wildlife Refuge is scattered in checkerboard fashion. Parts of the refuge can be found in Jackson, Woodruff, Prairie and Monroe counties. The Cache River NWR stretches along Bayou DeView and the Cache River from Grubbs to Clarendon.

In the 39,000-acre refuge, individual blocks range from 20 acres near Bayou DeView to 15,000 acres near Biscoe. What it lacks in continuity, it makes up for in function. The Cache River watershed is recognized as one of the most critical wintering waterfowl areas in North America. Duck hunters and other conservationists rallied around the Cache and Bayou DeView to stop a U.S. Army Corps of Engineers channelization project in the 1970s.

"There was a lot of public sentiment to do something with the Cache," said Dennis Widner, area manager. "The Fish and Wildlife Service proposed a refuge, and after holding public meetings, it purchased the first tract of 3,000 acres."

Since that time, the USFWS has continually bought land, adding to the refuge's size. The practice of buying land from willing sellers will continue in the Cache River watershed, Widner said.

The refuge features mostly hardwood bottomlands, which flood when the Cache leaves its banks. The biggest problem hunters face in the Cache River NWR is access. Widner believes that at least 20 percent of the acreage gets minor or no hunting pressure, because few hunters know where the land is. In other cases, some of the tracts are surrounded by private land. "There's a lot of land not being hunted," Widner said. "No one knows where it is or how to get to it."

That makes the Cache River NWR one of the best areas for hunters looking for new ground. The disjointed tracts don't have the crowds found in most public shooting areas.

Those adventurous enough to find unused tracts of the refuge will find exceptional shooting when the river is rising or holding stable. Most of the hunting is in flooded timber, but there is some main river hunting, mostly in river bends.

Most of the refuge boundaries are marked with signs, especially those that have the river as a border. Remaining tracts can be found by using a map, provided by a non-profit organization, Friends of Felsenthal. Although Felsenthal is many miles away, the organization raises funds to help NWRs, and funds from the purchase of the map go back into the refuges. The map can be purchased at stores in the surrounding area or at the refuge office, located 16 miles south of Augusta on Highway 33 at Dixie. Phone orders can be made by calling 870-347-2614.

Hunters on the refuge must have a permit that can be obtained at the refuge office.

Rice & Duck Capital of the World

NO PLACE ELSE ON EARTH CELEBRATES DUCK SEASON LIKE STUTTGART, ARKANSAS

Johnny Mahfouz of Stuttgart won the 1988 World's Championship Duck Calling Contest.

As you drive by the rice fields that surround this town of 10,000 people, you might tune in the local radio station. Its call letters are KWAK, of course. As you enter the city limits, a sign reads, "Welcome to Stuttgart, Rice and Duck Capital of the World."

A stage camouflaged as a duck blind blocks Main Street during the week of Thanksgiving. This is where the "World's Champion Duck Caller" has been chosen since 1936. During this annual "Wings Over the Prairie Festival," Main Street also features circus tents packed with vendors offering everything for the waterfowl hunter, from duck calls to dogs.

You might begin to think it has always been this way in Stuttgart, but it hasn't. That may help explain why duck season is embraced with such fervor now. Before rice came to the Delta, Stuttgart resembled most of the other farming communities in the area. Arkansas County was known for hay and cattle.

Arkansas' Grand Prairie occupies a unique niche in the Delta. Tallgrass prairie vegetation dominated the landscape when Rev. Adam Buerkle moved his congregation here in 1878. Because the grass was so thick and tall, it was common for men to get lost during a day of cutting hay for livestock. Buerkle, a Lutheran minister born in Stuttgart, Germany, applied for a post office in 1880 and named the town after the city where he was born. (While Stuttgart was founded by German immigrants and named after the German city of the

◀ Pintails and mallards take flight near Frank Freudenberg's outside Stuttgart, circa 1930.

Photo courtesy Melvin Spann

same name, it's pronounced "STUT-gart" here, not "STOOT-gart.")

Why do ducks come here? Location, location, location, as the real estate agents say. Geography demands that ducks winter in the bottomlands around Stuttgart.

The Mississippi Flyway is often described as a funnel that narrows just as it reaches the northern boundary of Arkansas. The funnel within that funnel is formed by the convergence of the three largest Delta streams in the state — the Arkansas, the White and the Mississippi. Arkansas County lies at the top of the funnel's throat.

That helps explain why Arkansas County has the highest duck harvest rate per square mile in Arkansas, 73.9, according to Arkansas Game and Fish Commission figures from the 1970s.

But until the arrival of rice, the town of Stuttgart wasn't fully able to take advantage of this prime location. When the 20th century began, Arkansas County led the state in beef cattle production. Ducks don't exactly flock to cow pastures.

In 1904, W. H. Fuller of Carlisle discovered the Grand Prairie of Arkansas had the perfect soil for growing rice. "Hardpan" is the term often used to describe this alluvial soil with a base of clay. It holds water, which makes it easy to flood fields; and it also has a firm foundation, which expedites harvest.

In 1906, the first rice was grown in Arkansas County. Three years later, Grand Prairie rice acreage was up to 27,000; by 1919, rice covered 143,000 acres of the Grand Prairie.

Ducks flocked to the rice fields. Their winter migration to Arkansas coincided with the rice harvest. In the early years, rice was left in the fields to dry after it was cut with a binder. Bundles were

Rice drying and storage facilities dominate the skyline of Stuttgart, population 10,420.

Stuttgart — A Timeline

1880	1904	1919	1927	1935
Rev. Adam Buerkle, a Lutheran minister and German immigrant, applies for a post office and names the community Stuttgart, after his native town in Germany.	W. H. Fuller of Carlisle harvests the first commercial rice crop on the Grand Prairie. A 70-acre field yields about 74 bushels per acre, well over the 35 per acre required to earn a $1,000 bonus from the citizens of Hazen and Carlisle.	More than 143,000 acres of rice are planted in the Grand Prairie, as rice fields rapidly replace the cattle pastures that once dominated the area.	Verne L. Tindall builds the first reservoir in Arkansas County for use in growing rice. Tindall is surprised when wintering ducks congregate on the 450 acres of flooded pin oak timberland.	Joseph and Herbert Pulitzer lease Freudenberg's Maple Island Reservoir, rent the ground floor of the Riceland Hotel, plus two houses in Stuttgart — all for use during duck season.

stacked into shocks. Ducks could wipe out an unprotected field in one night.

At the time, farmers paid a standard wage to anyone who would spend the night in their fields, keeping the ducks away — $5 and all the shotgun shells you could shoot.

The first wells dug to pump groundwater for flooding rice fields were less than 100 feet deep. But as the water table dropped and wells had to be dug deeper, farmers began looking for ways to offset the increasing cost of pumping water to grow rice.

Verne Tindall completed a shallow 450-acre reservoir just seven miles outside the Stuttgart city limits in 1927. By holding spring rain and runoff in it, he developed another source of water for his rice fields. When the ducks arrived that fall, they piled into Tindall's Reservoir. It was an unexpected bonus.

"The first few years it seemed as if all the ducks in the country tried to get into it," Tindall once told the Stuttgart *Daily Leader*. "It was quite a sight to see. Eight to 10 acres of the reservoir would be a mass of ducks."

Tindall expanded his reservoir to 750 acres, and he became an avid duck hunter. Soon there were reservoirs like Tindall's all over Arkansas County. The commercial hunting opportunities were obvious. And it didn't take long for Stuttgart to separate itself from all the other farming communities in the Delta.

When Tindall, Thad McCollum and Dr. H. V. Glenn combined to promote the first World's Championship Duck Calling Contest in 1936, the foundation was firmly in place for "The Rice and Duck Capital of the World."

Images of ducks are everywhere, even radio station call letters, in the 'Duck Capital'

The image of a mallard duck is omnipresent in the town of Stuttgart. The newspaper, the Stuttgart *Daily Leader*, incorporates a pair of mallards lighting in rice stalks in its front page flag. Similar images adorn many of the local businesses.

There's a Mallard Restaurant, and the Best Western goes by the title The Duck Inn.The mayor, Butch Richenback, is a duck call-maker and past world's champion duck caller. On the southeast side of town near the Riceland Foods main office, a duck crossing street sign stands near the highway.

To top it off, the town's radio station call letters are K-W-A-K. Since the station went on the air in 1948, ducks have been a major part of its format.

Melvin Spann started the station in 1947 with that thought in mind. In the beginning he wanted the KWAK call letters but couldn't get them. They were assigned to a ship. The ship was at sea at that time, and Spann couldn't get the KWAK letters released for use. Spann had to settle for KCUD, duck spelled backwards. That might have worked okay. But Spann got lucky. Lucky as a duck. Just before the radio station went on the air, the ship returned and released the use of the call letters KWAK.

It has been that way ever since, although there was a period when the owners of a California radio station attempted to buy the call letters. They too wanted to be KWAK, but not for the duck overtones.

For them, the call letters KWAK came closer to the word "quake," and where better to have them than in California, a state known for its earthquakes? Spann, of course, refused to sell.

The call letters weren't the only ducky part of the Stuttgart station. At one time, Mel Blanc, the voice behind Donald Duck and Daffy Duck, did all of the station's promos and station breaks.

STUTTGART — A TIMELINE

1936
Thomas Walsh of Greenville, Miss., uses his natural voice and hands, in lieu of a call, to win first place and a $6.60 hunting coat in the first "National Duck Calling Contest."

1944
M. T. McCollum II decides to take the hunting equipment out of his hardware store and opens a full-line sporting goods store in the building previously occupied by Ben Franklin's.

1945
D. M. "Chick" Major wins the World's Championship Duck Calling Contest with his Dixie Mallard duck call, which would become one of the most popular calls in the U.S.

1960
Pat Peacock, Major's stepdaughter, becomes the first person to win every World Duck Calling title when she caps her career with the Champion of Champions crown.

1994
Butch Richenback, maker of Rich-N-Tone duck calls and winner of the 1972 World's Champion Duck Calling Contest and 1975 Champion of Champions crown, is elected mayor of Stuttgart.

World Championship of Duck Calling

First champion was mouth-caller, first prize was a $6.60 hunting coat

The year after live decoys were banned by the federal government, Stuttgart held its first duck calling championship. While the live decoy ban did increase the importance of duck calls, it wasn't the main reason a trio of Stuttgart men decided to promote duck calling. It probably had more to do with the fact that DeWitt, which shares the Arkansas County seat with Stuttgart, held a calling contest the year before.

Whatever the ultimate motivation, Thad McCollum is credited with the idea of developing the contest as a way to celebrate the opening of duck season. He conferred with Verne Tindall and Dr. H. V. Glenn about joining forces to promote it.

"Sportsmen of the area liked the idea, but general interest didn't seem too great until the event took place," Tindall once told the Stuttgart *Daily Leader*.

In 1936, it was called the National Duck Calling Contest, and it attracted 17 entries to downtown Stuttgart on Nov. 24. First prize was a hunting coat valued at $6.60. The winner was Thomas E. Walsh of Greenville, Miss., who used his voice, rather than a duck call, to imitate the sounds of a mallard hen. "Mouth-calling," as it's commonly known, is a lost art. (One other mouth-caller won the World's Championship — Herman Callouet, also of Greenville, Miss., in 1942.)

Jake Hartz Jr. remembers attending that first duck calling contest as a young boy. It was broadcast over the radio. To ensure that enthusiasm for the contest was transmitted over the airwaves, a group was recruited to applaud on command.

"There were only about 15 or 20 of us," Hartz recalled. "We were freezing our butts off. They'd hold up a sign, and we'd all clap."

Even though the end of live decoys and the beginning of the duck call contest were mostly coincidence, the timing helped gain national publicity for the event at Stuttgart. It was recognized for encouraging sportsmanship and conservation at a time when the duck populations were attempting to rebound from the era of slaughter that marked the beginning of the century.

Photo courtesy Garner Allen

Gov. Orval Faubus appeared on stage to congratulate Pat Johnston after she earned one of her many titles at the World's Championship Duck Calling Contest. Johnston's success began at age 12 with a Junior World's title in 1950. She won the first of two World's Championships in 1955, at age 17. By then, Arkansas politicians like Faubus had recognized the importance of attending the duck calling contest on Thanksgiving weekend in Stuttgart.

Other events were added to the duck calling contest over the years as it evolved into the Wings Over the Prairie Festival of today. Dr. S. A. Drennan, a Stuttgart resident and Arkansas Wildlife Federation president, pioneered the sport of alligator gar fishing on the lower Arkansas and White rivers. Deep-sea tackle was used to catch these huge fish, which were then killed at boatside with a .22 pistol or bow-and-arrow before landing. (The Arkansas record alligator gar is 215 pounds from the Arkansas River in 1964.)

In 1939, in recognition of this growing sport, a contest was held to determine the largest alligator gar caught that year in Arkansas. An award for a 190-pounder was presented to Dick Diekhoff of Stuttgart. But fishing pressure on these long-lived freshwater monsters soon reduced their numbers and ended

Photo by Edgar Queeny

An alligator gar fishing contest was added to the 1939 World's Championship Duck Calling Contest in recognition of the increasingly popular sport. Entries had to be caught in Arkansas waters on rod-and-reel during the calendar year. The Arkansas and White rivers became famous for holding huge numbers of these large, prehistoric-looking fish. Gar fishing was promoted as having all the thrills of deep-sea fishing at a fraction of the cost. Dick Diekhoff of Stuttgart won first prize in '39 with a 190-pounder from the White River.

promotion of the sport.

By the late 1940s and early '50s, the season-opening celebration in Stuttgart was attracting nationally known celebrities, like baseball great Ted Williams and actor Robert Taylor.

The Stuttgart skyline was often dark with ducks during these early calling contests. Rice harvest methods left much more grain in the fields then.

Movie star Wallace Beery was a judge for the 1948 event. This contest is often remembered for the "duck salute" it received. Just as the finals were ending, a huge flight of ducks appeared on the horizon west of Stuttgart and flew directly over the judges' stand at low altitude.

Some of the best-known men in Arkansas duck hunting history were winners of the early contests. Names like Kenneth McCollum, W. H. Claypool, M. T. McCollum, Clyde Hancock, Chick Major and Jake Gartner were among the first dozen winners.

(See complete list in Appendix.)

It took one very young lady, however, to take the World's Championship Duck Calling Contest to a new level of national recognition. Chick Major's 12-year-old stepdaughter, Pat Peacock, won the Junior World's Championship in 1950. Five years later, as a high school senior, Peacock (now Johnston) won the first of two straight World's Championships.

The novelty of an attractive young woman duck caller helped put Peacock's picture in *Sports Illustrated* magazine and earned her an endorsement contract from Servus Rubber Company, which made duck hunting boots. Peacock traveled the U.S. for the next two years, appearing at sporting goods shows in all the major cities, blowing her duck call and promoting the World's Championship Duck Calling Contest.

Stuttgart residents bagged over 100 ducks in '73 without firing a shot

It's often recalled as "the day the ducks fell." A violent storm roared through Stuttgart on Nov. 26, 1973, smashing grain bins, uprooting trees and damaging homes. Also listed among the storm damage were over 100 ducks that were knocked from the sky.

Large hail was blamed for many of the duck deaths, but lightning and high winds were also part of the story. Several ducks were found encrusted in ice.

Because the storm hit during daylight hours, about 4 o'clock on a Friday afternoon, there were many eyewitnesses to the duck destruction. The Stuttgart *Daily Leader* reported 18 phone calls in the first half hour after the storm, all concerning the dead and injured ducks that littered the town. One man found a banded gadwall. Duck season would open the following morning.

Lloyd McCollum, then a member of the Arkansas Game and Fish Commission, was asked about the legal ramifications of claiming the dead birds. In most instances, wild game killed or injured by automobiles or unusual circumstances must be turned over to AGFC wildlife officers.

But McCollum ruled for the practical side, and said if those who found the ducks had an Arkansas hunting license and a duck stamp they could keep them.

In January 1974, Roland R. Roth of the University of Delaware surveyed Stuttgart residents for information about the unusual rain of ducks. A summary of his work, entitled "Effects of a Severe Thunderstorm on Airborne Ducks," was published in *The Wilson Bulletin* in December 1976.

The 106 ducks found after the storm included the following: 32 mallards, 29 pintails, 11 wigeons, 5 gadwalls, 2 redheads, 2 wood ducks and 1 blue-winged teal. Twenty-four weren't identified.

At least nine of the grounded birds were only temporarily dazed. They recovered and were released or escaped.

One unusual report included four ducks with head feathers that were "kinky, as if burned," which could have been due to lightning.

The music and mania of duck calling

Spirit of duck hunting, calling celebrated at Wings Over the Prairie Festival

The Wings Over the Prairie Festival is more than a duck calling contest. It is a celebration of the spirit that makes duck hunting one of the great American adventures.

It's a chance for duck hunters from all over Arkansas and the United States to come together and revel in their common bond. A chance for the duck-mad to delight in the peculiar mania that infects them.

The World's Championship Duck Calling Contest is the heart and soul of the Wings Over the Prairie Festival. But the festival is so much more.

"For over half a century, everybody's been coming home for Thanksgiving and having a party," said David Ruff, who has served as chairman of the Wings Over the Prairie duck gumbo cookoff. "This is our rite of spring."

It just takes place in the fall, that's all. The cook-off, held at the Grand Prairie War Memorial Auditorium, is a combination old-time bake-off and fraternity toga party. Many consider it to be the highlight of the season-opening weekend. Crews of cooks brew kettles of steaming duck gumbo while duck season celebrants mingle and dance in one pulsating throng.

The gumbo cookoff has been called one of the great parties in America. And like all great parties, it operates on the brink of chaotic meltdown. The rasp of duck calls competes with high volume rock-and-roll.

"It doesn't matter whether it's hot, cold, rain or sunshine, we'll be here," Ruff said. "If the world's going to come to an end, it will have to wait until tomorrow."

Elaborately decorated booths fill the auditorium. Judges taste every batch of gumbo. At the end of the evening, a champion is crowned. Everyone still capable of walking moves over to Main Street to catch the final of the World's Championship Duck Calling Contest.

Camouflage is the dominant clothing pattern. Hats are not an option but an essential statement of panache. Baseball caps are for the meek. Some favor cowboy hats, but the hard-core prefer felt duck hunting hats with mallard tail feathers stuck in the leather bands.

John Whiting of DeWitt wears a round cloth camouflage hat plastered with Ducks Unlimited pins.

"I've had this hat for 10 years," Whiting says. "During duck season, I wear it everywhere I go. I sleep in it."

The other badge of honor is the duck call, worn on a lanyard. Occasionally, merrymakers blow these at top volume,

Stuttgart's Main Street becomes center stage for the World's Championship Duck Calling Contest on Thanksgiving weekend.

much the way two-steppers shout "yee-haw" in a crowded honky-tonk. After all, calling ducks is why they are here. All had hunted that morning, trying to blow the tune of duck love that would coax reluctant mallards out of the sky.

Duck calling is an art and a science, as any contest caller will tell you. It's an art and science that has grown from the flooded timber and rice fields that have made Stuttgart famous.

In 1936, Thomas E. Walsh of Greenville, Miss., won the first World's Championship title. At stake was a new hunting coat. Many of the callers, including Walsh, used their natural voices to imitate mallard hens.

There's more at stake for the modern championship. Handmade wood and acrylic duck calls are the primary tools. Winners sometimes parlay their victories into successful call-making businesses. Champions like Buck Gardner have turned titles into careers in the duck call business. His mentor is Harry "Butch" Richenback, maker of Rich-N-Tone duck calls.

The winning package now includes cash, shotguns and an assortment of hunting equipment — all for blowing the perfect series of duck quacks.

"None of the calling we do would work in the duck woods," says Rick Dunn of Beebe, maker of Echo Duck Calls and 1997 World's Champion. "This is more like playing an instrument and hitting all the notes in a scale just right."

Regardless of the contest calling techniques' ineffectiveness in the field, duck hunters from all over the country flock to Stuttgart to listen to the music being played. The contest is held on Main Street. Callers are positioned on a stage fashioned like a duck blind, where they blow their routines in front of crowds estimated at 10,000.

"If you listen to a real good caller, it is like music," says Tommy Akin of Collierville, Tenn.

Thousands stand in the dark to watch as the new champion is crowned. Duck calling may be the most unlikely spectator sport, but the music of the call weaves a spell that hunters cannot resist.

Buck Gardner won the 1995 Champion of Champions event at the World's Championships.

Calling ducks drastically different than calling judges

The difference in Buck Gardner's duck calling was noticeable. Three weeks earlier, similar notes flowing from his duck call produced loud reverberating sounds, red bulging cheeks and an intense stare. Gardner had been focused on making the right duck sounds in what contest callers refer to as a winning routine.

Six days after winning the World's Championship Duck Calling Contest, Gardner's calls were more subtle. There was no strain and no constant noise, but rather soft sounds that seemed to coax mallards into a glide as they circled over dozens of decoys. Gardner was proving that he calls equally well to judges and ducks.

"Calling ducks is easier than calling to judges any day," Gardner said.

As in contest calling, there are rules to follow when coaxing ducks to decoys.

"There are two big mistakes I see many duck hunters make," Gardner said. "One is calling too much, and the other is not knowing when to call. If the ducks are coming in, there's no need to call."

Gardner said the biggest key to successful duck calling is being where the ducks want to be. He relies on the field and decoy spread to bring the ducks within calling range. He rarely blows his call while ducks are flying high. Although he's a world champion, he knows he's not that good. No one is, he said.

"There's a layer of air, about 100 yards high, and sometimes it seems if you call them before they get under that layer, it spooks them," Gardner said.

Gardner offered some other tips that bring in ducks:

■ Use a jerk string, a string attached to one or more decoys and jerked as ducks pass. The movement in the decoys creates ripples on the water and adds a more realistic appearance to the spread.

■ Keep your call in tune. Most calls are manufactured with a cork that holds the reed in place. The sound of the call is directly related to the cork. If it goes flat, it can change the sound.

"Cork is to a duck call what spark plugs are to a pickup truck," Gardner said.

■ Go to the field and listen to real ducks. "That's the easiest thing to do, but nobody does it anymore," Gardner said. "This isn't rocket science. It's just calling ducks."

Major development in calling ducks

D.M. 'Chick' Major became integral part of Arkansas duck hunting history

Walter Will Bryant never had to go far from his home to hear ducks quacking. Bryant, renowned for his knowledge of the woods and willingness to share it, grew up just across the road from Swan Lake in the Wabbaseka Scatters.

"One day I kept hearing this duck, 'Quack, quack, quack, quack,' right down on Swan Lake," Bryant recalled. "I said, 'I'm going to sneak up on that duck.'"

Bryant followed the sound and crept closer and closer, until he got close enough to see it wasn't a duck making the quacks.

"It was Chick Major," Bryant said. "He sounded just like a duck."

Coming from a man who has spent his life in the woods, like Bryant, it's the ultimate compliment to the abilities of Darce Manning "Chick" Major.

In the unsurpassed duck call-making history of Arkansas, Chick Major's story adds another important chapter. Major's Dixie Mallard calls were used to win hundreds of calling contests from coast to coast.

With his wife, Sophie, daughter, Dixie, and stepdaughters, Pat and Brenda, Chick was the head of a household that became known as the "World Champion Duck Calling Family." Chick won Stuttgart's World's Championship Duck Calling Contest in 1945. Over the next three decades, the Major family, including son-in-law Eddie Holt, would collect 28 titles in various duck calling contests.

Twenty of those titles are world championships, including Women's World's Championships by Sophie, Pat, Brenda and Dixie.

"We used to joke that we couldn't sit down at the dinner table unless we could blow a duck call," Pat Johnston said.

Chick Major's interest in duck calls began on a hunt along the Arkansas River near Conway.

"A friend was having trouble getting his sugar cane duck call to work and he asked Chick to take a look," Johnston said.

Photo courtesy Garner Allen

The World Champion Duck Calling Family, from left, Pat, Dixie, Sophie, Brenda and Chick in a photograph taken after Pat won the World, Women's World and Arkansas titles and Brenda won the Junior World title at Stuttgart in 1955.

Major became intrigued with how the call was put together.

"He grew up loving to work with wood," Johnston said. "And it wasn't long before he started trying to make one of his own."

Major borrowed a lathe and learned how to make a barrel, then an end piece. A jig was next. It was formed out of wax; a metal shop in Conway built it. At the time, Major lived in Conway and call-making was just a hobby. He worked as a truck driver for Cotton Belt's Southwestern Transportation Co. Major's route carried him from North Little Rock to Stuttgart to Gillett. Along that route, he met Sophie Word.

They married and moved to Stuttgart.

The relationship between a town, starting to become known for its duck calling, and a man talented enough to make an exceptional call was a natural. Major set up shop in the garage at his home, where he tinkered with making calls.

"Chick was a natural hunter," Johnston said. "He was one of those who hunted for the food. He'd hunt a lizard if he thought he could get some food out of it. He hunted constantly."

For that reason, his calls were designed to appeal to hunters.

The World's Championship Duck Calling Contest was still in its infancy. Duck call-making didn't begin to flourish in Stuttgart until 1945, when Major won the World's Championship.

"That's when his reputation as a duck call-maker kicked in," Johnston said.

The reputation was justified.

"The Dixie Mallard was the best call made at that time," said Butch Richenback, a student of Major from the time he was 8 years old until Major passed away in 1974. "He taught me how to blow a duck call and how to do everything to a duck call to make it do different things.

"You'd have thought I was his kid. I swept his shop. I spent as much time there as I did at home. I was like a shadow, he couldn't move without me being right behind him.

"He used to let me tune duck calls. When I started making them, people already knew me."

Richenback, maker of Rich-N-Tone duck calls, didn't start making a call of his own until 1976. He said he had too much respect for Major to even attempt making a call while Chick was alive.

Today, Major's daughter Brenda and her husband, Don Cahill, continue to make Dixie Mallard calls.

Chick and Sophie Major will always be part of the Wings Over the Prairie Festival. The Chick and Sophie Major Memorial Duck Calling Contest is held the Friday evening preceding the World's Championship Duck Calling Contest. The contest is open to high school seniors, and the winner receives a $1,000 scholarship.

For those who knew Chick Major well, he is remembered for more than duck calls.

Photo courtesy Garner Allen

Chick Major, his stepdaughter, Pat, and his Irish water spaniel, Stinker.

Of particular note was his ability to train dogs. Major owned an Irish water spaniel named Stinker that he trained to do a variety of tricks. Major and Stinker were a hit in elementary school classes, where Stinker would perform tricks like fetching specific articles of clothing. Major carved a small duck call that would fit in Stinker's mouth. The dog could hold it and blow the call on demand.

"He could sit all day and work with Stinker," Johnston recalls.

Garner Allen once wrote of Major:

"Chick Major was no fireside sportsman. Years afield in quest of quail and duck brought the crinkles born of greeting thousands of Grand Prairie sunrises to the corners of his eyes. A natural man, full of gentle mischief as anyone ever startled by Chick's phenomenal ventriloquistic talent can testify. He was genuine, as true as the tone of any duck call his manual and vocal wizardry ever produced."

Johnston is first lady of duck calling

Unmatched list of titles includes world champion, champion of champions

It's only right that a member of "The World Champion Duck Calling Family" would be the only person to win all five major competitions held in Stuttgart's annual World's Championship Duck Calling Contest.

Duck talk was the primary language in the Chick Major household. Pat Johnston got her love of calling from her mother and stepfather. Sophie and Chick were married when Johnston was in the fifth grade.

"I didn't know what duck hunting was until Mother married Chick," Johnston said.

In 1950, at the age of 12, Johnston won the Junior World title. In 1951, she took the first of five straight Women's World titles. In 1955, Johnston won the Arkansas title and the first of two straight World's Championships. In 1960, she capped her duck calling career with the Champion of Champions crown. (Intermediate and Chick and Sophie Major Memorial competitions have since been added.)

And Johnston has one other trophy from the annual Wings Over the Prairie Festival. In 1956, she won the first-ever Queen Mallard beauty contest.

Johnston started learning to blow a duck call when Major set up a woodworking shop in their garage. Johnston would hang around while Chick made his calls.

"Curiosity has always killed me about everything," Johnston said. "I would just stick around. Finally, one day he gave me a call and said, 'You need to learn how to do this.'"

Johnston said she "fiddled with it" but didn't think much of it. That changed in the fall during the World Championship Duck Calling Contest.

"I thought, 'Hey, I think I can do this,'" Johnston said.

But it would be Sophie Major, with more patience than Chick, who taught Johnston to blow a call.

"Mother was a natural-born teacher," Johnston said. "So, with her patience and his ingenuity, they worked with me."

Her interest in calling ducks led to hunting trips with Major. But it was after her first World's Championship at the age of 17 that duck hunting really became a part of her life.

"I hunted with everybody," Johnston said. "It was a novelty at that time to hunt with a female, especially a young female who was a champion caller."

"Every time I called they came in, and every time I shot I hit. It was just a wonderful morning."

One of those first hunts included a trip with reporters from *Sports Illustrated* and *Progressive Farmer* magazines. The morning of the hunt, temperatures were near freezing and sleet was falling.

"Going in, all I had on was hip boots," Johnston said. "The water was only up to my knees. But during the walk in, I stepped in a stump hole and filled my boot."

Johnston said no one saw the misstep; she wasn't about to say anything.

"I was with all of these guys," Johnston said. "I knew they weren't going to feel sorry for me."

The hunt continued, and it turned into one of those special mornings.

"Every time I called they came in, and every time I shot I hit," she said. "It was just a wonderful morning. But by the time it was over, my leg was numb."

On the walk out, the numb leg caused her to trip, and this time she went completely under. When she came up, she was minus her shotgun. She went underwater again to retrieve it.

"I survived, and it turned into the best experience I've ever had," Johnston said.

The next issue of *Sports Illustrated* carried a photo of her walking from the flooded woods. That picture would change her life.

The president of Servus Rubber Company saw the photo and noticed Johnston was wearing Servus boots. After signing a contract, Johnston traveled to all the major boat and sporting goods shows in the U.S., endorsing Servus boots. Johnston was gone so much she had to complete her senior year of high school and freshman year of college while on the road.

Even after her duck calling days were over, Johnston continued to promote duck calling and Stuttgart.

She is recognized as a driving force behind the Wings Over the Prairie Festival and the duck calling contest, and has been nicknamed "the Duck Lady."

In 1994, Gov. Jim Guy Tucker named Johnston as the first woman to serve on the Arkansas Game and Fish Commission. It wasn't just ducks that Johnston was interested in when she began her work on the commission.

"I am not just for ducks, and I want to make that clear. I am interested in anything that will make our outdoors better," Johnston said when she was appointed. "I am interested in today, but I am more interested in the future."

She proved that point well during her short tenure. Many AGFC employees count her as the best commissioner the agency has had. You wouldn't expect anything less from a woman who has excelled so well in a game mostly played by men.

"I have approached all of those situations with the idea that they're not judging me as a woman, they're judging me as a person," Johnston said. "I don't look at it as a woman versus a man. I think we're all equal."

But, at least in the history of the World's Championship Duck Calling Contest, Pat Johnston's record stands unequaled.

Richenback duck calls are rich in tone

Major's disciple carries call-making tradition to the next generation

The duck call sounded perfect to Butch Richenback. But the customer insisted there was "some little something missing on the low end."

"Can't you hear it?" the man said.

Richenback couldn't, but he took the customer's word for it.

"You think it's not right, huh?" said Richenback, who then blew the duck call once more, from the high end of the calling scale to the low end. The call sounded so good it turned the heads of a few competition callers in Richenback's Rich-N-Tone shop.

"What about that?" Richenback said. "Is that right?"

"No, it's still missing that some little something on the low end," the customer said.

"Then it's not right," Richenback said, and once again blew the call, while moving away from the customer. The competition callers in the shop, all of whom knew Richenback well, started backing up.

"How about now?" Richenback said. "Is that right?"

"That little something is still not there," the customer said, shaking his head, and then widening his eyes in disbelief as Richenback turned to a band saw, and cut the call in half.

"If it ain't right, it doesn't go out of this shop," Richenback said. "Come back tomorrow and I'll have a new one for you."

Richenback delivered on his promise, and the next season when the customer returned to the shop, the first words out of his mouth were, "The duck call is just fine."

Duck call-maker Butch Richenback was first elected mayor of Stuttgart in 1994.

There's not much middle ground with Harry M. "Butch" Richenback. He is cantankerous, yet lovable, soft-hearted yet hard-headed. He calls himself "the asshole of duck call-makers." At times he is cursed, but he is always respected.

"Butch is a special person," said Buck Gardner, 1994 World's Champion and 1995 Champion of Champions duck caller. "He will tell you how the cow ate the cabbage, and you have to respect that. People who know him will tell you he has a heart of gold. And when it comes to helping someone who needs it, he will give you the shirt right off his back."

Richenback's endearing and straightforward qualities are a big reason he was elected mayor of Stuttgart in 1994, a position Gardner predicts Richenback will hold for as long as he desires.

But his political standing takes a backseat to his skill at producing duck calls. Among those who know, it's generally agreed that Richenback makes the best hand-crafted duck call in modern times. That's another title Richenback will hold for as long as he makes duck calls.

"Other call-makers don't understand, Butch was born to make duck calls," Gardner said. "He puts his heart and soul into it, because he believes in the craft. To him, it's not about making money, but about making the best there is. That is the way duck call-makers used to be. Each call was a work of art with the call-maker's signature on it.

"Butch is a holdout from that old school, and you can see it in the calls he makes."

Watch Richenback cut and form a call from acrylic, cocabola or bois d'arc and it's easy to see that each call is a work of art. In reality, each call is different, even though, side by side, the forms may be identical.

"I don't do anything like the other guys," Richenback said. "I don't measure anything, I just go."

If you were to put a micrometer on each call, you might see the difference, but even that is doubtful.

While making the calls, Richenback measures with his eyes and the nub of his left index finger. The finger is cut off to the first knuckle.

"I like to never cut it off to fit," Richenback said.

He first cut the finger when he was 2 years old, on a lawnmower blade. A tablesaw took two more slices, and another two were lost to a bandsaw. The end result is a wide, rounded nub that Richenback places between his signature Coke bottle rim and the base of the barrel of his calls.

Richenback credits the quality of his calls to the lessons he learned from Chick Major, who made the Dixie Mallard call. Major is described by Richenback as a father figure. Richenback was 8 years old when he started hanging out at Major's shop.

"I went everywhere he went," Richenback said. "People thought I was his son."

It stayed that way until Richenback was 29 years old, and Major passed away. But during that time, Major taught Richenback to blow a duck call. He used the Dixie Mallard call to win the 1972 World's Championship and the 1975 Champion of Champions contest.

But more than that, Major taught Richenback the craft of making a duck call. When customers came to Major's shop to have a call tuned, it was Richenback who was given the job.

Richenback credits the quality of his calls to lessons he learned from Chick Major.

Major was still alive when Richenback won his world championship. Not long after, other callers began asking Richenback to make his own call.

"But I wouldn't do that out of respect for Chick," Richenback said. "I knew how to make a call before Chick died, but I couldn't."

The year after his Champion of Champions title, Richenback decided to prove a point to a few detractors. He bought a lathe and produced his first call, without using a jig. Richenback's uncle, Clyde Hancock, helped design the body. The shape of the lip came from a Coke bottle. The rubber reed standard of calls in that day was replaced with mylar, a synthetic material Richenback found in a mail-order catalog.

The name Rich-N-Tone was provided by a family friend, who combined Richenback's name with the tone of the call. Rich-N-Tone calls are known for producing every note of the scale a duck caller might need, from the high-pitched high ball of a rice field hunter, to the soft quack of a timber hunter.

"I want the call to do everything so you only need one," Richenback said. "And I really try to put the duck in the bottom of it, the rattling, raspy bottom end."

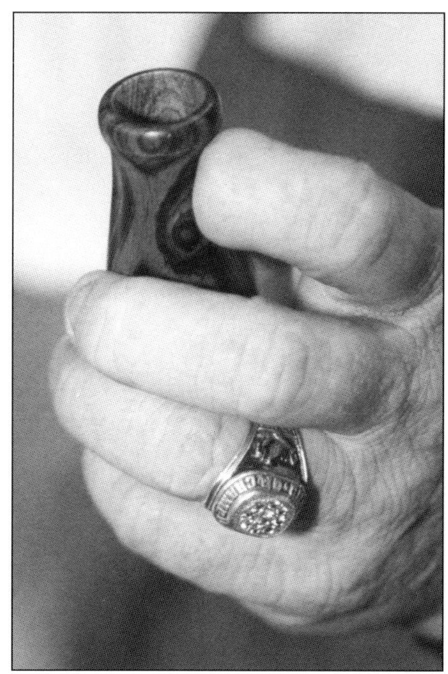

The end of Richenback's left index finger has been cut off five times. He uses it as a measuring device for making duck calls.

The first calls made in 1976 were smaller than traditional handmade calls and could fit easily in a shirt pocket. While other call-makers made fun of the small call, Marion McCollum of Mack's Sport Stop in Stuttgart saw its quality. McCollum took the first 12, and soon Richenback was behind in filling orders.

He is still behind today. In all, he produces about 2,000 calls a year; the exact number is unknown.

"I don't count anything," Richenback said. "I just keep up with the money, because the government is kind of picky about that stuff."

They are almost as picky as Richenback is about his duck calls. He still says he will cut one up in a "New York second" if it's not right. Rich-N-Tone duck calls have to their credit almost three dozen world calling titles, two Champion of Champions titles and more than 300 state and regional contest titles.

But Richenback is quick to add that the call is just a piece of equipment.

"If you put it on the shelf, it won't call a duck for you," he said. "You still have to know how to use it, know when to call and when not to."

Richenback's youth duck calling clinic about more than simply calling ducks

They come in all shapes and sizes — tall ones, short ones, big ones and little ones. There are cowlicks and ponytails, buck teeth and braces. Every one of them is different, except for the smiles on their faces and the duck calls hanging from their necks.

Each year, the traditions of duck calling in Stuttgart are passed down by Butch Richenback through his youth duck calling clinic.

The roots that keep the World's Championship Duck Calling Contest strong and growing can be traced to a youth center on the outskirts of Stuttgart. That's where Richenback, a World's Champion and Champion of Champion caller, passes on the skills that helped put Stuttgart on the map.

For four weeks, he teaches a calling clinic for kids ages 7 to 13. Each year, approximately 40 to 50 kids attend. On the Monday night preceding the World Championship, the kids perform before parents and relatives. Every kid goes home with a trophy, a duck call and a feeling of accomplishment. While the clinic is centered around duck calling, it goes deeper than that for Richenback.

"I've just got a soft spot for kids," said Richenback, who served as the youth center's director for more than 20 years. "When it comes to doing something for those kids, that comes first. You hear all of these things about dope and kids in trouble and that you're supposed to help them. Well, if (the clinic) will keep them from getting in trouble, I'll help them."

Richenback's method of keeping kids out of trouble is to get involved. He also coaches youth football and baseball. Richenback feels strongly about the personal touch.

"You want to help?" Richenback asks, "You want a drug-free community? Then get involved with the kids. Do something for them.

"I was taught when I was young that you don't help people just to get something. It's just that you're supposed to help others."

Richenback's work hasn't gone unnoticed by those who count. At the conclusion of one contest, a 7-year-old boy handed him a note. Richenback had given the boy a duck call when the youngster showed up with one that didn't work. Written on gray paper, taken out of a first grader's Big Chief notebook, the note visibly moved Richenback. It simply read:

"Thank you for the duck caller. I like it very much. Thank you for spending so much time with us at duck calling lessons."

It was signed "Your friend."

Others also recognize the importance of what Richenback does, including Johnny Mahfouz, the 1988 World's Champion, and Trey Crawford, the 1976, '86 and '93 World's Champion. They often judge the clinic's contest.

"This is where I learned to blow a duck call, just like these kids," Mahfouz said. "There's nothing to compare with the work that Butch does with the youth of this town. You just can't give him enough credit."

"If it wasn't for Butch and these kids, the interest (in the World's Championship Duck Calling Contest) would die," Crawford said. "People would just get away from it. I wish there were other people who cared like Butch and put as must into it as he does."

On the wall of his Rich-N-Tone shop hangs a framed thank-you from the parents of Stuttgart. It reads:

"We appreciate you Butch. Your tireless and unselfish work with our children over the past 20 years, while appreciated, has gone largely unsung.

"We appreciate you Butch — youth duck calling classes, direction of the Stuttgart Youth Center, coaching PeeWee football and baseball programs, as well as day in and day out just being a friend and pal when the kids needed one the most.

"A few of us know about the kids who have benefited from your generosity when they couldn't afford lessons, duck calls, uniforms, etc. If you, a man of modest means, didn't have the funds to help, you found someone who did.

"Truly this adage applies to you — 'No one ever stands so tall as when he stoops to help a child.'"

The birth of commercial duck hunting

Stuttgart's hunting tradition can be traced through McCollum family

When the fee for a guided duck hunt in Bayou Meto bottoms increased from $12.50 to $15 in the 1950s, skeptics were quick to howl.

"Everybody griped like hell," said J. W. McCollum. "They said you would never be able to book enough hunts."

They, of course, were wrong. Today, similar duck hunts start at $100 and run as high as $375.

The increase in cost is just one indicator of how far Arkansas duck hunting has grown in popularity. Many of those paying customers are from out of state. They pay the price because the hunting lives up to its reputation.

The roots of that reputation and Stuttgart's commercial duck hunting can be traced through one family: the McCollums.

The end result has been a town that reigns supreme as the "Duck Capital of the World." Duck hunters everywhere are as familiar with Stuttgart as baseball lovers are with Cooperstown, N.Y.

At the turn of the century, however, Stuttgart was nothing more than a farming community, surrounded by other farming communities. Arkansas County, which lies in the middle of the Delta's Grand Prairie, was best known for its vast hay fields.

When rice arrived in the Delta, in the early 1900s, the ducks that flew down the Mississippi Flyway and wintered in the White and Arkansas river bottoms became a nuisance. Rice was cut, shocked and stacked in the fields to dry. Rice shocks stacked three feet high would be leveled by morning if farmers didn't do something to protect them.

"We shot the ducks by the moonlight to keep them out of the rice fields," J. W. McCollum said.

McCollum said ducks were such a problem that Frank Freudenberg installed a rotating beacon, like those at airports, to keep the ducks out of his fields. In many ways, the farmers around Stuttgart hated ducks. That wasn't the case for the McCollum family, especially two half-brothers, Otis and Roy McCollum. They might well be considered the fathers of Stuttgart's commercial duck hunting.

"My father loved ducks," said J. W. McCollum, Otis' son. "He was the most knowledgeable man there was about ducks. The only problem was, he was about 20 years ahead of his time."

Otis McCollum never owned an acre of land. But he developed more than 7,000 acres along Bayou Meto, north of Highway 79 and due west of Stuttgart. Bayou Meto and Buffalo Ditch, or Big Ditch, as it is commonly known, cut through the heart of the land.

Roy McCollum did own land — 1,500 acres of flooded timber known today as Slick McCollum's. Slick was actually Kenneth McCollum, Roy's son.

Photo courtesy Bud McCollum

From left, Lloyd, Kenneth and Maurice McCollum after a successful hunt. Lloyd served as a member of the Arkansas Game and Fish Commission. Kenneth "Slick" McCollum's commercial hunting operation began on 1,500 acres his father, Roy, bought.

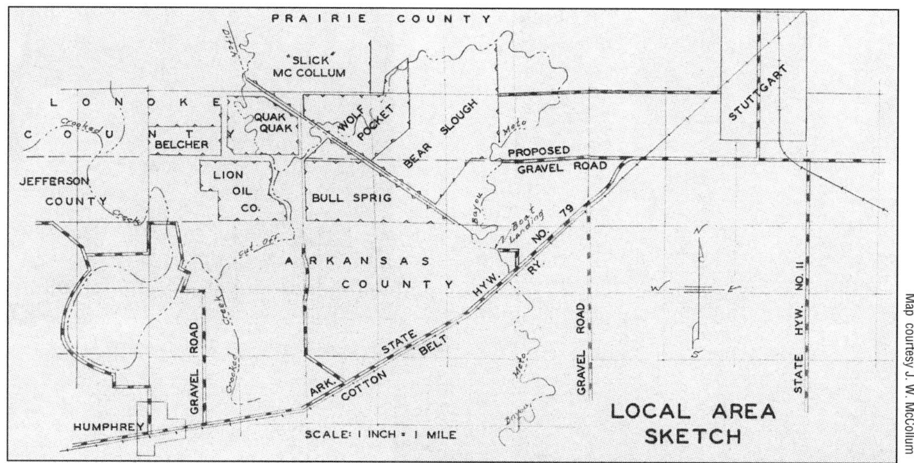

Map courtesy J. W. McCollum

The northwestern corner of Arkansas County, through which Highway 79 runs from Stuttgart to Humphrey, contains some of the state's best-known duck clubs. This area of the Bayou Meto bottoms includes the commercial operations started by Russell McCollum (Bear Slough on map) and Slick McCollum, plus private clubs, such as Quak Quak, Lion Oil and Bull Sprig. Otis McCollum built the levees and developed the area for duck hunting after World War II.

The land was originally the Stuttgart Hunting Club, owned by Roy McCollum, Roger Crowe and Wallace Claypool. McCollum bought out the others and developed the land for duck hunting.

Before World War II, much of the area surrounding it was considered "open land." The parcels that did have an owner had been sold for taxes, most for $1.25 an acre.

Hunters came by train. There was a depot at a place named Brummit, and hunters would go by wagon from there to a camp in the woods.

"They would kill all the ducks they could carry," said Elmer Grant, a neighbor of the McCollums.

Although there were limits, Grant said no one paid attention to them.

"There was only one game warden and he had half the state to look over," Grant said. "He never did catch anybody."

But the open land status started changing when Otis McCollum began leasing everything that wasn't owned by relatives. At one time, he controlled more than 7,000 acres.

That seems impossible today. Acre for acre, this northwestern corner of Arkansas County is the most sought-after duck hunting land in the U.S. It is the site of legendary duck clubs, such as Million Mallard, Quak Quak, Bull Sprig, Lion Oil and the commercial operations of Russell and Slick McCollum.

Otis McCollum leased the land for duck hunting. But the quality of the hunting depended entirely upon the whims of Mother Nature. During dry seasons, McCollum was forced to go to the lakes in the White River bottoms.

When rain was abundant, this northwestern corner of Arkansas County, attracted hundreds of thousands of ducks.

"Wherever it would flood, that is where he hunted," J. W. McCollum said.

Along with his seven brothers, Otis McCollum shot ducks for the market when it was legal. They had contracts with several hotels in Hot Springs.

After market hunting became illegal, Otis McCollum kept his love for duck hunting. But it became obvious to him that if exceptional duck hunting was going to be guaranteed, he would have to give Mother Nature a helping hand.

After World War II, McCollum decided he would develop the Bayou Meto-Big Ditch bottoms. In those days, the idea of forming levees to hold water for green-tree reservoirs was unheard of. Today, it is common practice. But it might not be, if not for Otis McCollum's work.

"It amazes me just to think about his ability to comprehend the possibilities of what he could do," J. W. McCollum said. "If he'd had just a little bit of capital, he could've done wonderful things. But for an old country boy who didn't get past 10th grade, he did pretty good."

Keeping up with McCollum family can be confusing, even for the McCollums

Bud McCollum and Marion McCollum are the same age. They are second cousins, which would lead you to believe the two spent their childhoods together in a small town like Stuttgart (pop. 10,420).

"I never met him until we started going to the fifth grade," Bud McCollum said.

That's partly explained by the fact that several miles separated their parents' homes. But it's also due to the large number of people with the last name McCollum in Arkansas County.

The present-day edition of the McCollum clan began with M. T. McCollum Sr. He fathered four sons in one marriage — Roy, Earnest, Robert and Johnny — and four more sons in another marriage — Otis, Gilbert, Thad and M. T. Jr.

M. T. Jr. fathered Marion McCollum III; Roy had Dick, Lloyd, Kenneth (better known as Slick), Roy Jr., Maurice and Russell McCollum. Roy Jr. fathered Roy III (Bud).

Keeping track of all the members of the McCollum family is tricky, even for members of the family. When Roy "Bud" McCollum III was a young boy, Otis McCollum would often refer to him as Charlie.

"Whenever we'd get ready to go somewhere, he'd look at me and say, 'Come on, Charlie,'" Bud said.

Otis McCollum probably knew Bud's name, but you can understand the need to develop your own tracking system.

M. T. McCollum owned McCollum Hardware, the forerunner of Mack's Sport Shop, now owned by Marion McCollum. Marion McCollum was named to a seven-year term on the Arkansas Game and Fish Commission in the early 1990s. Lloyd McCollum served on the commission in the late '60s and early '70s. Thad McCollum was one of the founders of the World's Championship Duck Calling Contest. Kenneth "Slick" McCollum won the fourth championship in 1939. J. T. McCollum finished second that year. M. T. McCollum won the title in 1941.

In other words, it's difficult to do anything involving duck hunting in Stuttgart and not bump into a member of the McCollum clan.

Concept of green-tree reservoirs started on Grand Prairie; commonly used now

Green-tree reservoirs symbolize the evolution of Arkansas duck hunting. You can chart that path in three steps: 1) the natural flooding of bottomland hardwood timber; 2) the creation of irrigation reservoirs for rice; 3) man-made versions of flooded timber, which are known as green-tree reservoirs.

While it's difficult to pinpoint the first green-tree reservoir, there's no doubt it came from the Grand Prairie region.

After Verne Tindall discovered the extra benefit of a rice irrigation reservoir — ducks flocked to it — many more were built on the Grand Prairie. Excluding Corps of Engineers and Arkansas Game and Fish Commission lakes, Arkansas County has 15 percent by number and 11 percent by area of all lakes over five acres in the state, according to the AGFC.

Early rice irrigation reservoirs, like Tindall's, held water most of the year. With advances in levee-building heavy equipment, some of these reservoirs were made several feet deep. The hardwood trees in the lakes died from the water covering their roots during the growing season. Peckerwood Lake, the 3,500-acre reservoir built by Edgar Queeny and Arkansas Irrigation Company, serves as the biggest example of what are often called dead-timber reservoirs.

Normally, late winter and spring are the heaviest rainfall seasons in Arkansas. One study by waterfowl biologist Ken Reinecke determined that good water conditions for mallards occurred in the White River National Refuge bottomlands only 31 of 53 winters (58%) from 1932-85. Often there is no overflow anywhere in the state on November duck season openers. That's why the rice irrigation reservoirs attracted so many ducks initially.

It didn't take much of a leap to go from dead-timber reservoirs to green-timber reservoirs. The next best thing to naturally flooded bottomland hardwoods is artificially flooded bottomland hardwoods. By building short levees around hardwood stands and, most importantly, draining the water quickly after duck season ended, it was possible to keep the timber alive year after year, hence the name green-tree reservoirs. It's the ultimate duck hunter's manipulation of Mother Nature.

The ideal place for a green-tree reservoir is a pin oak covered flat of clay-based soil. This provides food for ducks in the form of acorns. And it allows for relatively easy water manipulation, because the soil holds water. Arkansas' Grand Prairie region of the Delta fits that description perfectly.

But the green-tree concept can be put to use with other variables. By the 1950s, the use of green-tree reservoirs had spread to several other lower Mississippi River valley states.

As hardwood timber becomes more and more valuable, the importance of proper green-tree reservoir management increases. Research continues on how to best achieve the delicate balance of managing for ducks, long-term forest health and the desires of duck hunters.

The maximum depth of a green-timber reservoir should be 12 to 18 inches. Dabbling ducks, like mallards, tip up their tails to feed underwater. They don't completely submerge, as diving ducks do. Therefore, any food deeper than their outstretched necks is unavailable to them.

It's also well-documented that mallards are attracted to rising water and the "feather edge" of flooded timber. Along this edge they can best utilize acorns, seeds from moist-soil plants and invertebrates. Green-tree reservoirs permit gradual flooding that attracts ducks over a longer period of time.

By 1997, there were approximately 83,000 acres of public land under green-tree management for ducks by the AGFC. It's important to note that green-tree reservoirs remain relatively new, especially in terms of managing the health of 100-year-old hardwood trees.

Another step in the evolution of Arkansas duck hunting is likely to center on this conflict between man and nature: White River bottomlands naturally flood only about two of every three years, but public land duck hunters want flooded timber hunting every season.

Indeed he did. There are more than 15 miles of McCollum-built levees in the Bayou Meto-Big Ditch bottoms. All of them, which were laid out with a hand-held sight level, are still in use today.

The 7,000-plus acres McCollum flooded are where commercial hunting in flooded timber and the legend of Stuttgart began. In developing this area for duck hunting, McCollum also saved one of the area's critical wetlands. Since that time, most of the land around those bottoms has been cleared for crops. Today, those 7,000 acres have several owners, but this area is one of the largest privately owned contiguous blocks of timber in east Arkansas.

There are more than 15 miles of (Otis) McCollum-built levees in the Bayou Meto-Big Ditch bottoms. All were laid out with a hand-held sight level and are still in use today.

Almost without exception, the other large blocks of forested land in the Delta are owned by the Arkansas Game and Fish Commission or the U.S. Fish and Wildlife Service.

To pay the leases for so much land, McCollum began guiding. Hunts were \$5, \$7 or \$10 a day. Clients came from word-of-mouth advertising. Even with that primitive form of promotion, the reputation of Stuttgart duck hunting began to grow.

A big boost came from *Movietone News*, news clips shown as trailers for feature-length motion pictures. One of the segments highlighted the World's Championship Duck Calling Contest, duck hunting and Stuttgart.

"After that, we had people from all over the world coming to town to hunt," J. W. McCollum said.

The first clients included John Olin, head of Winchester-Western and the Olin Corporation, who started hunting with the McCollums before he set up his

Photo courtesy Bud McCollum

These ducks were killed in the Long Water Hole on Bayou Meto south of Highway 165, according to information written on the back of the photo. The men, from left, are Roy McCollum Sr., M. T. McCollum Jr., Thad McCollum and an unidentified hunter.

own Greenbriar Club. After Olin developed Greenbriar, he would lease out the second floor of the Riceland Hotel and bring in guests. When there were too many hunters for Greenbriar, the McCollums would get the spillover for their guide service.

The railroad also served as a source for providing hunters. As automobiles became more popular, the railroad companies began looking for ways to keep people traveling by rail. Hunting ducks in Stuttgart became a successful promotion for the railways and the McCollums. There was a station located on Highway 165 between Humnoke and Stuttgart.

J. W. McCollum remembers seeing rail cars full of people who had come to hunt ducks at Stuttgart.

No roads led to the acreage they hunted. Access was gained along Bayou Meto from a boat ramp at Highway 79. To carry hunters the two to five miles up Bayou Meto, McCollum would load them in Army M-1 personnel carriers, outfitted with five-horsepower motors. The carriers would accommodate 21 hunters.

"And believe me, it took a long time with only a 5-horsepower motor," said McCollum, noting he thought he'd hit the big time later with the purchase of a 22-horsepower Evinrude-ELTO.

Fifty percent of these clients had never hunted ducks before, and many of those had never shot a shotgun.

Most of the clients stayed at the Riceland Hotel. When they needed to be outfitted for hunting, they visited McCollum's Hardware, the forerunner of Mack's Sports Shop. Black gum boots sold for $6.50; a hunting coat cost $7; and a box of shotgun shells was $2.50. If you needed a shotgun, a Winchester Model 12 could be purchased for $65.

"That was a lot of money in those days," McCollum said.

All that for a duck hunt that seldom lasted longer than a couple of hours.

"Either you got your ducks early or you didn't get them," McCollum said. "You never hunted past 10 o'clock."

Otis McCollum required no hunting past 10 a.m., reminding J. W. that his father had an instinct for waterfowl behavior. Those were the days when ducks were numerous, and few people managed hunting places. Ducks filled the woods readily, so it seemed overly cautious to limit the shooting there. But Otis McCollum insisted. In addition, he always left one-third of the acreage as a rest area, another unusual practice at that time.

J. W. McCollum said his father did those things out of love for ducks

"To him it was a way of life," McCollum said. "He probably knew he was doing some good, but I doubt he ever thought he was changing duck hunting to the point it is today."

Mack's Sport Shop has grown with tradition of Stuttgart duck hunting

In the early 1930s, McCollum's Hardware was a good place to buy a hoe handle or keg of nails. There was no such thing as a sporting goods store.

When duck hunters started coming to Stuttgart en masse, McCollum's Hardware began stocking items to outfit them. You could still get a hoe handle and a keg of nails, but the shelves also included the following: black gum boots, $6.50; hunting coat, $7; long underwear, $1.50; hunting shirt, $2.50, wool socks, $1; and a box of No. 6 or 7 shot, $2.50. A Winchester Model 12 shotgun cost $65.

Business was good, too. Business was so good that M. T. "Mack" McCollum II decided to take sporting goods out of the hardware store and open a separate store in 1944.

McCollum's Hardware was on Main Street, next door to Ben Franklin's. Each building had about 1,500 square feet of floor space. When Ben Franklin's went out of business, McCollum cut a hole in the wall between the stores and moved his sporting goods into that space.

"At the time, a sporting goods store was unheard of," said Marion McCollum, Mack's son. "It's been said many times that it was the first full-line sporting goods store anywhere."

By 1970, it was time to expand again. Marion McCollum moved the business to Highway 79 in a 3,200-square-foot building. Decorated with various animal and fish mounts and filled with every item available for the duck hunter, the store became a tourist attraction during the hunting season.

It became even more of a draw after 1993, when McCollum added a mail-order catalog business. The catalog is mailed to more than 600,000 duck hunters worldwide. The store was enlarged again in 1997 to encompass more than 18,200 square feet, most of it in inventory waiting to go on the shelf or through the mail.

One fact says it all about today's version of McCollum's Hardware: More steel shotgun shells are sold at Mack's Sport Shop than any other retail location in the world.

Queeny's place on prairie fit for a king

St. Louis industrialist was an important influence on ducks, Grand Prairie

Edgar Queeny asked Carl Hunter to accompany him on a trip to El Dorado one day. Hunter, who managed Queeny's Wingmead Farms at Roe, was glad to oblige. Queeny and his wife, Ethel, came to Wingmead every year for duck season. Their primary residence was in St. Louis, where Edgar Queeny was president of the Monsanto Chemical Company.

When the Queenys visited Wingmead, they usually kept to themselves. Edgar Queeny hunted ducks every morning of the season and hunted quail in the afternoon.

Queeny didn't tell Hunter the reason for the trip that day. He simply asked him to go. Queeny was a man of few words. Several miles down the highway, after it became obvious that no explanation for the drive was coming from Queeny, Hunter asked, "Why are we going to El Dorado, Mr. Queeny?"

"I'm going to buy Lion Oil Company," Queeny said.

Later that day, he did exactly that.

"Edgar Queeny was one of the 10 richest men in the country at one time," said Hunter, who still smiles in amazement when thinking about Queeny's low-key manner. "You don't go buy Lion Oil Company on borrowed money."

Edgar Queeny was an equally powerful influence in the world of duck hunting. Most of Hunter's travels with Queeny took place in wooden canoes, through flooded timber on the 11,000-acre Wingmead estate along LaGrue Bayou. After Queeny purchased the land in 1939, the reputation of Arkansas' Grand Prairie duck hunting began a steady rise.

Queeny's "hunting shack" at Wingmead had 8,000 square feet, nine bedrooms, nine bathrooms and a separate dining room. Certainly no other place on the Grand Prairie required formal dress for dinner.

Few other places could match the illustrious guest list here either. It included outdoor writer Nash Buckingham, legendary film animator Walt Disney, waterfowl artist Richard Bishop and countless leaders of American business.

The story of Edgar Monsanto Queeny and Wingmead is about one extremely

Queeny's 11,000-acre Wingmead estate bordered LaGrue Bayou on the Grand Prairie and included 3,500-acre Peckerwood Lake.

wealthy, highly intelligent man's love for ducks and Arkansas. Other than his primary residence in St. Louis, Queeny had, at various times, three other homes, all in his favorite wild places — one on the Miramichi River in Canada, another in Alaska and Wingmead on the Grand Prairie of Arkansas.

Under the guidance of Edgar Monsanto Queeny, the Monsanto Chemical Company, founded by his father and named for his mother, grew from a small chemical company to a billion-dollar corporation. After 32 years under Queeny, Monsanto's assets were 100 times greater than when he began. Monsanto became a success story surpassed only by the chemical company giants of Du Pont, Union Carbide and Allied Chemical.

Initially, saccharin was the foundation for Monsanto. In 1901, John F. Queeny, who had been in the drug business as a salesman and buyer, attempted to challenge the German monopoly of the artificial sweetener. He had only $5,000 in capital. The company lost money until 1905. World War I cut off German supplies of saccharin and greatly increased demands for all other chemicals.

Edgar Queeny, born in 1897, was 22 when he went to work for Monsanto. He had studied chemistry for two years at Cornell University and served in the Navy two years during World War I.

His time at Cornell gave Queeny a chance to explore photography and journalism. He started work at Monsanto as the advertising manager. Queeny created the company's in-house newsletter, "Monsanto Current Events," and always took an interest in it and public relations in general.

Photo by Edgar Queeny

Photo courtesy/ Carl Hunter

Edgar Monsanto Queeny — 1897-1968

When his father named him president in 1928, Edgar Queeny was 30 years old and had been with the company only nine years.

Queeny referred to public relations as "business manners and morals." Throughout his presidency of Monsanto, Queeny wrote his own annual reports. He preferred a straight-forward, easily understood style, which was radically different from the standard of the day.

"I don't know what I'm going to do with that boy Edgar," John F. Queeny once said of his son. "He wants to change everything. He's going to ruin Monsanto."

Edgar Queeny never feared change. Experimentation was the theme in his life. He was as adept as a naturalist as he was as a businessman. In 1950, Queeny financed an African safari sponsored by the American Museum of Natural History. He came back to the U.S. with film documenting the African legend of the "Honey Guide," a bird that led men to bee trees. He also shot footage of a little-known and vanishing tribe, the Latuko. During that trip, Queeny remained focused through the camera lens as a bull elephant charged him.

"He wasn't afraid of anything," said Hunter, who would work 20 years for Queeny. "Nothing scared him. And he liked to be on the leading edge of everything."

That was what led to Queeny's association with Walt Disney. They shared a passion for producing color motion pictures. Hunter said Disney was once invited on a hunting trip at Wingmead.

"What? Me, kill a duck?" the creator of Donald Duck replied. "I couldn't live with that."

Disney did create the emblem for "The Pelican" — Queeny's World War II surplus "ruptured duck" PBY amphibious airplane. Aviation was another passion of Queeny's. He customized The Pelican into the ultimate hunting and fishing plane. It held a small boat packed with gear under each wing.

Queeny was often described as quiet

Photos by Edgar Queeny

The 8,000-square-foot home had nine bedrooms and nine bathrooms. Formal attire was required in the evenings for dinner.

Queeny's *Prairie Wings* continues to raise money for Ducks Unlimited

Anyone who shot a mallard hen at Wingmead paid Edgar Queeny a $25 fine, which was donated to Ducks Unlimited. In the 1940s and '50s that was more than a trifling sum. But it was a tiny fraction of Queeny's philanthropy toward DU, the waterfowl conservation organization that Queeny once served as a trustee. In fact, Queeny's work is still raising funds for DU.

In 1946, Queeny combined with waterfowl artist Richard Bishop to produce the book *Prairie Wings.* Through Queeny's photographs and Bishop's sketches, it detailed the intricacies of waterfowl flight.

Queeny shot many more ducks with a camera than he did with a shotgun. Documentary film-making was one of his passions. Queeny made films on everything from spearing lions with Masai warriors in Africa to the life history of salmon along the Gaspe Peninsula in Canada.

He also made a film with the same title as his book. After it was completed in 1948, the 25-minute *Prairie Wings* film was often used as part of Ducks Unlimited chapter organizational meetings around the country. The combination of full-color and slow-motion footage from the flooded timber of Arkansas made this an eye-opener for DU.

In 1986, Roy Hunter of Pine Bluff began trying to find a copy of *Prairie Wings* that could be converted to videotape. A Monsanto secretary remembered where a few originals were stored. Working with a film restoration expert, Hunter was finally successful in making videotape copies.

"I want the people of Arkansas to recognize what Mr. Queeny contributed to wildlife in general and ducks in particular," Hunter said. "Duck hunters everywhere recognize Stuttgart as the best duck hunting place in the country, and I want them to have the opportunity to see this classic film."

The *Prairie Wings* videotapes, with a short introduction added to the original, cost $35 each, which includes shipping. All proceeds go to the DU Pine Bluff chapter.

Mail orders are accepted at: DU Tape Project, P.O. Box 1002, Pine Bluff, AR 71613.

— supposedly a shy man who tried not to show it. He did, however, have a sense of humor and a spontaneous side, best illustrated by an incident involving The Pelican. Queeny and two other Monsanto executives were flying along the Alaska coastline, scouting for places to fish. Someone noticed crab traps had been set in a cove, and Queeny decided crab would be the perfect main course for dinner. The amphibious plane landed in the cove and taxied to each trap. Every crab removed was replaced with a fifth of fine Scotch whiskey that had a large greenback wrapped around it. The Pelican departed the cove without leaving any note of explanation.

Edgar and Ethel Queeny began taking "travel-trailer" trips to Arkansas' Grand Prairie in the early 1930s. Ethel is said to have been able to handle a shotgun almost as well as her husband. Edgar soon began looking for property. After hunting with Tippy LaCotts on Mill Bayou near DeWitt, Queeny tried to buy some land there.

Hard feelings still exist over the way Queeny purchased the 11,000 acres on LaGrue Bayou that became Wingmead.

Verne Tindall's Reservoir, built in 1927 near Stuttgart, had created the wave of the future on the Grand Prairie. Rice production was on the rise, but the water table here was already showing signs of stress. Irrigation wells had to be dug twice as deep as they were 30 years before. Tindall's Reservoir had shown that ducks were also attracted to these shallow lakes built to hold water for rice irrigation.

That's what most interested Queeny, the ducks. He formed Arkansas Irrigation Company and proposed the construction of a 3,500-acre lake on LaGrue Bayou. Roger Crowe of Stuttgart helped put together the deal. Arkansas Irrigation gained the power of eminent domain. Several farmers in the Slovak area were forced to sell their land to make room for the new impoundment, which became Peckerwood Lake.

Ethel Queeny enjoyed putting the official titles on the Wingmead property. "Wingmead" refers to the "meadow of wings" the Grand Prairie becomes each year when ducks migrate. Peckerwood Lake got its name from the thousands of woodpeckers that tapped out tunes on the acres of standing dead timber created when the lake was impounded. Edgar Queeny built three green-tree reservoirs on the property — Wingmead, Greenwood and Paddlefoot. He allowed no outboard motors; the wooden boats and canoes had to be paddled or pushed through the shallow lakes.

Carl Hunter believes Wingmead was possibly the first green-tree reservoir on the Grand Prairie. It was at least one of the first in which wooded areas, especially pin oak flats, are temporarily flooded to attract ducks. This re-creates the setting that has attracted mallards to the overflow bottomlands of Arkansas for centuries.

Peckerwood Lake was used primarily as a rest area for waterfowl. Queeny enjoyed flooded timber hunting, not open water. When all the construction was finished at Wingmead, Queeny literally had a place where he could step out of a mansion wearing his house slippers and kill a limit of ducks in some of the finest flooded timber hunting anywhere.

After she found out that Pinkerton security men had checked on her background, Mary Ann Hunter knew her husband, Carl, was a serious candidate for the job as manager at Wingmead. Mary Ann taught school in Little Rock, where Carl was employed by the Arkansas Game and Fish Commission.

There were many applicants for the job of running Queeny's farm in 1957, after Atlas Porter of Roe retired. Hunter had a big advantage. Born in 1923, he had been employed part-time by the AGFC as he was completing a bachelor of science degree in agriculture at the University of Arkansas.

In 1945, Hunter went to work full time for the AGFC and helped complete "A Survey of Arkansas Game," which detailed the state's wildlife resources. Much of Hunter's work involved waterfowl, including the planning, surveying and construction of small reservoirs. Hunter had also worked with quail. Thus, he filled all the qualifications Queeny required.

Recalled Hunter: "Mr. Queeny said, 'Do what you want about the farming. Just make sure the hunting is good.'

"He wouldn't walk off the porch to shoot the biggest deer in the woods. Ducks and quail — that was it."

It was the perfect job for a hands-on wildlife biologist like Hunter. Queeny continued to experiment, and one of the first they tried was establishing Canada geese, which were no longer migrating to the Grand Prairie in significant numbers. Locally raised captive Canadas were placed in rest areas. Wild-trapped young geese were held in pens at Wingmead over the winter. With this imprinting, the flock of Canada geese that migrated to Wingmead each year grew to as many as 2,000.

Hunter built up a population of 30 quail coveys on the property. Whether it was ducks, geese, quail or growing crops, Queeny was always willing to invest the money to try something new.

"Everybody looked to Wingmead to see what we were doing," Hunter said.

Hunter became vice president and general manager of Wingmead Farms, Inc. Mary Ann Hunter and Ethel Queeny became great friends. It was the perfect setting for the Hunters to raise two sons. The Queenys, who had no children, came to Wingmead every October and stayed through March.

Jess Wilson had been guiding for LaCotts on Mill Bayou when Queeny hired him as a guide and groundskeeper. The Hunter and Wilson families were two of 16 living on the Wingmead acreage.

Hunter and/or Wilson hunted ducks with Queeny every day of the season. Shooting always stopped at 10 a.m., which was another reason the 1,000-acre rest area on Peckerwood Lake held as many as 500,000 ducks.

Edgar Queeny died from a "heart ailment" on July 7, 1968, at his suburban St. Louis home. Carl Hunter continued to manage Wingmead until it was sold in 1977.

"Mr. Queeny was the most intelligent man I've ever been around," said Hunter, who retired from the AGFC as an assistant director in 1986. "I duck-hunted every day of the season, except Christmas Day, for 11 years. I was

Photo courtesy Joe Coogan

Frank Lyon Jr. had heard all his life about Edgar Queeny, Wingmead and the hunting there.

When Wingmead went up for sale, rumors of potential buyers included Elvis Presley

Edgar and Ethel Queeny had no children. Barnes Hospital in St. Louis and the Washington University Medical School associated with it had long been favorite charities for them. The 17-story Queeny Tower was dedicated at the hospital before Edgar died in 1968.

When Ethel died in 1975, Barnes Hospital became the owner of Wingmead. Barnes announced the estate would be sold by sealed bids on Jan. 8, 1976. And rumors quickly spread about who the next owner would be. Elvis Presley, Johnny Cash and Anheuser-Busch Inc. were included in the gossip. The story of Wingmead's sale, however, would center upon who didn't bid on it.

Frank Lyon Sr. and his son, Frank Jr., of Little Rock were among those who actually were considering the purchase. The Lyon family company owned, among other businesses, Coca-Cola Bottling Co. of Arkansas.

"We had heard about it all our lives," said Frank Lyon Jr. "Everybody had always been scared to death to come within 20 miles of the place."

The Lyons had kept memberships in various Stuttgart area duck hunting clubs for many years. They had a membership at Freudenberg's Reservoir after the Pulitzer brothers quit hunting. This, of course, would be the ultimate duck club membership.

The Lyons and longtime employee Maurice Eason looked over the property a couples of times. Wingmead is often summarized as an 11,000-acre estate. Peckerwood Lake takes up more than 4,000 acres of it. The land totals about 6,800 acres.

"We spent several weeks going over what we could afford to bid and have an economically viable farm, based on the tillable acreage and assets," Frank Lyon Jr. said.

Their ballpark figures ranged from \$6.1 million to \$5.7 million. Lyon said he and his father went back and forth — adding, then subtracting \$100,000 here, \$100,000 there.

The bids were to be sent to St. Louis by registered mail or personal agent. The Lyons put their bid in the mail on the designated day.

"Dad and I were sitting around talking," Frank Lyon Jr. said. "He said he had a funny feeling about registered mail."

As insurance, they sent a Lyon Co. representative with another copy of the bid. At the designated hour, only two bids had arrived by mail, and the Lyon Co.'s wasn't one of them. With a representative there to deliver the bid, the Lyons had made the highest offer. The total wasn't disclosed.

The next day a large number of bids arrived. They were returned unopened.

Photo by Edgar Queeny

Bishop always welcome at Wingmead

Renowned waterfowl artist and Edgar Queeny shared many interests

All guests at Edgar Queeny's Wingmead estate were weekend guests. The routine never varied: Arrive on Friday in time for cocktails and a formal dinner; hunt ducks Saturday and Sunday mornings, with a quail hunt possibly on Saturday afternoon; depart Sunday.

Only waterfowl artist Richard Bishop was allowed to vary from that routine.

"It was always open house for Dick Bishop," said Carl Hunter, who managed Wingmead Farms, Inc., for 20 years. "They were buddies. They'd get out there and laugh and joke. Dick Bishop could stay as long as he wanted."

The book *Prairie Wings* is the result of work Queeny and Bishop did together. Queeny writes in the preface that he wanted Bishop's name to appear as a co-author, but Bishop declined the request.

With Richard Bishop's background in engineering, interest in waterfowl flight and love of duck hunting, it was natural that he and Edgar Queeny would become friends. Both had attended Cornell University, too. The result of their friendship provides a significant chapter in U.S. waterfowl history.

In 1936, Jay "Ding" Darling, chief of the U.S. Biological Survey, asked Bishop to submit a design for the third federal duck stamp. Darling's mallards were featured on the first stamp. Canvasbacks by Frank Benson appeared on the second stamp.

Bishop's etching of Canada geese on the third stamp remains notable for two reasons. One, Bishop insisted on complete control of the reproduction, which resulted in no lettering within the borders of the design. It marked the first and only time an artist was given complete authority on the final image. Secondly, it was the first federal duck stamp published as a separate print. Bishop was the first to recognize the money-making potential in prints. The value of print sales has made the federal duck stamp competition so fierce among artists today.

The link between railroad men and waterfowl hunting, so evident in Arkansas, existed in Bishop, too. His father was a chief engineer on the New

Edgar Queeny took this photograph of Richard Bishop, as he made a sketch in the flooded timber at Wingmead.

York Central line. He loved waterfowl hunting and introduced his son to it at an early age. Bishop was born in Syracuse, N.Y., in 1887. His route to artistry included a mechanical engineering degree from Cornell in 1909.

Bishop started drawing in 1920 while working for his father-in-law at a Philadelphia manufacturing plant. He picked up a copper plate in a stack that was to be melted down, took it home and etched a portrait using a phonograph needle.

Four years later, a Bishop etching of Canada geese was honored by the Philadelphia Print Club. By 1933, he had quit the manufacturing business to become a full-time artist.

By following his interests, Bishop was able to form a perfect partnership of work and play. He remained an avid waterfowl hunter. After the shotgun was put away for the day, Bishop shot ducks with a camera. His high-speed movies applied the highest technology of that era to the study of avian flight. His films documented the uncanny movements of flying ducks that had previously been only rumors.

Wrote Nash Buckingham: "Thanks to the painstaking Bishop curiosity and his searching slow-motion cameras, we have the waterfowl and their ways not as we suppose them to be, but as God made them."

And it was this waterfowl photography that marked the meeting point for Queeny and Bishop.

Bishop often advised, "Don't say ducks never do that. Say they seldom do it."

Queeny recalls this advice in *Prairie Wings*. He describes how Bishop's high-speed camera had caught ducks "flying backward, standing still in the air, and looping the loop." The human eye sees only a quick hitch in a duck's flight pattern. *Prairie Wings* delved into the specifics of how the various wing and tail feathers functioned in allowing a duck to make such previously unheard-of moves.

Queeny mentions a slow-motion picture of a mallard hen performing what World War II pilots called an "Immelmann turn." The hen was frightened by the sound of Queeny's camera as she approached. He writes: "She flew four wingbeats on her back and winged over, righting herself when headed safely away."

Bishop annually sketched Christmas cards for the Queenys. Two other Bishop cards appear in this book inside the front and back covers. They are from Carl Hunter's personal collection.

The depth of the friendship between Queeny and Bishop appeared in many other ways. Ethel and Edgar Queeny commissioned Bishop to sketch an annual Christmas card for them. The series stretched over two decades.

Bishop accompanied Queeny on the two Africa safaris done through the American Museum of Natural History in 1950 and 1953. They hunted quail and ducks together all over the U.S.

Bishop's work is noted for its accuracy in reproducing the wing action and flight of waterfowl. High-speed photography aided the eye of an artist.

Richard Bishop died in 1975. His last book, *The Ways of Wildfowl*, was published in 1971. His first book, *Bishop's Birds*, had been published in 1936.

Bishop's long career provided a link from the early waterfowl masters, such as Benson and Roland Clark, to the contemporary greats, like Maynard Reece and David Maass.

Photo courtesy Melvin Spann

Pulitzers brought attention to Stuttgart

Brothers Joseph, Herbert leased Freudenberg's Reservoir for 25 years

They don't shoot ducks there now, but in the 1940s and 1950s Freudenberg's Reservoir was the toast of the town.

Frank Freudenberg built the reservoir in 1931 to save water for rice irrigation. But in a few short years it would be the duck hunting paradise of Joseph and Herbert Pulitzer. They were the sons of Joseph Sr., the newspaper publishing giant who endowed the Pulitzer Prize for journalism. Like his father, Joseph Jr. would also serve as publisher of the St. Louis *Post-Dispatch*. The Pulitzer brothers entertained people from all over the world at Stuttgart during duck season.

The beneficiaries of the Pulitzers' love of duck hunting were Freudenberg, who had gone bankrupt twice, and the town of Stuttgart, which was thrust into the limelight of the jet-set crowd.

Freudenberg's Reservoir had enjoyed some attention as a duck haven before Pulitzer leased the hunting rights in 1935. Early 1930 newspaper articles indicate the reservoir, also known as Maple Island, had operated as a commercial enterprise.

A July 7, 1935, Memphis *Commercial Appeal* article noted: "The duck club known as the Maple Island reservoir, owned by Frank Freudenberg will not be available to guns of the public during the coming winter. Joseph Pulitzer has bought shooting rights on the property for the use of himself and friends. The column is glad to see this change come over the property, for the simple reason that no doubt fewer duck (sic) will be killed on the property that supplied better hunting than most similar places in the rice belt."

The shooting rights on the property weren't the only change that came with leasing of the reservoir. The presence of the Pulitzer brothers seemed to usher in a new respect for Stuttgart duck hunting. The fact that the Pulitzers leased the property was reported all over the Southeast.

And duck hunting got some unusual attention. When the Pulitzers came to town it was big news. Take for instance the following Nov. 26, 1935, news story in the *Arkansas Gazette*, which appeared under the headline, "Pulitzer Brothers Go for Duck Hunting in a Big Way":

"Stuttgart – Herbert Pulitzer of New York and Joseph Pulitzer of St. Louis, sons of the famous New York publisher, have gone in for duck hunting here in a big way.

"They have rented the ground floor of the Riceland Hotel here, also two houses in Stuttgart and leased a 1,500-acre tract, including a large reservoir on the rice plantation of Frank

This rice field full of pintails at Frank Freudenberg's farm is part of what attracted the Pulitzer brothers to Stuttgart in 1935.

Freudenberg, six miles east of Stuttgart.

"The brothers have positively declined to see would-be interviewers and have made as few contacts as possible among the residents of Stuttgart. Also, persons with whom they have conducted business negotiations have been instructed to refuse to answer any questions.

"It is reported that the brothers have installed a retinue of attendants, including a hair-dresser, in the hotel here while they and their wives and guests are occupying the homes that they have rented. Freudenberg said that he had leased the hunting privileges on his farm and reservoir for the present season only, but declined to give any additional information, explaining that he had made this agreement with the Pulitzer brothers."

In fact, the Pulitzers had paid Freudenberg $100,000 for a 10-year lease. The Pulitzers and their duck hunting always made good copy. One newspaper story reported during the season that most of the Pulitzers' bag went to "hospitals and poor people." Another article recounted how Herbert Pulitzer and Grace Amory flew 1,000 miles to go duck hunting near Stuttgart, then another 700 miles "to eat the day's kill at Palm Beach, Fla."

"(Joseph) Pulitzer would come down in railroad cars and bring people from all over the world," said Rollie Remmel, who sub-leased the property from the Pulitzers in 1960.

The arrival of the Pulitzer brothers and their guests was big news in a small town. Even today, Pulitzer is one of the first names mentioned when old-timers refer to the dignitaries who visited Stuttgart to hunt. The pride is still there, regardless of the fact that Joseph Pulitzer also made headlines in 1943 for being charged with shooting over the bag limit and shipping ducks by express illegally. He pleaded guilty to the last charge and paid a $500 fine.

Freudenberg's Reservoir became highly regarded as a duck hunting hot spot. An entire wall of the Riceland Hotel dining room was adorned with a picture of ducks from the reservoir. And Freudenberg gained respect as a duck hunting expert. He was often quoted in regional newspapers and was featured in the Dec. 12, 1949, edition of *Life* magazine.

His first reservoir was 180 acres. He expanded it into a cluster of three reservoirs of 230, 260 and 420 acres. The Pulitzers continued to lease the Freudenberg reservoirs for three decades at $10,000 a year.

"It was about the 25th year when a group of us got together and sub-leased the property from them for $2,500," Remmel said.

Not long after, Freudenberg died. His widow sold the land to Lloyd and Carlton Baker. Today it is known as the Baker Brothers reservoir. The brothers continued to lease the property to individuals like Remmel until 1981 when Arkansas Best Freight leased the property. Since that time, ABF has made the reservoirs a part of almost 2,000 acres of rest area for waterfowl.

Pulitzer remained a duck hunter after eyesight failed

Being able to see a duck to shoot it is not altogether necessary. Joseph Pulitzer was an avid duck hunter, but as he got older his eyesight began to fail. It got so bad that seeing ducks come into decoys was almost impossible.

In a sport where some hunters with 20/20 vision have trouble hitting a flying duck, it would seem that Pulitzer's hunting days were doomed. That wasn't the case.

"In those last days Pulitzer would have a guide sit next to him while he hunted," said Garner Allen, retired managing editor of the Stuttgart *Daily Leader.*

"The guide carried a long cane fishing pole and tied a rag to the end of it. Pulitzer could see well enough to identify the rag at the end of the pole, but that's about all he could see.

"When the ducks would come in, the guide would turn Pulitzer in that direction and wave the rag toward the ducks."

Pulitzer would then shoot. He killed ducks, too, Allen reported.

Fifty-cent plastic Olt was too expensive, so Grant whittled corncob

Elmer Grant eyed the duck call and immediately determined that 50 cents was too much. It was during the 1920s. Grant was just a boy, but he had seen an Olt duck call and thought he needed one.

"But I couldn't afford it," Grant said.

To take care of the problem, Grant stole his mother's celluloid comb, broke it in half and shaved the handle down to make a reed.

"I got my ass whipped over that," said Grant, who was 80 years old when he relayed the story. "It was a big comb, with a big wide base. At that time, there really wasn't anything else you could make into a reed."

Grant said the whipping was worth it. He had no alternatives. And he knew he could make a duck call if he just had the right materials.

"All the old-timers around here made their own calls, so I had an idea of what I was doing," Grant said.

With the costly reed acquired, Grant hollowed out a corn cob, made an end piece from wood and had a duck call.

"It worked, too," Grant said.

It worked so well that Grant would use it for many seasons in guiding for clubs around the Bayou Meto-Big Ditch bottoms. During that time, Grant's payment for a day of guiding was 50 cents.

No one has done more in Arkansas

Rollie Remmel has been a lifelong cheerleader, fund-raiser for ducks

The question was posed at a Ducks Unlimited meeting in Little Rock: "With the exception of Rollie Remmel, who in Arkansas has done the most for ducks?"

That question said it all. Roland Roe "Rollie" Remmel undoubtedly occupies a class by himself when it comes to raising money in Arkansas for ducks.

"Rollie Remmel is a North American classic whose passion for life and wildlife is so infectious he inspires everyone he touches in a very memorable manner," said Matt Connolly, executive vice president for Ducks Unlimited. "He is our grandest human resource."

Remmel sums up his fund-raising efforts simply, saying, "If you hunt, you need to put something back. There are no buffaloes, I guess, because there was no Buffalo Unlimited."

Ducks Unlimited has long been Remmel's favorite cause. He became Arkansas' Ducks Unlimited state chairman in 1966.

"I'm a member of anything and everything that will help ducks," Remmel said. "My real love is Ducks Unlimited. It didn't take me long to figure out that if we save the waterfowl resource, my children and other people's children would have the option of hunting."

Remmel was born in Little Rock and lived there most of his life. But his love of duck hunting and raising money for ducks has made him a recognized figure all over Arkansas' duck country, especially Stuttgart.

"Enthusiastic" is the word most often used to describe him. One newspaper account in Stuttgart's *Daily Leader* described him as "energetic and voluble." Remmel has never been bashful about making the rounds with a collection plate. "Give 'til it hurts. It's for mama duck," is his rallying cry. But Remmel has always backed that up with his own actions.

Both Rollie and his wife, Ruth, are DU sponsors in perpetuity, which requires a donation of $25,000. By showing how much it means to them, they've set the example that others have followed. Their method might be described as "put up and shut up."

"We don't do a lot of yakking," Rollie said. "Nobody's going to do much listening anyway. Ruth once raised $50,000 for Ducks Unlimited in about five minutes."

Both Ruth and Rollie have been honored by The Nature Conservancy for their work in obtaining habitat and raising money. When the Arkansas Outdoor Hall of Fame inducted its inaugural class, the Remmels were obvious choices.

"Give 'til it hurts" has been the rallying cry for Rollie and Ruth Remmel in their support of DU.

Remmel, Tommy Hillman and Frank Thomas, after a successful hunt near Carlisle in 1997.

Before Remmel took over as state chairman, it was difficult to raise $5,000 a year in Arkansas for Ducks Unlimited Remmel raised $20,000 his first year and vowed to do 20 percent better every year after that.

"When I was first involved in DU, they were only raising a million dollars nationally," Remmel said. "I guess there were no more than 20,000 members. Now there are over 600,000 members. In 1996, we probably raised $88 to $90 million. In Arkansas alone, we raised $2 million."

Remmel fully expects to see a $3 million year in Arkansas. Every dollar raised is built on a foundation he started.

"Rollie has been an incredible supporter of Ducks Unlimited as long as I can remember," said Lt. Gov. Winthrop Paul Rockefeller, chairman of a September 1997 fund-raiser held in celebration of Remmel's 80th birthday. "He has been King Duck in Arkansas."

It was only natural that King Duck would celebrate his 80th birthday by raising money for Ducks Unlimited. As further testament in appreciation of Remmel's long years of dedication, the party raised almost $300,000.

Those funds were used to underwrite the Bittern Lake North Project in Alberta, Canada, and the Arkansas River Care project along state flyways. The Canada project encompasses more than 2,000 acres of breeding grounds for waterfowl and was dedicated as the Rollie Remmel Project in October 1997.

The area was almost lost during the drought years of the 1980s. Those were the years when few ducks were being produced in Canada and Arkansas hunters were seeing far less cupping into flooded timber. The Rollie Remmel Project restored 6,100 acres, and every year insures that as many as 200 "mama ducks" per square mile can produce thousands upon thousands of ducks, most of which will play a role in Arkansas' duck season.

Remmel's walking sticks have become trademark, fund-raiser for ducks

Rollie Remmel carries a walking stick wherever he goes. But rather than a tool to help him walk, Remmel's walking sticks have functioned as fund-raisers for ducks. A "Rollie Stick" is often the highlight of a Ducks Unlimited event.

"I was in a Ducks Unlimited meeting in Hope about 30 years ago," Remmel said. "I saw these fellows walking with these split hickory hoe handles."

Remmel found out that a man named Lockhart owned a factory that made the hickory handles and ash "show sticks" used at livestock auctions. Remmel had always appreciated the value of a good walking stick when wading through flooded timber, where one false step can turn a good duck hunt into a miserable day. He met Lockhart and began ordering sticks from him.

Rollie began carrying a hoe handle as part of his DU outfit, which also includes a vest and a hat covered with hundreds of pins from all over the world. When various wildlife artists added their marks to them, Rollie Sticks jumped in value.

Remmel was present at a DU meeting also attended by waterfowl artist Lee LeBlanc. LeBlanc penciled some images of mallards along the edge of Rollie's stick. Before the night was over, Remmel put the stick on the auction block, and it sold for more than $1,500.

The list of notable personalities who possess a Rollie Stick includes President Bill Clinton, Hillary Clinton, former President George Bush, former Vice President Dan Quayle, Supreme Court Justice Sandra Day O'Connor and actor Ted Danson.

"My sticks are bipartisan," Remmel said. "I give them to Democrats and Republicans alike."

The Rollie Stick has evolved from a hoe handle to gnarled wood of every make. Some are painted and others have carved duck heads at the top.

When auctioned at Ducks Unlimited events now, they always bring big money. Rollie Sticks have sold for as much as $5,000 at national DU meetings.

An Inland Sea

WHITE RIVER OVERFLOWS ARE ARKANSAS' BIGGEST KEY TO HOLDING BIG NUMBERS OF WINTERING DUCKS

The White River gauge at Clarendon is the most-watched figure in Arkansas during duck season. Flood stage is 26 feet; 28 feet is a magic number for many duck hunters; and every reading means something to one duck hunter or another.

Except for the Mississippi River, which spread the foundation of the Delta, the White River deserves more credit than any other for Arkansas' unmatched duck hunting.

Elevation, or lack of it, explains the freshwater sea created when the White River overflows. The three major rivers in the Arkansas Delta are the Mississippi, Arkansas and White. The Arkansas and White rivers flow into the Mississippi within a few miles of each other, in a complex and ever-changing relationship. Because the White River lies lower in the Delta than the other two, it begins backing up during any rise in the Arkansas and Mississippi.

This starts a chain reaction. Black River, Cache River, Little Red River, Bayou DeView, LaGrue Bayou and countless other small streams and bayous begin losing their capacity to move water downstream, and they start to overflow. The result is a vast, shallow body of water bordered by the Ozark Mountains on the west and Crowley's Ridge on the east.

◄ Dozens of oxbow lakes in the 154,000-acre White River National Wildlife Refuge offer excellent duck hunting.

Photo courtesy Brian Robbins

The forested bottomlands of the White River provide excellent habitat for wood ducks.

Simply put, a little water causes a lot of flooding in the White River bottoms. That's why the ducks have been coming here for centuries.

And it's also the reason why man didn't begin ditching and draining these bottoms at the turn of the century, as was done in the St. Francis River floodplain. The "Great Swamp" moniker given the St. Francis basin would be even more appropriate here. Or maybe the White River bottomlands should be called the "Greater Swamp," simply because they kept man at bay longer.

The biggest drainage problem in the Arkansas Delta was saved for last. By the time it got to the top of the list, in the form of the Cache River-Bayou DeView channelization project, the perceived value of wetlands had begun its U-turn.

The White River National Wildlife Refuge today is another reminder of the significance of the Cache River battle. The White River NWR began as a 113,000-acre tract in 1935. If the Cache and Bayou DeView had been channelized, the White River NWR was positioned downstream to take a heavy blow, too, in the form of increased siltation, warmer water temperatures and high-velocity floods.

Instead of that, the White River NWR got 41,000 acres added to it in 1992 in a land exchange coordinated through the federal government with the Potlatch Corp. Ducks carried a great deal of clout in the land swap. With waterfowl numbers dropping throughout the 1980s, protecting their habitat was given high priority. The new 41,000-acre tract connected the existing White River NWR with the new Cache River NWR.

At times, there are so many ducks in the White River bottoms that mid-air collisions are unavoidable. The lower White and Cache rivers sometimes hold 45 percent of Arkansas' wintering ducks.

Two Arkansas native species provide the best measuring stick for determining the 'wildness' of a Delta river bottom. No. 1 is the black bear... No. 2 is the river rat.

The lower White River and the Cache River are looked at as one unit in the Arkansas Game and Fish Commission's North American Waterfowl Management Plan. It is the most important unit in the state for wintering ducks. Aerial surveys during the 1970s documented an average of 496,103 ducks here, which represented about 45 percent of Arkansas' total, and as much as 10 percent of the wintering ducks in the entire Mississippi Flyway.

Most importantly, this area represents the largest contiguous tract of bottomland hardwoods remaining in the Delta.

Because of all these characteristics, the Cache-Lower White River unit is the "Flagship Project" for the Lower Mississippi Valley Joint Venture Plan that is contained within the North American Waterfowl Plan. In other words, the highest priority is maintaining and enhancing this area as the best of the best wintering waterfowl habitat in the Mississippi Flyway.

If you want to understand both the beauty and terror early settlers found in the vast bottomlands of eastern Arkansas, begin wandering through the White River National Wildlife Refuge. This 154,000-acre tract along the lower White River represents the closest thing remaining of the bottomland hardwood forest that once covered the Delta.

Two Arkansas native species provide the best measuring stick to determine the "wildness" of a Delta river bottom.

No. 1 is the black bear. Arkansas was once known as "The Bear State." The few descendants remaining from that original black bear population are roaming through the White River bottoms. (The black bears found in the Ozarks and Ouachitas now are the offspring of Minnesota and Canada transplants.)

No. 2 is the "river rat." A river rat usually lives on a houseboat and gets everything he needs from the river and its bottoms by fishing, hunting, trapping and farming. Like the black bear, this native species has dwindled, but you'll find more houseboats and river rats along the White River than any place else in Arkansas.

From black bears to river rats to bottomland hardwood forests to mallard ducks, this truly is Arkansas' last great wilderness.

WHITE RIVER, FEDERAL LAWS — A TIMELINE

1903	1918	1933	1934	1935
President Theodore Roosevelt establishes the first federal refuge on Florida's Pelican Island to protect egrets, herons and other water birds.	The Migratory Bird Treaty Act signed by the U.S. and Great Britain (for Canada) prohibits the sale of waterfowl and sets bag limits and season lengths. The first season is 107 days with a daily limit of 25 ducks.	Photographs of George Wilcox and the thousands of mallards he protects in Wilcox Lake along the White River appear first in the St. Louis *Post-Dispatch* on Dec. 31, then in newspapers around the world.	Congress passes the Migratory Bird Hunting Stamp Act, authorizing the annual issuance of a duck stamp. The first stamp, which costs $1, features a sketch by Jay N. "Ding" Darling, who spearheaded the campaign for the stamp.	White River National Wildlife Refuge established with land bought from several large timber companies. Much of the 113,000 acres has been heavily logged, and the purchase of this decimated land is questioned by many.

'Boat ride from hell' usually worth it

Hurricane Lake WMA known for rugged trips and hellacious duck hunting

It's 4:30 a.m. and headlights of vehicles unloading boats at the only ramp leading into the Hurricane Wildlife Management Area look more like a convention of four-wheel drive trucks than the starting point for a duck hunt.

A quick count revealed 42 trucks and trailers before Steve Stansberry and Brian Urtle jumped into the boat. More vehicles were coming toward the ramp, and with one-and-a-half hours to go before shooting time, it was a good bet more were on the way.

When Hurricane Lake is hot, no line is too long and no time too early to get in on the massive waves of mallards that produce great hunts for the hundreds, sometimes thousands, of hunters who travel here. The WMA is located along the confluence of the White and Red rivers. Rice and soybean fields surround it, making it a premier stopping-off place for migrating ducks.

Hunters here set up in flooded timber openings along ridges that naturally pull ducks through the treetops. The openings have been present since before 1950 as logging decks, where timber companies pulled logs to have them loaded and moved out. Hurricane Lake is full of those places. During early morning hours, mallards can literally fill the treetops.

But as shooting time came and went, you could see the worry in Stansberry's face. Ten minutes later, the first mallard appeared, a scout that must have been leading the charge for the waves behind it. The first flocks answered calls readily, circling over the decoys, wings fluttering, not quite wanting to land, before they lifted and flew away.

Killing ducks is easier when greenheads are three feet off the water, and it gives you the satisfaction of knowing you have fooled that duck.

But after two weeks of dipping into holes filled with decoys, and being met with loads of steel shot, the ducks were starting to get smarter. Shots would have to be taken after they broke the treetops, looked at the decoys and began their lift-out. It's not the classic style of duck hunting, although Nash Buckingham, the legendary outdoor writer, wrote fondly of shooting ducks at treetop level with his full-choked double-barrel shotgun.

It worked this day. An hour after the

HENRY GRAY/ HURRICANE LAKE WMA

Acres: 17,524
First purchase: 1958
Location: Near Augusta and Georgetown in White County.
Topo maps (7.5 series, U.S. Geological Survey): Augusta SW, Georgetown.

Hurricane Lake WMA gets its name from an oxbow lake within its boundaries. But most hunters drop the word "lake" and refer to it as simply "Hurricane." As one old duck hunter put it, "during duck season, it's just Hurricane, because there's a whirlwind of ducks that come here." (Don't say "hur-i-KANE" unless you want to identify yourself as a newcomer; locally, it's pronounced "hur-uh-kun.")

The area is situated along the confluence of the White and Little Red rivers. It has a series of creeks, most notably Glaise Creek, running through it. The rivers and the creeks provide most of the floodwater that fills almost 6,000 acres of hardwood timber. The WMA is dotted with oxbow lakes that attract ducks from great distances.

Although it was one of the first WMAs purchased by the Arkansas Game and Fish Commission, its reputation as a duck hunting paradise didn't start growing until the early 1990s. Its popularity is evident by the number of vehicles parked at Mitchell's Corner, one of the area's only access points. Other access points are from the White and Red rivers, where boats launch at Nemo Landing on the Little Red River or at Georgetown on the White River.

Hurricane Lake WMA is named in honor of Henry Gray, a former director of the Arkansas Highway Department. Gray worked in the AGFC real estate division when many of the WMAs were purchased and served as the first director of the Arkansas Game and Fish Foundation.

White River, Federal Laws — A Timeline

1935
U.S. Biological Survey Bureau announces the most rigid regulations in waterfowl hunting history, including a 30-day season, a ban on live decoys and hunting over bait and a restriction on automatic shotguns to a maximum of three shells.

1990
Ramsar Convention names the lower White River-Cache River-Bayou DeView floodplain a "Wetland of International Importance." It joins the Everglades and Okefenokee Swamp among only eight U.S. areas so designated.

1992
A land swap between the federal government and Potlatch Corp., adds 41,000 acres to the White River National Wildlife Refuge, and links it to the newly formed Cache River National Wildlife Refuge.

1994
The 14,900-acre Bald Knob NWR, located along the Little Red River near its confluence with the White River, becomes Arkansas' ninth national wildlife refuge. It opens to waterfowl hunting in 1997.

1996
The federal duck stamp, which now costs $15, has raised half a billion dollars, 98 percent of which has been used to acquire more than 4.5 million acres of wetlands for the national wildlife refuge system.

hunters saw the first mallard, six limits of greenheads followed and the group was heading home through a maze of brush, standing timber and cypress sloughs. The ride was a constantly winding adventure, as the flatbottom boat brushed against trees and scooted under overhanging limbs, while its occupants got their hats knocked off and their ears clipped by a variety of limbs, twigs and vines.

It was easy to see why regulars call a trip through Hurricane WMA the "boat ride from hell."

Back at the boat ramp, with the advantage of daylight, a glance at the vehicles included license plates from Tennessee, Illinois and Indiana. They provided more evidence that Hurricane Lake has become more and more popular as a duck hunting paradise.

For today's hunters, it is much like Bayou Meto was in the 1970s — a place where new duck holes could be found without the limits imposed by crowds walking in from every direction and spreading out. Hurricane Lake WMA is crowded, but most of the access is by boat, which leaves pods of hunters dotted within the more than 6,000 acres of flooded timber.

"Hurricane Lake was unknown about 15 years ago," said Don Akers, former chief of wildlife management for the AGFC. "The locals hunted there, but there was very little outside use."

That started to change when conditions in other areas were dry during early parts of the season. Hurricane floods from backwater of the White and Red rivers, and from a water control structure on Glaise Creek, where runoff centers. Those conditions made Hurricane the only alternative for hunters seeking public land for duck hunting in that area. But once they found out how good it was, they kept coming back every season, dry or wet.

Mike Wallace of Little Rock grew up near Hurricane and has seen the area slowly become more popular. He began hunting here as a 10-year old, when his grandfather would pull him in a boat through the woods.

"We'd Indian hunt like that and kill ducks," Wallace said.

As a teenager, Wallace and Wendell Bennett, who farms near Mitchell's Corner, would arrive at 4:30 a.m. and be the first or second vehicle putting in to hunt for the day.

"Now, if you show up at 4:30 a.m., especially on the weekends, the parking lot is filled up," Wallace said.

He estimates that on a typical opening morning as many as 200 vehicles are parked at the launch ramp by 4:30. Competition for hunting places on the oxbows is often so fierce that duck hunters spend the night in their boats.

Before the '96 season, Wallace noticed one hunter in a prime oxbow sitting in a boat crappie fishing a full two days before the season opened. Although he was fishing, his decoys were already spread. The man was working his "shift" among a group of hunters holding the oxbow for opening day.

"Everything is changing," Wallace said. "There used to be a lot more duck-hunting etiquette. People wouldn't put in right on top of you. Right now, it seems that anything goes."

Wallace attributes the changes to new people starting the sport, who don't know any better. He worries what it will be like as these problems grow. But he plans to hunt here always.

"I have so many memories from this place," Wallace said. "When I go down there, I'm a teenager again. You forget about all your business worries, and it's a new day."

Hurricane Lake WMA encompasses 17,000 acres. It was purchased in 1959 by the AGFC from the Woods Lumber Co. Before the purchase, the company used timber from the area primarily to build sewing machines and bodies for cars like the Model T.

To meet its needs, the company cut the best timber in the area. It's a harvest method known as "high-grading."

After a more than 20-year hiatus in timber management, the AGFC began a program in the early 1990s that Akers said should help return the area to its natural state.

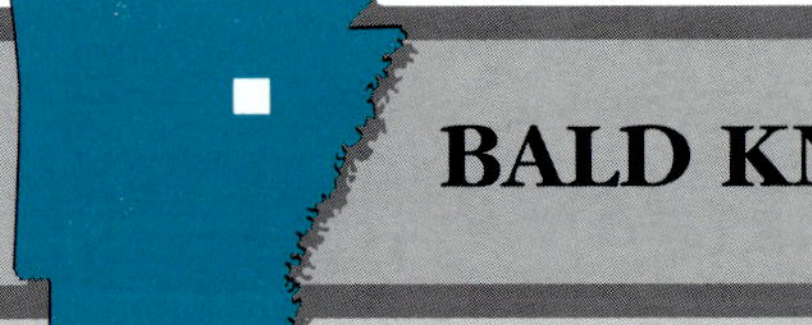

BALD KNOB NWR

Acres: 14,900
First purchase: 1994

The Bald Knob National Wildlife Refuge is one of the more unusual wildlife refuges within the state. The majority of it, 12,000 acres, is agricultural land.

Originally known as the Huntsman Farm, the 12,000 acres was purchased from the John Hancock Insurance Company. An additional 1,800 acres of bottomland timber as well as a few other tracts of land have been added to the refuge since 1994.

The refuge is located in White County, between Bald Knob and the Little Red River. Shaped like the letter "L," its southeastern border meets the Hurricane Lake Wildlife Management Area.

All of the refuge was opened to hunting during the 1997 waterfowl season. Prior to that, it was a rest area for waterfowl. During the 1996 duck season, the agricultural fields, much of which were flooded by backwater from the Little Red River, held large numbers of ducks.

There are some water-control structures on the area, and, according to Dennis Widner, the area manager, there will be others added to allow for flooding of additional acreage.

The refuge is divided into two units — the Farm Unit and the Mingo Creek Unit.

The Mingo Creek Unit is 1,800 acres of overflow bottoms. It gets its name from a creek that flows through the middle of it. The Mingo Creek Unit borders the Little Red River for seven miles.

The Farm Unit is still farmed by cooperative farmers. They grow crops on a share basis. The farmers harvest their share, and leave the USFWS's share standing for wildlife. Crops include rice, soybeans, and milo. Hunting is allowed on most of the refuge, but hunters are required to have a refuge permit available at the Cache River NWR office.

Deer stand duck hunt opens some eyes

Hi-Tech Redneck Club specializes in the unorthodox to assure good hunting

Warren Carpenter enjoys watching the reaction of first-time visitors to the Hi-Tech Redneck Hunt Club.

"You take people out in the dark and strap them in a small lock-on deer stand with 14 feet of water under them and it tends to get their attention," Carpenter said.

The deer-stand hunting is just one unique aspect of the Hi-Tech Redneck Hunt Club, which is actually just a nickname for the Lost Bend Hunt Club.

"We do whatever it takes to make it work," Carpenter said, hence the nickname.

The club really doesn't have a proper name because there is nothing proper about it. It's made up of six men, most of whom were boyhood friends in Searcy.

"We just like to hunt together," Carpenter said. "We get along so well. We don't have any rules. It's not looked at as an investment or used for business. It's just us and friends with no other purpose than to enjoy what we have."

The club started in 1981 when Larry McCall of Searcy got the other members together to buy a 60-acre tract on the White River that was bordered on three sides by Hurricane Lake Wildlife Management Area. McCall's description of the land sold Carpenter over the phone. It was within a quarter-mile from where Carpenter went on his first duck hunt.

This club is like many that have started over the years since the Arkansas Game and Fish Commission first began purchasing land for public duck hunting. Before that, most duck clubs were located on large blocks of private land. That trend has shifted as small groups of hunters are able to buy small tracts that border AGFC wildlife management areas. Without the WMAs, these small private areas couldn't count on good hunting.

"None of us could afford it," Carpenter said. "But we knew we had to do it."

Looking back, Carpenter realizes their timing was perfect. At that time, the reputation of Hurricane Lake WMA was a shadow of what it is today.

"You would tell people you hunted near Searcy and they thought you were crazy," Carpenter said. "They didn't know how good it was. Which was probably a good thing. We couldn't have thought about buying the same type of land near Stuttgart."

The members, who include McCall, Carpenter, Keith Webb, Bobby Reynolds, Wayne Ridout and Art Rand, have to put in at Nemo Landing on the Little Red River, then motor up the White River to get to their land. Shortly after they bought it, one of the members mentioned building a cabin.

"And within the next nine months we had a cabin," Carpenter said. "We worked every Thursday, weekend and holiday until we got it built. Those first years things were kind of crude."

The cabin encloses 1,000 square feet. It's built on stilts six feet high. A recre-

The Hi-Tech Redneck cabin stands six feet high over the White River bottoms near the Hurricane Lake Wildlife Management Area.

David Bell shot the white mallard in Hurricane WMA and had it mounted with a black duck.

White duck had big following in Hurricane

When the group of mallards flew treetop-high over David Bell, one duck in particular caught his eye. He shot, watched the duck fall and thought, "I've killed a little snow goose, or I've killed somebody's pet duck."

When Bell retrieved the duck, he wasn't sure what he'd killed. All but a half-dozen feathers were solid white. The duck's eyes were gray. Everything else looked like a mallard — from its body shape and size to its orange feet and yellow bill.

Bell was hunting in Hurricane Lake Wildlife Management Area with friends from Batesville. As they loaded their boat to go home, another hunter saw the white duck and said, "You got our duck."

He told Bell that several hunters had seen the white duck flying with mallards in Hurricane WMA in previous weeks, and everyone was trying to shoot it. Bell took the white duck to a taxidermist and had it mounted in a display with a black duck.

Said Bell, "I've always told people it was a mallard, and nobody has said, 'Well, you idiot, it is not.'"

Bell is probably right, according to Dr. Jim Johnson, who directs the Cooperative Fish and Wildlife Research Unit on the University of Arkansas campus.

Mallards have successfully crossbred with more than 40 other duck species. The wood duck is the next most successful cross-breeder at 20-plus. Identification problems are common. This ability to hybridize has produced, for example, ducks with the green head of a mallard drake and the long distinctive tail feathers of a pintail drake. Black ducks, mottled ducks and mallards have crossbred to the point they are difficult to distinguish genetically.

According to Johnson, without the pinkish eyes and complete lack of color in the feathers that would distinguish an albino, Bell's duck most likely was the offspring from a "barnyard stopover." A hen mallard may have been bred by a white "domestic" duck on a farm pond.

Johnson noted that these domestic ducks are mallards that have had the color bred out of them. The hen could also have mated with another domestic species, the Muscovy, to produce a nearly-white duck.

Frank Bellrose accumulated 25 years of experience in aerial waterfowl counts while working for the Illinois Natural History Survey. He estimated that one in every 100,000 mallards he saw was solid white and about one in 10,000 was partially white.

ational vehicle generator ran the lights or a water pump but not both. Because it was so loud, the generator was hung in a tree 40 yards behind the cabin. The club eventually had to build a shed with a deck leading from the cabin to the generator, because McCall slipped from the tree and broke his ribs.

"On those cold, frosty mornings, it was kind of slippery climbing the tree to start the generator," Carpenter said.

Today the deck stretches from the bank of the river to the house and back to a generator shack, covering a distance of 100 yards. A diesel/propane generator was added, and now the club can run water and lights at the same time, plus a satellite dish.

It has cell phone service too, by way of a 12-volt hook up running from a truck battery to the cabin. Sometimes the phone works only in one corner of the cabin, and then only if you stand on a chair.

Through the years the club's land has expanded to 260 acres, some in timber, the rest in soybeans.

"We've all got one-sixth of 80 acres of beans," Carpenter said. "We figure all of our expenditures by how many bushels of beans it will cost. We think we're a bunch of farmers."

Carpenter said the only real problem at the club is not having the ability to manipulate water. Lost Bend relies on overflow from the White River.

"Since we've been here there's only been one year when it hasn't flooded at least during some part of the season," Carpenter said.

The problem lies in the extent of the overflow.

"There are days when you can park a Bronco under the cabin," Carpenter said. "And then a few days later you can motor your bass boat up to the deck."

It's those high-water days when visiting duck hunters are often put in treestands — three feet square and 14 feet high. After the initial shock of duck hunting from a deer stand over water, they usually leave thinking the thrill was worth it.

This 1955 AGFC map shows lakes along the White River, including Big Hurricane, which is now part of Hurricane Lake WMA. ▶

Meacham killed ducks to save rice crop

Waterfowl were a menace in days when harvest extended into December

(Editor's note: Wiley Meacham of Brinkley has recorded on audio tape the history of his family and the duck hunting they enjoyed. The tapes were made in Meacham's farm office, which is located within 100 yards of his birthplace and within a half-mile of where most of his hunting takes place. This is an excerpt from his story, in his words.)

Duck hunting has been a passion most of my life. But I started hunting ducks because my father told me to do it. That was around 1940, when I was about 12 years old.

Cotton was our main crop, it brought about $5 a pound. By 1940, we owned about 4,000 acres and my dad decided to try rice farming. About 3,500 acres was bottomland overflow land.

We started clearing land, 60 acres to start, to grow rice. It turned out to be profitable, and each year we added to the 60 acres.

It took about five months for rice to get ready to harvest. We didn't have the combines we have now. You would take what they called a binder and cut the rice. It threw the rice out in a bundle on the ground. Then you would hire people to come along and pick up these bundles, and put five, six or eight of these bundles in what we called a shock. It had to sit there two or three weeks until the sun dried it enough for it to be stored.

By the time the rice got ready to be cut, it was usually October. By the time we were through cutting it and got it shocked, it was usually November, and the weather would be getting bad. A lot of times it would be Christmas or after before we completed the harvest.

The reason it took so long is at times we would be out of the field a week because of bad weather. Even in good weather, it would be noon before you could start the threshing process because the dew and the frost had to dry off it. Because of that, you only got four or five hours of actual harvest time before sundown. So it took forever to harvest a crop.

It was during that same period of time the ducks were coming here. They would come by the thousands. The only place there was water was in this overflow land after a rain. The ducks would land in these rice fields, especially if it had rained and there was some water standing in them, but they would also land in the dry fields.

The ducks would tear down the shocks and they would eat it all. They were worse than a bunch of hogs. You could wind up losing a whole field of rice from the ducks. So someone would have to walk around in the field with a shotgun and shoot to scare the ducks off.

This was during the second World War. Dad gave me a double-barreled LeFever, a bird gun. I didn't know anything about duck hunting and didn't care anything about it.

On weekends and holidays and after school, he would have me get the gun and sit in the fields and shoot to keep the ducks out of there. I was there mornings and afternoons mostly, but

Meacham hunts ducks in more traditional ways today, including hosting groups of dignitaries like these during the 1993 Waterfowl USA Celebrity Hunt. From left, Wiley Meacham, Don Thompson, Steve Wilson, Steve Smith, Rollie Remmel, David Harville and John McDaniels.

sometimes I would stay all day.

After a while I got to wanting to kill them. But the only way to get ammunition was to get an allocation. Because of the war, everything was rationed. So the shells were nearly always No. 8 bird shells

I couldn't kill a duck more than 30 yards away. I'd let them land and crawl a quarter-of-a-mile through the mud to try and kill me one. After a while I got a passion for killing ducks.

It was about this time I got to noticing, especially after rainy weather, all of this shooting going on in the woods where the water was backed up.

Sometimes there would be 30, 40 and 50 shots at a time. The only way I knew to hunt a duck was crawl up on him, I'd never seen a duck caller. Occasionally I could shoot one out of the air.

So this was new to me. I could hear all this shooting, and I could see off in the distance all these ducks flying.

I started wanting to go back there. From home, it was three miles, a mile or two over open fields and the rest through the woods.

A friend and I tried to go back there to see what was going on. We found along this old log road a couple of piles of ducks. I mean there would be 40, 50, 60 ducks in a pile with nothing but their heads pulled off.

It didn't bother me much then, but as I got older it did bother me a lot. What it was, was occasionally people out of Little Rock and Memphis, they would come and hunt ducks. But they would have more ducks than they wanted or could carry out. These people would kill all these ducks, take a few to eat and pull the heads off the rest to show the people back home the good duck hunting they had.

It bothered the local people, because if a duck was killed by a local, it was used for food.

Above, Meacham calls ducks in the same woods he's hunted all his life. Below, in the early years of rice farming, rice was cut with a binding machine and left in bundles on the ground. Farm hands would pile the bundles into shocks, which became an easy target for ducks.

Photo courtesy Riceland Foods Inc.

Wilcox Lake known round the world

Photos taken in 1930s made George Wilcox a highly-sought guide

Albert Wilcox remembers the day his father shot two duck hunters. George Wilcox "had a temper and he could get pretty nasty at times," Albert Wilcox said. Especially when people started messing with his ducks.

This was in the 1930s, and George Wilcox had become renowned worldwide for his duck sanctuary on the White River. The reputation brought with it both good and bad.

In this case, it was two duck hunters wanting to get at the throngs of ducks sitting on Wilcox Lake. To do that, the hunters motored their boat down the White River. Most of the motors used at the time were single-cylinder Fairbanks and Moore engines. When those outboards were slowed and shifted into reverse, they backfired.

"It sounded like a shotgun," Albert Wilcox said.

The noise was just the thing to get a bunch of ducks off the water and winging their way to other duck holes on the White River where hunters waited.

"A couple of guys kept doing it and doing it," Wilcox said. "But (George) stopped them pretty good. He delivered a load of No. 6s to their backsides. They were just lucky he didn't have his rifle, or he might have killed them."

The story provides a glimpse of George Wilcox's nature. Any description would have to start with the title "river rat," the bottomland version of a mountain man. A river rat literally lives off the river and the land around it. George Wilcox did just that, from his houseboat on the White River. But he was also a conservationist, a businessman and an ambassador for Arkansas.

This widely-recognized photograph of Wilcox Lake and the two-page photo on the previous pages were taken in 1928. Both appeared in a *New York Times* photo essay about the lake on Jan. 21, 1934.

What made him all of those things was a lake that went by various names: Wilcox Lake, Little Round Pond and Open Lake. In the 1920s and 1930s, it was the best-known duck hunting lake in the world. It's still well-known, thanks to some popular old photographs of hundreds of thousands of ducks in a cypress-lined lake. Most duck hunters have seen it in restaurants, hardware stores, books, hunting camps or just about anywhere that mentions duck hunting and/or the White River. Despite the popularity of these images, the place and the story behind it have been mostly forgotten.

Wilcox Lake is located on the west side of the White River, upriver from Crockett's Bluff. It is part of the North Unit of the White River National Wildlife Refuge.

When George Wilcox acquired the lake and approximately 2,500 surrounding acres in 1930, it was close to a small town called Mount Adams Landing. Wilcox was born there in 1899, a few years after his mother and father rafted down the Mississippi River and set up a blacksmith shop on the banks of the river.

"How they got here the Lord only knows," said Lynn Christine, Wilcox's daughter, who now owns a fish market in West Helena.

At the time, the land was mostly wilderness. But it suited George Wilcox perfectly. The only time he left was to serve a year with the American Expeditionary Forces in France during World War I. Once back home, he did what he could to live off the land. Wilcox bought and sold timber, fished commercially, trapped and, during duck season, worked as a guide.

Wilcox Lake was the forerunner of Peckerwood Lake near Stuttgart and Claypool's Reservoir near Weiner. In the 1930s, there was very little rice grown outside of the immediate area around Stuttgart, and the twisting, turning White River had yet to make some of the oxbows that are now upstream from Wilcox Lake. There were few reservoirs, and even less land outside of the river valley that held enough water to hold ducks.

For that reason, hundreds of thousands of mallards went to Wilcox Lake every winter. Many people thought Wilcox baited the lake and managed it in other ways to draw ducks.

"You didn't have to do anything," Albert Wilcox said. "There was enough food there for them. They would just come; there were so many of them that you could have knocked down your limit with a club."

"He did everything he could to protect the ducks. We protected everything. We hunted almost all the time, but we didn't waste anything."

And George Wilcox did everything he could to keep them there.

"He never allowed anyone to fire a shot around the lake," said Albert Wilcox, who is now retired in Arizona.

If they did, they might meet the same fate as the two duck hunters with the back-firing boat motor.

"He did everything he could to protect the ducks," Wilcox said. "We protected everything. We hunted almost all the time, but we didn't waste anything. We did what we could to make sure everything was taken care of.

"I might shoot a couple of squirrels for breakfast on just about any morning, but if it was time for squirrels to have their litters we wouldn't shoot them. He insisted on things like that. We were good stewards of the game."

George Wilcox learned there were benefits to being that way. Hunters were willing to pay $10 a day to hunt there, and during the days when the Great Depression still had a strong hold in Arkansas, it was a livelihood that couldn't be passed up.

He was intent on keeping it that way. It didn't matter who you were, you were dealt a heavy hand for messing with the ducks on Wilcox Lake.

For instance, a photo essay on Wilcox in the Dec. 31, 1933, edition of the St. Louis *Post-Dispatch* reported Wilcox "studies the flight habits of the ducks and no less important, the activities of hawks and other enemies. He and his helpers have killed close to five thousand hawks in the last seven years."

An accompanying letter from editor O.R. Bovard advised Wilcox that the reference to the killing of "5,000 hawks and eagles" was edited out with the advice that some people didn't think killing eagles was acceptable. But Wilcox did it anyway, and in many newspapers that practice was well reported.

"Back then it wasn't illegal to kill eagles," Albert Wilcox said.

Killing those birds in itself gave Wilcox notoriety. Christine has boxes of letters from people all over the world who wrote to Wilcox in the 1930s. Most were simply addressed George Wilcox, White River Bottoms. Some were from Native American chiefs, asking Wilcox for the eagle feathers so they could be used to make headdresses. A few, including one written in German and mailed from Berlin, criticized Wilcox for the practice.

"I think it said that one eagle was worth 100 ducks," Albert Wilcox said.

George Wilcox didn't pay them much attention. The ducks were feeding his family, and that was the most important thing.

He used Wilcox Lake as a rest area and hunted around it. South of the lake is Poplar Creek. In the summer, it goes mostly dry. But each fall, Wilcox could dam the lower end and it too would fill with waterfowl.

"He cut shooting lanes in the treetops," Albert Wilcox said. "Then we would get at one end and scare the ducks up. Most would fly toward the Open Lake through the shooting lanes. Some would mill around and settle right back from where they came."

The process produced some unbelievable shooting. In one 1934 newspaper account, 18 men shot 450 mallards in a little over an hour.

"It didn't take long," Albert Wilcox said. "They would get their limits or run out of shells."

In another unusual aspect to the hunting, Wilcox built a blind more than 100 feet high in a bitter pecan tree.

"The year he did that, I got to go to school one day," Albert Wilcox said. "The rest of the time I had to stay at home and

Photos courtesy Lynn Christine

help him get the materials up the tree."

Wilcox had been shooting from trees for years. Albert Wilcox said his father knew many flyways in the bottoms, where he would climb up a tree from his horse's back and shoot ducks.

Wilcox had a Chesapeake Bay retriever that would pile the ducks at the base of the tree.

"That dog would bite the first two ducks' heads completely off, then leave the rest of them alone," Albert Wilcox said.

The dog proved invaluable when shooting took place in the tree blind, where good shots, especially on windy days, were tough to come by in the swaying treetop.

"People loved to do it," Albert Wilcox said.

Shooting from the tree blind added another unique aspect to the hunting. So much so that Joseph Pulitzer insisted on hunting at Wilcox Lake and shooting from the heights of the tree. Others came from all over the country to shoot there as well.

Wilcox's popularity only heightened when the St. Louis *Post-Dispatch* sent a photographer to the lake and recorded the massive numbers of ducks in the photos that are shown everywhere today. The newspaper ran the photos on a Sunday and made them available, for a price, to other newspapers around the country.

"Every major newspaper in the country picked them up," Albert Wilcox said.

Metro-Goldwyn-Mayer Corporation saw the photos and paid Wilcox $500 for the rights to film on his lake. That resulted in a short film that letters indicate was shown in movie theaters all over the country. Some of it was used in *Movietone News*, the news trailers shown before movies at that time. In addition, newspapers in Australia, Italy, Germany and Great Britain ran the photos. Magazines like *Popular Mechanics* and *National Geographic* ran the photos as well.

"It was the first time Arkansas duck hunting was ever publicized on a national, or really, an international scale," Albert Wilcox said.

The result was rich clients for George Wilcox's guiding service who poured in from every corner of the country.

"The biggest part of my education came from hunting with and talking with all those big-money hunters," Albert Wilcox said.

Requests on how to set up similar refuges came from as far away as Chile. Christine's letters indicate that a wealthy Chilean, possibly a dignitary, offered Wilcox a job to set up a bird sanctuary in that country.

"He actually thought about moving over there," Albert Wilcox said.

It might have been the realization that the job would have been almost impossible, or just the fact that there was no place like the wilderness of the White River bottoms.

Wilcox knew the bottoms better than anyone. Almost every meal he ever ate came straight from the bottoms.

Photo courtesy: Lynn Christine

Photographs of George Wilcox and Wilcox Lake appeared in every major newspaper in the country in 1933 and '34. Wilcox was asked to help establish a similar lake in Chile.

"We raised everything there," Albert Wilcox said. "We had a garden. We had fish. We even raised hogs in the bottoms. There's still nothing better than pork raised on acorns."

Ironically, it would be the bottoms that killed George Wilcox. He owned a big black horse that he would ride through the bottoms. He would also hunt on horseback.

During one of those hunts, Wilcox was thrown and hit his head on a tree. He survived, but a metal plate had to be put in his head. As a consequence, Wilcox suffered from occasional seizures. On one horseback trip into the flooded bottoms, he somehow fell from the horse and into the river's current. Christine believes he must have had a seizure while he was in the water.

"We raised everything there. We had a garden. We had fish. We even raised hogs in the bottoms. There's still nothing better than pork raised on acorns."

Wilcox was only 44 years old when he drowned. Soon after, Wilcox Lake began to die, too. Wilcox's wife, Bobbie, leased the lake to several companies until financial problems forced her to sell the land to the Townsend Lumber Co., which later turned the land over to Potlatch Corp.

Wilcox Lake occasionally attracts ducks today. But farming practices and the construction of other reservoirs have changed the ducks' flyway habits.

"They've just spread out, and they've really stopped using this side of the river," Christine said. "It's nothing like it used to be."

But the way it used to be, promoted by a river rat with a lot of business savvy, helped put Arkansas duck hunting on the map.

WHITE RIVER NWR

Total acres: 154,000 acres
South Unit: 101,000 acres
First purchase: 1935
North Unit: 53,000 acres
First purchase: 1992
Topo Maps: Crockett's Bluff, Ethel, Weber, Henrico SW, Turner, Indian Bay SE, Henrico NE, Snow Lake, Yancopin.

The White River National Wildlife Refuge is considered one of the most critical waterfowl wintering areas in the world. Likewise, it is one of the most important waterfowl hunting areas in the state.

In most years the White River is considered the key to holding ducks. The long winding river, once out of its banks, can house hundreds of thousands of mallards, and the current of the river almost always insures open water during bitter cold periods. That is an important benefit when shallow water fields and reservoirs freeze over. Without the open water of the White River, there would not be many places for ducks to rest and feed. The result would be most of the state's population of ducks pushing further south.

The tendency for ducks to head to the White River during cold spells is easily noted during drastic temperature drops. White River hunters testify that you can see an increase in flights of ducks along the river as soon as the thermometer begins to move down.

"It's almost as if they expect the fields to freeze over, and some of the ducks decide they are going to get a jump on the rest," said George Cochran of Hot Springs, who hunts the river once it leaves its banks.

In addition, the importance of the White River can be seen by the habits of mallards during normal years when the river leaves its banks from mid December to late January. Up until the point when the bottoms become flooded, rice fields and green tree impoundments in the Grand Prairie usually have good populations of ducks.

"But you can see them leave and head to the river as soon as it leaves its banks," Cochran said.

Made up primarily of bottomlands with many oxbow lakes interspersed within its boundaries, the refuge offers a variety of hunting opportunities for hunters all over the state. Running from Clarendon in the east-central region of the state to the Mississippi River, it makes up one of the longest-running blocks of protected river bottomland in the Southeast. The only larger National Wildlife Refuge in the Southeast is the Okefenokee Swamp.

The area's size and location in the heart of east Arkansas' prairie region allow hunters to see and work flocks of ducks that number into the hundreds.

"Flight ducks, those huge flights of ducks riding a cold front or a rise in the water, are what the river has over any other area in the state," Cochran said.

The majority of the hunting takes place north of Highway 1 at St. Charles in what is referred to as the North Unit. The majority of this land was acquired in 1992 through a land swap with Potlatch Timber Co. Access to the area is made at several locations, including Clarendon, Preston's Ferry, Maddox Bay, St. Charles. There is also a drive-in area near St. Charles. In addition, there are several primitive ramps along the course of the river.

When the river is out of its banks, classic flooded timber shooting can be found. But most of the shooting takes place in and around one of the oxbow lakes that are primarily on the east side of the river. In dry years the oxbows attract large numbers of ducks, but conditions are often crowded.

The South Unit can be accessed from Jack's Bay and from the Arkansas River Canal near Lake Merrisach. Hunting in the South Unit is allowed only on Tuesday, Thursday, Saturday and Sunday.

A popular hunting spot is 5,000 acres in a dead timber reservoir just off the Canal. The area is usually guaranteed water, since it is flooded by gravity flow from the Arkansas River.

All hunters on the area are required to carry refuge permits available at the White River NWR at St. Charles.

'Flight ducks' are late season bonanza

Hunting gets better in the woods the colder it gets, according to Cochran

The main flock of mallards sailing over the treetops was in a tight formation, while others were scattered and trying to catch up.

The lead hen would bank left, beat her wings a half dozen times, then sail toward a break in the trees before lifting out and making the circle again. Each time the string of ducks behind her mimicked every move.

They were a swarm of ash-colored breasts and brown bodies working an ever decreasing circle, trying to find the right air stream and opening in the trees to break through.

Below, three hunters hugged up against trees surrounding a set of two dozen decoys and softly chuckled out feed calls. Two of the hunters kicked the black water, sending ripples across the open hole, while the other jerked a string tied to three decoys, adding to the movement that more than anything attracted the circling ducks.

The scene is the same almost every day of duck season in Arkansas' flooded timber. But on this day, there was one big difference.

In the early season, a typical flock might include a couple of dozen ducks. The mallards in this scene numbered well into the hundreds.

These are what timber hunters call "flight ducks," large groups of mallards fresh into the state after riding a cold air current from the north.

"When I think about duck hunting, this is what I think about," George Cochran said. "I get excited about opening day, because that's when everything gets underway. But from there the excitement just builds. I can't wait for the later part of the season; that's when things get right. And right means big bunches of ducks making so much noise coming through the trees it makes your heart skip a beat."

◀ Camouflaged amidst the thick woods of the White River National Wildlife Refuge, Dale Singleton calls to passing ducks.

George Cochran (left) and Rob Kilby display the results of a cold-weather duck hunt.

Late season and big flocks of ducks come together. And it's worth the wait.

Cochran, of Hot Springs, is better known as a two-time BASS Masters Classic champion. His status as a professional angler is recognized across the country. But when it's duck season, fish are the last thing on Cochran's mind.

That fact was evident when Cochran won the 1996 BASS Masters Classic. His second Classic victory put him in high demand for appearances at boat and tackle shows across the country, where his presence was worth as much as $2,000 a day.

Rather than cash in on the opportunities, Cochran refused any public appearances during Arkansas' 50-day duck season, choosing to hunt each day in one of the state's public shooting grounds.

Cochran fishes to make money, but he makes money in order to duck hunt.

In many ways, the two sports are related. Some of the knowledge Cochran uses to locate, pattern and catch fish is used to find, pattern and shoot ducks. In some circles, his ability to find ducks in highly-pressured public shooting grounds overshadows his fishing.

That ability is highlighted as the season grows longer. Cold fronts become more predictable, and water, a big factor in duck movements, is usually present in most of the river valleys. Added to those is the vast amount of land available along the major duck flyways of the state. To pattern ducks you have to have a lot of land at your disposal, and in Cochran's case that is thousands of acres of public ground.

"I hunt almost exclusively on public ground," Cochran said. "I like moving around, learning new areas, but most of all, that is what you have to do if you are going to stay with the ducks. Plus, I hunt every day. That keeps me in touch. That's how you stay successful in public ground.

"You can't kill ducks day in, day out, every season by standing beside the same tree every day. You can have some good days, but at some time the ducks are going to leave. If you want to

keep having good days, you have to go with them."

By moving with the ducks during the past 40 years, Cochran has learned much about their habits. At the top of the list is one simple rule — late season is the best season. While excitement peaks during the early days, Cochran marks three periods when duck hunters should be on their toes. All of them occur late in the season.

"Duck hunting is hit or miss until about December 15th," Cochran said. "That is usually about the time we get our first major flights. The second comes around Christmas, and the last sometime during the first or second week of January. And each time duck hunting just gets better and better, especially in timber."

Cochran said water and weather conditions may change those flights some, but those three periods are normally peak times.

These peaks usually occur when rain has filled river valleys and spilled out into stands of timber. Water levels are usually the most important key to finding ducks in the late season. Flights moving from the north are common, and the first places that get hit will be those WMAs along the river valleys. The most important of those are the White, Black and Cache rivers and, on a lesser scale, the St. Francis, L'Anguille and Ouachita rivers and Bayou DeView.

In each of those, Cochran concentrates on the water level.

Foremost will be whether the rivers are rising or falling. When they rise, they flood new cover, opening up what Cochran calls "the candy store." Ducks stay with the rise of water, Cochran said, just like fish will.

"I love to be in Hurricane, Dagmar, or Black Swamp, right after a major cold front when the water is rising or is stable," Cochran said. "You can bet that those big groups of flight ducks will be there. I'm talking hundreds of mallards at one time. That is pure duck hunting at its best."

"If you call a lot, you can forget it. One comeback call, a feed call and kick some water, and then never holler at them again."

Many Arkansas hunters, especially those in the WMAs located along Arkansas' river valleys, have seen these flights. Most often they occur during a few special days, and then are gone. But if you're like Cochran, you can stay with them as they make their way through the state.

"If you eliminate the pressure and the water is stable or rising; then the ducks will stay there," Cochran said. "Once it starts falling, the ducks will leave. If you want to stay with them, you have to follow the river and its rise just like the ducks. They follow the level all the way down, and then start filtering out into the fields.

"Likewise, if the river leaves its banks, the ducks will leave the prairie and go to the river."

Mallards rest on a frozen rice field. Ducks flock to open water in the woods when winter creates ice-covered fields like this one.

While each year is different, some things can be counted on as the water rises. Those areas closest to the river will see the highest degree of change. For that reason, day-to-day changes in water level, as indicated in daily newspapers, can tell you when it's time to change locations.

"But you can count on it; if the water level is stable in the White and Cache rivers, the ducks will be there," Cochran said.

Water can get too high for some areas. The White River, for example, at times rises well above good duck hunting stages. During those times, look to the Cache River, where backwater will start to spread over typically higher ground. Then, too, areas like Dagmar don't flood until the White River is well out of its banks. But when they flood, hunter pressure is typically light until the word gets out.

Bayou Meto WMA adds another factor to consider. It has the benefit of many water control structures and usually remains stable when the rivers are rising and falling.

Although water levels give a good indication of how ducks can be patterned with weather and water conditions, they don't account for the pressure of the constant shooting that takes place as ducks move along the river.

"Pressure moves ducks as much as anything else," Cochran said. "And if more hunters would learn not to exert as much pressure on the ducks, they would stick in an area much longer."

Late-season ducks have typically run the gauntlet. They have heard the best and worst of calling, and survived the best and worst of shooting. By the time they get to Arkansas, they are educated. As they learn, they start to change habits. Many duck hunters fail to change with them.

Knowing how to approach late-season ducks can mean the difference between success and failure.

Cochran uses a fishing analogy to explain hunting pressure. He believes ducks loaded up in a 100-acre tract of a WMA are a lot like fish loaded up in a cove.

"If I go into that cove and catch everything I can, then I won't have the fish to last me over the course of a tournament," Cochran said. "But if I go in there and catch a limit and then leave, I will be able to come back every day for many days to get a limit."

Fish feel the pressure from getting caught. Ducks feel it from getting shot at, even though shooting is a common occurrence all the way down the flyway. The pressure that Cochran means is the type of pressure that can actually run ducks out of the area.

"It never fails to happen: a large group of ducks is occupying 100 acres of flooded timber," Cochran said. "I find them and for a day or two, I hunt the edge of where those ducks are wanting to be. And every day I kill my limit. But then somebody else find those ducks, and they can't stand it. They have to run in the middle of them with their boat, or set up right where the ducks want to be, and all of the sudden the pressure has multiplied so much they leave.

"That's when I move, too. But if people would realize that the hunting can be just as good for a longer period of time by staying on that edge, they could have much better duck hunting."

Other changes in pressure can make a day more productive as well. The most common mistake is calling too much. The call is usually the most obvious clue to a duck that things are not right in the woods.

"Most people who hunt public land, go in, hunt until 9 or 10 o'clock and then leave," Cochran said. "But if they would spend more time in the woods, they would learn a lot about ducks.

"One of the first things you realize when you are slipping through the woods is that ducks are not as loud and boisterous as they were during the early part of the year. You don't hear a lot of calling once the hunters have left the woods. If the ducks are there, you can slip through the woods, and if you do it quietly enough, you might see 500 mallards. Of those, 250 will be sleeping on logs, and the others will be playing or chasing hens.

"They really don't feed much in the woods; of 1,080 ducks we killed in 1996, about 80 of them had acorns in their craw, and they were wood ducks. Ducks are like us; they eat in the kitchen and that is the fields, but the woods are the living room where they sit back and relax."

In the woods, Cochran said every once in awhile, you might hear the lonesome quack, quack of a hen. But for the most part, the woods will be free of loud duck noises.

Early in the year, a lot of calling works because ducks can't see through the canopy of trees as well, and they are listening more than looking for ducks.

"But late in the season these ducks get smart," Cochran said. "If you call a lot, you can forget it.

"One comeback call, a feed call and kick some water, and then never holler at them again."

Cochran said late in the year it is best to use more decoys, along with a jerk string and stay away from calling.

It is another example of Cochran's late-season approach.

"Being successful means breaking habits," Cochran said. "Stop calling, pay closer attention to the water, and, above all else, be ready to move. A mobile duck hunter is a successful duck hunter."

Larry McCall, Keith Webb, Bobby Reynolds and Warren Carpenter look for the large flocks of mallards they have come to expect when winter cold fronts enter the state.

Leading ducks into decoys on a string

Jerk strings are a simple way to make decoy spreads look convincing

Every duck hunter has seen it some time during the course of the season. Flocks of mallards circle a decoy spread once, twice, three times, dipping at intervals and almost locking up before lifting off and leaving sight.

The immediate reaction is a look around to see what spooked them. At times the accusatory finger is pointed at a hunter more intent on watching the show in the air than staying hidden. Others blame the caller, the location, decoys set in a wrong pattern, or someone who moved. The list runs the gamut.

There are many reasons a flock of ducks spooks from a spread of decoys. But the decision to go elsewhere can most often be blamed on a lack of realism.

As much as every duck hunter would like to believe his calling is enough to convince ducks the water below is full of lovesick hens and a buffet of acorns or rice, in reality, the best of calling is useless if the whole picture doesn't pass muster for just one lead duck.

As ducks come down the flyways they are greeted by all types of danger, including the well-equipped hunter who sounds as good, and in some cases better, than a real duck.

When ducks respond to calling and are met with shotgun blasts, they quickly learn to avoid similar mistakes. That education includes relying on all their senses, especially sight.

As a whole, duck hunters assume spreads of life-like decoys sitting on the water and adequate calling are enough to bring in wary ducks. But they forget what the duck is really looking for.

"Ducks look for movement," said George Cochran.

As strange as it sounds for a segment of hunters who go out of their way to remain motionless, that statement comes from years of experience hunting ducks in highly-pressured shooting grounds.

Cochran, a professional bass fisherman who suspends his fishing time to hunt every day of the duck season in

Photo courtesy Gregg Patterson

George Cochran uses some of the same philosophy to hunt ducks as he does to catch fish.

the public shooting grounds, utilizes movement to kill more ducks.

"Early in the season, ducks that are flying over are listening for the sounds of other ducks," Cochran said. "Safety is in numbers, and that's where calling attracts them. But after a few days of being shot at, they get smart. You can get their attention with a call, but after that you better shut up and start being a little more convincing with the overall picture."

Even when most of a flock is resting, some ducks will be moving, according to Cochran.

Cochran has spent many days in the flooded timber of Arkansas' WMAs. And he has watched ducks rafted in flooded fields. In each case, movement is constant, and most of the time calling is at a minimum.

"If there are 500 ducks sitting on the water, 150 will be asleep; the rest will be split between feeding and chasing hens," Cochran said. "It's constant activity."

But when duck hunters toss out decoys, unless the wind is blowing, action in the spread comes nowhere close to resembling the real thing. Movement can make a big difference, a fact that the sporting goods industry has taken advantage of.

In the past few years, products that shake and move to produce ripples across the water have been common. In addition, other items that attach to decoys to impart movement or make splashes are available. They all work to some degree.

More enterprising hunters, especially those who hunt from a fixed-blind position, use 12-volt trolling motors to send constant wave action through a spread. And then there are those who simply kick water.

One of the most effective tools to put movement in a spread is a jerk string.

"There is probably no better duck call than a good jerk string," said Buck Gardner, 1995 Champion of Champion and 1994 World's Champion duck caller, who markets Rich-N-Tone duck calls.

Cochran agrees with the summation. The jerk string is an ever-present part of his decoy spreads. Its use is simple.

Cochran ties a bungee cord to a tree trunk on one side of the duck hole. On the other end of the cord he ties a mallard hen decoy and a few feet down the line attaches a drake decoy. From the drake decoy, Cochran attaches a nylon string and runs it to the opposite side of the duck hole, stretching the string tight.

"Many times, when they see this, they lock up and fall right in. It's really effective."

"When the ducks are working and can see the decoys, I release the cord so the hen and drake are pulled quickly across the hole," Cochran said. "Then they hit the end of the cord and bob around on the surface.

"I think this looks like the drake is trying to catch the hen to mate with her. This really tears those circling ducks up. Many times, when they see this, they lock up and fall right in. It's really effective."

The realistic presentation of ducks, not only moving but participating in a mating ritual, is more convincing than the best of calling. When it comes to getting ducks through the treetops or past that invisible barrier over a rice field, calling them in on a string can be the best thing.

Red legs indication of hormone change, rather than new ducks

You don't have to hunt ducks long before you hear a standard yarn about red legs on mallards. The words usually come from a hunter examining several bagged birds. Especially late in the season, the legs and feet of one duck may be more brightly colored than the others. They appear more red than orange.

"Look here at the red legs on this one," a hunter will say. "We must be getting some new ducks."

The theory is these red-legged ducks have come from the more frigid north, thus the red legs. Or they have not been here long enough to spend much time in the rice and soybean fields of east Arkansas, and their normally red legs have not been discolored by the muddy water.

An inspection of the legs is common in dry years that lack cold fronts. Those years leave many hunters working the same flocks of ducks each day. Educated ducks are hard to hunt, and many hunters begin looking forward to better days.

When a red-legged duck shows up, it is a cause for a celebration of sorts since it is looked upon as a sign of new, less-educated ducks coming down the flyway.

In reality, the color of a duck's legs has nothing to do with the time spent in any region of the country or where the duck has been during the migration. A mallard that has been in the state for months, spending every hour in a muddy field, will eventually have red legs.

The color of the legs is a direct result of hormones and how far along the ducks are in the breeding stage. Leg colors normally go hand in hand with the plumage of a mallard drake's green head and its greenish-yellow bill, which also start becoming more brilliant during the late season.

If deer were migratory, we might say the same thing about the hardening of their antlers and the rubbing that takes place along with that stage of breeding. But we see them day to day, and we know these characteristics have nothing to do with migration.

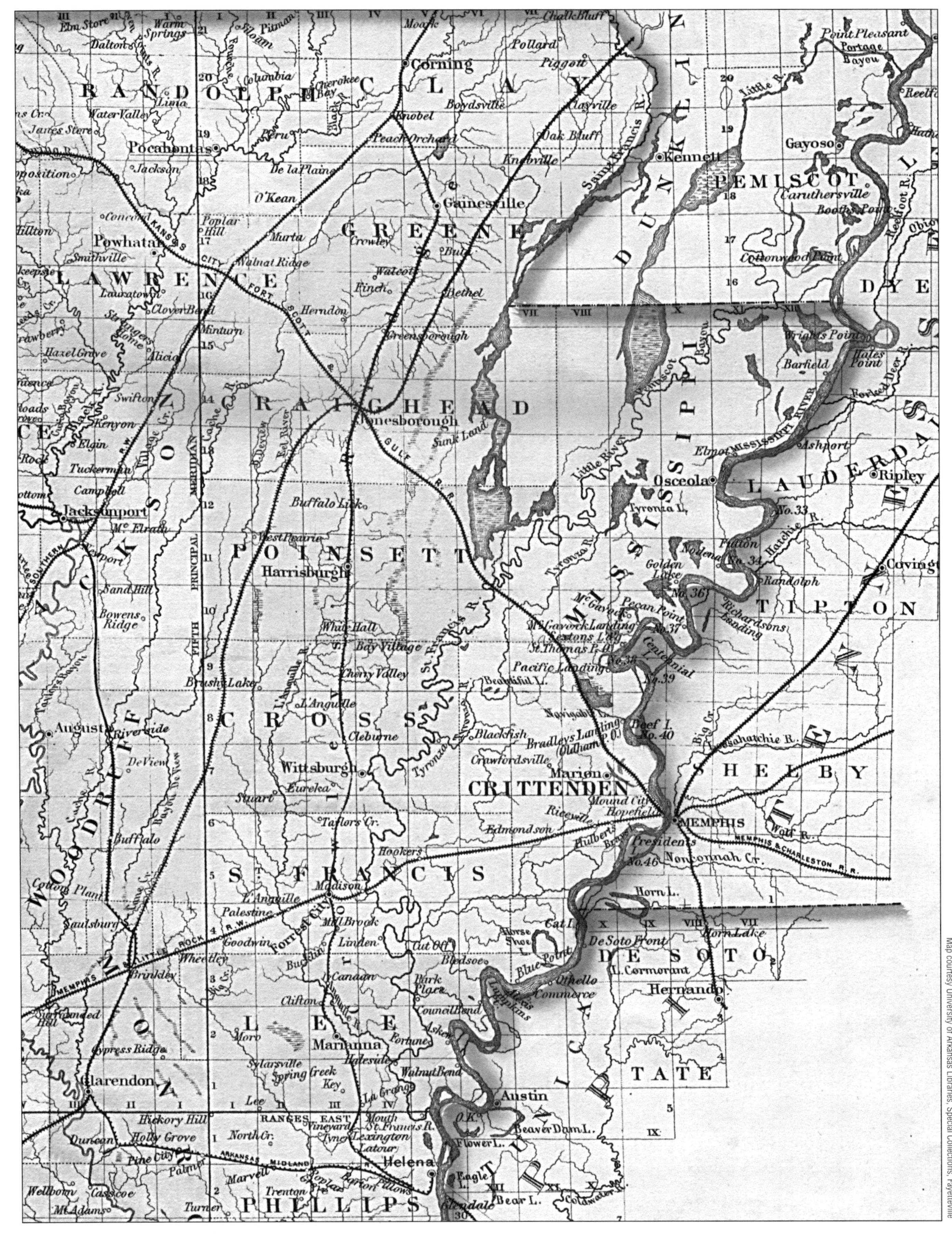

Map courtesy University of Arkansas Libraries, Special Collections, Fayetteville

A White River cabin-boat trip in 1892

Railroads, rivers transported hunters into sportsman's paradise of Arkansas

(Editor's note: In 1893, the Missouri Pacific Railway Company printed a complimentary booklet entitled "Ideal Hunting and Fishing Grounds," which provided a sportsman's opportunities along the "Iron Mountain Route" in Missouri, Arkansas and Louisiana. The booklet included depot-by-depot details and how best to take advantage of them. One recommended method, once you had taken the train to the "jumping off point" of your choice, was the cabin boat. The following is a description of a White River cabin-boat trip, as it appeared in the railway booklet.)

A third plan of procedure is to build a cabin-boat near the headwaters of one of the streams and float downward with the current, finding something of interest to the sportsman in every mile of its course. A skiff or large canoe is sometimes used in place of the larger craft, accomplishing a longer distance in a specified time, but entailing more of a hardship and exposure upon the voyagers. The size of a cabin-boat is only limited by the width of the smaller streams in which it is to be used, or by the amount of money set apart for its purchase or construction, and its cost is comparatively small compared with the advantages of a floating camp of ample size to furnish living and sleeping room for three or four men. With such a craft the choicest of hunting and fishing grounds can be reached, and as the fall rains flood the low grounds, forcing out the deer from their summer range, the creeks and bayous afford splendid cruising grounds, with assurance of a rich harvest on the outlying cane ridge now transformed into miniature islands, each with its four-footed Crusoes awaiting the subsidence of the floods.

In this connection it will, perhaps, be interesting to read the account of a

DUCK SHOOTING IN ARKANSAS.
St. Louis, Iron Mountain & Southern Railway.

THE GREAT IRON MOUNTAIN ROUTE

Runs Through the Famous Hunting and Fishing Grounds of Arkansas. No State offers a larger variety of Game.

H. C. TOWNSEND,
General Passenger and Ticket Agent
ST. LOUIS, MO.

This 1884 railroad map illustrates how hunters and anglers could use the rails to gain access to a "sportsman's paradise."

cabin-boat trip down White River, undertaken and accomplished in the autumn of 1892, by two sportsmen from a Northern State. The particulars, as given, were originally prepared by one of the gentlemen for publication in a sportsmen's journal, from memoranda jotted down on the "voyage," and may be accepted as mirroring with remarkable fidelity the everyday occurrences of a delightful trip:

Allan had started southward on the morning of October 28, and three days later I followed expecting to join him at Little Rock. My train into St. Louis was a few minutes late, and I had scarcely time left for purchasing my ticket over the Iron Mountain Route and attending to my baggage, if I hoped to get away on the "cannon ball," due to depart at 8:20 p.m., but by dint of a good deal of rushing, I managed all right, saw everything stowed in the baggage car and my Irish setter securely tied to the biggest trunk, and was climbing into the smoker when a thought suddenly struck me. Allan had proposed wiring me at St. Louis of any change of plan. Possibly I had been a bit neglectful in not inquiring for a telegram at once.

A rush to the Western Union's room; a rush back to the smoker, and then the train was under motion, threading its way through a net work of switches and among hundreds of locomotives, coaches, box cars and flats, tacking westward in search of room to swing its ponderous length and bear away towards the equator, with a clear track and the world before it. I had found a telegram — and, luckily it was prepaid, for I would have had no time for making change. Tearing it open I read as follows:

"To Frank S., Union Depot, St. Louis, Mo.:

Stop at Newport. Have got a sure thing worth millions.

Allan D."

This was highly encouraging, though somewhat vague; but nevertheless, I was glad to learn that there was even a prospect of sport ahead. I consulted my folder and found that Newport was on the main line, at or near the crossing of White river, and eighty-five miles north of Little Rock, then, my mind satisfied on this point, I lighted my cigar and puffed complacently until the conductor came along after my ticket, when I acquainted him with the change in my destination and requested him to share the information furnished with the monarch of the baggage car. After this I felt entitled to a bit of intelligence in return, and, as it happened, the conductor was able and willing to answer in a very few words the half-dozen queries that I propounded.

"Yes; good place to stop off. Hunting everywhere. All sorts of game, from bear to snowbirds. Go up towards Batesville if you want quail — see you've — got a fine dog in the baggage car. Better hunt deer, though; there's more fun in it. Next — Ticket, please."

Duck Shooting

There is no better duck shooting in United States than lower White River Bottom. Excellent for Mallard Ducks. Game can be sent to any place in U. S. Terms very reasonable. Season November, December and January.

Address all communications to

Kleinschmidt Bros., Duck Hunting Lodge

621 East 16th St. Little Rock, Ark.

I smoked some more, inventoried my fellow passengers and found a fair sprinkling of sportsmen — incipient or pronounced — but none from Arkansas; bought a paper from the newsboy and read the special telegrams; smoked again and then went back to the sleeper and took a nap that lasted till the porter aroused me at five o'clock with the information that Newport was only thirty minutes away.

It was not yet day when we slowed up at the depot, but Allan was on hand, and, early as was the hour, he had a drayman ready to take my baggage as soon as it touched the platform.

"Where's Pat; did you bring him?"

"He's in the baggage car. How's the pup?"

"Square as a barrel-hoop. Here, you fellow, look lively there and get the trunk over. There, I'll lead the dog and take your gun. Bring your grip in your hand."

"How far's the hotel?"

"Hotel, nothing; it's a country residence, and we're sole proprietors, come on — right across the track."

The drayman drove away to a street crossing farther down, but we simply lugged our loads across a half-dozen tracks, dodged between some freight cars, stumbled a few yards over a soft, yielding turf, and then found ourselves on the bank of a big river, the farther side of which was obscured in the gloom. Below us I could see the gleam of flowing water, and a dark blotch that looked like the roof of a house with a glow of ruby-colored firelight showing through a foot square window.

"Hello, Bud! Lend a hand with this luggage, will you? The bank is a bit steep for us greenhorns."

It was a "bit steep" — if straight up and down is "steep" — and how the two trunks were lowered down that twenty foot bluff I never learned. Their weight would have carried them down, no doubt, but there were no indications that they had been roughly handled, and the contents of both were found intact when I opened them two hours later. Of my own descent I shall say nothing, save that it was accomplished with all due celerity, and that the momentum I acquired carried me over a short gang plank, through a narrow doorway, and almost over a small kitchen stove that was unexpectedly encountered. I don't think the stove was injured in the collision, for it stood sufficiently rigid to repel my charge, but it was certainly the warmest stove for its size and looks that I ever saw.

I stumbled over to a folding cot and sat down to collect my scattered thoughts, while Allan busied himself collecting the scattered contents of my grip, which had suffered much more than its owner. A small brass lamp was burning dimly on a rude table in one corner of the little room but its light was insufficient, so Allan struck a match and ignited the wick of a campaign torch swinging by a wire from the ceiling. Then I had an opportunity for looking around but could gather no satisfactory knowledge for the scrutiny.

"Cabin-boat," said Allan, replying to my look of inquiry. "She's small, but I think she'll answer. Twenty feet long, over all. Twelve foot beam. Cabin, twelve by twelve."

So this was a cabin-boat — and it was twelve feet square, and twenty feet long the other way. In an ordinary state of mind I might have understood all this; but just now I was slightly rattled.

"It was a happy thought of mine — don't you think so? I just stopped off here a minute to look around and the first thing I saw was the 'Palace.' That's her name, you know."

I was growing more and more mystified. Leaving my seat on the cot I opened the door and attempted to pass out, but paused at the threshold. In front of me, and seemingly on every side, there was water. Beyond the doorway the bow of the boat extended a scant four feet, nothing but a platform without bulwarks, a stout pin, to serve as a row lock on either side, while the long oars hung on hooks over the door. It was daylight now, and I could see that, in the short time that had passed since my embarkation, the boat had cast loose from the shore and swung into midstream, heading downward. On the left bank were the white walled houses of Newport; on the right a thin fringe of willows and sycamore; beyond them an opening which might be a cultivated field or a swampy lake, I could not tell which. My two trunks were on the boat's bow — extremely close to the edge it seemed to me; Pat, the Irish setter, still chained, crowded between them. In the water, dead ahead, floated a tree trunk with one ragged limb that threatened to rake dog and trunks from the boat. I made a step forward with some hazy idea of averting the catastrophe, but just then the craft on which I stood swung sharply to the right, passing the obstruction without touching.

"Who's steering this ark?" I inquired of Allan, who had joined me.

"Bud, the former owner of the Palace. He is a fisherman and a trapper; one of the three who built the boat on upper Black river, intending to spend the winter in the woods. They reached Newport all right, and then the other two went on a spree, and, as a result, are locked up on a charge of attempt to kill, which will insure them warm quarters until the spring term of court. I bought the craft of Bud for twenty dollars, and for twenty more he is to stay with us till our hunt is over."

We went back into the diminutive cabin and called Bud to join us. He was typical backwoodsman, tall and lank, with a straw colored beard that clung closely to his lantern jaws, and spread, in a thin fringe, over the breast of his black overshirt. His age neither of us ever attempted to guess, but he was certainly past middle age, and though his strength was considerable his movements were commonly slower than those of many an octogenarian. He shook hands cordially, spoke flatteringly of the "purty dorg" I had brought on board with me, examined my hammerless Greener and commented on the "sure enuff wire barrels," and then busied himself in the preparation of breakfast, while Allan and I got my trunks inside, and took Pat back to the dry goods box, at the stern, which he was to share in company with Allan's "Pup," a foxhound of uncertain age but many accomplishments.

Then we unpacked my trunks, throwing the blankets and pillows together in a corner, arranged our ammunition on a shelf over our bunk — Bud was to sleep on the cot or the floor as he liked — put our guns together and declared ourselves ready for business.

Meanwhile the boat had been floating at will with the current, broadside and stern on, and often as in the proper way, but Bud was keeping a weather eye open and if danger threatened from contact with either shore or a floating log, a powerful sweep of the single steering oar would set us right again without delay. At length, after a glance ahead, our "man Friday" informed us that a "hull passel" of ducks were floating close to the right shore and that we were fast nearing them. Here was a chance for a first shot at Arkansian game. A hasty inspection verified Bud's intelligence. The ducks were certainly there and if there was not a "hull passel" there must have been at least a half of one.

"Mallards," muttered Allan. "Let her float on, till they rise; then pick your bird and make a sure shot."

We waited, and floated, but the ducks did not rise. Perhaps they thought our craft was a "runaway" without crew or pilot; at all events, they just sidled out of our way a bit with the evident intention of letting us pass. But just as we were even we sprang into view with a yell that put a hundred wings in instant motion and our first barrels rang out together. I won't know how many ducks fell, for the number of those down were augmented next instant by a second harvest from the demoralized flock, but there were ten plump mallards to retrieve when the smoke had cleared. Bud gathered them in with the aid of a canvas boat that lay, already stretched, on the sloping roof of our cabin; and as Allan and I piled the victims of our bloodthirstiness together in a heap on the floor we registered a vow to shoot no more ducks until the day before our return homeward, and I am glad to say that we kept to our resolutions in spite of temptations such as

On Board The Houseboat

WALTER ADAMS

We have one week in which we can take care of a few individual guests. A great many of you have written me saying you could not get up a full party of at least ten members, so here's your chance. Exclusive Shooting Privileges on 25,000 Acres. The greatest Mallard Duck Shooting in America. Rate $125.00 each per week.

J. A. WILKIN Watson, Ark.

few gunners are ever called upon to resist.

"We're gittin' clus ter ther railroad bridge," said Bud a few minutes later. "There's good quail shootin, in a big field on ther right. Ef you'l take that bird dorg of yourn in that field you'll kill a bushel in an hour." I looked at Allan inquiringly, but he shook his head.

"We're not here to exterminate all the small game in the country," he said, "big game is what we're after, and outside of killing a few squirrels or birds for our own use, we'll stick to big game exclusively. Just now our larder is pretty plentifully supplied with fresh meat" — with a glance at the pile of mallards — "and I favor letting the quails slide." And so they slid.

That night we tied up our boat in an eddy at the mouth of a dry slough, undoubtedly quite a river itself in a time of high water. We had floated a great many miles during the day, but the river's bends were many and sharp and it seemed to us that our actual progress had been but small. Bud assured us that there was game in the vicinity, and so, more to please him than for any other reason, we landed and made a short detour through the woods.

It was certainly a wild looking locality. Along the river's bank there was a growth of low ash, elm and hackberry trees, with here and there a giant gum or cottonwood; then we came to a narrow ridge thickly grown with cane, some of it shoulder high, and, in places, matted into a dense tangle with briars and vines. Beyond we could see the lofty trunks and brown red foliage of a line of cypress trees and we struggled on until we stood in semi-gloom beneath them at the verge of a narrow mud-margined lake.

The sun was down, but enough of daylight remained to permit us to examine the footprints, marking the soft earth on every hand, but our ignorance of woodcraft prevented us from gleaning half the significance of the tell-tale marks. There were squirrel tracks everywhere — we had hunted squirrels before and recognized those at a glance. Then there were other tracks of the same size, but rounder and deeper; others longer and resembling the print of a baby's foot, except that the marks of long claws were plainly evident. "Minks and coons," remarked Allan sagely. "I once lived on a farm in Michigan where such animals were common. Here's a new one on me, though — unless it's an otter; and here's another that might be a wildcat, judging from its size and shape. It's all guess work with me, but I'll bet I'm not far from the truth."

By this time I had made a discovery of more importance and I was not long in making the fact known. A bear had walked along the water's edge, in the soft mud. There was no disputing the fact for the marks of the great paws could be distinguished easily. Bruin had entered the water, presumably to drink, then waded alone for a distance and returned to the cane, heading towards the river. The tracks were not particularly fresh but the fact of their existence was quite enough for us. Further on the discovery was duplicated, and as there was a noticeable difference in the size of the tracks our spirits rose still higher. There was certainly two bears in the vicinity — or there had been within the past forty-eight hours.

"We'll look for them in the morning," said Allan as we turned away. "It's too late to find 'em to-night."

"Lucky for us that it is," I replied, "for we haven't a charge of buckshot with us."

It was a fact. In Bud's anxiety to drive us ashore he had hurried us out with nothing in the way of ammunition save the shells in our guns. Four loads of duck shot in a range where bears were as plentiful as flies in August.

We again pushed our way across the cane ridge, but the forest of "fish poles" seemed taller than before, and we were longer in reaching the farther side. At length we burst forth into an opening but it was only a narrow one; a sort of dry slough, with the cane beyond higher and thicker than ever.

"We've missed our way a little," remarked my friend. "Suppose we follow this slough, it is easier walking and must lead us to the river."

We turned to the right, made a dozen steps in the direction indicated, and then something happened. In the midst of the rattle of flying hoofs and breaking cane four shots rang out in quick succession, and we stood in mortified silence looking blankly in each other's faces. I was the first to speak.

"It was a big buck. I saw his horns."

"And we shot him with chilled sixes," replied Allan. "Let's go back to the boat."

That was our first shots at deer, and it was two days before another opportunity of the kind was granted us. We were both willing and anxious to tie up at that particular landing for a month, or until we had loaded the boat with venison and bear meat; but Bud, in his superior wisdom, willed that it should be otherwise. He admitted that there was some game in the vicinity, but not enough to "fool" with. It would pay us to drop farther down the river where the bottoms were wider and big game more plentiful. So we floated on, occasionally landing to kill a squirrel or two — for we had given our ducks to a trapper who had passed by, going up the river in a dugout. The canvas boat was kept floating at the stern and proved very handy on many occasions, particularly when we wished to make a landing to inspect marks on the shores that our keen-eyed boatman suspicioned of being deer or bear tracks. A half-dozen times we found spots that seemed, from all indications, to promise favorable for sport, but Bud was intractable and doggedly kept our craft in mid-stream, aiding the current at times with the long bow oars.

"No use stoppin' afore we reach Ergusty," he would say. "Thar's some game along hyar, but we'uns want a heap of it."

At length, Augusta was reached, and as we passed under the bridge of the Memphis Branch, we both heaved sighs of relief. We were a mile or two ahead of the cabin-boat at this point, trolling from the canvas boat for big mouth black bass and catching a good many more than we cared to keep; but the river had a renewed interest for us now and we dropped our rods and pulled on rapidly; leaving the town behind and getting again where brakes of blue-stemmed cane lined the shores on either side and no sound reached our ears save the harsh chatter of a million woodpeckers, fluttering from tree to

This group of hunters traveled down the Mississippi River and up the St. Francis River on a steamboat in 1885.

tree, the bark of an impudent gray squirrel, or a musical outburst from a passing choir of blackbirds.

We had but one firearm with us in the boat, a 45-90 Winchester, taken along expressly for killing the bears that might be found swimming the river. Possibly, we might have killed a bear in this way by patrolling the river from early youth to extreme old age, though the chances would have been against us after all; but we were over sanguine at the time and in our extreme watchfulness narrowly escaped shooting a black sow of the "razorback" type that was contentedly hunting mussels and crawfish beneath the bank in the shallow water.

Pulling on until we fancied ourselves as far as Bud could drift by midday, we landed on a sandbar, lifted our boat out and tilted it end wise against a log so that our guide could not pass without detecting it. Then we sallied forth in search of adventures, bearing directly away from the river through the open bottom — for there are broad belts of open oak woods interspersed between the cane brakes and lakes and we had accidentally struck one of these clear strips, locally known as "overcup glades" from the overcup oaks that constitute their principal timber growth.

The earth was hard and dry, for it was yet too early for the fall rains and not even a respectable shower had fallen for weeks. A good many deer tracks could be found, but they were all very old. If a deer had passed that way within a week or ten days the closest of scrutiny failed to find evidence of the fact. Yet there were deer — lots of em — as we afterwards found, in this very range that we had stumbled upon by the merest chance, and it was not many minutes before we had ocular proof of their existence.

Without the slightest warning, a deer stood before us in the open glade and not a hundred yards distant. He may have been lying down and arose at the sound of our approach, or he might easily have been feeding there in plain sight of us both for several moments before we saw him, for we were walking with extreme caution and there were but very few fallen leaves to rustle beneath our feet. However, we did not stop long to speculate on how the deer got in his present position. The fact that he was there was quite enough knowledge for one dose. We were content to accept matters as they stood and ask no questions.

When the hero of a dime novel draws a head on big game of any kind, the rifle barrel "trembles and wavers for an instant and then becomes rigid as a bar of steel." The barrel of my 45-90 was exactly as "rigid" as the aforesaid steel bar, but after it "wavered for an instant" it began wabbling and describing eccentric circles, making wheels, as it were, of which the deer constituted the hub. I dropped my arm, drew a long breath and then tried it again, but with no better results.

"Shoot, you idiot!" whispered Allan fiercely. "He's going to run."

That decided me on the proper course to pursue. I pulled the trigger, and, sure enough, the deer ran, just as my friend had prophesied. I had expected to see a fair rate of speed exhibited by a frightened deer, but this one managed to exceed my expectations. I emptied the magazine of my repeater as he ran — it had a short magazine holding only five cartridges — but when our game passed out of sight, around the end of a mudhole thickly grown with elbow brush, he was traveling as briskly as ever.

I expected that Allan would comment on my poor marksmanship, but he had nothing to say. Instead he offered to carry the now empty rifle and there was a certain peculiar twinkle in his eye that made me suspicion the friendliness of his thoughts. Was it possible that he was hugging himself over my ill-luck and looking ahead to the time when the first deer should be slain, and by his own unerring hand. I believe it was this thought more than any hope of having touched the deer that prompted me to follow on and look for signs that my shot or shots had taken effect.

There was no blood where the game had stood when first discovered. A few hairs were scattered among the fallen leaves but Allen suggested that they had been rubbed off against a tree as the deer turned. Further on we found where one of my bullets had entered a persimmon sapling eight feet from the ground.

"Shooting too high," I said. "I have heard that that is a common occurrence with inexperienced shots."

Allan said nothing, but pointed to a long furrow plowed in the earth a few yards beyond. I thought of accounting of this low shot by the fact that I had not raised my sights but as it was made at point blank range — if there is such a thing — I concluded to hold my peace, and I was glad I did so when, on going around the pond we stumbled on the deer lying dead, with a bullet through the ribs from side to side and another bullet hole in the left flank, ranging forward and lodging against the shoulder. This must have been from my last shot, for from the course my game had run I could not have struck it in the left side with any of the previous ones.

I don't know how many ducks fell, for the number of those down were augmented by a second harvest...but there were ten plump mallards to retrieve when the smoke had cleared.

It was a fair sized buck, but in my excitement I could have carried it to the river bank without assistance. I suppose we should have dressed it on the spot but our ideas of the operation were vague and so we carried it as it was and tumbled it down on the sand bar beside our boat just as the Palace "hove in sight" around the bend above. We had killed our first deer and felt reasonably proud of our achievement, though Bud persisted in speaking of "that little ol' deer you'uns happened ter hit," just as though the killing was an accident and the game itself so small as to be beneath the notice of a true sportsman.

It would be useless to relate all the incidents of the next few days. Before the week was out Allan and I had each two deer to our credit. We might have made a better score, perhaps but for one circumstance that weighed heavily against us. In driving his bargain with Bud, before my arrival, Allan had foolishly allowed our guide the privilege of setting and attending to a few traps as a means of increasing his earnings, and we more than suspicioned that, in selecting our stopping places, Bud was guided more by the amount of "coon sign" visible than by the probability of big game being found in the neighborhood. More than once I consulted Allan as to the practicability of making a new trade with the "rights and privileges" left out, but we both shrank from broaching the subject to the "party of the second part." Bud was a trapper, dyed in the wool, and if we had hinted at hanging up his traps for the season he would certainly have thrown up his important position on board the Palace and mapped out a campaign in which we would have had no part. So we held our peace and hunted with unabated vigor, while Bud's store of furs increased daily, and the cabin of our craft grew almost uninhabitable from the pervading odor of musky mink and malodorous polecat.

About three days was the limit of our stay in any one place, just time enough to get practically acquainted with the lay of the surrounding country. In one place — it was where the cut-off from Seven Mile lake entered the river — our halt was extended to a week, for game and fur both were abundant. At this point I killed four turkeys out of a flock of twenty or thirty, and Allan shot three deer, only one of which he secured. The others were badly wounded but escaped into the thick cane where without dogs it is impossible to follow them.

We passed Des Arc and DeValls Bluff, two towns of considerable local importance. At the place last mentioned we layover a couple of days while awaiting a renewed supply of provisions and other necessaries, ordered from

Little Rock; but our time was not lost, for some of the planters in the neighborhood invited us out to their farms for quail shooting, giving Pat a chance to show the sort of work of which he was capable. We found the birds extremely plentiful and so tame that they would hardly flush until fairly kicked out of the grass. The only drawback, that could be called such, was the extreme rankness of vegetation, which rendered it difficult at times to keep our dog in sight; but Pat worked tirelessly, in spite of the burrs and briars encountered at every turn, winning the good opinion of all.

So far, Allan's hound, which answered to the plain and unadorned name, Pup, had signally failed to distinguish himself in any way, mode or manner. Once he had been started after a wounded deer, and ran merrily until he discovered a hollow log containing a wildcat. Then the pursuit was changed to a siege; but when the cat was smoked out of its retreat and made a rush for free air and less restricted quarters, Pup's grit failed him, and the expected fight ended with the first round. Pup went one way and the wildcat another, until overtaken by a load of buckshot.

Our last week was spent at a point which possessed sufficient attraction to the over-particular Bud to make him concur in our desire to linger. There were more deer here than at any place previously visited, but we spent very little time in their pursuit. On the day of our arrival, Allan discovered a pool a mile or so from the river, where a bear family had been watering, and we thought our days would be best employed in watching for their return. Winter was rapidly approaching, and the beginning of the rainy season might be expected at any hour. Therefore, if we wished to try our hand at what Bud called "water-hole shootin'" we must needs lose no time. Our opportunity might vanish forever at any minute.

As the food supply — acorns and persimmons — was very scarce in all parts of the cane region it is possible that the bears were ranging a wider scope than is usually the case. Bud assured us that "b'ar allus drink ou'n ther same hole," but if these did it must certainly have been "a long time between drinks" in their case. Every hour for three days and nights we kept that muddy little pool under our watchful eyes but nothing in the shape of a bear materialized. We had made us a snug blind behind an old log, occupied by both of us at night, while we watched by turns during the day, and if even a squirrel had ventured down to quench its thirst it could not have escaped our notice.

We held our peace and hunted with unabated vigor... and the cabin of our craft grew almost uninhabitable from the pervading odor of musky mink and malodorous polecat.

The morning of the fourth day we spent in our cots on board the Palace, too worn from loss of sleep to care whether we hunted or not. Bud had caught a couple of beavers the night before, and we had a sumptuous dinner, consisting of beaver-tail soup, roast venison, fried squirrel, potatoes, rice, and canned fruits, with our choice of corn bread or hot biscuits. Bud called the repast a "scrumptious feed," so it will be seen that there existed all around a marked unanimity of opinion in regard to the matter. After dinner we smoked our pipes and read some week old Memphis dailies until the sun marked the hour for our afternoon's hunt; and then, for the first time during our trip down the river, all three of us started together, Allan with his Winchester and Bud carrying his 32-caliber Marlin, while I brought up the rear, bearing the Greener with an ample load of buckshot in either barrel.

This world is full of coincidences, and the unexpected encounters us at every turn. At or about the time we stepped from the door of our floating camp an old she bear and three half-grown cubs scrambled from their lair beneath the canes and vines and took a course that brought them to their old-time drinking pool just as we reached it from another direction. Perhaps our surprise at the meeting was greater than their own. At all events, before we had had time to collect our thoughts Mrs. Bruin was leading her interesting family in full retreat toward the nearest brake.

"Shoot," yelled Bud; and the spiteful report of his little rifle was followed by the fall of the nearest cub. Instantly I threw my gun forward and both triggers were pressed almost simultaneously, but I had only a stern shot, and the No. 8 buck lacked penetration for this sort of work. By a rare piece of carelessness on his part, Allan's rifle was unloaded, and before he could throw a cartridge into the chamber the old she bear had disappeared in the cane, dragging one hind-leg that had been broken by my shot. The cubs were slower and another fell at the joint reports of the two rifles; but, only wounded, it struggled on and two more shots were required to finish it.

Allan and I, if we had been alone, would have undoubtedly lost the wounded bear and the remaining cub, but Bud had been in many a bear hunt and knew exactly how to proceed in every contingency.

"Run around the p'int of ther ridge," said he, "they'll ha'ter cross ther slew an' you kin head 'em off. Go ahead an' I'll foller 'em up."

He plunged into the cane, while we dashed away in compliance with his instructions a run of two hundred yards brought us into the slough just as the remaining cub attempted to cross; but a shot and a yell turned him back, and we could see blood on the cane leaves where he had entered the brake.

Both of the bears were now wounded and we had them between two fires. Of course it would be possible for them to attempt to escape along the narrow ridge, but a bear makes considerable noise in breaking its way through tangled cane, and by carefully listening we would be able to discover the direction

Map courtesy University of Arkansas Libraries, Special Collections, Fayetteville

they were going and cut them off.

Minutes passed, however, before any noise disturbed the oppressive silence, save the wheezing escape of a steamboat ascending the river, miles away, and the honk, honk, of a flock of geese hurrying southward. Suddenly we heard Bud's rifle again, and then his loud, deep-chested yell.

"Look out, fellers! I've done shot off tew more of her legs, but she's cumin' on ther stumps."

Something was coming. We could hear it tearing through the cane like an incipient cyclone.

"Stand fast Craig-Royal and we'll weather it," quoted Allan under his breath; and then three shots were fired as fast as fingers could press the triggers; the cub fairly rolled out of the cane, his hide riffled with bullet and shot, whiles the old bear, open mouthed, dashed by so close that she struck the barrel of my gun, broked down for the reception of more cartridges.

(Left) This 1836 map included steamboat routes through Arkansas. (Below) These hunters are from a later era, but White River hunting trips remained popular then, too.

How I wished for a repeater! It takes time to reload a shotgun, and instants seem like hours at such a time as this.

Bang!

A 45-caliber bullet struck Bruin in the shoulder but a trifle too far forward to break the bone. The blow, however, checked her for an instant and she turned half around facing us — and just in time to catch three ounces of buckshot in her breast. That was a "finisher." At such short range no rifle can equal in life-destroying powers a heavily loaded shotgun.

Thus ended our bear hunt and, as it proved, our last day after big game of any description. That night the wind blew sharply from the northeast, a fall of snow and sleet followed, and it was with the greatest of trouble that we got our bulky game to the boat. Bud constructed a rude sled, and the sleet-coating on the earth favored us to some extent, but still we were quite exhausted when all our meat was safely housed and quite willing to rest for the time being.

With the storm came the ducks and geese, and, if we had liked, we could have loaded our boat with wild fowl. On the second day the cold moderated and the sleet changed to rain but still the migration of ducks continued. Flying overhead and swimming with the current they passed us by thousands; unmolested, too, save by an occasional shot from one of the rifles, fired in a vain hope of equaling the feats credited to Leatherstockings and Dan Boones of fiction.

Three days before the date set for the end of our hunt, a steamboat passed, with Newport as its objective point, and we decided to grasp that opportunity for our return. Fifteen minutes sufficed to pack our small belongings; a small army of ebony-hued roustabouts stood ready to hoist our trunks and boxes on board the larger craft; and then the engineer's bell rang, the big stern wheel revolved, and we began slowly forcing our way against the swollen current of White river, leaving the Palace to peacefully float at her moorings, once more, by our free gift, the property of that most inveterate of trappers, Bud.

Photo courtesy Jake Hartz Jr.

The Scatters

AGFC'S INITIAL LAND PURCHASE REMAINS THE CROWN JEWEL AMONG PUBLIC DUCK HUNTING AREAS

The scene has greeted hunters at Bayou Meto for decades. At five o'clock on almost every morning of duck season, for as far as you can see, trucks pulling boats are lined up to launch at one of the ramps leading into the 34,000 acres of woods.

For a first time visitor it can make an impression that will last a lifetime. Spotlights dance through the woods. Angry shouts and occasional shotgun blasts in the darkness warn wading duck hunters they are getting too close to a group already set up. Before first light, shadows of ducks crisscross through the treetops.

By full daylight, ducks come in every direction. For a hunter used to seeing ducks come from one general direction, it is a sight as mesmerizing as it is addicting. Through the years, that addiction has been unshakable for many, despite the circus atmosphere.

Bayou Meto has become so popular among Arkansas duck hunters it is often called "Bayou Metro" or just "The Metro." Traffic jams of boats and motors are as common as those in the skies among passing mallards.

◄ Billy Jeter, Tracy Lyons and John Godwin hunt from a typical hole in the flooded timber of the AGFC's Bayou Meto WMA.

Photo courtesy Arkansas Game and Fish Commission

Hunters have been lining up to get into Bayou Meto since the land was acquired in 1948.

It will remain the same for as long as ducks migrate south. Because Bayou Meto, even to those who don't hunt, means ducks. You might assume that ducks flocked to Bayou Meto before man first waded through its flooded timber. But the Bayou Meto that so many hunters have fallen in love with hasn't always been so popular.

History of this area is sparse, especially leading up to the time when early settlers attempted to tame the wilderness

Bayou Meto's 34,000 acres are covered mostly in timber, which stands in stark contrast to the cleared agricultural land surrounding it.

of eastern Arkansas. The little history available shows if anything Bayou Meto did not tame easily. In fact, history has shown us the only thing Bayou Meto is suited for is wildlife, especially ducks.

The reason? Water, nature's element that was so effective in forming the Delta and Bayou Meto, was also man's biggest hazard. Water in Bayou Meto often came too fast and stayed around too long.

For a duck hunter today, Bayou Meto's main problem continues to be water. Many times it comes too late, but when it comes so do the ducks. No other duck hunting area in the state produces so many ducks by the simple ability to hold water.

Before the area surrounding Bayou Meto was developed, the water was more likely to produce swamp fever. The hardship did little to build a love for Bayou Meto, but it played a part in developing it.

Bayou Meto was part of 7,686,575 acres of land transferred to the State of Arkansas under the Swamp Land Acts of 1849 and 1850. Most of the land was sold at prices that ranged from 50 cents to $1.25 an acre. The proceeds from the sale of the land were supposed to be used to construct levees and drainage districts for flood control.

To some extent it worked that way, but by Trusten Holder's account in a 1970 report to the Arkansas Planning Commission entitled *Disappearing Wetlands in Eastern Arkansas*, it had other impacts as well.

The AGFC and Bayou Meto — A Timeline

1915
On March 11, Gov. George Washington Hays signs Act 124, which creates the Arkansas Game and Fish Commission and, among a long list of game laws, sets the first-ever bag limit on ducks — 25 per day.

1927
The great flood backs up the Arkansas River from the Mississippi, bursting levees from Little Rock south. A levee break at Swan Lake washes away the logging town of Anerpt, which in 21 years will be part of the first purchase of Bayou Meto.

1937
Pittman-Robertson Act is passed, calling for an excise tax of 11 percent on sporting guns and ammunition. The funds are to be used in restoring wildlife habitat and will eventually allow the AGFC to buy land for its WMAs.

1944
Constitutional Amendment 35 passes, giving the Arkansas Game and Fish Commission independent authority to regulate wildlife through revenues from hunting and fishing licenses and fines.

1947
Changes in the federal aid program allow Arkansas' annual allocation to jump from $31,387 in 1946 to $131,821 in 1947, and the AGFC begins buying land.

"For some struggling farmers, who had been trying to clear enough land to make a living, the formation of a drainage district was but another hazard," Holder wrote.

"To begin with, drainage of the lowlands was a difficult task. Then, with human nature being what it is, with the politicians and the richer landowners dictating the courses of events (frequently with the sheriff doubling as the collector of the drainage taxes), one can imagine some of the results. Even at best, without any planned favoritism or accidental boondoggling, it probably would have been impossible for all benefits to precede the collection of the drainage taxes, or to provide simultaneous and equal drainage to all landowners in the district.

"Also, in many instances, it would have been impossible to drain water from one tract without flooding another man's land. Frequently, therefore, individual farmers within some drainage districts were damaged instead of benefited....Then too, the activity within one drainage district often necessitated the formation of another district downstream."

Seventy years later, for better and worse, the drainage districts had created one of the most productive agricultural regions in the country. They allowed the clearing of the lands that are now mostly rice and soybean fields.

But the Bayou Meto bottoms survived. During the first part of the century, Bayou Meto was considered free range for cattle. Fences, one in Lonoke County and the other at the floodgate of Big Bayou Meto, were constructed to keep the cattle from ranging out of the bottoms onto agricultural land.

While the farming interests were growing, others saw uses for the timber of Bayou Meto. One of those uses was duck hunting. W.M. Apple, a former outdoor columnist for the *Arkansas Democrat*, often relayed stories of trips from as early as 1916 taken to Bayou Meto Flat to shoot ducks.

Apple would travel in a Model T from Little Rock, a trip that would take almost 12 hours. Lodging was nonexistent, so Apple and hunting buddies made do.

"After the rice had been shocked they would come along with a threshing machine," Apple said. "Then there would be a haystack — usually about 15 feet high and 50 feet in diameter. You would just bore a hole back in those things and crawl in. They were the warmest things in the world to sleep in. The only trouble was crawling out into that predawn cold."

Not everyone was interested in the bottomlands for the hunting. Timber was a valuable commodity.

When settlers first started carving out

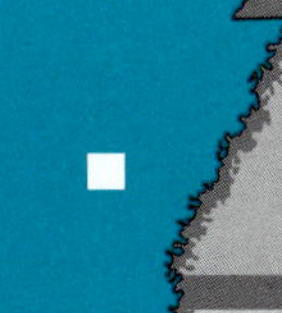

BAYOU METO WMA

Acres: 33,832
First purchase: 1948
Location: Between Pine Bluff and Stuttgart in Jefferson and Arkansas counties.
Topo Maps (7.5 series): Humphrey, Humphrey SW, Cornerstone, Lodge Corner, and Reydel.

Bayou Meto is the largest state-owned public shooting ground in the country and is primarily known for its excellent duck hunting. (Don't say "by-you me-toe." The Arkansas pronunciation is more like "by-o me-duh.")

Approximately 10,000 to 12,000 acres of hardwood bottoms are flooded with the aid of a series of levees, ditches and water control structures designed to capture heavy fall rains. In addition, two areas, Halowell Reservoir and the Wrape Plantation, are set aside for rest areas.

Due to Bayou Meto's large size it can be accessed from several highways including U.S. 79, southwest of Stuttgart, and State Highways 11, 152, 88 and 276.

Much of the area has walk-in access from the Vallier School Impoundment, Buckingham Flats, Mulberry Turnaround and Long Bell Turnaround. But many hunters use boats to get to prime spots by using one of the launch ramps that are on every side of the area, including at Halowell, Tipton, Vallier Impoundment, Mulberry and Long Pond.

Although Bayou Meto is the most popular duck hunting area in the state, it has had to withstand attempts to channelize its tributaries since the AGFC first purchased land in the area.

Bayou Meto's ability to hold water has also created problems for surrounding farmers trying to get their crops out. But the area has withstood the test of time and is expected to remain the top public duck hunting area in the country.

THE AGFC AND BAYOU METO — A TIMELINE

1948
AGFC purchases Bayou Meto Flat for the purpose of providing public duck hunting land. Most of the 34,000-acre wildlife management area is obtained for $7 an acre.

1957
Halowell Reservoir, part of a private hunting club, is purchased by the AGFC. The 600-acre reservoir initially serves as a green-timber hunting area; after the timber dies, moist-soil plants are established and it serves as a waterfowl rest area.

1981
AGFC creates the Arkansas Duck Stamp. The $5.50 stamp features a Lee LeBlanc painting of seven mallards in Bayou Meto.

1995
The Walter Will Bryant-Cannon Brake water control structure is dedicated. The AGFC project allows controlled flooding for waterfowl in a southern section of Bayou Meto that previously was dependent on fall and winter precipitation.

1996
Due to over-crowding in Bayou Meto, AGFC passes regulations forbidding out-of-state guides to operate on state-owned public hunting grounds.

Bayou Meto WMA holds many well-known areas within its boundaries

It's called Bayou Meto, but when hunters talk about it, they most often mention the various sections that comprise this wildlife management area. In some respects, the names of these areas within Bayou Meto are as well-known as the WMA itself.

Here's how a few were named:

■ **Wabbaseka Scatters.** This is a general term for all of Bayou Meto. It is often shortened to simply "The Scatters." Wabbaseka Bayou flows south from the town of Wabbaseka and spreads or "scatters" in several directions as it enters the woods of Bayou Meto. The name was used long before 1948, when the Arkansas Game and Fish Commission began purchasing land for the WMA.

■ **Buckingham Flats.** Another popular area of Bayou Meto was a favorite of outdoor writer Nash Buckingham, according to Trusten Holder. Over time, the flat woods became known to almost everyone as Buckingham Flats.

■ **Lower and Upper Vallier School Impoundments.** Yes, there was an old schoolhouse in the woods here, according to Holder. The Vallier School once stood near the boundary of Bayou Meto.

■ **Government Cypress.** While there is no formal record of how the area got its name, it's believed this tract was owned by the federal government, which harvested the cypress timber here.

■ **Long Bell.** Named after the Long Bell Lumber Company. Most hunters know the area as Long Bell Turnaround. Prior to Bayou Meto being purchased, the woods surrounding the turnaround were heavily logged. Signs of that logging still exist today, including a shallow trough where oxen teams pulled logs to the logging deck.

■ **The Tram.** This serves as a landmark for frequent visitors. The Tram marks the remains of a railroad that carried timber from Bayou Meto.

a place for themselves in eastern Arkansas, they cut some of the timber to build homes. The rest was just in the way, keeping them from planting the fields they wanted most. In most cases, settlers built their homes and cut their fields near or on canebrakes. Canebrakes were located on fertile soil, and clearing them was as simple as lighting a match and burning them.

But as more settlers moved to the area, timber increased in value. Sawmills started popping up all over, including in the heart of Bayou Meto. One of these mills was located at the end of Wabbaseka Scatters Road. It was operated by Long Bell Lumber Company, a name that remains attached to the site today. Most know it as Long Bell Turnaround.

There are other signs of its existence as well. The area is well-known for its walk-in access. Hunters here may be familiar with an old roadbed running north and south just east of the turnaround. That roadbed represents the remains of the railroad that served the Long Bell Lumber Company.

A few other signs might not be as noticeable, including a shallow trough north of Long Bell that extends for almost a mile from the upper end of Government Cypress to the Long Bell railroad.

The trough is said to have been made by teams of oxen dragging the huge logs out of Bayou Meto.

The oxen and the cross-cut saw did their jobs well. By 1927, most of the virgin timber had been cut

Although many duck hunters mourn the loss of the timber, that procedure probably insured that Bayou Meto would be around for future generations.

Once the timber was cut, many of the companies sold the cut-over land at very low prices. In some cases, buyers couldn't be found and in others, the land was abandoned and eventually reverted back to the state for the nonpayment of taxes.

By 1948, when the Arkansas Game and Fish Commission began acquiring land for Bayou Meto Wildlife Management Area, or Bayou Meto Game Restoration Project as it was labeled

From left, Vincent France, Mikey Beale and Melissa Bowman were among the hunters in Bayou Meto WMA during the 1996 Youth Waterfowl Hunting Day, Dec. 24.

then, the cost of the first purchase of 1,305 acres was $27.50 an acre. Approximately 25,000 acres were bought for $7 an acre.

Those purchases varied greatly from an 80-acre tract that was added in 1969 at a cost of $150 an acre.

That initial 1,305 acres included the remains of a small town. As mentioned earlier, Bayou Meto is often referred to as "Bayou Metro" because at times there are so many hunters filling the wilderness area it often seems like a downtown rush hour.

But the metro title also has some historical basis. In the early 1900s, Anerpt, a small town was located in part of what is now Bayou Meto. The town of about 100 people was considered a thriving community. It had a post office, a sawmill and its own railroad.

But its residents have forgotten about Bayou Meto's ability to attract and hold water. In 1927, on Easter Sunday, Mother Nature gave them a wet reminder. The Farelly Lake Levee, built from the funds of the Swamp Lands Act, broke near Swan Lake.

The break was so massive it was still visible in 1970, when Holder was writing *Disappearing Wetlands of Eastern Arkansas*.

The citizens of Anerpt were able to move to high ground, believing that the flood would not be too bad. But by the middle of the week, the water had risen fast enough that it swept away most of the tenant homes.

Holder's 1970 report stated that two or three of the houses were still lodged in the woods about a mile from where they once stood. They now serve as a reminder of Bayou Meto's occasional fury.

Today, flooding on Bayou Meto is controlled by a huge number of water control devices, if you count all of the culverts, gates, levees, and concrete structures.

Even with all of those man-made helpers, Bayou Meto still shows an occasional wild streak, inundating crops and trapping duck hunters. But those wild streaks and the hassles of long lines at boat ramps aren't nearly enough to thin the crowd at the best public duck hunting ground in the U.S.

Flooding Bayou Meto at the whim of Mother Nature

When the start of duck season rolls around and water levels in Bayou Meto Wildlife Management Area are less than ideal, duck hunters often ask why the Arkansas Game and Fish Commission doesn't attempt to install a pumping system that will ensure the area gets enough water.

Even when it's dry, or at least not full of water, many hunters have very few options left in the immediate area. That is why pumping Bayou Meto seems like a worthwhile endeavor.

But that is not altogether feasible. Scott Yaich, assistant director of the AGFC and one time Wetlands Coordinator, put together figures that explain why pumping is a pipe dream.

If the AGFC could undertake the job of pumping Bayou Meto, it would take 60 10-inch wells, all pumping 3,000 gallons per minute.

With those pumps in place, it would take 30 days of nonstop pumping to fill 10,000 acres.

In some years, that wouldn't have helped anyway. Often 30 days before the season there isn't enough water available to pump.

To put it in financial perspective, the fuel costs for 30 days of pumping would be approximately $180,000. The total cost, including wells, labor, etc., would add up to just under $1 million.

What many people don't realize is just how much water it takes to flood the area. To fill 10,000 acres, which is the equivalent of 7.8 billion gallons of water, it would take 1.6 billion duck hunters each carrying a five-gallon bucket of water.

Of course there are not that many duck hunters in Arkansas. On average, there are about 50,000 duck hunters. So, in an average year it would take each duck hunter carrying 2,120 five-gallon buckets of water to get the area in shape to duck hunt.

One thing should be certain. There are no substitutes for the work of Mother Nature.

Stranded overnight, hunters burn decoys to avoid being dead ducks

(Editor's note: Duck hunters get lost in Bayou Meto every season. The names of the three hunters in this incident have been deleted. The story appeared in the December 17, 1996, edition of the Arkansas Democrat-Gazette, written by Judd Slivka.)

STUTTGART — The tale reads like a bad joke: Three hunters walk into the woods, pockets full of ammo and decoys. It starts to pour and the hunters have to stay the night.

The next day, they walk out of the woods wet, tired and hungry, their decoys burned the night before to keep warm. But they did shoot two ducks. The three men, all of Pine Bluff, went into the woods of the Wabbaseka Scatters in Arkansas County off Arkansas 88 on Sunday morning to hunt for ducks.

"They walked over to their usual place and didn't get any ducks, so they walked over to somewhere they hadn't been before," said Melvin Case, the Office of Emergency Services coordinator for Arkansas County. "It started to rain, and everywhere they went there was water over their waders. So they found some higher ground and tried to camp for the night.

"They told me they burned their decoys to keep warm."

Officers from the Arkansas County and Jefferson County sheriff's offices searched the area until about 4 a.m. Monday. That's when the three men and their dog, Ace, were discovered on a hill deep in the woods.

"We got within a quarter-mile of them, but we couldn't get to them," Case said. "We could hear them, but we couldn't get to them. The water was too deep. So every half-hour or so, I would get in the rescue truck and sound the siren. When it started getting light at about 6:30, I would sound the siren about every five minutes. They walked out about 7:30.

"They needed that siren to tell them where to go. They told me they weren't even going to attempt to walk out. They were just going to wait for someone to come and get them."

Case said all three men were none the worse for wear.

"They just came out tired, wet and hungry. But they got their ducks. I guess that's what mattered to them."

Always willing to share 'The Scatters'

Walter Will Bryant had crowd waiting for him every morning of duck season

Arkansas Governor Jim Guy Tucker looked over the crowd gathered along a gravel road in the Bayou Meto Wildlife Management Area. It was opening day of the 1995-96 duck season. It's certainly not unusual to draw a crowd in Bayou Meto on opening day.

But it was 11:30 a.m., a time when most duck hunters should have been long gone. The party that is Stuttgart's Wings Over the Prairie Festival would soon be revving up for Saturday night.

For the 250 people gathered near the new Cannon Brake water control structure on Little Bayou Meto, this was an opportunity to pay respect. And it simply could not be missed.

"How many of you went on your first hunt with Walter Will?" asked Gov. Tucker.

Hands were raised all over the lot. One observer guessed that at least 50 grown men held a hand in the air.

"Mister Walter Will" is the way most people address Walter Will Bryant, whose name was honored with the Cannon Brake dedication that day. He was born in "The Wabbaseka Scatters," as the Bayou Meto Wildlife Management Area is also known. Wabbaseka Bayou flows into the Bayou Meto woods then spreads or "scatters" in several directions, hence the name. It is often shortened to simply, "The Scatters."

Bryant has lived most of his life within sight of his birthplace. They say Mr. Walter Will knows every tree in The Scatters. Only the thousands of hunters who have been lost in the 34,000 wooded acres of Bayou Meto WMA can truly

Those who have hunted with Walter Will Bryant claim they've never heard a better duck-caller or seen a finer shot.

appreciate that statement. But you don't have to get lost in Bayou Meto to appreciate Walter Will Bryant.

Bill Bridgforth remembers walking in the woods one day with Bryant. Bridgforth, a Pine Bluff lawyer, has hunted and fished all his life. They were near the confluence of the White and Mississippi rivers on this day, not Bayou Meto. As they approached a pecan tree, Bryant tapped Bridgforth on the arm and said, "Look at that."

"I hate to admit this," Bridgforth recalled, "but all I saw was a pecan tree. I said, 'Mr. Walter Will, what do you see?'

"He started showing me how deer had come and gone; how a raccoon had been there and a place where it had stood on its hind legs; he pointed out the color and the dryness of the pecan shells and showed me which ones had been eaten that day and which ones had been eaten the day before. That whole tree just came alive."

When the Arkansas Game and Fish Commission announced plans to build the Cannon Brake water control structure, just down the road from Bryant's house in Bayou Meto, many people urged that it be named for Mr. Walter Will. As an AGFC commissioner in 1995, Bridgforth made sure that happened. The Walter Will Bryant/Cannon Brake structure added dependable water control on Little Bayou Meto for flooding a large section of Bayou Meto WMA.

Since meeting Bryant in 1968, Bridgforth has tried to spend as much time with him in the woods as possible.

"First of all, he's such a wonderful man," Bridgforth said. "He is also the most woods-wise man I've ever met, and I've spent a lot of time in the woods during hunting seasons over the last 45 years."

Bryant was born on Nov. 14, 1918. His father farmed 140 acres here through the Depression and taught Walter Will the basics of woodsmanship at an early age. He has always lived off this rich bottomland.

For most everyone who comes here now, The Scatters is a place to get away. But you can't learn to read the woods on weekends and holidays. To gain Bryant's vision, you have to live here and you have to depend on the woods to put food in your belly. Only then do you begin to see.

Walter Will Bryant represents the last of a generation. He seems to have been aware of this for a long, long time. Mr. Walter Will passes along some woodsmanship every chance he gets. He gives everyone a glimpse of Bayou Meto magic. How else are they going to see it?

"There's been more game killed over that kitchen table than anywhere else in the United States," said Juanita Bryant.

For decades, especially during duck season, men and boys have gathered in the early morning darkness outside the Bryants' home on Cornerstone Road. They waited until Mr. Walter Will came out to take them hunting. When they returned, of course, the stories flowed

The Walter Will Bryant/Cannon Brake water control structure honors a man who took thousands of people hunting and provides a dependable way to flood the timber here.

over the Bryants' kitchen table.

"You know how it is," Juanita said. "They'd kill the same duck six or eight times. Every one of them has to tell his side of the story."

Juanita and Walter Will Bryant were married in September 1946.

"He trapped to make a living when we first married," she said. "He'd get up at four o'clock in the morning to go run his traps. One month he got 47 coons and 27 mink. The coons were worth about $4 or $5 apiece and the mink about $20.

"He'd let me stretch the coon, but he wouldn't let me stretch the mink because it was worth so much."

She too qualifies for the dignity of address that is a dying Southern tradition. Here in The Scatters, no matter if the words come from a teenager or a 50-year-old man, it's always "Miss Juanita" and "Mister Walter Will."

In answer to a newcomer's question, Walter Will says he was born just 150 yards from his current home.

"He's come a long way in his life, hasn't he?" Juanita says with a smile.

It helps to have a sense of humor when your husband attracts bands of hunters at ungodly hours of the morning. Juanita and Walter Will have shared many hours in the woods.

She recalled a time in the late 1940s, when the deer population in Arkansas was just beginning to show signs of life again. Juanita and Walter Will were hunting squirrels.

"He was always trying to sneak up on me because he didn't think I had any sense," she said. "Of course I didn't have any sense; I married him."

As Juanita turned to see what she assumed would be her husband sneaking through the woods, she saw a whitetail deer instead.

"He hadn't ever seen one, so I didn't tell him about this one," she said.

The legal deer kill during the 1940s averaged 1,500 per year, for the entire state. The good old days weren't always so good.

There's a P.S. Olt duck call somewhere along the Rhine River in Germany. It belongs to Walter Will Bryant.

The only extended period of time he's spent away from Bayou Meto was during World War II when he served under General George S. Patton's Third Armored Division. Bryant packed his duck call when he went overseas. He got to do a little duck hunting before he lost his call near the Rhine.

"We hunted a couple of times in little potholes," Bryant said.

His duck gun was a .30-caliber Winchester carbine. Bryant claims he once killed 23 ducks with 25 shots from that rifle. No, he didn't shoot them on the water.

"I shot them in the air," Bryant said. "I was a pretty good shot. I still am, but not as good as I used to be."

No one who has hunted with Bryant doubts that story.

"He's as good a shot as I've ever seen," said Bridgforth. "He had eyes like a hawk."

"His shooting skills are legendary," said Vernon Tarver of Fayetteville. He has known Bryant since 1968. As a longtime member of the Shady Oaks Duck Club, located near Long Pond, Tarver too has spent many days in the duck woods with Bryant.

"Nobody I know of has spent as many days and nights in the Wabbaseka Scatters," Tarver said. "He'll be describing some place in The Scatters and he'll say, 'You remember that old mossy stump sittin' there don't you?' Nobody else does, but he does.

"We call him Mr. Duck. He is a damn duck."

That's what everyone says after they've heard Bryant blow on the little black Olt. He's owned only three duck calls in his life. All were P.S. Olts. When he's not using it, Bryant keeps the hard-rubber call in a mason jar filled with water. The lid is screwed on tight. He claims this prevents the cork that holds the reed from drying out.

Bryant's other "secret" to calling ducks is wearing a cotton glove on the hand in which he holds his call.

"It muffles down the sound," Bryant said. "It makes it sound different. You're not supposed to call a duck loud."

Nobody can tell you what notes Walter Will Bryant blows differently than anyone else. Not only can you not see the woods without his experience, you can't hear the subtle sounds either.

"He's the only person I've ever seen who could blow a hail call and ducks would keep lighting on the water all around him," Bridgforth said. "It's almost like he understands game."

A computer is tucked in the corner of Juanita's "office" just off the kitchen in the Bryant's home. In 50-plus years of marriage, she has gone from stretching coonskins on cane to running farm accounting software on a computer. The Bryants' farm is 770 acres now. Through the years they've grown cotton, corn, soybeans and rice, educated three kids and saved enough to buy a second home on Lake Hamilton near Hot Springs.

"I remember when it took half your ground to raise feed for your mules, cows and hogs," Walter Will said.

When so many duck hunters began showing up on his doorstep every morning, Bryant started using his tractor to haul them to the woods. He cut off the bed of an old pickup truck and made a trailer out of it. He could carry 10 or 12 people.

Bryant never charged anyone to take them hunting. In over 40 years of duck seasons, he missed only a half-dozen days, he reckons. Multiply those numbers out. You'll see that it's no exaggeration when someone says Walter Will Bryant took thousands of people duck hunting.

"I wouldn't go duck hunting if I had to go by myself," said Bryant. "I've always tried to take some kids every time I went. I just wanted to show them what it's like."

Mr. Walter Will's duck hunting days were all but over by the 1996-97 season. He got out a few days with friends like Bridgforth and Tarver.

He has never quit blowing a duck call though. During the fall of '97, Walter Will and Juanita were staying at their place on Lake Hamilton. He kept seeing a few mallards on the lake, so Bryant took his Olt out of the jar and walked down to the dock one Sunday afternoon.

"The ducks covered me up," Bryant said with a laugh. "They were landing on top of the boathouse."

The master had not lost his touch.

Halowell Reservoir changes with time

Water control essential part of moist-soil management for waterfowl

Moist-soil management is a term that you will hear more and more frequently when it comes to providing good habitat for wintering ducks. To see it in action, climb upon the Arkansas Game and Fish Commission's observation tower at Halowell Reservoir.

The 600-acre reservoir near Bayou Meto has a long history of heavy use by ducks. Halowell was constructed in the early 1950s. It was a private duck hunting club when the AGFC acquired it September 1957.

The changes it has undergone form a timeline of how AGFC waterfowl management practices have evolved. At first, Halowell was used as a green-tree public duck hunting area. After the timber died in the mid 1960s, the lake was also managed for fishing and was noted for producing huge bream.

In 1976, the reservoir was drained and aerially seeded with rice to provide food for waterfowl. Results were mixed because of varying availability of water each year and the uneven level of the land within the reservoir. By 1980, a plan was in place for promoting moist-soil plants, which provide both shelter and an abundance of seeds.

"Ducks evolved to rely on natural foods like acorns, herbaceous plant seeds and invertebrates," said AGFC waterfowl biologist Jon Schneider. "Although ducks now rely heavily on farm row crops for energy, these are not as nutritionally complete as natural foods.

"Ducks rely on rice for a good portion of their diet in Arkansas, but natural foods are essential if they are to return north in healthy condition to breed. Seeds and invertebrates produced in moist-soil habitats, like Halowell, provide amino acids, vitamins and minerals that are all but absent in other foods."

A cooperative project with Ducks Unlimited recently added cross levees to improve water control and provide ideal water depths and foraging habitat for ducks. Because the topography of the reservoir varies over three feet from east to west, flooding to an optimal depth for feeding waterfowl was impossible in more than half of the impoundment until the cross levees were added.

"Mallards prefer four to eight inches of water in moist-soil habitats, and anything over 12 to 16 inches or so is really too deep for most dabbling ducks to exploit," Schneider said. "Like contour levees used by rice farmers, the cross levees allow us to provide an even distribution of water throughout the reservoir.

"With better water control, we can also manipulate water levels to encourage moist-soil seed-producing plants and control unwanted vegetation. This type of control is essential to managing moist-soil impoundments for optimal duck habitat."

To flood Halowell, the AGFC uses water relifted from Bayou Meto to the east, as well as water that backfloods into the reservoir from Little Bayou Meto on the west. Because the elevation in the reservoir slopes east to west, the two cross levees were placed on contours running north and south.

"About two-thirds of the reservoir can be naturally backflooded from the west, so dividing Halowell into three separate impoundments allowed us to more efficiently flood the reservoir," Schneider said. "Instead of pumping the entire reservoir including the western two-thirds that floods naturally, now we can pump one impoundment at a time depending on water conditions."

Ducks get up from the 600-acre Halowell Reservoir, one of the few waterfowl rest areas in Bayou Meto WMA.

A 1940's look at Tent Camp (upper photo) is not much different than a 1990s look (left). Pictured in top photo; from left,Vernon Jackson Jr., Vernon Jackson, Sr, and Ewing Jackson. Left photo, Andy Jackson, Cache River Elwood Blues, and J.D. Simpson III.

Traditions of the past preserved

Tent Camp hasn't come up with any way better than the way it used to be

In the movie *Land That Time Forgot*, viewers get a make-believe look at what it would be like to step back into the past.

At the Gillett Hunting Club, members get the real thing.

"We're just a bunch of goony birds," said J.D. Simpson III, who has hunted here for 47 years. "But that's the way we like it."

The way they like it is the way things used to be.

The Gillett Hunting Club, also known as the Tuf Nut Hunting Club or Tent Camp, was started in the 1920s. Two of the founding members, Vernon Jackson Sr. and James D. Simpson Sr., were co-owners of the Tuf Nut Garment Manufacturing Co. and Little Rock Tent and Awning.

Given the men's positions and the economic times, a campsite made from tents was a reasonable and perfect idea. So reasonable and perfect that their sons and grandsons haven't changed the camp in more than 70 years.

The tents, the duck blinds and the traditions of hunting are still mostly the way they were decades ago.

"People remember our club because it's so different," Simpson said.

In place of the standard house at the average duck club, tents, complete with wood burning stoves and smokestacks, line the camp area. Modern amenities are almost non-existent; you won't see much of a change in today's scenery from that recorded in 60-year-old black and white photos. It's like stepping back in time.

"When you bring someone to camp, they remember it for the rest of their lives," said Andy Jackson of Little Rock, who has also hunted here for 47 years.

"It's a regular gawk-off," Simpson said.

That type of memory is what Tent Camp is all about, preserving the way things used to be. But it's not a sideshow; the club doesn't want publicity. Its members have turned down repeated requests by Ducks Unlimited and others to auction hunts here.

Tent Camp consists of three main tents, Tuf Nut, Hog and Cook. The tents are 17 feet wide, 27 feet long and 11 feet high. They are taken down and stored after each season.

"We are kind of stingy about the things we have," Simpson said.

Most duck hunters have a touch of romance attached to the traditional old ways. The members of Tent Camp have decided to live it. Every day of duck season grasps tradition and holds onto it.

"We want to keep it the way it was in 1920, as long as there is duck hunting in Arkansas," Simpson said.

"We do nothing half-assed."

That much is evident by the extremes they take to keep things the way they were. The things that have changed are those things the members have no control over.

In the early days, members traveled to the tent camp by passenger train. The trip started at Main Street in North Little Rock and, six to seven hours later, with stops at Scott, England, Stuttgart, Almyra and DeWitt, they would arrive in Gillett.

The first tents had wooden sides and floors. It took six men to bring the structures to the campsite. They were transported on a log wagon pulled by a team of horses.

At the camp, there was no electricity and no plumbing. Heat came from pot-bellied stoves. Dead ducks were stored at Youngblood's Ice House in Gillett.

"The way it used to be is the best way," Simpson said. "We haven't come up with any way that is better than the way it was."

The Tent Camp consists of three main tents (17 feet wide, 27 feet long and 11 feet high). The names for each, then and now, are Tuf Nut, the Hog and the Cook tent. Another tent was erected for the caretaker. Since the 1920s an additional tent, the Honeymoon (originally named the Terry tent after Congressman David D. Terry) has been added to accommodate hunters with snoring problems.

The tents offer the bare necessities for camp life — a place to sleep out of the weather. They are heated by wood-burning stoves. In 1972, electricity was added. The lines were run underground and out of sight.

"We didn't want anybody to know we had it," Simpson said.

The decision to add such a modern comfort as electricity was not an easy

At Tent Camp, custom and gentlemanly tradition overshadow formal rules

Part of the Gillett Hunting Club's History has been documented in a pamphlet the club printed in 1991 entitled, "Hunter's Heaven." A letter that Bill Terry, attorney for the group, wrote to a new member comes as close as anything to defining the rules of the club:

"The intent of the trust agreement has always been to operate an old-time Arkansas duck hunting camp for the benefit and enjoyment of the owners and their sons and friends who are personal hunting buddies with no commercial or business overtones involved...annual dues and assessments are to be paid for by the individual owner with no subsidies from any company. The ownership of the club is by and for each individual owner and his personal friends."

Other than that, as one member said, "There are no rules. Therefore we don't break any."

To some degree that is true. Andy Jackson likes to tell the story about Justin Matthews III and the time he became a member in the 1960s. Matthews was visiting with long-time member Ewing Jackson and asked: "Now that I'm a member, what are the rules?"

To which Jackson replied: "Justin, there aren't any rules, but, by God, you better not break one of them."

The club is operated with Southern hospitality at its core. And when it comes to hunting, blinds are not drawn for but assigned. The system works perfectly.

"One of the things you discover is duck clubs cannot be democracies. Somebody's got to be in charge," Jackson said.

If there are problems, they are solved in a gentlemanly fashion. At the heart of every solution is the question: "What would a gentleman do in this situation?"

"There are no factions, no bickering," the late Vernon Jackson Jr. said. "Everybody defers to the other fellow on use of the best blinds and such. It's always been the custom."

And that's why, when Gillett Hunting Club members depart for a few days at Tent Camp, they often say, "Bye, dear, I'm on my way to Heaven."

Duck hunter's Heaven.

one. The primary reason was for the aid of the cook. Plus, it was hard to keep clean without running water, an additional comfort that could be had with electricity.

According to Jackson, the final decision was made when the original brass Coleman lanterns needed maintenance. When the club sent the lanterns to the Coleman Lantern Co., the manufacturers wrote back asking to purchase the antique lanterns from the club. The lanterns were so old that parts weren't available to fix them.

"They hadn't seen lanterns like that in a long time," Simpson said.

Despite the addition of electricity, the members still strive to keep everything as original as possible. Electric lines in tents run to bare light bulbs. And recently when the lights needed to be replaced, Jackson spent a great deal of time finding identical parts to wire them in the same manner.

"You won't believe the time we spend on figuring out how to not change things," Jackson said.

With electricity, came a television. "But we don't watch T.V.," Simpson said. "It's there to watch only for the weather and any Razorback athletic event. Besides, we only get one channel."

This is a hunting camp, a place to get away from everything else. One of the main rules is "no business."

"You don't bring business to camp," Jackson said, and Simpson verified.

But that doesn't mean they don't take the camp to business. The walls of Simpson's office in downtown Little Rock's Stephen's Building are almost totally covered with photos and memora-

A World War II command car provided a back drop for a day's limit at Tent Camp. Hunters are, from left, Ewing Jackson, Somers Matthews and Vernon Jackson Sr.

Command car kept club out of the mud

In the early days hunting club members made their way to the club by railway. Once in Gillett, wagons and horses carried hunters and equipment to the camp site.

But as modernization swept over the countryside, the train and horses were soon replaced by the automobile. That was fine until it rained. Dirt roads turned to muddy bogs, and the four-wheel drive vehicle was not as common then as it is today.

To take care of the problem, the club purchased a U.S. Army command car, complete with the Army star on its side. The car was parked at the gate so members could get in and out of Tend Camp without getting stuck.

bilia from Tent Camp.

"We like to hunt and we don't want anything to get in the way of that," Simpson said. "Basically we want to selfishly protect these things because of the pleasure it brings us."

Hunting takes place on and around Jacob's Lake in some of the same blinds that have been in use since 1919. The most notable is called Big Willow, built six feet off the water, amid seven large cypress trunks. It is said to be one of the most famous duck hunting blinds in this part of the country.

Other blinds include the Thorn Thicket, the Lake, and the White Line.

Transport to the blinds is made in flatbottom boats pushed by three- and four-horsepower motors. Anything larger is too new and too loud. And the club insists on not using a motor in its wooded area after 10 a.m.

"We wouldn't go to all the trouble if the hunting wasn't as good as it has always been."

All of this, and the hunting is good, too. The natural cypress brake on Mill Bayou is one of those areas that has always drawn ducks. It's surrounded by the Grand Prairie, and within eyesight of a mallard flying high over the Arkansas River.

It is a convenient dropping-off spot for migrating ducks following the river and resident flocks filtering their way out of rice and bean fields and down Bayou Meto.

The members of Tent Camp take their hunting as seriously as all the other traditions at this campsite.

"There is no doubt that we take the hunting seriously," Simpson said. "We wouldn't go to all of the trouble if the hunting wasn't as good as it has always been.

"When people come to hunt with us, they know we are serious."

To illustrate the point, Simpson related a story from a hunt that included the Episcopal Bishop of Arkansas. Having a

Vernon Jackson Jr. with one of the last live decoys used at the Gillett Hunting Club.

Live decoys convenient part of early hunts

Not everything at the Gillett Hunting Club can be the way it was in the 1920s. One of those is the use of live decoys, a common practice at the club during the early days.

Live decoys were outlawed by the U.S. Fish and Wildlife Service in 1935. Until that time, the club kept mallards in a pen on club property. Several hens and one drake were kept for the purpose of drawing ducks.

On hunting days, the ducks were taken to the blind, where a weighted leather tong was attached to their feet. Once in the water, the live ducks would preen and swim around while calling, a sight most wild flocks couldn't resist.

In those days, "Ducks were so thick you could hear their humming five miles away. They sounded like a sawmill in operation," recalled Wilbur Wallace, a nephew of the club's first caretaker.

Wallace's comment and a description of the use of live decoys were included in a pamphlet the club printed in 1991 entitled, "Hunter's Heaven: A History of the the Gillett Hunting Club."

Dr. W. H. Miller trained the live decoys. Dr. Miller's training of the decoys was so complete that by the end of the morning the ducks would jump into the boat when he rapped a paddle on the gunwale.

Having live decoys is much easier than what the club has to do these days. Tent Camp uses 360 magnum decoys. Like the live decoys that required constant care, the artificial decoys require the same.

The water levels of Jacob's Lake and Mill Bayou are at the mercy of Mother Nature and the U.S. Army Corps of Engineers.

Mill Bayou flows into Bayou Meto, which empties into the Dumas Pool of the Arkansas River. Water levels often change here, depending on whether the Corps is pushing water through Lock and Dam No. 3 or holding it at Lock and Dam No. 2.

One day the water can be high, but the next it can drop a foot or more. Each time the level changes, the club is forced to restring the decoys, a job that can take most of the day.

"We have to," J. D. Simpson said. "It's a lot of work. But we know exactly how to set the decoys to draw the ducks.

"If you don't change them, you wind up with a big mess."

dignitary of that caliber in the blind, one might think that special treatment would be called for. But after the Bishop accidentally dropped his gun on the floor of the blind, Simpson looked sternly at him and said, "If that gun goes down again, Bishop, we're out of here."

Added Simpson, "This is not a training ground."

"But it is a great place for young hunters to experience duck hunting," Jackson said. "They get something special here, and when you grow up hunting like this you learn to respect the sport much more."

It's been said that you can never really know where you're going if you have no idea where you've been. Every season, Simpson, Jackson and the members of Tent Camp go back to the way duck hunting used to be. Fun is part of the reason for the trip back in time, but most of it is about respect.

"It's got a hold over me that I can't break," Jackson said.

(Above) Vernon Jackson Sr., J.D. Simpson Sr., Vernon Jackson Jr. and J.D. Simpson Jr. after a successful hunt. (Below) V.L. Jackson Sr., Ewing Jackson, Claude Baker and Jimmie Simpson warm themselves by a wood-burning stove in November 1941.

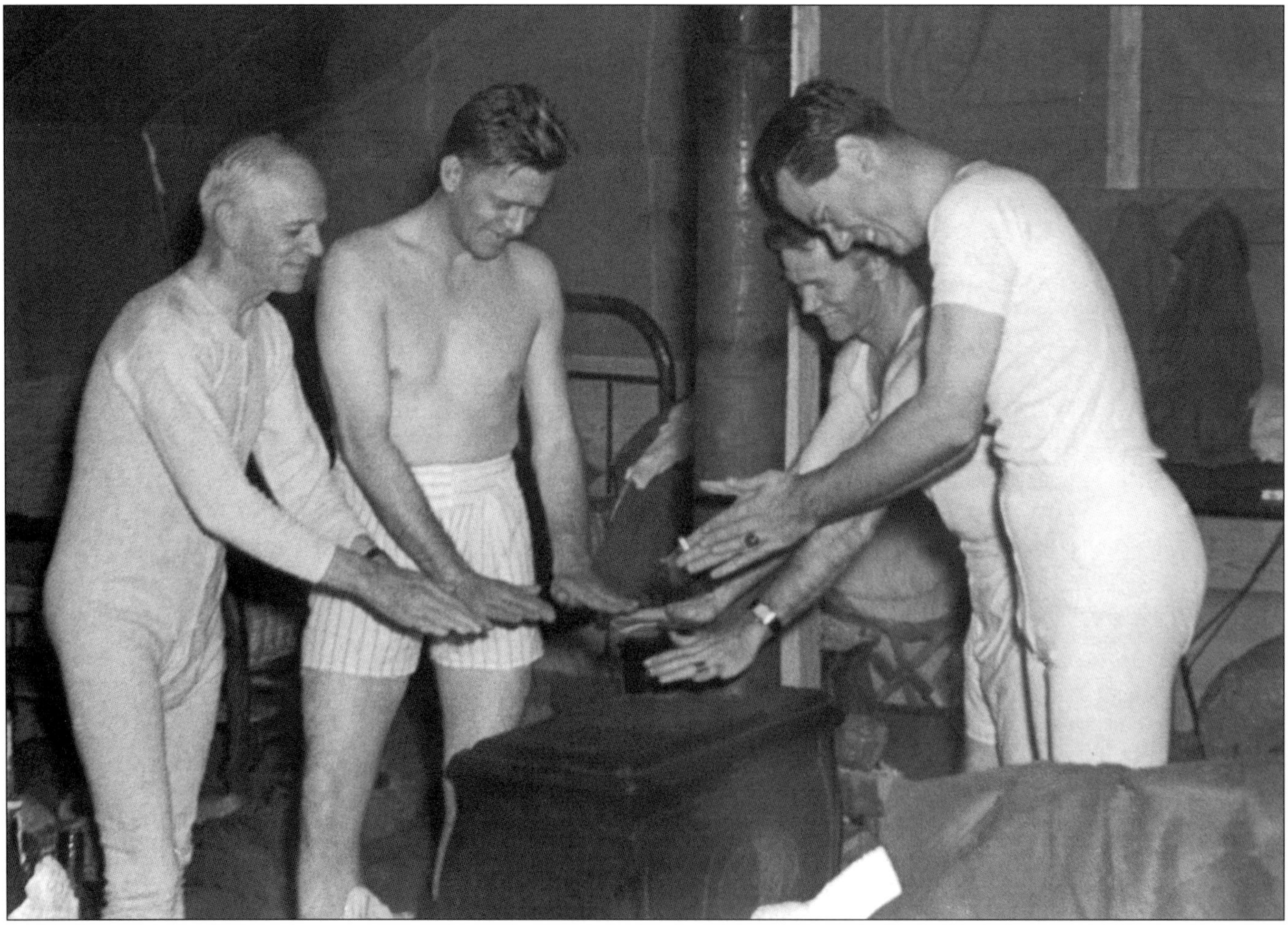

Ducks as thick as gnats in a swill pail

Buckingham, Queeny, 'millionaires and senators' hunted with LaCotts

Tippy LaCotts can't imagine a better way to get an education. All he had to do was lead people into the pin oak flats along Mill Bayou, where the ducks were "as thick as gnats in a swill pail." The rich and famous came calling on LaCotts.

"I was privileged to be associated with a lot of good folks, through my old, black P.S. Olt duck caller," said LaCotts. "There's no other way I could have ever got as complete an education as I did from being acquainted with those people. I saw how they conducted themselves, and I learned about their business interests."

LaCotts was known by the company he kept. It included the most famous waterfowl hunting writer of all time — Nash Buckingham — and one of the 10 wealthiest men in the U.S. during the first half of the 20th century — Edgar M. Queeny. LaCotts kept a scrapbook that is filled with photos, letters and notes from U.S. senators, foreign ambassadors, millionaire businessmen and even beauty queens. LaCotts' story explains just how far Southern hospitality and unparalleled duck hunting can take you.

"My family settled at Arkansas Post," LaCotts said. "All those people came up these streams, like LaGrue Bayou."

Clarence Elmer "Tippy" LaCotts Jr. was born between DeWitt and Almyra on Sept. 8, 1914. Stuttgart has earned its reputation as the duck hunting capital. But you could argue that DeWitt (pop. 3,553) has a better location. Where could be better for hunting ducks than smack in the middle of Arkansas County near Bayou LaGrue, with Stuttgart to the north, the White River to the east, the Arkansas River and Bayou Meto to the west and the confluence of the Arkansas, White and Mississippi rivers to the south?

And there's also Mill Bayou. After Clarence Elmer LaCotts Sr. left the hunting club he established at Stinking Bay on the White River, he decided to "fix up" some land his father owned on Mill Bayou, a Bayou Meto tributary five miles west of DeWitt.

"Back in those days you didn't have all this heavy equipment," LaCotts said. "It was quite a job to go out in the woods and make levees that would hold water at a decent level. That's what you called fixing up a place."

Without modern equipment, there was only so much fixing up you could do. The natural lay of the land was essential to having a good place to duck hunt. There is no doubt that the LaCotts family's 270 acres on Mill Bayou was a place ducks wanted to be.

Before Queeny bought Wingmead north of Stuttgart and made it famous for duck hunting, he hunted on Mill Bayou and wanted to buy property here, according to LaCotts.

"He said, 'Let me buy your place and I'll build a clubhouse,'" LaCotts recalled. "I said, 'I just can't part with it.' He called me again the last minute before he closed the deal at Stuttgart."

Queeny, the man who led the Monsanto Corporation's rise to prominence, didn't stop calling on LaCotts for help. After Wingmead was established, Queeny asked if he could hire one of

'Settin' on a log in a pin oak flat' is the tradition linked to Arkansas duck hunting

Tippy LaCotts calls them "legal duck bait." He is referring to the small acorns that have long attracted mallards to the flooded timber of Arkansas.

"I've shot ducks that had such a craw full of them that you wondered how they could fly," LaCotts said. "Their craw looks like a sack of marbles."

Almost every reference to Arkansas flooded timber hunting mentions ducks feeding on "pin oak" acorns.

Nash Buckingham's book *Blood Lines* includes a story about hunting with LaCotts in the pin oak flats around Mill Bayou. A picture of Buckingham in the first pages of the Derrydale Press edition incorporates an old Arkansas expression in explaining that it was taken while the author was "settin' on a log in a pin oak flat."

However, pin oak to a duck hunter and pin oak to a botanist mean two different things. To a duck hunter, pin oaks are any species of oak tree that produces an acorn small enough for a duck to eat. The list includes pin oaks, willow oaks, water oaks and laurel oaks. All are in the red oak family.

To a botanist, pin oak means just that — one species (*Quercus palustris*). The pin oak is a medium size tree. In his book *Trees, Shrubs & Vines of Arkansas*, Carl Hunter describes pin oak leaves as having "long, pointed lobes separated by very deep curving indentations...seldom over 5 inches long, lobes often at right angles to the midvein."

Hunter, a former Arkansas Game and Fish Commission biologist and assistant director, notes that pin oak flats are seldom found in the deep bottoms. They are more common on the edge of overflow lands. For instance, the White River National Wildlife Refuge has few bottomland hardwood stands with high percentages of red oaks.

Ducks gather to feed on acorns where they are abundant. One study documented the acorn production from a 120-year-old, 98-foot-tall water oak tree. In one year, it produced 28,360 acorns.

Tippy LaCotts leads the way through a flooded pin oak flat along Mill Bayou.

LaCotts' top guides, Jess Wilson.

"I told him if he'd pay Jess more than he was making for me, I'd tell Jess to come talk to him," LaCotts said.

You can watch Queeny's short film *Prairie Wings* and know that Wilson went to work for Queeny. He stayed with him for many years.

With Nash Buckingham's help, hiring guides became a necessity at LaCotts' Duck Hunter's Paradise. Buckingham wrote in his book *Blood Lines* about hunting with Elmer, i.e., Tippy, in the pin oak flats of Mill Bayou. The story "Wax and Wane" paints a vivid picture of DeWitt the day before duck season opened in 1937, introduced as follows:

"Every hamlet or city has its big moment, and the evening before duck-shooting season opens is by long odds DeWitt's — and a truly delicious experience."

Opening day included a duck hunt with Tippy. Buckingham wrote:

"'Take trees,' laughs Elmer. 'We don't need to go any farther.' By now the heavens are literally alive with mallards. 'Look out,' warns Foy. 'They'll knock your hats off in a minute.' I want my companions to see this sight. And seemingly in a trice ducks begin lighting all about us, completely filling the open pools for an acre."

A picture of Elmer LaCotts is included in the story. Buckingham definitely spread the word about LaCotts' place on Mill Bayou.

"Nash came over here and hunted and just fell in love with it," Tippy said. "Nash hunted at a lot of different places and he was a judge at field trials. My name was circulated everywhere he went. I was able to build up a clientele from that. Nash treated me just like a prince."

A signed copy of *Blood Lines* dated Christmas 1938 is one of LaCotts' most prized possessions.

As the sign on the previous page indicates, LaCotts' Duck Hunter's Paradise was originally a single-day commercial hunting operation. There were no accommodations.

"Day-hunters, that's what we called them when Daddy first started taking commercial hunters," LaCotts said. "We'd take people out in an old jalopy of a car. Whenever we got stuck, we'd just get out and hunt."

Coffee was served in a tent after the hunt.

LaCotts' father died in the mid 1930s. When Tippy returned from the service after World War II, he had decided to quit commercial hunting.

"I'd been shot at enough," LaCotts said.

Some wealthy businessmen from Memphis leased the land and helped LaCotts build a clubhouse. It was called the Mud Lake Club; some of the members had been connected with another Mud Lake Club in the Hughes area.

LaCotts enjoyed this relationship for almost 35 years. He didn't have to leave DeWitt to learn about the ways of the world. A Christmas card from a British ambassador to the U.S. lies among the mementos that LaCotts collected during this time.

The 1997-98 season opened with ducks once again filling the pin oak flats along Mill Bayou. Two of Tippy's grandsons were set to guide hunters there. It was easy to see why they would want to follow in their grandfather's footsteps.

This 1955 Arkansas Game and Fish Commission map shows the lower Arkansas and White river areas, including Bayou Meto and Mill Bayou.

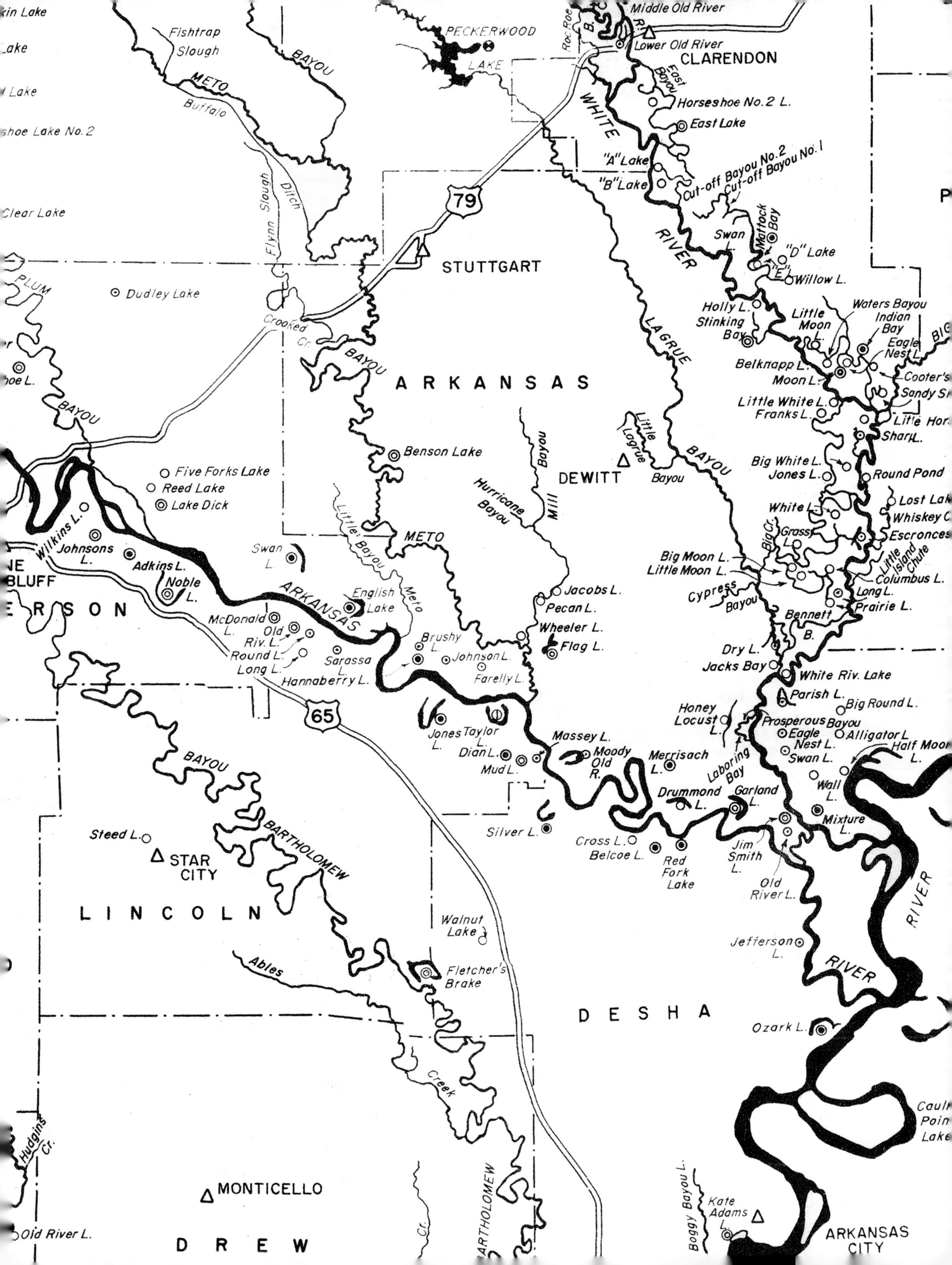

Middle Old River
Fishtrap Slough
PECKERWOOD
LAKE
BAYOU
METO
Buffalo
Lower Old River
CLARENDON
East Bayou
WHITE
Horseshoe No.2 L.
East Lake
"A" Lake
"B" Lake
Cut-off Bayou No.2
Cut-off Bayou No.1
Flynn Slough
Ditch
79
Clear Lake
RIVER
Swan L.
Mattock Bay
"D" Lake
"E"
Willow L.
STUTTGART
Dudley Lake
PLUM
Crooked Cr.
BAYOU
LAGRUE
Holly L.
Stinking Bay
Little Moon L.
Waters Bayou
Indian Bay
Eagle Nest L.
Belknapp L.
Moon L.
Cooter's
Sandy
ARKANSAS
BAYOU
Little White L.
Franks L.
Little Lagrue Bayou
Sharp L.
Benson Lake
Bayou
Mill
BAYOU
Big White L.
Jones L.
Round Pond
Five Forks Lake
Reed Lake
Lake Dick
DEWITT
Hurricane Bayou
Lost Lake
White L.
Whiskey
Little Bayou Meto
METO
Big Cr.
Grass L.
Escronces
Wilkins L.
Johnsons L.
Adkins L.
Swan L.
Big Moon L.
Little Moon L.
Little Island Chute
Columbus L.
BLUFF
Noble L.
English Lake
ARKANSAS
Jacobs L.
Pecan L.
Cypress Bayou
Long L.
Prairie L.
McDonald L.
Old Riv. L.
Round L.
Long L.
Sarassa L.
Hannaberry L.
Brushy L.
Johnson L.
Farelly L.
Wheeler L.
Flag L.
Bennett B.
Dry L.
Jacks Bay
White Riv. Lake
Parish L.
Big Round L.
65
Honey Locust L.
Prosperous Bayou
Eagle Nest L.
Alligator L.
Jones L.
Taylor L.
Dian L.
Mud L.
Massey L.
Moody Old R.
Merrisach L.
Laboring Bay
Swan L.
Half Moon L.
BAYOU
Wall L.
Drummond L.
Garland L.
Mixture L.
BARTHOLOMEW
Steed L.
STAR CITY
Silver L.
Cross L.
Belcoe L.
Red Fork Lake
Jim Smith L.
Old River L.
LINCOLN
RIVER
Walnut Lake
Jefferson L.
Ables
Fletcher's Brake
RIVER
DESHA
Ozark L.
Creek
Hudgins Cr.
MONTICELLO
BARTHOLOMEW
Cr.
Boggy Bayou L.
Kate Adams L.
Old River L.
DREW
ARKANSAS CITY

Central Flyway Turn Lane

THE ARKANSAS RIVER VALLEY CONNECTS THE CENTRAL FLYWAY WITH THE MISSISSIPPI FLYWAY

As the Arkansas River trickles out of Colorado's Rockies and gains life through Kansas and Oklahoma, it becomes a left turn lane for ducks heading south from Canada and the Dakotas.

Arkansas is always linked with the Mississippi Flyway. As the key state for wintering mallards in the 14-state Mississippi Flyway, that's an accurate portrayal. But people don't consider the fact that this state also gets a booster shot of ducks from the Central Flyway.

The Arkansas River is the most underrated factor in this state's reputation as the epicenter of duck hunting in North America. It's also another example of why you have to look at the whole picture before you can understand the individual parts of Arkansas.

The Arkansas River Valley forms a west-to-east funnel for ducks. The light at the end of the funnel is the Delta. Specifically, the Arkansas Game and Fish Commission's 34,000-acre Bayou Meto Wildlife Management Area stands prominently as a visitor's center after the narrow river valley corridor opens into the Delta.

◄ Most people don't associate Arkansas duck hunting with mountains, but Petit Jean WMA proves the combination exists.

Retrievers are invaluable in open water hunting conditions, like those found along the Arkansas River Valley.

Banding data show the Central Flyway and Arkansas River Valley make significant contributions to the duck population in the Grand Prairie region of Arkansas. That also indicates how good the duck hunting can be along the Arkansas River Valley. The Western Arkansas River unit of Arkansas' North American Waterfowl Management Plan has the state's highest duck harvest rate, in terms of density. Of Arkansas' 10 units, the narrow band of land along the Western Arkansas River has an average of 68.8 ducks killed per square mile. The Bayou Meto/Lower Arkansas River unit is second with 61.0.

It should be emphasized that those figures are weighted heavily by the fact that this is such a narrow strip of duck habitat. In terms of total ducks in Arkansas during the mid-winter surveys, the Western Arkansas River unit has an average of only 4.1 percent, based on 1970s averages. That's less than one-tenth of the Cache River/Lower White River unit.

But the Western Arkansas River also has about one-tenth the number of duck hunters as the Cache/Lower White. And maybe the most impressive feature of the Arkansas River valley is potential. Since the completion of the McClellan-Kerr Navigation System in the 1970s, the river valley hasn't been subject to the extreme water levels that characterized it previously.

The Arkansas River Valley continues to define its new personality in terms of

Photo courtesy George C. Graham

Hunters paying attention to flight patterns of ducks can find sand bars along the Arkansas River that will produce fast shooting.

duck habitat. Two features are highly favorable for its continued improvement. First, the Western Arkansas River unit has a higher percentage of public land (36.7%) than any other in the state because of the U.S. Army Corps of Engineers' presence along the McClellan-Kerr system. Permanent water and potential green-tree reservoir habitat abound.

Secondly, there is also a high percentage of agricultural land along the river. Water holds the key to this potential. As more landowners begin to see the continually rising profits available in managing for waterfowl, the number of ducks that linger on their way down the Arkansas River Valley will increase.

GALLA CREEK WMA

Acres: 3,358
First purchase: 1960
Location: Near Atkins in Pope County
Topo maps (7.5 series, U.S. Geological Survey): Atkins, Holla Bend.

The Galla Creek Wildlife Management Area is best reached by State Highway 105 south of Atkins or by State Highway 247 and county roads south of Pottsville.

About 400 acres of hardwood timber are flooded each fall to attract ducks. Due to the small size of the area and heavy hunting pressure, the quality of duck hunting varies considerably from day to day.

Galla Creek has many old fields which are managed as upland and small game habitat. The area offers some good quail and rabbit hunting, although its small size does limit hunting opportunity. Galla Creek also offers some good squirrel hunting within the hardwood timbered portion and has a fair deer population.

Camping on the area is restricted to designated areas.

Arkansas River Valley — A Timeline

1687
A year after Arkansas Post was founded at the mouth of the Arkansas River by Henry de Tonti, another Frenchman, Henri Joutel, writes of the "turkeys, bustards, swans, teal and other game" along the river.

1751
French explorer Jean Bernard Bossu travels the Arkansas River and notes, "game of all kinds is plentiful...wood pigeons, swans, geese, bustards, ducks of all kinds, teals, divers, snipes, water hens...and other birds not known in Europe."

1819
Naturalist Thomas Nuttall travels the Arkansas River from its mouth into what is now Oklahoma and hunts geese along the way. He describes the Arkansas Territory as "one vast trackless wilderness of trees."

1820
Naturalist John James Audubon explores the Arkansas River and records 50 species of birds, including green-winged teal, pintails and mallards.

1902
The Morrilton Hunting and Fishing Club, better known as the Fish Lake Club, is incorporated. The club is located about six miles west of Morrilton in Arkansas River bottomland.

Keeping up with ducks in the corridor

Weather, water changes create feast-or-famine routine for hunters

Any other place in Arkansas, and the ducks would have been written off as long gone. A minute before, the flock had shown an interest in the spread of decoys. The line of ducks winging its way east above the Arkansas River had started breaking and pulsating.

"When those high bunches start doing that, you know they are interested," Bob McAnally said. "When they start widening the line and moving back together it means they are wanting to come down and rest or feed."

The flock of ducks had been doing that. And they had started losing altitude. But now they were a half mile away. They had to be gone.

But they weren't. The ducks tipped their wings, started a slow bank and headed back toward the decoys.

"Seeing ducks work like that is a big reason why I like hunting the Arkansas River," McAnally said. "You see so much more of the ducks working."

McAnally is a wildlife biologist with the Arkansas Game and Fish Commission. He works from the AGFC office in Russellville, an area where all of the duck hunting revolves around the Arkansas River.

The Arkansas doesn't get the attention the White, Cache and Black rivers receive. But Central Flyway ducks have always flown down the river from Oklahoma and crossed over into the Mississippi Flyway.

Before the Corps of Engineers built the dams of the McClellan-Kerr Navigation System, the river often overflowed in the winter, providing hunting opportunities down its length. But now the river lacks the overflow bottoms found along other rivers in the state, and most of it flows through areas known more for other wildlife than ducks.

Despite that, year in and year out, the waterfowl harvest is higher per square mile along the Arkansas River than in any other place, McAnally said.

"It's open water hunting, so you have to do things a little different. Decoys are important, because a lot of the ducks you will be trying to decoy are high."

"It doesn't get a lot of attention around the state, but it gets hunted hard," McAnally said.

The Arkansas River figures greatly in how ducks come through the state. A big part of the flocks that frequent Stuttgart and the Bayou Meto area get there by way of the Arkansas River. And when the river is high, it can have an impact on whether or not those areas see a lot of ducks.

The best example of that came during the 1996 duck season. Rain and high water arrived early, and every lowland in the state had enough water to hold ducks. But there were few in most places. The exception was the Arkansas River. It was high, and it stayed high for most of the early season. While east Arkansas hunters were crying the blues, river hunters were quietly enjoying a great start.

"We had ducks like nobody's business," said Jerry Williams of Conway, who hunts near Coal Hill.

Then the water level dropped and the hunting changed. Stuttgart and Bayou Meto started seeing more ducks, and flights along the river went back to normal.

Normal means good hunting overall, with a lot of highs and lows in between.

"The things that control hunting along the river are the same things that control it elsewhere — weather and water," McAnally said. "But we see the sudden changes more. You can go from feast to famine to feast in no time at all.

"You will have periods of time when it's as good as it gets anywhere, and then others when you have to really hunt for them."

The best times are when water is high and cold fronts are pushing through.

"We see the flight ducks then," McAnally said.

"And when there's extra water, you've got a lot of places where ducks are not being bothered."

McAnally said there are two types of hunting along the western Arkansas River

Arkansas River Valley — A Timeline

1939
A delegation of sportsmen from Pulaski and Faulkner counties asks the AGFC for assistance in establishing a 6,000-acre duck refuge east of Mayflower. Years later, it would be impounded to form what is now Lake Conway.

1951
The AGFC approves expenditure of $25,000 to impound approximately 1,000 acres in the Nimrod area for duck hunting. Construction begins on what will be known as the McClellan-Kerr Navigation System.

1957
Holla Bend along the Arkansas River becomes the state's third national wildlife refuge after conservationists and hunters push for the designation to land that had been declared "government surplus."

1970
The 449-mile McClellan-Kerr Navigation System, which is built at a cost of $1.3 billion and includes 12 locks and dams, is fully opened to barge traffic on Dec. 31.

1989
A cooperative effort between Ducks Unlimited, The Nature Conservancy and the AGFC reclaims more than 8,000 acres of land in Blackwell Bottoms. It is established as the Ed Gordon/Point Remove WMA.

— river valley and main river hunting.

River valley hunting is a lot like that found in east Arkansas. It includes WMAs like Galla Creek, Petit Jean, Nimrod, Blackwell Bottoms, Harris Brake and Bell Slough. Most of the areas have flooded timber.

They are also mostly small, creating crowded conditions. This usually results in too much pressure to hold many ducks. But when ducks are moving in large flocks, they do find their way to the WMAs, and then the hunting is comparable to that east in Arkansas.

Arkansas River Valley hunting also includes oxbows and cypress and buckbrush brakes. Other areas in the valley attract ducks with thousands of acres of soybeans and rice, which are grown from the Oklahoma line to Little Rock. Soybean and rice fields that hold water draw ducks. These fields would attract more ducks if they were managed for waterfowl.

"That is changing," McAnally said. "It's becoming more attractive for landowners to develop fields to hold ducks. One of the commission's private land goals is to make western landowners aware of the opportunities. The bottom line is the more land you get under management, the more ducks that will be attracted."

It's in the river itself that Arkansas River hunting varies from the Delta.

"You have to stay on your toes if you hunt the river," McAnally said. "It's not like hunting any other place.

"You stick to the same spot every day, and chances of consistent shooting are slim."

McAnally said ducks along the Arkansas River are like ducks everywhere in that they feed at night and in the early morning. Most of the feeding activity is done in the river valley. The ducks then use the river to rest and get grit to help in digesting food.

The main species found on the river are mallards, ringnecks and gadwalls.

Hunters along the Arkansas River usually find a wide variety of waterfowl species.

NIMROD WMA

Acres: 3,550
First purchase: None, lease agreement since 1949 with U.S. Army Corps of Engineers.
Location: Near Danville in Yell County
Topo maps (7.5 series, U.S. Geological Survey): Nimrod Dam, Plainview.

Nimrod Wildlife Management Area is a small hunting area located near the upper (western) end of Lake Nimrod. The area can be reached off State Highway 28, just west of Plainview.

Several dirt roads lead into developed parking areas located along the edge of the area. Travel is by foot or by boat when Nimrod is flooded.

A series of levees catches rainfall and floods the pin oak timber each fall, making the area attractive for ducks. The Nimrod area also offers good squirrel hunting and some good quail hunting in the higher elevations.

"When you have a flooding situation it can be tremendous," McAnally said.

The lock and dam system holds water in pools. As these pools rise and spread, they inundate many backwater areas that provide both food and shelter.

"Traditionally, the later, the colder and the nastier it gets, the better the duck hunting gets."

During these times, hunters should watch flight patterns of ducks using the river and place large decoy spreads around islands.

"It's open water hunting, so you have to do things a little different," McAnally said. "Decoys are important, because a lot of the ducks you will be trying to decoy are high."

McAnally said most often his spreads number around 50 decoys.

"The way you place your decoys on the river may be more important than how you place them any place else," McAnally said. "You need to set up with the wind at your back or crossing. You have to use hook or 'J' sets. You can't throw them out haphazardly like you can in the east.

"Most Arkansas duck hunters are so spoiled. You get in a hole and here they come. You lose a lot of that need to pay attention to the wind and other details."

McAnally said attention to those details kills more ducks on the Arkansas River than anything else.

"You have hot spots, but they change day to day," McAnally said. "They change with the wind, with the water level and with pressure. You have to constantly watch the birds and find out what they are using right then, and tailor your hunting to that. You can't get set in your ways."

Remember that high water attracts ducks, and falling water forces them to leave. Wind currents dictate flight paths, and successful hunters get under them. Cold fronts are also a big key, since the river is the main corridor for ducks winging their way down the flyway.

"Traditionally, the later, the colder and the nastier it gets, the better the duck hunting gets," McAnally said.

Photo courtesy George C. Graham

HARRIS BRAKE WMA

Acres: 2,866
First purchase: 1957
Location: Near Perryville in Perry County
Topo maps (7.5 series, U.S. Geological Survey): Thornburg, Perryville.

The small Harris Brake Wildlife Management Area lies adjacent to State Highways 10 and 300, one mile south of Perryville. Only two all-weather roads enter the area, so most of the travel is by foot or boat. The 1,200-acre hunting area is separated from a 1,300-acre lake by an earthen dam with built-in water control structures that make possible flooding of the hunting area for ducks. The lake serves as a waterfowl rest area, and also provides some excellent bass, bream, and crappie fishing. Additional fishing can be found in the Fourche LaFave River, which borders the hunting area on the north. A public boat launching ramp to the river is next to the Highway 10 bridge.

When flooded, Harris Brake's oak-hickory woodlands provide good duck hunting opportunities, but the small size of the area and its proximity to Little Rock and other populated areas result in extreme hunting pressure at times.

Good squirrel, rabbit and raccoon hunting can be found on Harris Brake when it is not flooded. Camping is restricted to designated camp sites.

Arkansas River becomes only source of big water during dry duck seasons

Dry conditions in Arkansas bring adverse attention to duck season. The lack of water has an impact on the hunter's ability to find and hunt concentrations of ducks.

But ducks don't like dry years any better than duck hunters do.

Studies have shown that when rainfall is above normal and habitat on unmanaged private land increases substantially, greater portions of Mississippi Flyway mallards are attracted to the Mississippi Alluvial Valley, mallard body weights increase, pair formation and molting occur sooner, mortality rates decrease and subsequent recruitment rates may increase, according to *Habitat Management for Migrating and Wintering Waterfowl in North America.*

If conditions remain consistently dry, they can have an impact on how many ducks will come back next season.

Scott Yaich, assistant director of the Arkansas Game and Fish Commission and former U.S. Fish and Wildlife Service waterfowl biologist, is one who worries over that prospect.

In dry conditions, many ducks will fly over Arkansas to central and south Louisiana, where wet conditions are normally found. So there is usually enough water along the flyway for ducks to get their legs wet, but that's about it. Those areas don't offer the food value found in Arkansas' river bottoms and farm fields.

Ducks have to fly farther to get there, expending more energy, leaving them somewhat poorer for the return in the spring. This will cut into the number of eggs a hen can produce.

"It can be significant, but it won't be disastrous," Yaich said.

If breeding conditions are good we will still see progress, but not at the same rate we might if wintering conditions were better, Yaich said.

The bright side is things can turn around quickly. And ducks have as late as February and March to find enough water to get in good condition for breeding.

Cold conditions make hunting hot

Overlooked places along Arkansas River backwaters attract migrating ducks

The snow was almost blinding. You could look down and see what you were doing, but if you looked up, the thick flakes made it difficult to keep your eyes open.

Jerry Williams tried turning his shoulder to the snow and wind as he threw decoys from the boat, but the wind was so strong that it washed around and hit him in the face anyway.

The snow was an unexpected surprise. Clear skies had been expected and desired for this trip in a small backwater lake along the Arkansas River. The land is referred to as Dardanelle Wildlife Management Area, but in a formal sense it's not like most other WMAs.

Dardanelle WMA is cooperatively managed by the Arkansas Game and Fish Commission and the U.S. Army Corps of Engineers. The Corps owns the land and makes it available to the AGFC to manage just as it would other WMAs. WMAs like this are found on almost every Corps lake in the state.

"Usually we don't have what you would call a resident duck like they have in the eastern part of the state. Our ducks are just passing through."

In most areas, they are a forgotten resource of public land. In many cases, the areas are believed to be private. But along the edges of most of these lakes, public land that is often ideal for waterfowl hunting can be found. That is especially the case for Dardanelle WMA and all the Corps land along the Arkansas River.

The lake is formed by the McClellan-Kerr Navigation System along the Arkansas River. The river, which begins in Colorado and snakes through Kansas and Oklahoma before getting to Arkansas, is a major corridor for ducks migrating through the state.

Most duck hunters are under the impression that every duck killed in the eastern part of the state follows a course that is tied into the Mississippi River. But banding information has shown many of the large numbers of ducks killed in the Stuttgart and Bayou Meto areas first

Blinding snow makes for good hunting conditions along the Arkansas River, where cold fronts funnel ducks down the river valley.

come down the Arkansas River.

The impact of the river is seen during seasons when the water level is high and other areas in southeastern Arkansas are holding few ducks at season's start. Those along the Arkansas River, especially those in Dardanelle WMA, usually have good hunting.

That is especially true when the river is out of its banks, and small backwater areas are filled with water and ducks. A lack of cold weather and the abundance of food found in the flooded land keep ducks in the river basin.

They stay there until the river starts dropping. Many years it is only after the level drops and a cold front passes through the state that large concentrations of ducks start moving into the Grand Prairie.

"The ducks will stick around if the conditions are right," Williams said. "But usually we don't have what you would call a resident duck like they have in the eastern part of the state.

"Our ducks are just passing through. We are the first hunters they see when they come into the state, and there is not enough food and habitat around here to keep them."

Williams said the location along a major corridor in the flyway allows Dardanelle WMA hunters to see and work flocks of mallards that number well into the hundreds.

"But you might sit here all day and not see a thing," Williams said, "Then, all of the sudden, there are 200 mallards cupped in front of you."

For that reason, Williams preaches patience to hunters sitting in his blind. Blinds are legal in Dardanelle WMA.

"I've sat here many times and not had a duck at 10 o'clock, and at 10:30 had hundreds of mallards buzzing over me," Williams said. "It can happen real quick."

For that reason, hunting in this area can be an all-day affair. Hunters go to their spots with the intention of waiting until they have killed their limit.

Coffee can, rubbing alcohol provide makeshift heater for freezing duck blind

On freezing duck hunts, makeshift heaters can be the difference between warm toes and chattering teeth.

On cold days, Jerry Williams relies on a heater made from a coffee can that provides hours of warmth. The can is stuffed with a roll of toilet paper, which is then soaked with rubbing alcohol.

One-pound coffee cans are best, because a standard size roll of toilet paper will fit snugly inside them. Once the paper is in the can, a container of 70 percent rubbing alcohol is poured over it. Anything less than 70 percent won't burn long, Williams said.

The paper is lit with a match after it is thoroughly soaked. The heater can be recharged with alcohol at intervals.

Jerry Williams knows from experience that ducks can drop in at any moment when pushed by cold fronts along the river valley.

Enjoying the beauty of Petit Jean

Historical mountain top presents unique backdrop for traditional duck hunt

In the duck hunting kingdom of Arkansas, going west is the wrong way. At least that is the accepted thought of most state hunters.

The primary arteries for ducks migrating south are in the east, and the agricultural fields of the Delta act as magnets for hungry waterfowl.

In comparison, the western portion of the seems lacking in so many ways. The west has more mountain ranges than fields, and there are few waterways that double as duck highways.

The one thing it has is the Arkansas River, which affords a sprinkling of classic river bottom havens and agricultural fields along its path.

Its presence funnels ducks from the Central Flyway to these areas, and hunters awaken each morning to see the sun turn golden over mountain vistas rather than over flat land interrupted only by rice field levees. For them, going east just doesn't offer the same feeling.

Although once mallards float over decoys, with wings cupped like they are carrying suitcases and planning to stay awhile, the background is secondary. Your heart races regardless of where you are.

In the west's Petit Jean Wildlife Management Area, the sun peaks over a portion of the Petit Jean mountain range — a sight that seems particularly strange to one used to hunting flat areas. But everything looks familiar when the sky is busy with ducks.

Standing on the edge of a flooded sage grass field in the Petit Jean WMA, it is easy to see why hunters in this part of the world are not easily excited about heading east for ducks.

Bill and Crutch Aikman are included in that group. They have never spent a morning in Bayou Meto or in a flooded rice field, both considered traditional duck hunting mainstays in Arkansas.

Traditional for them are small creeks that flood fields, creeks that on drier days would appear to be more of a home for a quail than a duck.

But ducks find them.

"I've limited out several mornings just by setting the decoys out and pulling on a jerk string," Crutch Aikman said as constant flocks of ducks passed overhead.

In the east, one could expect part of

Central Flyway ducks are attracted to areas like Petit Jean Wildlife Management Area.

those flights to drop in at any moment. But here, an effort has to be made because decoying ducks and passing shots are not as common.

If you want to kill ducks, you have to stay alert, which is harder to do when working flights are sporadic. The mind wanders.

It is then when scattered flocks of mallards drift into decoy spreads without the coaxing of calls, wigeons swing by and wood ducks and scaup dive-bomb hunters' positions without warning.

"Isn't that the way it always goes?" said Crutch Aikman as four mallards flew out of the decoys.

Seconds earlier they had moved in unseen, passed over the decoys and almost touched down before suspecting something was awry and heading to safer water.

While they were sneaking in, Aikman had been in the middle of a childhood story that had a party of four hunters listening intently.

A half hour later, another flock drifted into the decoys, interrupting the constant string of stories being passed between the hunters. This time their approach was noticed. Because Pete Perkins was on his first duck hunt, he had been chosen as the first man to shoot.

But as the ducks hovered over decoys, Perkins waited for someone else to lead the way and the chance was missed.

"On days like this, you can't afford to lose those opportunities," Aikman said.

"I've limited out several mornings just by setting the decoys out and pulling on a jerk string."

Most of the surrounding water in the area was iced over, although temperatures for much of the state were well above freezing. Getting ducks to decoy to icy holes was difficult. It seemed the ducks could sense warmer climates to the east and along the Arkansas River Valley.

"Like anywhere, you have your slow days," Aikman said. "But if we had been paying attention, then we could have killed our limits on the groups of ducks that sneaked in on us."

PETIT JEAN WMA

Acres: 15,000
First purchase: 1953
Ownership: Arkansas Game and Fish Commission
Location: East of Danville, south of Dardanelle
Topo map (7.5 series, U.S. Geological Survey): Ola, Casa, Danville Mountain.

Access to the Petit Jean Wildlife Management Area is by county roads off State Highway 10, 7 and 154. The area is scattered along the Petit Jean River for more than 10 miles giving it a very irregularly shaped boundary, so watch for the yellow Game and Fish Commission signs.

Petit Jean has few all-weather roads, and many roads are closed due to flooding and bad weather during the winter. The area is about three-fourths bottomland and one-fourth upland forest and fields.

By using levees and gated culverts to catch rainfall, about 1,000 acres of the bottomland are flooded for ducks each winter. Duck hunting is generally good here. The WMA normally has good quail and squirrel hunting, too.

Annually, the area is used for quail, fox, and raccoon dog field trials. Dog pens and horse stables are available. Camping is restricted to designated ares.

Railroad influence on old hunting clubs not limited to the Delta

Names like Buffalo Island, Hatchie Coon and Wapanocca come to mind when you start compiling a list of legendary Arkansas hunting and fishing clubs that were established along railroad routes. Railroads provided the earliest reliable means of transportation into the bottomlands of the Delta in the 19th century. Sportsmen quickly took advantage of that.

Because of its path through the Ozark and Ouachita mountains, the Arkansas River valley west of Little Rock isn't usually associated with the tradition of hunting and fishing clubs found in the Delta. But the Morrilton Hunting and Fishing Club, better known as the Fish Lake Club, stands as an example of how the Arkansas River Valley contains all the elements of traditional Arkansas duck hunting.

The Morrilton Hunting and Fishing Club was incorporated on April 23, 1902. Membership was limited to 50 and remains that way today. A clubhouse was built near the Missouri Pacific Railroad line about six miles west of Morrilton.

Outstanding crappie fishing on cypress-lined Fish Lake, located near Point Remove Creek, gave the club its more commonly used nickname. But duck hunting was excellent too in nearby Blackwell Bottoms.

"Blackwell Bottoms was called Turkey Pond," said Edward Lee Eddy, whose father was a lifetime member of the club. "We used to say that Turkey Pond was the best-kept duck hunting secret in the United States. Only the locals knew about it. You could stand in the flooded pin oaks and shoot ducks all day long."

The Morrilton Hunting and Fishing Club owns the land around Fish Lake, which includes some good duck hunting. But it never controlled the prime duck hunting area of about 8,000 acres in Blackwell Bottoms.

Various attempts at farming Blackwell Bottoms ended in failure, which finally resulted in Arkansas Game and Fish Commission ownership of the land that is now called the Ed Gordon/Point Remove Wildlife Management Area.

Big river ducks drawn to little magnets

Small creeks and oxbows along Arkansas River pull in flocks of waterfowl

Hal Hunnicutt is certain he has never seen as many ducks in one place as he did the day before Thanksgiving in 1967.

These ducks weren't sitting on Claypool's Reservoir or one of the other famous duck ponds in Arkansas. They weren't packed in a Grand Prairie rice field or in a Delta pin oak flat. They were smack in the middle of Cadron Creek near Conway.

Hunnicutt and two friends were on the creek scouting for ducks. To get there the trio had traveled down the dirt foundation of Interstate 40. The interstate was under construction; its foundation was in place up to Cadron Creek.

At the creek, they slid a flatbottom boat and 18-horsepower motor over a fence, and headed upstream.

"We went around a bend in the river and came to a straight stretch, and it was packed full of ducks," Hunnicutt said. "You couldn't stick another duck on the water for more than three-quarters of a mile."

Hunnicutt said they were mesmerized by the sight of the ducks coming off the water.

"We just kept going right through them and they jumped up and parted right in front of us," he said. "You could have grabbed them from midair if you wanted to."

Hunnicutt's memorable moment serves as one example of how many ducks use the Arkansas River valley and the many finger flyways along its course. They include Fourche LaFave, Cadron and Palarm creeks and the Lollie and Plumerville bottoms.

Along the course of these Arkansas River tributaries are overflow bottoms of hardwood timber, agricultural fields, pockets of open water and even a few oxbow lakes. Hunnicutt has hunted all of them.

Because water is always a concern, regardless of what region of the state you are hunting in, the oxbow lakes are where most people hunt

"I have seen some of these places, especially the oxbows, just crammed full of ducks," Hunnicutt said. "In the lakes you are always assured of having water, and in a dry year it can be unbelievable. In a wet year it is mediocre."

Some hunters in the area float hunt along the winding creeks, jumping mal-

From left, Sam Snead, Russell Ratcliff and Hal Hunnicutt wait for ducks in an Arkansas River oxbow near Conway.

lards and wood ducks in bends of rivers where the bank has slipped into the channel. The areas provide cover and often have grass seed and other forms of vegetation to feed on.

In dry years, these floats can produce limits of ducks as well as crappie and bass. But that type hunting is not as popular as it once was.

Most of the hunting takes place in the oxbow lakes until the river backs up the creeks into stands of timber or soybean fields.

Hunting on the oxbows is a deep-water affair, so deep you can't wade.

"In the lakes you either need to build a blind or hunt from a boat," Hunnicutt said.

It is an open water style of hunting, where attention to wind pays big dividends. Big spreads of decoys are also a must.

"You have to have a lot of decoys because you are competing with a lot of water," Hunnicutt said. "A duck can sit down just about anywhere along the Arkansas River, so if you want to pull him to you, you'd better make it look like there's no better place to be."

Hunnicutt said ducks along the river valley are especially prone to ganging up, like those on Cadron Creek.

In other instances while hunting oxbows, Hunnicutt has allowed a group of mallards to land unmolested within the decoys. Within moments other flocks followed.

"It starts growing, and before you know it there's 5,000 ducks on the water," Hunnicutt said.

Large numbers of ducks are a fact that comes with the river. It is a major corridor for ducks winging their way from the Central Flyway in Oklahoma to east Arkansas. Cold fronts push ducks in large flights. Hunters in areas along the Arkansas River get the benefit of seeing ducks in numbers most hunters never see. By the time these big flights get to east Arkansas, they disperse across the abundant habitat.

"But everything is kind of limited here in the river valley," Hunnicutt said. "The Ozarks and Ouachitas bottleneck them right to us."

And there is a lot of underutilized habitat along the flyway.

"When the river gets up and backs up the creeks there is a lot of good flooded timber shooting," Hunnicutt said. "In some of these creeks, it's good many miles from the river."

Hunnicutt would like to see some of the land developed for waterfowl habitat rather than relying on the whims of Mother Nature. But the demand for that type of hunting ground isn't as high as it is in eastern Arkansas.

"But the hunting could be every bit as good," Hunnicutt said. "I've seen it, and it's worth seeing."

BELL SLOUGH WMA

Acres: 2,040
Ownership: Arkansas Game and Fish Commission and U.S. Army National Guard.
Top maps (7.5 series, U.S. Geological Survey): Cato, Mayflower.

Bell Slough, also known as Grassy Lake, is located on the southern end of Lake Conway and the northwest corner of Camp Robinson.

The hardwood bottoms of Palarm Creek offer surprisingly good mallard and wood duck shooting, despite the proximity of Interstate 40.

Flights of ducks filter into the area from the Arkansas River a few miles away, many feeding on nearby agricultural fields before resting on Lake Conway and in Bell Slough.

The small size of the area and its proximity to Little Rock and Conway often bring heavy hunting pressure on weekends. But good shooting can be found during the week, especially after a cold front pushes ducks down the Arkansas River.

ED GORDON/ POINT REMOVE WMA

Acres: 8,400
First purchase: 1989
Topo maps: Morrilton West, Hattieville, Moreland.

Point Remove Wildlife Management Area is also known as Blackwell Bottoms for the small town near its boundary. Almost entirely made up of agricultural fields now, it was once almost all hardwood forests. It was also renowned for the huge numbers of mallards it attracted.

But in the late 1950s and early 1960s the land was cleared to plant soybeans. Although the flooded timber hunting was gone, ducks continued to come to the bottoms.

The area floods when Point Remove Creek backs up from the Arkansas River and spills out of its banks. When that happens, as much as 4,000 acres of the management area are inundated. When the water level drops, levees allow from 600 to 800 acres to stay flooded.

Most hunting takes place during high-water times. Hunters set up in brush lines along high ground and around sloughs. Most build make-shift blinds in the tall grass around canals or hunt from boats in open water.

The majority of the hunting takes place in depths of one to four feet. The topography is not the typical flat area of most bottomlands, but has many variations.

In peak years as many as 30,000 ducks may use the area, the majority of which are mallards. Other species include wigeon, scaup, gadwalls and an occasional pintail.

Access is made from Highway 95 out of Morrilton to a boat ramp on the East Fork of Point Remove, and from the Blackwell exit off of I-40 to a boat ramp on the West Fork.

Food and shelter keep ducks lingering

Holla Bend, Dyer Lake, Johnson County rest areas benefit river flyway

There was a time when a duck winging its way down the Central Flyway had to be ready for a long haul if it took a left turn in Oklahoma to head for the wintering grounds of east Arkansas.

It was a non-stop flight because there were few resting places. But that is changing. Rest areas along the Arkansas River are becoming recognized as valuable habitat tools that enhance hunting opportunities. Those that are established are magnets to ducks.

"Without them there wouldn't be any places where a duck could put its feet down without getting shot at," said Bob McAnally, district wildlife biologist with the Arkansas Game and Fish Commission.

One of the first stops is Dyer Lake near Mulberry. The lake is about a mile long and 200 yards wide. Adjacent to the oxbow lake are four sections of crop land, managed specifically for waterfowl, totaling 457 acres.

"That habitat is real important to the waterfowl," said Randall Bullington, a biologist for the AGFC. "A food and water source is there all winter long and when they get ready to migrate back to the northern states and Canada in February and March."

The Dyer Lake project was started by Ducks Unlimited, which built the sections of croplands to be flooded. Farmers work the land, leaving 25 percent of the crops for the birds.

The added attraction has enhanced much of the hunting in the immediate Arkansas River valley.

"We are working to get more projects like it," McAnally said. "Once we convince people of the benefits, and make it worth their while, then we should be able to manage more land to hold more ducks."

The Johnson County Waterfowl Rest Area serves as another example. The rest area is approximately 400 acres, almost all of it in moist-soil plants. It was built in the 1970s and has continually attracted more waterfowl each year.

"At times we get covered up with ducks," said John Gallagher, AGFC wildlife biologist.

And that hasn't changed since the area doubled in size in 1996.

"Our biggest problem is the area has been too small," Gallagher said. "But we've proven it will work."

One of the biggest of the Arkansas River Valley rest areas is Holla Bend

Rest areas attract Canada geese too. Hunters take advantage of the relationship by setting Canada decoys to attract ducks.

National Wildlife Refuge. In the early 1900s this was a small community. As many as 65 families lived on the peninsula formed by the river.

Historical accounts say the land was fertile and the farms fared well. But that changed in 1927. It was the year of the great flood, and this farming community was one of its victims. The land that had been fertile was covered by layers of sand and most of the farmers left.

In 1954, the U.S. Army Corps of Engineers cut a channel across Holla Bend to improve navigation. In 1957, the land in the old river bend became Arkansas' third national wildlife refuge.

Holla Bend now provides an important resting area for migrating waterfowl. As many as 30,000 ducks have been known to winter on the area. A portion of those are trapped each winter, banded and released.

Providing a resting and feeding area is the primary goal of the refuge. A large farming operation is at the center of that goal. Like at Dyer Lake, local farmers plant soybeans, milo, corn and winter wheat. The soybeans and milo are harvested by the farmers, while the corn and wheat are left in the field for wintering waterfowl.

Scattered among the fields are several small shallow pools of water. In the summer the pools are drained, which allows the growth of moist-soil plants that provide seed for feeding waterfowl.

The largest body of water on the area is the old river channel, which forms the border for three sides of the refuge. Ducks feed in the fields and rest in the old channel.

Together all of these places provide an important link for waterfowl crossing from the Central Flyway to the Mississippi Flyway. Without them, McAnally believes Arkansas River hunting would suffer greatly.

"The river and the river valley have a lot to offer for migrating ducks," McAnally said. "But a lot of it depends heavily on high water and overflow.

"Once we get to a point where we manage for waterfowl outside of east Arkansas, then we will be able to not only winter more waterfowl, but provide more opportunity for hunters up and down the river valley."

Stan Gray holds a ringneck he shot in the Little Rock pool while watching a football game.

Busy Arkansas River provides convenient shooting areas for urban duck hunters

The ducks buzzed the decoys at the same time the Arkansas Razorbacks crossed the goal line. A minute later and they would have been dead ducks. Any earlier and they would have never been noticed.

Football games and duck hunting normally don't go together, except on the Arkansas River.

The Arkansas River's proximity to large cities makes unusual sights a little more common, one of which is shooting ducks within sight of the Little Rock skyline.

"I think most people would be amazed at how many ducks are killed in what some people would refer to as the city limits of Little Rock or North Little Rock," said Stan Gray of Little Rock, who has been known to set up a blind on a river sandbar, shoot ducks and watch a football game.

"And it's close enough to town to get good reception when there's a game on."

The same type of hunting, some within the shadows of highway bridges rumbling with the noise of traffic, can be found all the way down the river.

"One thing about river ducks, nothing seems to bother them much," Gray said.

Traffic along highways, bass boats roaring from spot to spot, barges chugging and sending out big waves are all part of life for a river hunter.

"At times it's distracting, but it's worth it," Gray said. "And besides, it only takes a few minutes from anywhere in Little Rock and I can be hunting."

Shooting is good, too. Most of the ducks are scaup, but mallards, gadwalls and an occasional pintail can be found.

"It's not an everyday thing," Gray said. "But if you only have a few hours in the morning or evening, it sure beats not going."

Hunting usually takes place on the ends of sandbars, formed between two jetties. Brush and driftwood are easily found to make a blind, and ducks decoy well.

"One thing about it, if you are close to Little Rock's skyline or a bridge, most people think it's too close for a duck to land," Gray said. "The ducks don't think that way, I guess because there's not that many people shooting at them."

The treasured jewelry of duck hunting

Metal bands function as important management tools for biologists

These small silver bands have caused worlds of pleasure and pain. No, they aren't wedding bands, but those are the only similar objects that can create this range of emotions — everything from hope and love to greed and hate.

These bands, though, are worn by birds. In layman's terms, they are called duck bands. They are the most sought after waterfowl hunting trophy. Duck hunters have argued, lied, cussed and brawled to determine who gets a duck band. A bride should feel so wanted.

The duck band, though, was not designed to bring out such emotions.

"It's a tool," said Jon Schneider, Arkansas Game and Fish Commission biologist. "And if it's something that provides a souvenir to a hunter, great."

The aluminum duck band began as a way for the U.S. Fish and Wildlife Service to determine travel routes and patterns of migrating waterfowl. It has been transformed into a way to monitor harvest rates. Somewhere in between, duck hunters started referring to the bands as jewelry, and stringing them on duck-call lanyards. They have become a badge of honor.

Shooting a banded duck is a rare occurrence. Of the almost 100 million ducks migrating, only about 200,000 are banded, or about 1 in 500. And only a small percentage of those end up in the hands of a hunter.

"But that's enough to give us invaluable information," Schneider said.

Each summer thousands of ducks are banded in the breeding grounds of the northern United States and Canada. The ducks are drawn into wire mesh traps shaped like a fish trap. They feature a large opening that necks down to a small opening. Ducks go in to feed, but can't find a way out.

A common misconception is that only mallards are banded. While the targeted species is the mallard, other ducks get into the trap, and all are banded.

Photo courtesy Brian Robbins

Thurman "Tadpole" Washington of Humnoke holds a banded mallard hen. Hunters should report band numbers to the U.S. Fish and Wildlife Service by calling, toll-free, 1-800-327-BAND.

"A band is slapped on every bird that gets in," Schneider said. "We try to use the mallard because it is the most common, and that seems to be what the hunters are mostly after."

Each band has a number; the species, sex and location of each duck is recorded as the band is attached. The path of migrating ducks can then be traced by marking their starting point and each location where a banded bird is killed. The information from those bands has revealed that a majority of the ducks wintering in Arkansas come from Saskatchewan.

The sight of a band on a duck's leg may cause unusual behavior among duck hunters.

But the bands are not just a one-way deal. In seasons past, ducks were banded in the wintering grounds to monitor the return trip.

"We learned that there is a pretty big difference in patterns that the males follow and those the females follow," Schneider said.

"Band recoveries provide us with a means to ensure that we maximize the harvest or do not over harvest."

Hens are primarily homebodies, returning to their birthplace year after year. But the drake doesn't have such ties — he follows the hen, wherever she may go.

While those patterns have been useful in determining where and when ducks travel, the band's contribution these days is as part of the methodology in determining harvest rates.

"Band recoveries provide us with a means to ensure that we maximize the harvest or do not over harvest," Schneider said.

It works like this. Let's say there were only 1,000 ducks in North America. If the U.S. Fish and Wildlife Service banded 100 of them and only 15 of the bands were reported, it would give an indication that the harvest rate was 15 percent, or a total of 150 ducks. Of course, that would hinge on how many of the bands were actually reported.

"There are a lot of bands that aren't reported," Schneider said. "I've talked to a hunter or two with lanyards full of bands that didn't report any of them. They said they didn't trust the federal government enough to report them."

The banding program has a system that accounts for unreported bands. Every few years the USFWS adds reward bands to the mix. Those bands are worth from $10 to $400 if they are reported.

"You can pretty much guess that everyone is going to turn in a high-dollar reward band," Schneider said. "They throw out a percentage of those and compute the rate in which they are returned."

Schneider said the last time a reward band study took place, it indicated that only 32 percent of bands found in Arkansas are reported.

"We assume that the return rate on the high dollar bands is the accurate rate," Schneider said. "They just provide a correction pattern."

Getting a band is special keeping them can be work

Most outdoor sports have trophies. The deer hunter has the Boone and Crockett buck, scored on the basis of antler size and mass. Turkey hunters measure spurs and beards. Anglers go by weight or length of their catch.

In duck hunting, though, the trophy is not measured or weighed. It comes in the form of a small metal band attached to a duck's leg. It's a trophy that isn't taken lightly among waterfowl hunters. Many adorn their duck call lanyards with bands. A full string of bands is considered a status symbol. The bands have become so highly-sought that almost anything can happen when a banded bird is shot.

Many one-legged ducks come back to the blind, the retrieving hunter having relieved the duck of the band before anyone else spots it. The tactic is so well-known that foot races to downed birds are common.

Bands are so prized that hunters will go to extremes to keep them, as well. So it was for Larry White of North Little Rock. One season, White leased and hunted a rice field near Humnoke. A veteran hunter, White had acquired a string of bands that began at his duck call and ended halfway up his lanyard on both sides.

On a hunt during the first week of the season, he didn't notice his duck call had become caught between two boards in the blind. It was stuck so fast that when White left the blind to retrieve a dead duck, the subsequent pull broke the lanyard. Duck bands spilled everywhere, most of them into the ankle-deep muck.

White immediately began trying to retrieve the bands. He got some but not all. Fearing the other hunters would step on his bands and push them deep into the mud, he forced everyone out of the blind. The hunt was over.

As a matter of fact, White suspended the hunting at the blind for the whole season, despite the high price of the lease. As soon as the field was dry enough, he returned with metal detector and shovel. "I managed to get most of them," White said. "I think it was worth it."

From the Mississippi to the Red

PUBLIC LAND WATERFOWL HUNTING OPPORTUNITIES ARE RISING FASTER HERE THAN ANYWHERE ELSE IN STATE

South Arkansas is better known for timber, deer, oil, watermelons and tomatoes than it is for duck hunting. But what it lacks in reputation it more than makes up for in function. The region is highlighted by a series of public areas that provide a mixture of everything that has come to symbolize duck hunting in Arkansas.

This public land trail begins in the southeast corner with Overflow National Wildlife Refuge and courses through areas with names like Seven Devils, Cut-Off Creek, Felsenthal, Sulphur River, Bois D'Arc and Millwood. This trail ends in the west at Pond Creek, the state's newest national wildlife refuge.

From a duck hunting standpoint, everything is here. There's flooded timber in Sulphur River, Cut-Off Creek, Bois D'Arc, Felsenthal and Overflow. Open water hunting is excellent on Millwood Lake, Seven Devils and the oxbows of Felsenthal. There are the swamps of Pond Creek, Sulphur River and Bois D'Arc, where Spanish moss clings to trees, giving you the feeling of stepping back in time. Where else in Arkansas can you shoot a mallard from the same spot where an alligator was sunning only a few warm days before?

◄ With his Chesapeake Bay retriever at his side and friend Bud Evans watching, Randy Atwell calls ducks in Felsenthal NWR.

In the shadows of an oil well, duck hunters return from a morning in Felsenthal NWR.

South Arkansas represents the old traditions of duck hunting, too. The Hempstead County Hunting Club, located on Grassy Lake near Millwood, was formed in 1897.

These areas have always attracted ducks. The land that is now Felsenthal was once part of a great lake stretching down through Louisiana, a natural hole of water that attracted waterfowl before the first settlers arrived. To the west, Bayou Bartholomew follows a path the Arkansas River cut 20,000 years ago. Just as the White River, Cache River and Bayou DeView converge to form a Delta waterfowl paradise, the Saline, Little and Red rivers meet in similar fashion in the southwest.

"Ducks have always come to this part of the country, and I'm sure they always will," said Danny Gulledge of Hamburg.

They may begin to come here more than in any other time in recent history. This region is best described as the new frontier in Arkansas duck hunting. In the last three decades more than 80,000 acres have been purchased for the management of waterfowl. There are more new waterfowl hunting opportunities here than in any other part of the state.

Unlike the northern half of Arkansas, the south can boast of excellent duck hunting from its west boundary to its east boundary. Lake Lewis, assistant area manager for Overflow NWR, calls it a "mixing pot" of ducks. They come down

From left, Jason Perry, Scott Perry and Terry Jerry try to remain motionless in Cut-Off Creek as mallards light behind them.

the Red River, Bayou Bartholomew, the Ouachita River and the Saline River. They come up from Louisiana and across from Texas and Mississippi. Central Flyway ducks mix with Mississippi Flyway ducks.

As in the Delta, where vast forests of hardwoods were cleared to make way for the pay off of growing soybeans and rice, south Arkansas hardwoods were cleared, too. But pine was put in its place. In both cases, what remains are the last parcels of wetlands that draw ducks for miles.

The only difference here is the timing.

"In south Arkansas, everything happens just a little bit later," Lewis said. "The ducks show up late and they stay late."

Duck hunting starts getting good at Christmas. It keeps getting better until the season ends. Just don't expect anyone from south Arkansas to promote it over watermelons, tomatoes and deer.

"We don't want anyone to know what kind of duck hunting we have," said Mark Morris of Hamburg. "They can just keep coming to deer hunt for all we care."

SOUTH ARKANSAS — A TIMELINE

1897	1930	1953	1955	1956
Wealthy timberman William Buchanan, who has a passion for duck hunting, buys the land around Grassy Lake and forms the Hempstead County Hunting Club.	On August 14, the Howard County game refuge is dedicated. Its creation involved substantial help from local citizens and the Dierks Lumber and Coal Co. (now Weyerhauser). It becomes the first of the AGFC's wildlife management areas.	Following the recommendation of federal aid coordinator Trusten Holder, the AGFC approves the purchase of 6,000 acres, entitled "the Bois D'Arc land," for a price not to exceed $25 an acre.	The AGFC purchases the 8,205-acre Rosenfield tract on Cut-Off Creek at a cost of $12.50 per acre.	The AGFC passes a condemnation order on the Moses and Cason tracts in the Bois D'Arc area for the purpose of building a fishing lake. A total of $50,000 is authorized for the construction of the lake.

Swamp holds a devilish attraction

Cut-Off Creek feeds seven lakes surrounded by pine to create Seven Devils

There is an attraction to Seven Devils Wildlife Management Area that is hard to explain. The name conjures up images of a wild place untouched by human hands. In many ways, it is an accurate image. Seven Devils is one of the few wildlife management areas that has seen little change since settlers first came to Arkansas.

Most folks would never dream of changing it. But in reality, Seven Devils probably has more to do with that than anybody's particular design.

Duck hunting around Monticello is always a unique experience. It's hard to get the feeling for traditional Arkansas duck hunting when you pass through forests of pine trees. Monticello is much better known for deer hunting than it is for duck hunting.

Locals enjoy the fact that few outsiders know about the great duck hunting here. In fact, some of the best duck hunting the state has to offer can be found in the middle of deer and pine country.

It's a setting that doesn't lend itself to beautiful mornings in the duck woods. Seven Devils has probably always been ugly. There is nothing ducky about it. It looks like the perfect home for nothing.

But Seven Devils, like the Black Swamp, is a natural duck magnet that attracts ducks from high in the sky.

"Sometimes it seems as if the ducks are miles up there, and they just let the bottom fall out," said Randy Morgan of Monticello.

Ducks that frequent Seven Devils find their way down Bayou Bartholomew and Cut-Off Creek, two waterways that flow south along the edge of the Delta.

It is close enough that ducks often feed in Delta fields at night and rest under the cover of buckbrush in one of the seven lakes here during the day.

"Seven lakes? Do you call them lakes? Those aren't lakes! They grab hold of your very soul and hold it captive! Seven lakes, you say? More like seven devils."

Seven Devils WMA is hunted almost exclusively by locals. It's really like a huge duck club with a membership of Monticello regulars.

The same duck hunters visiting the area season after season create some good-natured fun. One duck hunter following a marked trail through the swamp found himself at a dead end, surrounded by buckbrush and unable to turn around. Another hunter who left his decoys out overnight, watched as the sun rose on his spread and discovered that his decoys were painted fluorescent orange.

The good-natured fun accentuates the good duck hunting, where mallards, gadwalls and wood ducks decoy well most of the time.

Clear days attract ducks to the swamp. Ducks will respond to calls and decoys from as far away as they can be heard and seen. Like so many public hunting areas, the hunting gets better as the morning gets later.

Seven Devils Swamp is 3,500 acres of bottomland in the southeastern portion of Drew County. The swamp is fed by Cut-Off Creek, which flows in from the north.

There are seven lakes within the WMA. Boats are standard hunting platforms in the swamp. Some are outfitted with elaborate blinds and cleats that attach to trees, making for sturdy, safe places to stand and shoot.

This is an effective way to hunt deep water. You can move the boat to take advantage of the wind or get in a better body of water where ducks are more numerous. That system is common in the swamp, where the majority of the hunting seems to be around the deeper water of the seven lakes.

Why the area carries the name Seven Devils is a mystery. But there are several stories that help explain the title.

According to one story, there are seven creeks in the swamp, and if you got lost in the swamp you will have a

SOUTH ARKANSAS — A TIMELINE

1957
Sulphur River WMA is established with a $150,000 purchase of 9,000 acres. The AGFC also receives a bulldozer in the deal.

1964
The purchase of bottomland timber in an area known as Felsenthal is brought before the AGFC. The land totaling 10,560 acres is offered for sale by the Georgia-Pacific Corporation of Crossett.

1970
President Richard Nixon authorizes the establishment of 65,000-acre Felsenthal National Wildlife Refuge, located at the confluence of the Saline and Ouachita rivers.

1980
The 12,247-acre Overflow National Wildlife Refuge is purchased from The Nature Conservancy and established to preserve one of the remaining bottomland hardwood systems considered vital for waterfowl.

1996
In a land swap with Weyerhauser, the USFWS acquires 25,000 acres to add to the 2,300-acre Cossatot National Wildlife Refuge and renames the area Pond Creek NWR, Arkansas' 10th in the federal refuge system.

devil of a time getting out.

A more common story, printed in the book *7 Tales From Seven Devils,* is that, before the turn of the century, a trapper got lost in the swamp for more than two weeks. When he finally found his way out, a local farmer nursed him back to health. The trapper told the farmer of his experience in the swamp.

"It was easy for me to believe there was no escape," the trapper said. "Evil spirits seemed to draw me deeper and deeper into the swamp, and I went this way and that way but never the right way."

The farmer replied, "I've heard people say that there are seven lakes within the swamp."

"Seven lakes? Do you call them lakes?" the trapper said. "Those aren't lakes! They grab hold of your very soul and hold it captive! Seven lakes, you say? More like seven devils."

Once that story made the rounds, the name Seven Devils caught on.

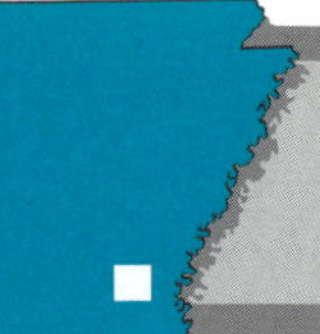

SEVEN DEVILS WMA

Acres: 512
Purchased: 1954
Topo maps (7.5 series, U.S. Geological Survey): Collins.

Seven Devils WMA is part of 3,500 acres of bottomland that make up an area commonly known as Seven Devils Swamp. The swamp is fed by Cut-Off Creek. Within the swamp are seven lakes, none of which is very large — Burton Lake, Royal Lake, Brushy Lake, Big Lake, Roberts Lake, Boggy Lake and Simpson Lake.

While their names sound harmless, the lakes are the reason for the name Seven Devils, according to local legend. The story goes that a man lost in the winding swamp cursed the lakes as devils and the title stuck.

Several small creeks course through the swamp, often creating confusion among newcomers. It is said that by dropping a leaf into one of the creeks, you can determine the general direction of flow. But in the next creek that direction of flow might change. The ever-changing directions of the many winding creeks is the reason many people become lost.

Duck hunting is most often done from one of these small lakes, using boats outfitted with pop-up blinds.

The swamp, made up of bald cypress, black willow, pin oak and hickory, is an anomaly among the pine tree forests around it. That obvious difference brings ducks from high in the sky as they push their way south while following Bayou Bartholomew and Cut-Off Creek.

Although south Arkansas is known for deer, Cut-Off Creek provides flooded timber duck hunting in the Arkansas tradition.

The 8:30 a.m. flight will arrive on time

Cut-Off Creek gets ducks that are frightened from traditional areas

If you didn't know better, you would have sworn the ducks could tell time. Their arrival was right on schedule. Randy Morgan said it would happen at 8:30 a.m., and within minutes the sky was filled with promising flights of ducks.

They first showed up in pairs, then groups of six and eight. As the minutes passed, the duckless skies of an hour earlier were filled with the silhouettes of working ducks.

Part of hunting in Cut-Off Creek includes waiting for the 8:30 flight. Hunters often refer to the particular times when flights of ducks start coming in. Usually that's more of a confidence builder or an attempt to keep friends in the woods when they are ready to go home.

But at Cut-Off Creek, the 8:30 flight is the real thing. More often than not, there are more ducks hovering over the timber of Cut-Off Creek at 8:30 than at any other time.

Locals believe those late-arriving ducks have been shot out of Bayou Meto by the mass of hunters who flock to the Arkansas Game and Fish Commission's most popular WMA. By evening, these ducks hovering over Cut-Off Creek will return to Bayou Meto. They make the round trip each day. That's the theory anyway.

While it is crowded in Bayou Meto, most Cut-Off Creek hunters have about 8,500 acres of flooded timber to themselves.

The best example of that was the 1991 season. Most Arkansas hunters experienced a poor season because of dry conditions. Cut-Off Creek was one of the only places that held ducks. But the secret never got out. Unlike other areas that get hot with activity, the word did not spread like it would for Bayou Meto or Hurricane WMAs.

At that time, Cut-Off was just like other traditional green-tree reservoirs. A hunter willing to walk could find great numbers of ducks in the large tracts of hardwoods.

John Ward of Monticello calls to the 8:30 flight in Cut-Off Creek Wildlife Management Area.

It was so good during the last week of the 1991 season that half a dozen hunters killed limits of greenheads every day. Before they left Cut-Off Creek each morning, they called in another thousand ducks, which lit among their decoys. On the last day, a common limit consisted of two mallard drakes and a black duck.

Since that time, a brutal ice storm hit south Arkansas. Cut-Off Creek was hit particularly hard. Almost every mature hardwood had its top broken from the weight of the ice, littering the forest floor. The debris has made walking through Cut-Off Creek difficult and almost impossible in waders.

But the heavy undergrowth is attractive to ducks, and the area often holds tremendous numbers of mallards. In many of the places where trees have fallen, the habitat has been enhanced with the planting of large food plots.

These are good places when cloud cover is present. And they are excellent vantage points to watch for new flights of ducks. When this day began, there were few ducks flying. At 7:30 a hooded

A flock of mallards is caught by the camera just as they lift off from Cut-Off Creek.

merganser found its way into the spread, and 30 minutes later a mallard floated in treetop-high.

It looked as if two ducks would be the extent of the hunt.

"Just wait," Morgan said. "Things will pick up. We still haven't seen the 8:30 flight."

The ducks didn't let Morgan down. Within minutes the hunt had renewed vigor. Of the several thousand ducks that flew overhead, 90 percent were pintails. That in itself added to the surprising aspects of the duck hunting in this region.

There is no way of knowing whether or not the 8:30 flight theory has any validity at all. But on a slow day, it seems feasible enough to make you want to wait it out.

CUT-OFF CREEK WMA

Acres: 8,937
First purchase: 1956
Location: Near Dermott in Drew County
Topo maps (7.5 series, U.S. Geological Survey): Line.

Cut-Off Creek Wildlife Management Area is one of the few state-owned public hunting areas in Southeast Arkansas, and therefore receives considerable hunting pressure during the deer and waterfowl seasons. Camping is restricted to a few designated areas, which quickly fill up with hunters.

Access to the west side of the area is by county roads, three miles south of the Collins community on State Highway 35. Access to the east side of the areas is from county roads along the west side of Bayou Bartholomew and off U.S. Highway 165 south of Dermott, near Jerome. Vehicular traffic on the area is restricted to maintained gravel roads.

Cut-Off Creek is flooded in the fall and winter to attract ducks and generally offers some good hunting. There is also a good deer herd on this WMA, as well as good numbers of squirrels and furbearing animals. This is a fairly typical bottomland hardwood area, containing numerous potholes and wetland acres.

Cut-Off Creek itself provides some fair to good fishing for a variety of species.

From left, Mark Morris, Danny Gulledge and Drew Baker push their boat near the boundary of Overflow National Wildlife Refuge.

Where the Delta meets piney woods

Overflow NWR last attraction for ducks migrating through east Arkansas

All morning Danny Gulledge had been waiting for the sight above him. Right at the top of the trees, 20 to 30 black mallard bodies were cupped and committed to dropping in.

It is a sight timber duck hunters relish. Mallards swing low over the treetops, set up on a hole with wings cupped, then start fluttering their wings as they begin to drop.

The only problem with this scene was there were two dozen decoys still in a decoy bag. And the rest of the hunting party was gathering the remaining gear from a hunting hole. Ten minutes earlier or later and they would have been in a perfect position to coax the ducks through the treetops and into the decoys.

Drew Baker, Mark Morris and Gulledge were hunting in Overflow National Wildlife Refuge. The refuge is an almost pristine tract of hardwood timber in the extreme Southeast corner of the state. Whereas Big Lake is the first stop in Arkansas for migrating mallards, Overflow is the last stop.

But unlike the areas to the northeast, Overflow often sees light pressure, while affording refuge for great numbers of ducks close to the end of their migration through Arkansas.

But even in an area where there are ducks, conditions have to be right. On this day in Overflow, they were far from it.

Clouds had brought rain to Overflow. The rain started almost as soon as the alarm clock went off and did not stop for more than five minutes throughout the day.

For as long as Gulledge can remember, duck hunting has been associated with nasty weather. But from a timber hunting standpoint, cold weather and clear skies are as nasty as they like to see it.

Rather than opt for a field hunt when presented with the truly nasty conditions, Gulledge and party set up in the middle of the bottoms and waited for the black skies to turn to dark gray. To them, a slow day in the bottoms of Overflow outweighs a good day elsewhere.

There were just enough ducks to keep it interesting. Less than 10 minutes after things started clicking, eight mallards sailed into the decoys like they were on a string.

When they were well within range, the group exhibited some exceptional shooting. But the hitting wasn't very good. When the shooting was over, only three ducks lay dead on the water.

There would be other chances. However, it seemed the ducks preferred another section of the woods.

To remedy the problem, they picked up the decoys and made ready to move. It was then that the 20- to 30-bird flock presented itself. And an opportunity was lost.

The rainy day ended at 11:30 with only the three mallards. Sitting in the wet woods trying to coax one of the hundreds of flocks to break through the treetops, it was obvious why south Arkansas hunters like Overflow so much. It's about 12,000 acres of the flattest timberland in the state.

Tommy Strebek of Crossett, who has hunted the area for the last 40 years, said that several years ago the land was surveyed, and from one end to the other there was less than two feet difference in land variation. That it hasn't been cleared is a miracle.

It is surrounded by some of the most treeless landscape in Arkansas. The whole region at one time was like Overflow. The area's extreme western border is a bluff where the Gulf Coastal Plain meets the Delta. Above the ridge, the land was like the hardwood forests of Overflow, but it has since been cut and reseeded in pine plantations. The piney woods, as it is called by the locals, is home to the biggest deer herd in the state.

To the east of Overflow is typical east Arkansas agricultural land, where soybeans and rice are grown. That land heavily timbered like Overflow before it was cleared for farming between 1937 and 1978.

Somehow Overflow survived the saw. According to Strebek, it was offered to the Arkansas Game and Fish Commission for about $2 an acre. Even though the price was cheap, the sale was turned down due to a lack of funds. A local farmer bought the area, and it was private until The Nature Conservancy bought it in the early 1980s and turned it over to the national wildlife refuge system.

Because it has been basically untouched for so long, the large tracts of oak are almost like virgin timber with huge trees similar to those found in Shirey Bay-Rainey Brake and Big Lake. The big trees offer a duck hunting scene that timber hunters envision when they think of the perfect hardwood bottom

OVERFLOW NWR

Acres: 12,247
First purchase: 1980
Topo maps (7.5 series, U.S. Geological Survey): Wilmot SW, Wilmot NW.

Overflow National Wildlife Refuge is located southeast of Crossett in Ashley County. It is bordered by the Louisiana state line on the south, cleared agricultural land to the east, and Mississippi Valley Alluvial escarpment on the north and west.

The escarpment, or bluff, is the dividing line between what is normally referred to as the "Piney Woods" and the Mississippi River Delta. Deer hunters on the bluff look out over hardwood bottoms made up primarily of red oak trees.

Migrating waterfowl see it as a large rest area amid a part of the country that has lost all of its hardwood.

The bottoms are flooded by Overflow Creek, which is fed from the north by Beech Creek and from the east by tributary sloughs. Overflow Creek feeds into Bayou Bartholomew, which feeds into the Ouachita River.

Flooding occurs when Bayou Bartholomew backs up, and runoff from agricultural land fills the sloughs.

Access is made from Hamburg, southeast on Highway 8, then south on Highway 8-173 Cutoff and west on Highway 173. A primitive boat ramp accesses Gaines Slough where hunters filter into the bottomland hardwoods.

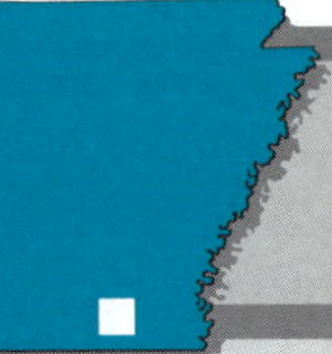

FELSENTHAL NWR

Acres: 65,000
Authorized: 1970 by Public Law 91-611, and signed by President Richard Nixon.
Established: 1975
Topo maps (7.5 series, U.S. Geological Survey): New Union, Hutig, Marais Saline, Felsenthal Dam.

Felsenthal NWR is located in Ashley, Union, and Bradley counties in southeast Arkansas, 53 miles west of the Mississippi River, three miles north of the Louisiana border and eight miles west of Crossett.

The area has three land types that include 39,000 acres in bottomland hardwood, 11,000 acres in upland habitat and 15,000 acres in permanent water.

The refuge lies within what is known as the Felsenthal Basin, a remnant of an enormous lake that once extended below Monroe, Louisiana.

The confluence of the Ouachita and Saline rivers is at the heart of the refuge, and each river helps flood the area. A dam on the Ouachita River holds enough water so that the 15,000 acres of permanent water and the 21,000 acres flooded by overflow create what the USFWS believes is the world's largest green-tree reservoir.

In addition, the two rivers' associated creeks, sloughs, oxbow lakes and bayous provide a chain of fishing and hunting opportunities for many species.

The area is accessed in several locations, including from Highway 82 west of Crossett and near the dam site one mile north of Huttig.

According to USFWS statistics, the area's average waterfowl population from October to December is approximately 30,000 ducks. A peak occurred in Nov. 1995, when more than 300,000 mallards wintered in the area.

Two factors influence the flooding potential of Felsenthal: the topography is relatively flat, and the refuge is lower than the surrounding area. Those factors result in the area being flooded most years for up to eight months.

The Saline and Ouachita rivers provide water for flooding thousands of acres in Felsenthal National Wildlife Refuge.

A 'mixing pot' of migrating ducks

Felsenthal's location and flood plan attract ducks from several directions

One minute there was not a duck in the sky. The next minute a flock of mallards was breaking through the tops of trees and settling down in one of the nameless sloughs in Felsenthal National Wildlife Refuge. The sudden change in scenery prompted the question: "Where did they come from?"

Felsenthal sits almost exactly in the middle of the south border of the state. Unlike the rest of the duck hunting refuges within the state that have agricultural fields surrounding them, Felsenthal is almost totally surrounded by south Arkansas' piney woods. The clearcuts and pine forests are good habitat for deer and turkey. But they are not suitable for ducks.

In the average refuge, ducks feed close by in flooded fields and use the woods of the refuge to rest. They stick to these areas mostly during the day, filtering out early in the morning or on moonlit nights to feed. It doesn't happen that way at Felsenthal.

"I don't know exactly where these ducks come from," said Lake Lewis, assistant refuge manager for Overflow NWR who hunts Felsenthal regularly. "I haven't ridden on their backs so it's hard to say."

Lewis has seen thousands of ducks come to Felsenthal and can only theorize about where they originate. The area's location allows many possibilities. Central Flyway ducks traveling the Red River to the west can find Felsenthal just a hop, skip and jump away from Sulphur River WMA. The Ouachita and Saline rivers that come together in the heart of the area are thoroughfares that stretch to the central part of the state. A hard right turn by ducks migrating down the Arkansas River puts them on course to follow those lesser-known routes. To the east, ducks along the Mississippi River and as far away as Stuttgart can make the trip in a few hours. And to the south, ducks filter up from Louisiana.

"It's just a mixing pot," Lewis said.

A mixing pot that has seen peak populations of mallards as high as 300,000 with an average of 30,000 ducks a day. The hunting is good, providing some of the only public-land opportunity in the region. In all, there are about 65,000 acres within the refuge. Of that, 15,000 acres are permanently flooded, and with manipulation of water another 21,000 acres are flooded for part of duck season. The total 36,000 acres was once billed as the world's largest green-tree reservoir.

"But not all of it is green today," Lewis said.

Part of the 15,000 acres is dead timber, and area managers are working to keep from losing any more. The dead timber is a result of water that remains on hardwood stands too long. At times the area is flooded for as long as eight months of the year. Oak trees are not water-tolerant that long, become stressed and die.

"We can't afford to lose any more trees," Lewis said. "We are trying our best to protect the woods as best we can."

For that reason, water management at Felsenthal is highly intensive. The area is flooded slowly.

Felsenthal's standard water level is 65 feet mean sea level. At that depth, 15,000 acres are flooded and at 70 msl, 36,000 acres are flooded. To get to that level, the water is raised in daily increments. For instance, look at one year's flood plan. From Nov. 15 to Nov. 30, 1997, Felsenthal was raised two-tenths of a foot with a target depth of 67.5 feet by Dec. 1.

After that point, the rise is regulated to one-tenth of a foot per day with a target depth of 70 msl by the first of January. While that plan doesn't always make local hunters happy, most of whom would like to see 36,000 acres flooded for the whole season, it could explain where Felsenthal's ducks originate.

Each increment of water inundates new ground, putting new food in the water every day.

Biologists tracking radio-collared birds have found that ducks, especially mallards, are prone to fly great distances to take advantage of newly-flooded ground. Those trips have been far enough to easily encompass a trip from Stuttgart to Felsenthal and back.

"Mallards love to exploit newly flooded habitat, and they will fly a long way to do so," Lewis said. "So that could be possible."

Either way, filling Felsenthal slowly enhances the duck holding potential.

"It's like opening the candy store," Lewis said. "You don't get the volume of ducks like you have on the Cache and White rivers until after Christmas."

That late timing is yet another reason for the incremental flooding. Things just happen later in south Arkansas.

"From a duck hunting standpoint it probably wouldn't help much to have it flooded early," Lewis said. "They get here late and they stay late."

That tendency makes Felsenthal one of the hottest hunting spots during the month of January. The hunting can be good even before that. Early season hunting occurs primarily on oxbow lakes in the lower end of the refuge.

"From a duck hunting standpoint it probably wouldn't help much to have it flooded early. They get here late and they stay late."

The best hunting takes place on lakes Pete Wilson, Wildcat, Redeye, Shallow Lake, Spring Bayou, and Grand Marais.

Most of the shooting is from boats outfitted with pop-up blinds and surrounded by big spreads of decoys. As the water level inches up, lakes to the north of those like Marais Saline start seeing more ducks. By the time the level reaches 67 msl, sloughs and low lying flat areas offer classic green-tree shooting. It stays that way and continually improves as more ducks arrive.

"The one thing about Felsenthal is it doesn't get the crowded conditions like most of the public shooting grounds," Lewis said. "It gets a lot of pressure, but the hunters aren't behind every tree."

Lewis said early in the season the permanent pool is crowded all the time, but once the water level gets up, the hunters scatter.

"You just get a lot more elbow room than in other public areas," Lewis said.

Ducks travel the sloughs and river channels in small groups up to about 25.

"It's a lot like Bayou Meto where you work three or four groups, with a large flock numbering a couple of dozen," Lewis said. "You really don't see the flight ducks of 200 or more at a time like you would on the Cache or White rivers."

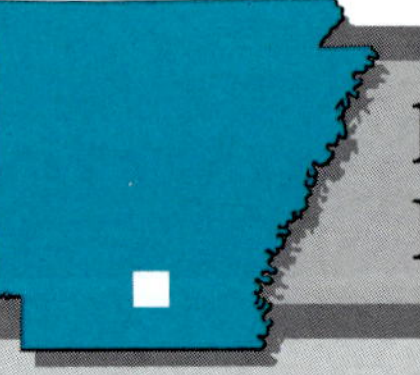

BERYL ANTHONY/ LOWER OUACHITA WMA

Acres: 7,069
First purchase: 1984
Topo maps: Felsenthal Dam, Huttig.

The Beryl Anthony Wildlife Management are is located in Ashley and Union counties. The area is almost entirely bottomland hardwood forest, with the exception of two lakes — Clear and Lock. Both are within the area's boundaries. The WMA is bordered by the Felsenthal National Wildlife Refuge to the north and the Ouachita River National Wildlife Refuge to the south. Both refuges are well-known for their waterfowl hunting. The same is true for the lesser known wildlife management area. Hunting on the area takes place when the Ouachita River leaves its banks, an occurrence that takes place most years and can last as long as six months annually.

The WMA lies within what is known as the Felsenthal Basin, a remnant of an enormous lake that once extended below Monroe, Louisiana. It has been attracting waterfowl for decades, with upwards of 300,000 ducks wintering near the area during dry years. The area is accessed from the Ouachita River below the lock and dam at Felsenthal and by a county road that runs through it. The road has several primitive camp sites along its length.

Hunting is traditional green timber shooting, but unlike some areas in Felsenthal and other WMAs, the water gets too deep to wade. Most of the hunting takes place from boats.

The best times to hunt are after Felsenthal floods. The minimum flows from Felsenthal Dam keep water in the bottomlands of Lower Ouachita WMA. The two areas complement each other, allowing hunters and ducks to spread out.

Ducks frequent the area to rest and to get away from the heavy pressure in the neighboring refuges. Hunters willing to scout can find concentrations of mostly mallards.

Bois D'Arc among best WMAs

Central Flyway sends ducks into flooded timber for traditional Arkansas hunt

Bois D'Arc is not considered to be in the heart of duck hunting country. Located near Hope, this area is better known for its watermelons, deer hunting and politicians.

But this 7,500 acre wildlife management area, about 800 of which is flooded for duck hunting, is as traditional a duck hunting place as there is in the state. It was recognized as such in the late 1940s when Trusten Holder, the Arkansas Game and Fish Commission's coordinator of federal aid, set out to buy this land for duck hunting. It was one of his top choices, along with Bayou Meto and Black River.

Bois D'Arc is located near the Red River, where large numbers of mallards funnel down from the Central Flyway through Oklahoma and into Arkansas. What the Black, Cache and White rivers are to east Arkansas, the Red River is to southwest Arkansas.

And the results are comparable, too. The majority of the ducks killed here are mallards. Further west on Millwood Lake, where the water is open, other species are hunted. But mallards in the timber of Bois D'Arc were the goal here.

It is a special experience. The timber is just like that of the more popular WMAs, but you get a real feel of being in a different part of the world as you travel along the ditches and bayous of Bois D'Arc. Cypress and oak trees are covered with Spanish moss, providing a swampy touch that is often lost in other areas.

There is a lot of that feeling in this part of the world. To the north of Bois D'Arc is the legendary duck hunting club, Grassy Lake, where swamp is almost too formal of a description.

"It's like stepping back into prehistoric times," said Phil Butler, who is a regular on Bois D'Arc, along with his son Drake, an Intermediate World's Duck Calling Champion.

Grassy Lake and areas around it like Bois D'Arc are known for their alligators. The huge gator on display at the Little Rock Zoo known as Arkie came from Grassy Lake.

Bois D'Arc was bought in 1953, when the Arkansas Game and Fish Commission was actively acquiring as much bottomland as possible. But the area was known for its duck hunting long before that.

Like Big Lake in northeast Arkansas, this is a community area, where locals utilize hunting holes with names like Pole Cat Meadow. At one time, blinds were allowed on the area, but the small

Phil (left) and Drake Butler take up decoys after a morning hunt at Bois D'Arc WMA.

Alligators are common in southwest Arkansas hunting areas, like Bois D'Arc.

size of the area caused conflicts.

As legend has it, an old timer had a blind in Bois D'Arc that everyone honored as his. The man hunted the area often, even though he was well into his 70s. But one day, an Arkansas State Trooper got to the old man's blind first. He wouldn't leave, nor would he allow the old man to stay and hunt.

Needless to say the old timer got his feathers ruffled and invited the much younger state trooper out to the levee, where the old timer intended to whip the trooper.

The scene made for quite a story and lots of controversy; by the next season, blinds were outlawed on the area.

Today, the local hunters compete over who gets to what hole first. Sometimes the race starts on the roads leading to Bois D'Arc. But more often, determined local duck hunters spend the night at the boat ramp. When they see lights coming down the road, they jump in their boats for a head start. All of this is legal, as long as boats are not on the area before 4 a.m.

There are differences hunting at Bois D'Arc from other WMAs. Hunters here believe in the word "hunt." A duck hunt is an all-day affair and lasts to the last possible second. In many other WMAs, ducks are so numerous that a hunt is often considered more of a shoot than a hunt. If hunters in those locations don't have their limits by 9 or 10 a.m., they leave the woods.

In Bois D'Arc you never know when the next flight of mallards coming down the Red River will appear, and it can be worth the wait.

BOIS D'ARC WMA

Acres: 5,883
First purchase: 1953
Location: Near Hope in Hempstead County.
Topo maps (7.5 series, U.S. Geological Survey): Spring Hill.

Bois D'Arc Wildlife Management Area is located about seven miles south of Hope and can be reached off U.S. Highway 67 or State Highway 355 in the vicinity of Spring Hill.

The bottomland hardwoods of the Bois D'Arc area offer good hunting for deer, squirrel, furbearers and — when flooded — ducks. The WMA lies only two miles from Red River, a flight path for ducks coming through Oklahoma and the southwestern corner of Arkansas. Several water control structures have been built to flood the area to attract ducks.

The 750-acre Bois D'Arc public fishing lake, formed by an earthen dam across Cedar Bayou, provides good fishing for bass, bream, crappie, and catfish — and also serves as a waterfowl rest area.

The area is heavily used by all types of hunters, so several camping sites have been developed to help disperse hunters. During wet periods, vehicle access is limited, and roads may be closed.

A way station for Red River ducks

Lake Millwood provides some of the only guaranteed water in SW Arkansas

In the 1940s the Arkansas Game and Fish Commission attempted to buy a large section of bottomland along Little River, Saline River and Pond Creek.

At the time, the AGFC was buying every acre of valuable duck hunting land that it could get its hands on. In this case, the bottoms were renowned for exceptional flooded timber duck hunting.

"Old-timers used to say you could walk across it on the backs of ducks," said Greg Mathis, AGFC wildlife biologist. "It was phenomenal."

The AGFC failed in its purchase attempts. The lumber company that owned it refused to sell.

It was just as well. The lumber company's decision was unfortunate only for itself. As it turned out, most of the timber in the bottoms was destroyed by the impoundment of Lake Millwood.

Although hunters in southwest Arkansas lost thousands of acres of overflow bottoms, they gained more than 30,000 acres of guaranteed surface water.

"Lake Millwood has since become vital, if not critical, to the average duck hunter," Mathis said.

It is a way station for every duck flying down the Red River. Local hunters say that when Lake Millwood has ducks, everyone around it has ducks. If Lake Millwood doesn't have ducks, no one has ducks.

The lake is totally public. And it provides the biggest part of the public hunting opportunity in southwest Arkansas. It's an opportunity a lot of people take advantage of.

"It is heavily hunted," Mathis said.

Hunting on the lake takes place in two forms. The most common is open water or lake hunting. Lake Millwood impounded several shallow fields, timber, buckbrush flats and winding sloughs. As a result, much of the lake is shallow.

That, combined with a healthy dose of aquatic vegetation, makes it a favorite stopping place for early migrants like teal.

Hunting on Lake Millwood is usually in open water, where big spreads of decoys work best,

Whether early in the season or late, hunters launch at many places on the lake and make their way to the shallow areas where they set out big spreads of decoys and stand in buckbrush or dead timber. Others make use of blinds attached to their boats.

"Years ago the Corps would allow you to build your own blind," Mathis said. "But it got out of hand, and they had to do away with that."

"Old timers used to say you could walk across it on the backs of ducks. It was phenomenal."

The second hunting method is similar. It occurs when the lake rises in the fall and spreads out. Most of the hunting continues to take place in shallow areas; there's just much more of it. Along with the extra flooded ground, there is also a return to the days of old in the form of flooded timber shooting.

"The majority of the ducks killed on Millwood are mallards, probably 60 percent of the kill," Mathis said. "But the gadwall hunting is really good at times."

Other species include redheads, canvasbacks, mergansers and scaup.

Construction began on Millwood Lake in 1961 and was completed in 1966. It is considered a key player in flood reduction along the Red River.

More importantly for area sportsmen, the lake is a vital link in holding ducks for surrounding clubs. Long-time clubs like Grassy Lake, Yellow Creek, Cypress Bayou and Po-Boy manage a large portion of hardwood bottoms near the lake. Along with Millwood, these clubs constitute the largest area of wintering habitat for waterfowl in that part of the Red River valley.

The area received a major addition with the purchase of Pond Creek bottoms, north of Millwood. The U.S. Fish and Wildlife Service bought approximately 26,000 acres in the area. The Pond Creek National Wildlife Refuge is expected to be managed to produce some flooded timber hunting. When it all comes together, this will create a wintering area rivaled only by the White River NWR.

Mouth calling, pirogues, among traditions still alive in Sulphur River WMA

Duck hunting in Sulphur River Wildlife Management Area is a return to the past in many ways.

The overflow bottomlands along Mercer Bayou in the Red River valley are like the Black River WMA in northeast Arkansas. Sulphur River WMA represents the remnants of the deep Red River bottomlands that were common 100 years ago.

Unlike most hardwood bottomlands, this area gets too deep to wade. Rather than the traditional way of hugging a tree and kicking water, hunters shoot from johnboats or pirogues. Homemade blinds are common fixtures on boats, and big spreads of decoys in likely areas attract ducks coming down the Central Flyway.

"Most of the hunters filter out into the wooded holes or small lakes," said Greg Mathis, an Arkansas Game and Fish Commission wildlife biologist. "A lot of the hunters use pirogues. They paddle out, set their decoys, back their boats into the brush and call the ducks down to them.

"It's an old style of hunting that works really well in Sulphur River."

One of those pirogue hunters is Mike Harris. His father, James, has hunted the bottoms for years.

"The Harris family lives and breathes duck hunting," Mathis said.

Mathis means that literally. When James and Mike Harris call ducks they do it with their own breath — no duck calls, just what their hands and lungs provide.

"Mouth calling is a lost art," Mathis said. "But they still do it."

Mathis said Harris doubles his thumb over and grips his fist around it tightly.

"His hand actually looks like he's holding a duck call," Mathis said. "But there's nothing there. He takes his fist and shakes it in the water and then blows through it.

"I don't know how it works. But it sounds real good."

The ducks like it, too. The hands-on process produces limits every season, just like duck hunters did it 100 years ago.

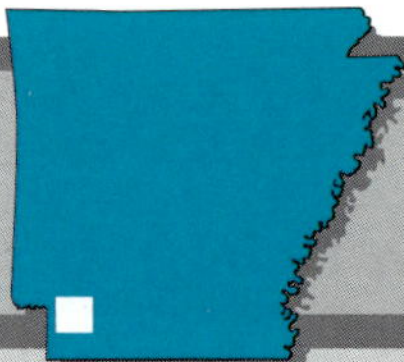

SULPHUR RIVER WMA

Acres: 16,520
First purchase: 1957
Location: Near Texarkana in Miller County
Topo maps (7.5 series, U.S. Geological Survey): Doddridge NW, Bloomburg, Domino, Fouke.

The Sulphur River Wildlife Management Area lies west off U.S. Highway 71, 15 miles south of Texarkana, near the Texas-Arkansas-Louisiana borders. Limited access is available off Arkansas Highways 237 and 160, as well as U.S. 71.

When flooded, Sulphur River WMA offers some of the best duck hunting in southwest Arkansas. Rainfall provides the bulk of the flooding; water control is aided by a series of dams and levees on Mercer Bayou. Most of the Sulphur River area is in the lowlands of Mercer Bayou, with a number of feeder streams winding through the bottomlands. Most hunting is in small open pools.

Because the water gets too deep to wade, hunting takes place from boats and makeshift blinds. Local hunters often use pirogues to slip quietly through the woods.

Bottomland hardwoods, such as oak and hickory, are the primary habitat, and provide good hunting for deer, squirrel, and swamp rabbits.

Most travel on Sulphur River WMA is by boat or foot. Camping is allowed only in a few designated areas.

There is limited sportfishing on the many lakes, creeks and sloughs of the area. However, commercial fishing is heavy in Mercer Bayou and Sulphur River.

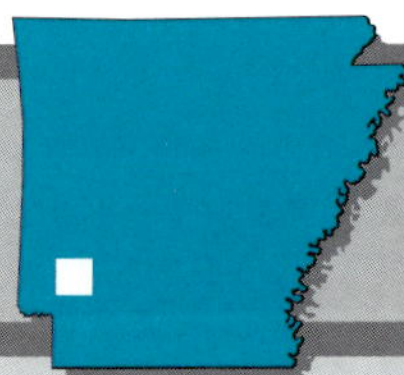

POND CREEK NWR

Acres: 27,300
First purchase: 1994
Topo maps (7.5 series, U.S. Geological Survey): Falls Chapel, Winthrop, Horatio, Lockesburg.

Originally named the Cossatot National Wildlife Refuge, the Pond Creek bottoms consist of 2,300 acres. In 1996, the Arkansas Land Exchange Act added an additional 25,000 acres. The land was part of a trade agreement between the U.S. Fish and Wildlife Service and Weyerhauser Timber Co.

Pond Creek NWR is 95 percent forested land — mostly oaks — with small areas of open water, shrub swamps, beaver ponds, open marsh and roads. Duck hunting is excellent when Little River leaves its banks.

Ducks use the area from the Red River flyway. In dry years, waterfowl can rest on Lake Millwood, which adjoins the refuge.

Once water-control structures are in place, Pond Creek coupled with Lake Millwood will hold untold numbers of ducks in southwest Arkansas, according to Arkansas Game and Fish Commission wildlife biologist Greg Mathis.

"It's a major plus for this part of the world," Mathis said.

Hunting in the NWR takes place in traditional form in the overflow bottoms. But there are also many small beaver ponds, and there is some open marsh hunting, reminiscent of Louisiana.

In the past, some individuals attempted to turn part of the area into a private duck club, Mathis said. But the efforts met little success.

The ability of the USFWS to manage the unit as a whole should improve duck hunting and end the individual efforts.

A series of roads throughout the refuge provides access. Hunters are required to carry a refuge permit, available at the Felsenthal NWR office.

Arkansas' ultimate step back in time

Primeval swamp of Grassy Lake preserved by a duck hunter in late 1800s

Primeval. It's the word you hear in almost every description of Grassy Lake. It's one thing to get deep in the White River Wildlife Refuge and imagine a 19th century steamboat rounding a bend in the river. It's quite another to look over an ancient swamp and think how natural a *Tyrannosaurus Rex* would appear here. That's primeval.

Of the unaltered wonders remaining in Arkansas, Grassy Lake represents the biggest step back in time. And if not for a duck hunter, it wouldn't have aged nearly so well.

There must be 100 lakes named "Grassy" in Arkansas. But there is nothing like this 6,000-acre swamp located in the bottomlands below Millwood Lake, between Hope and Texarkana. Apparently, William Buchanan thought the same thing when he saw it in the late 1800s. The owner was going to harvest the impressive stand of cypress trees when Buchanan made him an offer that matched the value of the land, plus the timber on it.

Buchanan had already become a wealthy man through the timber industry. By this time, he was more concerned with using that fortune to feed his love of the outdoors. The ducks that flocked to Grassy Lake made this one of Buchanan's favorite places.

In 1897, he formed the Hempstead County Hunting Club and built a lodge near the lake. Duck hunting was done in grand style. In the book, *Southern Timberman*, Archer H. Mayor recounts the daily routine during hunting season. Black servants began cooking breakfast at 2 a.m., woke up the hunters at 4 a.m. and pushed or paddled them to their blinds before dawn.

During this era before daily bag limits were set, the shooting was limited only by the strength of your desire.

Herbert Railey was born the same year the Hempstead County Hunting Club was founded. He lived on the ridge above Grassy Lake. Local residents were allowed to hunt on the lake, but they couldn't use a boat. These "bank hunters," as they were called, helped keep the ducks stirred up for the members who hunted from blinds on the lake. Railey began frequenting Grassy Lake as a "bank hunter" in the 1930s.

"I was allowed to hunt, but I couldn't carry anybody with me," Railey said. "Grassy Lake was duck heaven. It was my favorite place. The mallards were thick. Every once in awhile you killed a wood duck."

Wading along the banks of Grassy Lake wasn't as inviting as it might sound. Alligators, big alligators, added to the primeval sights of Grassy Lake, both then and now.

"Those alligators wouldn't bother you," said Railey.

Federal regulations, including bag

The Hempstead County Hunting Club was founded in 1897. Duck hunters depart from these boat houses after drawing for blinds.

Photo courtesy Bill Routon

Ralph Routon of Hope displayed the bounty from a morning's hunt at Grassy Lake in this photo from 1914, before daily bag limits were set.

limits, were set in 1918, but it would be many years before enforcement would put any teeth in those laws.

"Legal was all you could carry," Railey said. "I forget what the limit was. At the beginning, they didn't pay any attention to it, and neither did I."

Bill Routon of Hope has a picture (above) of his father, Ralph, with 50-plus ducks from a morning's hunt at Grassy Lake. In the photo, Routon is holding a 12-gauge Remington automatic shotgun with a nine-shot extension. A cypress "box" boat, which was commonly used in that day, appears in the foreground.

Bill Routon joined the Hempstead County Hunting Club shortly after he moved here from Alabama in 1910. Although his father died in 1934, when Bill was only 10 years old, he remembers several hunting trips with his father on Grassy Lake. And he remembers his father canning both duck and quail, so they could enjoy the meat year round. The results of successful hunts didn't go to waste.

All of the ducks identifiable in the photograph are mallards, mostly drakes.

"We always thought anything but a mallard was a trash duck," Routon said.

Routon sold his membership in the Hempstead County Hunting Club after he returned from the service in World War II. He's now a member of the Yellow Creek Club, which borders Grassy Lake and is located in the same bottomland.

William Buchanan's family still owns controlling interest in the Hempstead County Hunting Club. The presence of old money, a 100-year-old hunting club, mallard ducks and rich bottomland gives the southwest corner of Arkansas a Delta atmosphere. Cotton was king here, too, at one time.

You just don't hear much about the duck hunting here.

"This part of the Red River valley is so similar to the Mississippi Delta, but it's just on a smaller scale," said Charlie Walker, a Hope attorney and member of the Yellow Creek Club. "The Red River valley in Louisiana is a popular hunting area, but in Arkansas it's a well-kept secret."

Before Millwood Dam was built, the Saline, Little and Red rivers flowed together within a few miles of Grassy Lake.

"The Red River used to flood all the time and back up all over this country," said Routon.

But that has begun to change. Millwood Dam controls the Saline and Little rivers. Lake Texoma absorbs some of the Red River's rage. In the absence of periodic floods, the swamp at Grassy Lake is changing, too. Gadwalls have increasingly taken the place of mallards in the daily bag. The thick vegetation that has always been part of this swamp has changed character, too, Routon has noticed.

But the cypress trees haven't changed. And Grassy Lake still offers the best primeval view in Arkansas.

This 1955 AGFC map shows the southwest corner of the state before Millwood Lake was impounded. Grassy Lake is just north of Little River's confluence with Red River.

PIKE
MURFREESBORO
HOWARD
DE QUEEN
SEVIER
NASHVILLE
HEMPSTEAD
LITTLE
RIVER
ASHDOWN
HOPE
TEXARKANA
MILLER
LEWISVILLE
LAFAYETTE
Bizzil L.
Hollway L.
Lichford L.
Pond
Negro L.
Spring L.
Stag
Red L.
Red L.
Grassy L.
Mc Guire L.
Horseshoe L.
Mud L.
Clear L.
Yarber L.
Bairds L.
Grassy L.
Cypress L.
Hawkins L.
Johnson L.
Levoice L.
Scott L.
Trailer L.
Red L.
Clear L.
Walker L.
Clear L.
Orten L.
Pleasant L.
Winham L.
Harper L.
Mud L.
Upper Red L.
Fish L.
Old River L.
Buck Martin L.
Lower Red L.
Old River Lake
Clear L.
Cypress L.
27 Cut-off L.
1st Old River L.
2nd Old River L.
Adams Cut-off L.
Scott L.
Kuykendall L.
Purson L.
Moore L.
Cut-off L.
Meriwether L.
Bratt L.
Spirit L.
Bayou L.
Cypress L.
Kelley L.
Norman L.
Le May L.
Goss L.
Copeland L.
Lower Bayou L.
Goose L.
Maniece L.
Coker L.
Palmer L.
Birdewells Lake
June
RED RIVER
LITTLE RIVER
SULPHUR RIVER
COSSATOT
SALINE
Blue Bayou
Mine Cr.
Yellow Cr.
Hudson Cr.
Sandy Bois D'Arc Cr.
Creek
Bodcaw
Day Cr.
Boggy Cr.
Mercer Bayou
Maniece B.
Field B.
Walnut Bayou
Choctaw Bayou
Caney Cr.
Flat Cr.
Rolling Fork
Rock Cr.
Cane Cr.
Muddy Fk.
Prairie Cr.
Saline Cr.
Antoine
70
71
82
67

ARKANSAS DUCK SEASONS – YEAR BY YEAR

(Year represents when season began; for example, 1915 is 1915-16 duck season)

Year	Total Days	Daily Bag Limit	Mallard Limit	(Hens)	Start	End	Notes
1915	106	None			Oct. 2	Jan. 15	Arkansas only; no federal laws
1916-17	92	None			Nov. 1	Jan. 31	Arkansas only; no federal laws
1918-29	92	25			Nov. 1	Jan. 31	First federal waterfowl regulations
1930	92	15			Nov. 1	Jan. 31	
1931	30	15			Nov. 16	Dec. 15	
1932	61	15			Nov. 16	Jan. 15	
1933	61	12			Nov. 16	Jan. 15	
1934	30	12			Nov. 6	Dec. 15	Tuesday thru Saturday only
1935	30	10			Nov. 20	Dec. 19	C
1936	30	10			Nov. 26	Dec. 25	F
1937	30	10			Nov. 27	Dec. 26	F
1938	45	10			Nov. 15	Dec. 29	F
1939	45	10	3	(3)	Nov. 15	Dec. 29	F
1940	60	10			Nov. 2	Dec. 31	
1941	60	10	3	(3)	Nov. 2	Dec. 31	
1942	70	10	10	(10)	Nov. 2	Jan. 10	Wood ducks open; closed since '18
1943	70	10	10	(10)	Nov. 2	Jan. 10	
1944	80	15	5	(5)	Nov. 2	Jan. 20	D
1945	80	10	10	(10)	Nov. 2	Jan. 20	D
1946	45	7	7	(7)	Nov. 26	Jan. 6	A
1947	30	4	4	(4)	Dec. 8	Jan. 6	E, Noon start opening day
1948	30	4	4	(4)	Nov. 26	Dec. 25	
1949	40	4	4	(4)	Nov. 18	Dec. 27	
1950	35	4	4	(4)	Dec. 2	Jan. 5	
1951	45	4	4	(4)	Nov. 22	Jan. 5	
1952-54	55	4	4	(4)	Nov. 17	Jan. 10	
1955-58	70	4	4	(4)	Nov. 7	Jan. 15	A
1959	40	4	4	(4)	Nov. 30	Jan. 8	B, Noon start opening day
1960	40	4	4	(4)	Nov. 23	Jan. 1	B, Noon start opening day
1961	30	2	2	(2)	Nov. 24	Dec. 23	B, Noon start opening day
1962	25	2	2	(2)	Dec. 6	Dec. 30	B, Noon start opening day
1963	35	4	2	(2)	Dec. 2	Jan. 5	B, Noon start opening day
1964	40	4	2	(2)	Nov. 25	Jan. 3	C
1965	40	4	1	(1)	Nov. 25	Jan. 3	C
1966	45	4	2	(2)	Nov. 24	Jan. 7	D

ARKANSAS DUCK SEASONS – YEAR BY YEAR

Year	Total Days	Daily Bag Limit	Mallard Limit	(Hens)	Start	End	Notes
1967	40	4	2	(2)	Nov. 22	Dec. 31	D
1968	20	3	2	(2)	Dec. 6	Dec. 25	D
1969	30	4	2	(2)	Nov. 29	Dec. 28	D
1970	45	4	4	(4)	Nov. 27	Jan. 10	D
1971	50	4	4	(4)	Nov. 20	Jan. 8	D
1972	50	4	4	(4)	Nov. 25	Jan. 13	D
1973	40	4	4	(4)	Nov. 24	Jan. 19	D, Closed Dec. 9-25
1974	50	PS	3	(2)	Nov. 20	Jan. 18	D, Closed Dec. 8-17
1975	50	PS	3	(2)	Nov. 19	Jan. 14	D, Closed Dec. 10-16
1976	45	PS	4	(2)	Nov. 20	Jan. 14	D, Closed Dec. 12-17
1977	45	PS	4	(2)	Nov. 19	Jan. 7	D, Closed Dec. 12-16
1978	50	PS	3	(2)	Nov. 18	Jan. 18	D, Closed Dec. 11-22
1979	50	PS	4	(2)	Nov. 17	Jan. 5	D
1980	50	PS	4	(2)	Nov. 24	Jan. 17	D, Closed Dec. 8-12
1981	50	PS	4	(2)	Nov. 24	Jan. 17	D, Closed Dec. 14-18
1982	50	PS	4	(2)	Nov. 20	Jan. 13	D, Closed Dec. 13-15
1983	50	PS	4	(2)	Nov. 19	Jan. 17	D, Closed Dec. 12-21
1984	50	PS	4	(2)	Nov. 17	Jan. 10	D, Closed Dec. 10-14
1985	40	PS	3	(1)	Nov. 23	Jan. 13	D, Closed Dec. 9-20
1986	40	PS	3	(1)	Nov. 22	Jan. 12	D, Closed Dec. 8-19
1987	40	PS	3	(1)	Nov. 21	Jan. 11	D, Closed Dec. 7-18
1988	30	3	2	(1)	Nov. 26	Jan. 1	C, Closed Dec. 19-25
1989	30	3	2	(1)	Nov. 25	Jan. 1	D, Closed Dec. 18-25
1990	30	3	2	(1)	Nov. 23	Jan. 6	D, Closed Dec. 11-25
1991	30	3	2	(1)	Nov. 23	Jan. 5	D, Closed Dec. 3-13, Dec. 23-25
1992	30	3	2	(1)	Nov. 21	Jan. 3	D, Clsd Nov. 30-Dec. 11, Dec. 24,25
1993	30	3	2	(1)	Nov. 25	Jan. 9	D, Closed Dec. 6-17, Dec. 27-30
1994	40	3	2	(1)	Nov. 25	Jan. 15	D, Closed Dec. 5-9, Dec. 19-25
1995	50	5	4	(1)	Nov. 24	Jan. 21	D, Closed Dec. 11-15, Dec. 22-25
1996	50	5	4	(1)	Nov. 23	Jan. 19	D, Closed Dec. 9-13, Dec. 23-25
1997	60	6	4	(2)	Nov. 15	Jan. 18	D, Closed Dec. 1-3, Dec. 24, 25

PS - denotes bag limit determined by point system (In 1974-75, mallard hens 90 pts., drakes 35 pts.; '85-86, hens 100 pts., drakes 35; see page 89)
Shooting hours: A = 1/2 hour before sunrise to 1/2 hour before sunset; **B** = sunrise to sunset with noon start on season openers; **C** = sunrise to sunset; **D** = 1/2 hour before sunrise to sunset; **E** = sunrise to 1 hour before sunset with noon start on season openers; **F**= 7 a.m. until 4 p.m.

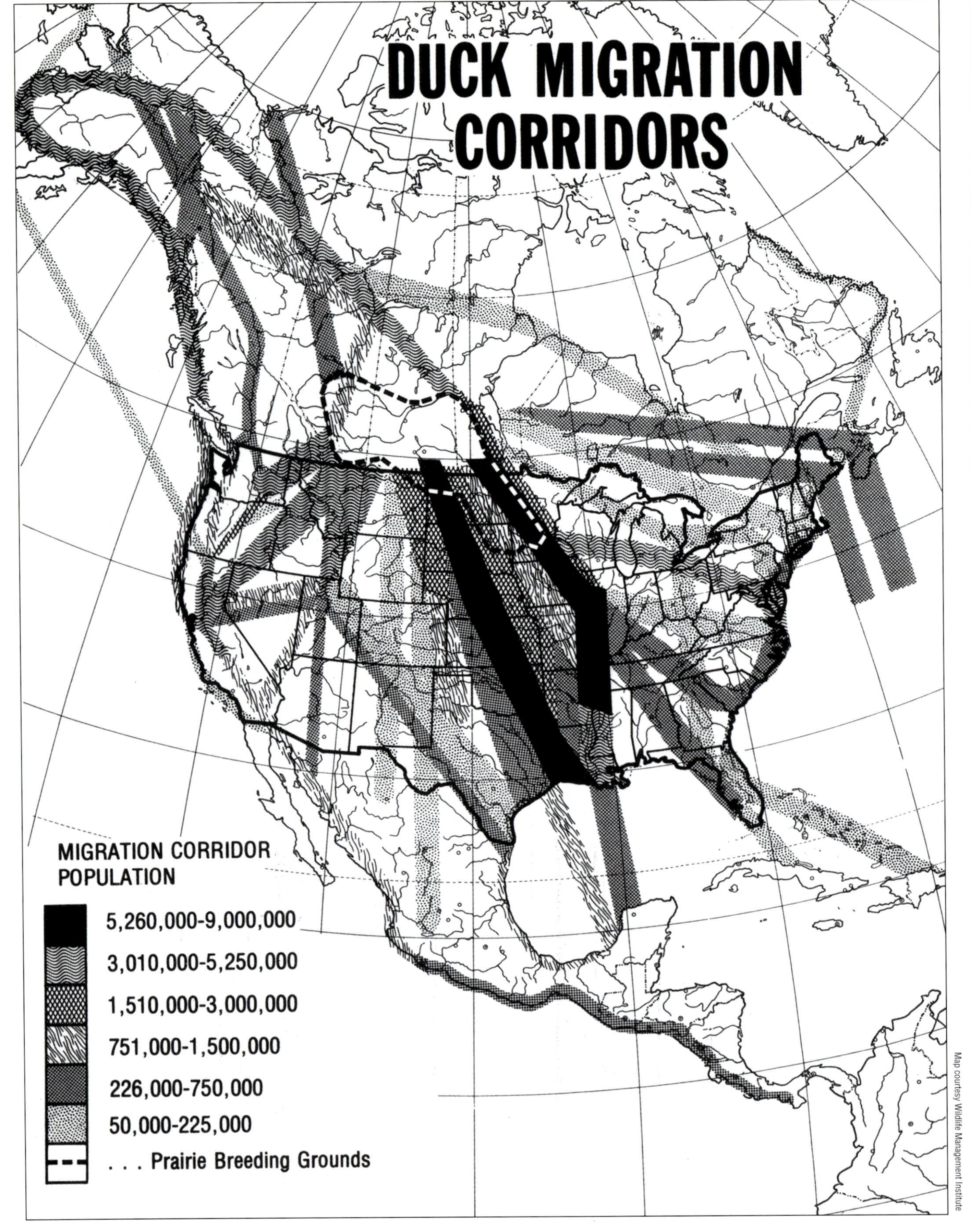
DUCK MIGRATION CORRIDORS
MIGRATION CORRIDOR POPULATION
5,260,000-9,000,000
3,010,000-5,250,000
1,510,000-3,000,000
751,000-1,500,000
226,000-750,000
50,000-225,000
. . . Prairie Breeding Grounds
Map courtesy Wildlife Management Institute

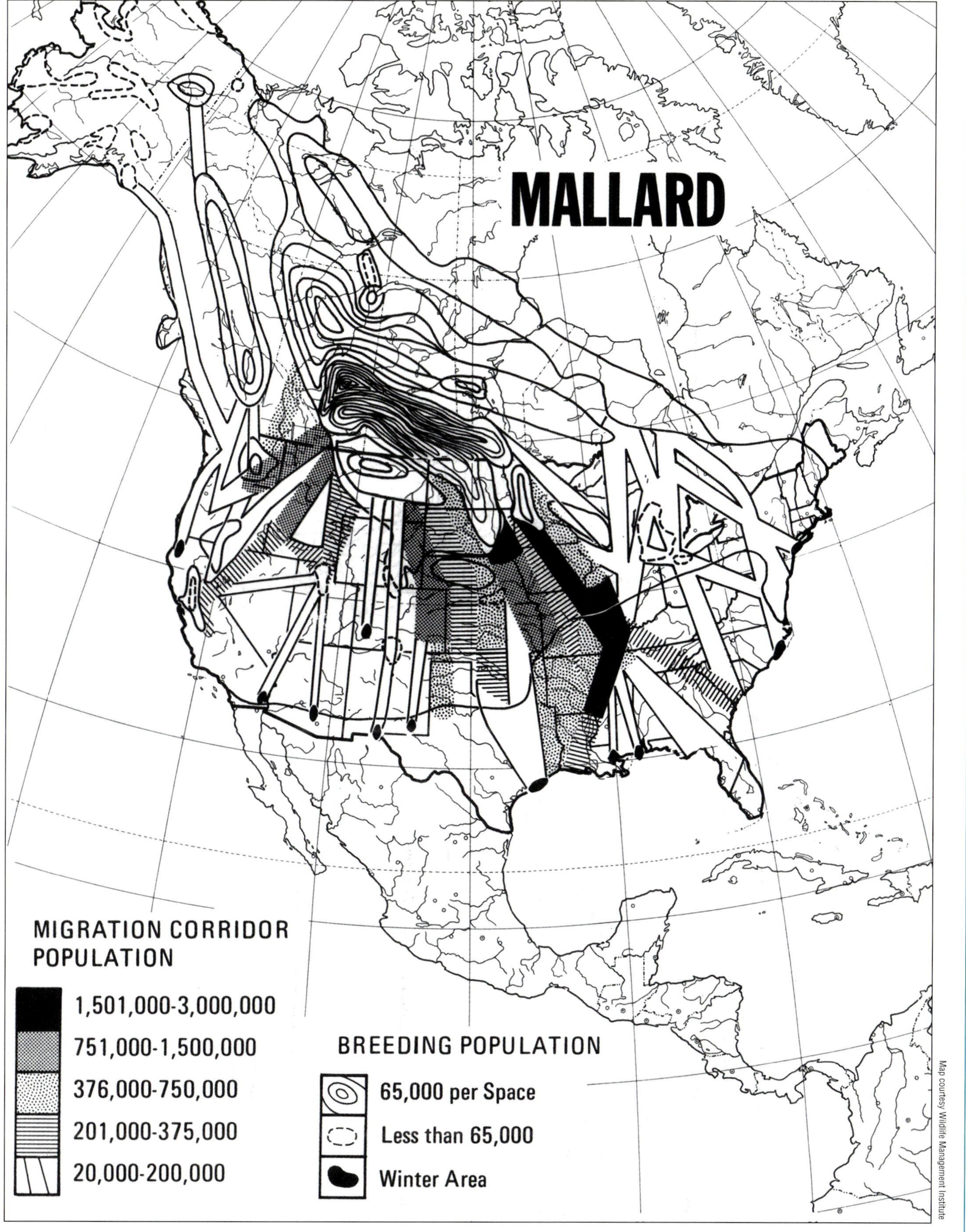
MALLARD
MIGRATION CORRIDOR POPULATION
1,501,000-3,000,000
751,000-1,500,000
376,000-750,000
201,000-375,000
20,000-200,000
BREEDING POPULATION
65,000 per Space
Less than 65,000
Winter Area
Map courtesy Wildlife Management Institute

A collection of Arkansas duck calls

Duck calls serve as a way to chronicle history of duck hunting in the state

Arkansas isn't the birthplace of duck call-making. That title probably belongs to Illinois. But Arkansas call-makers have been among the dominant influences in the craft since the end of the 19th century, when J.T. Beckhart began making his Big Lake style calls.

Because mallards are the most callable of all waterfowl and because mallards are the dominant species in the Mississippi Flyway, it's only natural that states along the Mississippi River would produce the great call-makers.

Arkansas' abundance of flooded timber further encouraged the development of duck calls. Even in the days when live decoys were permitted, a good duck call filled a need for hunters. Why mess with live decoys when all you had to do was hide next to a tree, kick some water and blow a duck call?

Louis W. "Biff" Morgan of Little Rock has always kept his own calls through the years. Duck calls become treasured personal mementos that mark times in your life. In the early 1980s, Morgan started seriously collecting calls made in Arkansas. His collection now numbers over 300.

"It gives me a chance to hunt all year long instead of just during duck season," said Morgan, who served as the president of the Callmakers & Collectors Association of American from 1994-96. "I enjoy hunting for them and meeting the people who have them. I like history, too, so it's a good combination."

Duck Calls: An Enduring American Folk Art, by Howard L. Harlan and W. Crew Anderson, provides an overall look at the development of duck calls.

It's important to note that "Arkansas style" duck calls aren't necessarily made in Arkansas. The term refers to the basic design of a duck call. Arkansas style calls feature a one-piece insert or stopper. (See photo above.) This one-piece insert style is common on most calls made today.

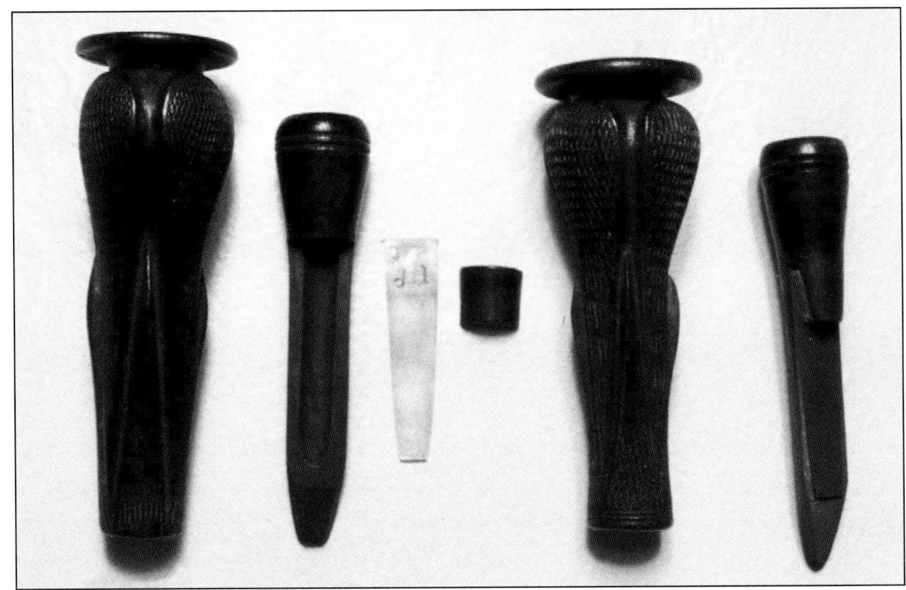

This photograph shows the difference between a "Reelfoot style" duck call (left) and an "Arkansas style" call (right). The main parts of a call are the barrel and the insert or stopper. The insert serves as a base for the reed, which is usually made of metal or plastic. The Reelfoot call uses a small, loose wooden wedge-block (shown in middle of the photo) to hold the reed in place. The Arkansas style call has a slit in the insert. A small piece of cork, inserted in the slit with the reed, holds the reed tightly in place, and no wedge-block is needed.

Both the Reelfoot and Arkansas style calls in the photo were made by Ira Green Ferguson of Hamburg from 1920-40.

The duck calls shown on the following pages represent an attempt to establish a base line of information about Arkansas-made calls. Craftsmanship separates Arkansas calls from those made in many other parts of the country. When early makers, like Beckhart and Pop Pickle, were turning out calls, it was the beauty of the hand-checkered wood and the various styles of the call-maker that often produced a sale.

Keep in mind that Big Lake in the state's northeast corner is the birthplace of Arkansas call-making. The far-reaching influence of Chick Major brought call-making to its extraordinary level in Stuttgart today. Other pockets of duck call-makers are sprinkled around the state.

Morgan selected the calls shown here from his collection. The order in which they appear follows a chronological format by general area. For instance, "Jonesboro area" starts with the earliest Big Lake and St. Francis River call-makers, like Beckhart and Ed St. Mary, and ends with current craftsmen, like Everett Baldridge of Hardy.

"Northeast Arkansas" might have been the best way to categorize these first four pages of calls. But that type of designation doesn't work as well when you try to separate Stuttgart, Pine Bluff and Little Rock call-makers. So the cities listed here are used as guidelines. Jonesboro is more or less the center point of the widespread northeast region. The "spheres of influence" are tighter around towns like Stuttgart and Pine Bluff.

If you've still got your grandfather's old duck calls in a shoe box in the attic, the following pages may help you determine exactly what you've got.

For identification, #1 is the call on the far left, the listings are left to right, so #6 is the call at the far right. The dates indicate the general period when each call was made.

JONESBORO AREA — 1. James T. Beckhart , Buck's Point, 1890s to 1922; **2.** Beckhart; **3.** Beckhart; **4.** Beckhart; **5.** Ed St. Mary, Manila, 1890s to 1920s; **6.** O.K. "Pop" Pickle, Otwell, early 1900s to 1939.

JONESBORO AREA — 1. O.K. "Pop" Pickle, Otwell, early 1900s to 1939; **2.** Pickle; **3.** Henry Kenward, Jonesboro, 1900s to 1930s, "New Bechart" ; **4.** Claude Stone, Hornersville (Mo.) 1909 to 1960s; **5.** Stone; **6.** John Henry Norris, Weiner, 1916 to 1940s.

JONESBORO AREA — 1. Mark Klusener, Otwell, 1920s to 1960s; **2.** Virgil Fryman, Weiner, late 1920s to early 1940s; **3.** Fryman; **4.** Fryman; **5.** Abner “Ab” Norris, Greenfield, 1928 to 1932; **6.** Leonard Pickle, Otwell and Jonesboro, 1930s to 1970.

JONESBORO AREA — 1. Melvin Shopher, Harrisburg, late 1930s to early 1940s; **2.** Roy Buttry, Jonesboro, late 1920s to 1940s; **3.** Warner Wiles, Jonesboro, late 1930s to 1960s; **4.** J.L. Tyner, Walcott, 1940 to 1965; **5.** Jack Carroll, Harrisburg, 1940s; **6.** Charley Brown , mid 1940s, Fisher.

JONESBORO AREA — 1. W. E. "Buck" Boyd, late 1940s to mid 1960s, Paragould and Mountain Home; **2.** Boyd; **3.** Willis Herndon, Leachville, 1940s to 1960s, Leachville; **4.** B.F. Brogdon, 1940s to 1960s, Blytheville; **5.** Dalton Elrod, Jonesboro, 1940s to 1960s; **6.** Robert L. Zirkle, Parkin, 1948 to 1996.

JONESBORO AREA — 1. W.L. "Aussie" Landers, Batesville, late 1940s; **2.** Kenneth A. Snider, Imboden, 1950s; **3.** Paul Stricklin, Paragould, 1950s; **4.** Robert A. White, Jonesboro, 1950s to mid 1960s; **5.** Ted Neal, Lepanto, early 1960s; **6.** Vinson Lay, Manila, 1966 to 1979.

JONESBORO AREA — 1. Hubert Barnes, Tulot, 1960s to 1992; **2.** Barnes; **3.** Unknown, Tuckerman area, early 1970s; **4.** Thurman McCann, Trumann, mid 1970s to 1990s; **6.** McCann.

JONESBORO AREA — 1. Everett Baldridge, Hardy, mid 1970s to 1990s; **2.** Grady White, Trumann, 1985 to 1990s; **3.** Blount Hohn, Diaz, late 1980s; **4.** Jerry Lane, Newport, mid to late 1980s; **5.** Shannon Hall, Jonesboro, 1990s; **6.** Randall Floyd, Monette, 1990s.

STUTTGART AREA — 1. Chick Major, Stuttgart, 1938, signed with ball burnisher; **2.** Major, 1939, rubber stamped; **3.** Major, 1939; **4.** Major, 1942, Dixie stamped; **5.** Major, 1950 to 1952, red and gold label, indented corners; **6.** Major, 1952 to 1959, red and gold label, round corners.

STUTTGART AREA — 1. Chick Major, Stuttgart, 1950s, Jake Gartner design; **2.** Major, early 1950s, Herb Parson call; **3.** Major, early 1960s; DuPont call; **4.** Major, 1960s, George Shaw call; **5.** Major, 1960s, Sportsman's One Stop call; **6.** Major, late 1960s, Princess Pat call.

STUTTGART AREA — 1. Chick Major, Stuttgart, 1960s, round label call; **2.** Major, 1971, North Little Rock Ducks Unlimited call; **3.** Major, early 1960s, Mel DeLang call; **4.** Major, early 1960s, Mel DeLang call; **5.** Major, early 1970s, laminated call; **6.** Major, early 1970s, "Save the Cache" call.

STUTTGART AREA — 1. Chick Major, Stuttgart, early 1970s; **2.** Major, early 1970s; **3.** Major, early 1970s; **4.** Sophie Major, Stuttgart, late 1970s, acrylic; **5.** Sophie Major, late 1970s; **6.** Sophie Major, 1979, mini call.

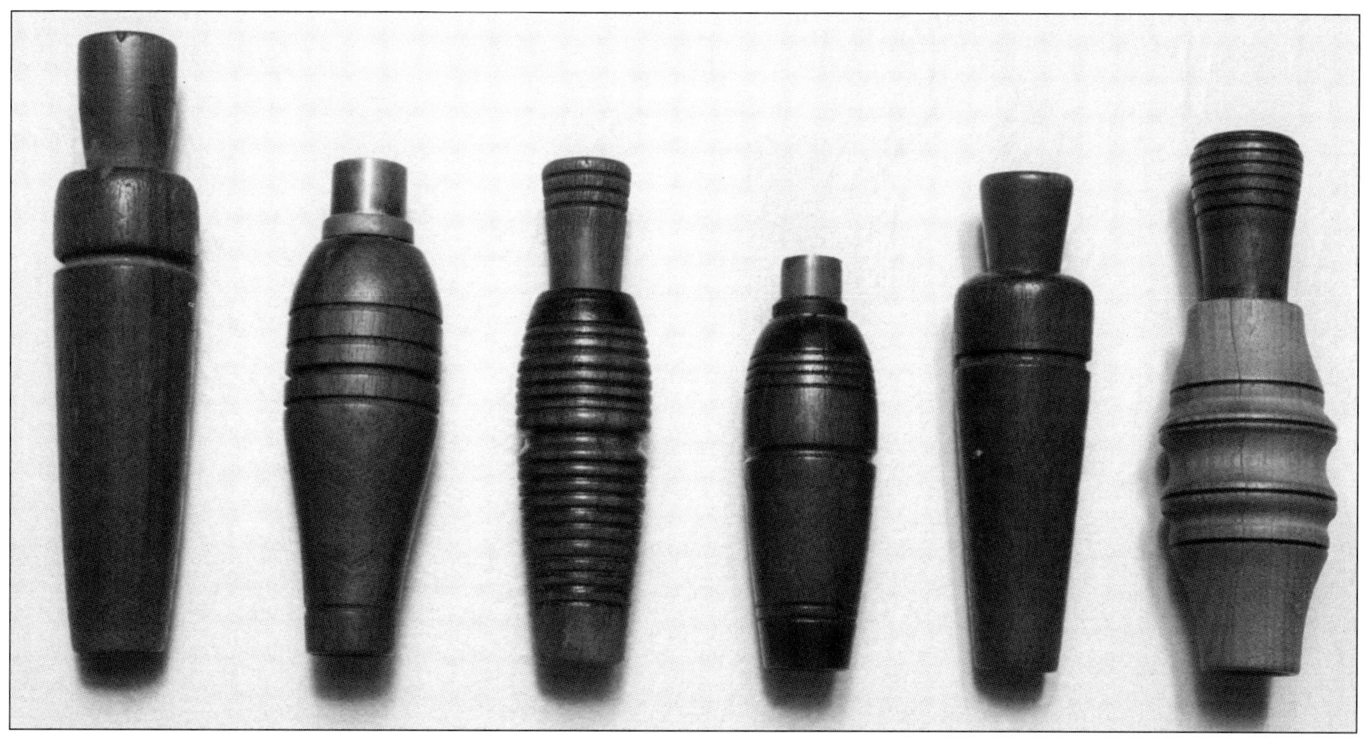

STUTTGART AREA — 1. Ruben Slifer, Stuttgart, 1915 to mid 1930s; **2.** William Lancaster, Stuttgart, late 1920s to 1950s; **3.** Lancaster, late 1920s to 1950s; **5.** Victor Selig, Stuttgart, late 1930s to 1950s; **6.** Frank A. Walton, Stuttgart, 1938 to 1950s.

STUTTGART AREA — 1. Clyde Hancock, Stuttgart, 1930s to 1950s; **2.** Hancock; **3.** Hancock; **4.** Hancock; **5.** Garland "Buddy" Rhodes, Stuttgart, 1940s to 1950s; **6.** Fred Wessels, Stuttgart, early 1940s.

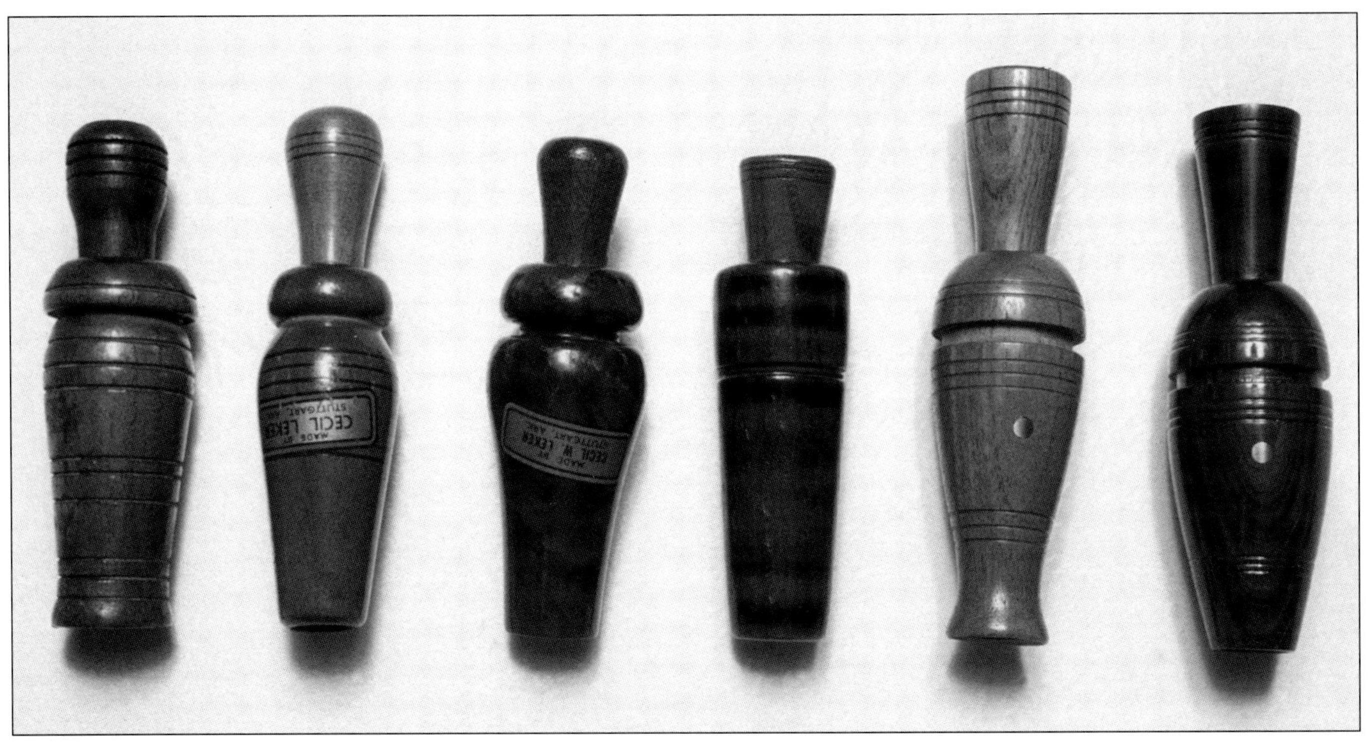

STUTTGART AREA — 1. Wade Grisham, Stuttgart, 1940s to 1950s; **2.** Cecil Leker, Stuttgart, 1940s to 1950s; **3.** Leker; **4.** Eddie Jacobs, Stuttgart, late 1940s to early 1950s; **5.** Tom Fricke, Stuttgart, 1947 to 1950; **6.** Fricke.

STUTTGART AREA — 1. Marion Bullard, Stuttgart, 1948 to 1950; **2.** Jake Gartner, Stuttgart, 1950s; **3.** Tip Masterson, Stuttgart, late 1940s to early 1950s; **4.** A.G. Duncan, Stuttgart, 1950s; **5.** Louis "Louie" Rabeneck, Stuttgart, 1950s; **6.** Irwin E. Millsap, Brummlt, 1950s.

STUTTGART AREA — 1. Pat Murphy, Stuttgart, 1950s; **2.** Raymond Staats, Stuttgart, 1950s; **3.** Norman Weatherly, Stuttgart, 1957 to 1980s; **4.** Danny Packabush, Stuttgart, 1960s; **5.** Waymond Ball, Stuttgart, 1960s to 1970s; **6.** Billy Starks, Stuttgart, #1 in a series of 25, 1980.

STUTTGART AREA — 1. Billy Starks, Stuttgart, mid 1970s to 1990s; **2.** Starks, "Wings Over the Prairie," #5 in a series of 50, 1986; **3.** Charles Marchand, Stuttgart, mid 1970s to 1990s; **4.** Harry M. "Butch" Richenback, Stuttgart, mid 1970s to 1990s; **5.** Richenback; **6.** Richenback.

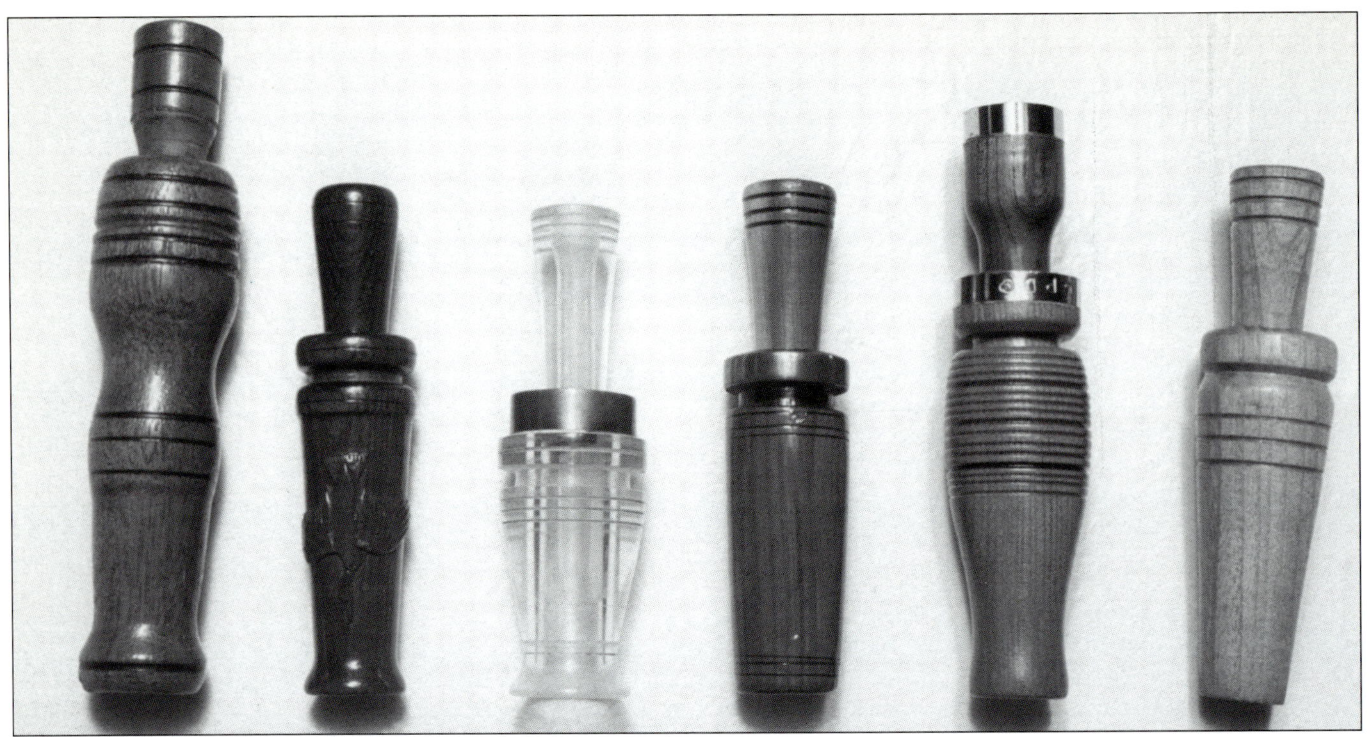

STUTTGART AREA — 1. Glen Rose, Stuttgart, 1980 and 1981; **2.** Norvell O. Peterson, Stuttgart, #5, 1981; **3.** James McCarty, Stuttgart, 1981 to 1990s; **4.** Don Hallinger, Stuttgart, 1982 to late 1980s; **5.** Glenn O. Rabeneck, Stuttgart, mid 1980s to 1990s; **6.** Andrew "Andy" Smith, Stuttgart, mid 1980s to 1990s.

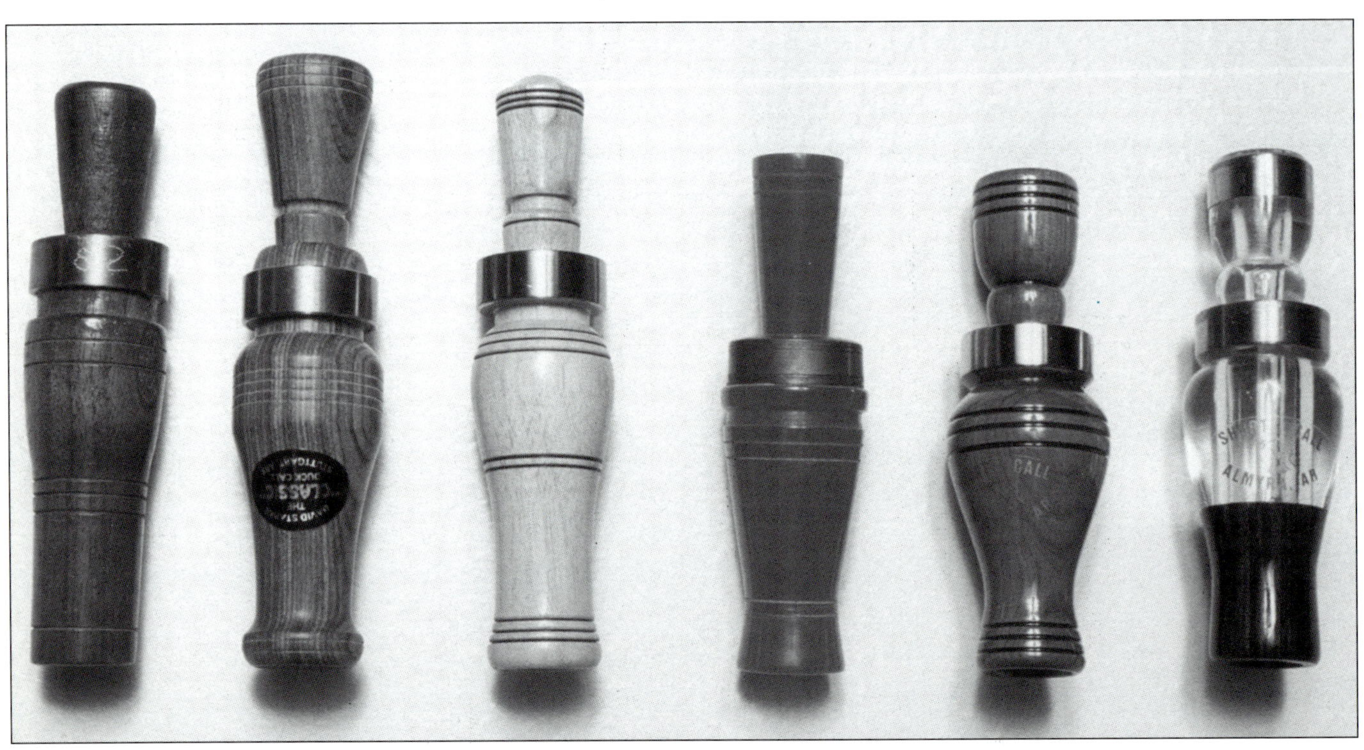

STUTTGART AREA — 1. Russell Calhoon, Stuttgart, #8, 1989; **2.** David Starks, Stuttgart, late 1980s to 1990s; **3.** Lloyd Snotzmeir, Stuttgart, mid 1930s to 1990s; **4.** Billy Starks, Stuttgart, mid 1970s to 1990s; **5.** W.A. "Short" Relyea, Almyra, early 1990s; **6.** Relyea, early 1990s.

STUTTGART AREA — 1. Henry Hollman, Gillett, 1930s to early 1940s; **2.** James Harold Rush, DeWitt, 1950s to 1960s; **3.** Pete Pittman, DeWitt, 1950s to 1960s; **4.** Roy Charles Goodwin, DeWitt, early 1970 to 1990s; **5.** Steve Goodwin, DeWitt, mid 1980s to 1990s; **6.** Lester Herman, DeWitt, 1990s.

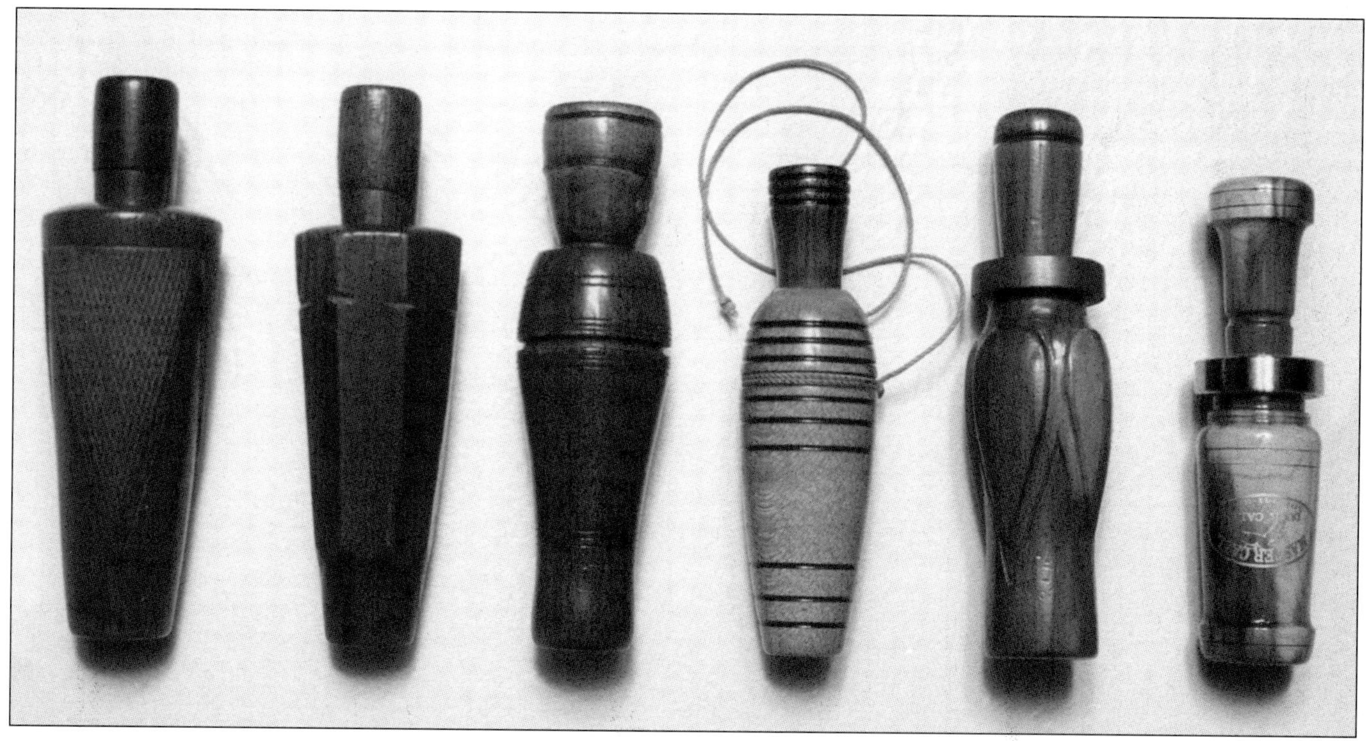

STUTTGART AREA — 1. E.A. Faifer, Clarendon, 1920s to early 1930s; **2.** Faifer; **3.** Jess W. Wilson, Roe, personal call at Wingmead Farm, 1940s; **4.** Ted Eans, DeValls Bluff, 1950s; **5.** John Walton, Roe, 1950s to 1980s, early style; **6.** Bill Lockridge, Roe, late 1980s to 1990s.

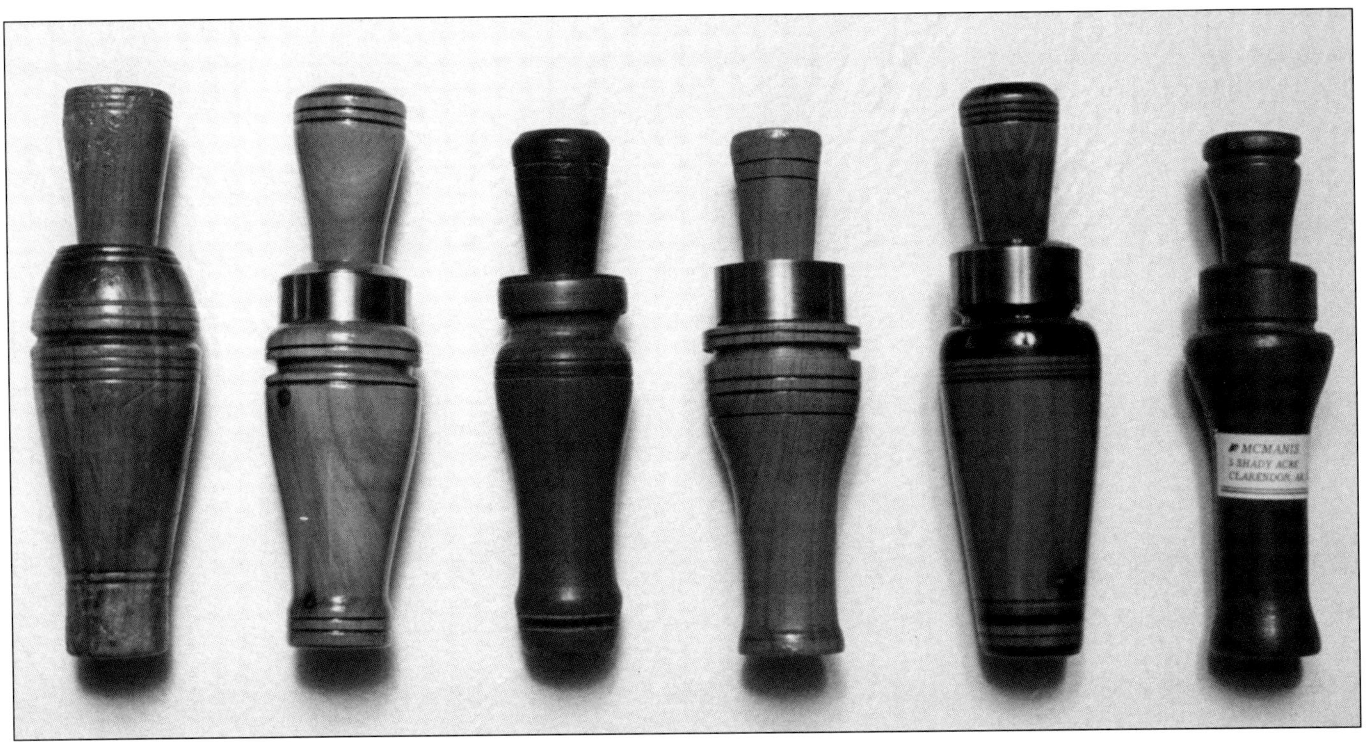

STUTTGART AREA — 1. Harrell Dean Vick, Hazen, late 1970s to early 1980s; **2.** Earl Jackson, Clarendon, early 1980s; **3.** Robert Kelly, Clarendon, early 1980s; **4.** Frank G. Keys, Clarendon, mid 1980s; **5.** Bobby Locke, Clarendon, mid 1980s; **6.** Bill McManis, Clarendon, mid 1980s.

STUTTGART AREA — 1. Clyde Tweedle, Clarendon, mid 1980s to 1990s; **2.** Alvin Taylor, Clarendon, mid 1970s to 1990s; **3.** Alvin Taylor, Clarendon, mid 1970s to 1990s; **4.** Virgil Gladish, Pepper's Eddy, late 1980s to 1990s; **5.** Grover Knoll, Clarendon, 1990s; **6.** Knoll, Clarendon, 1990s.

PINE BLUFF AREA — 1. Jo Willingham, Pine Bluff, early 1920s to 1930s; **2.** Ezra Cochran, Pine Bluff, late 1920s to 1940s; **3.** Cochran; **4.** Cochran; **5.** Cochran; **6.** John Jolley, Pine Bluff, Memphis and West Memphis, late 1920s to 1940s.

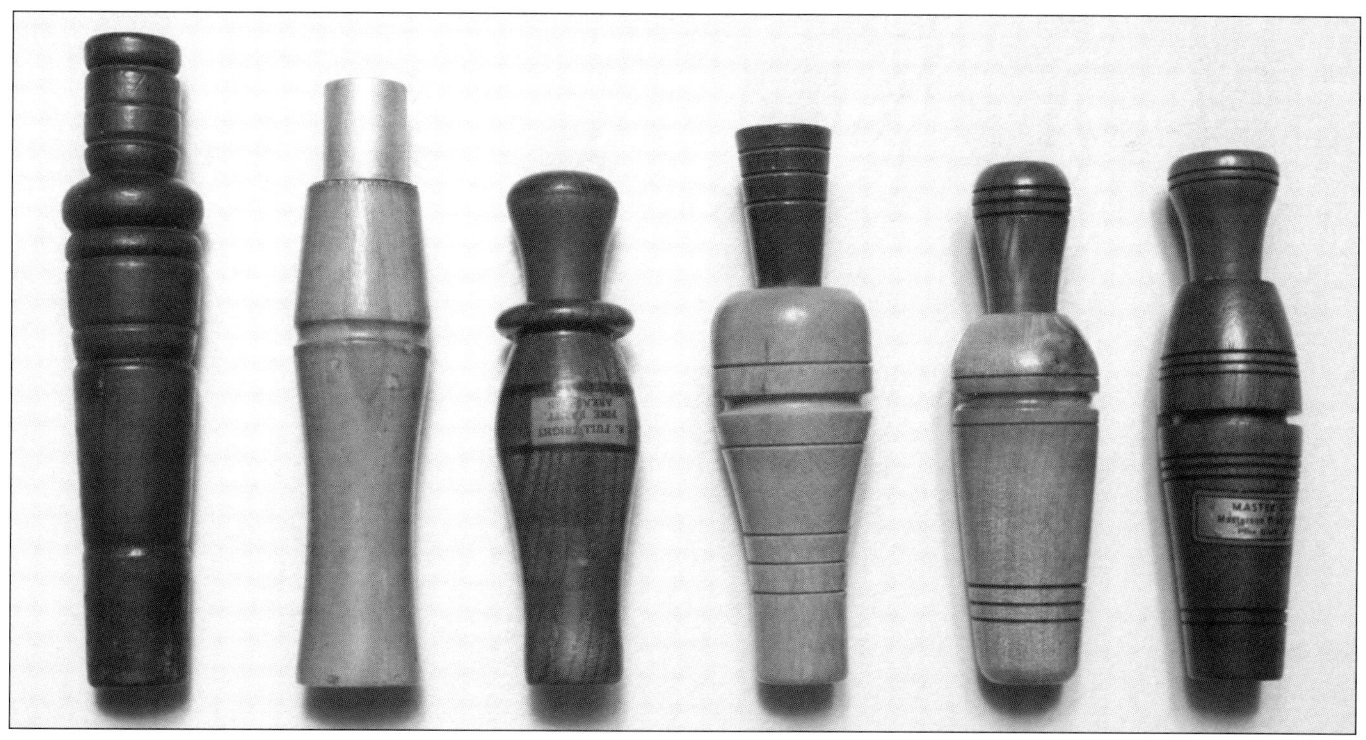

PINE BLUFF AREA — 1. T.J. Craig, Pine Bluff, 1940s to early 1950s; **2.** William M. "Bill" Carraway, Fordyce and Pine Bluff, 1930s to 1950s; **3.** Austin Fulbright, Pine Bluff, 1950s; **4.** Walter Bleau, Pine Bluff, 1950s; **5.** Buster Evans, Pine Bluff, 1950 to 1975; **6.** Tip Masterson, Pine Bluff, 1950s.

PINE BLUFF AREA — 1. Marvin Bell, Pine Bluff, 1950s to 1960s; **2.** Vedna Otis Johnson, Gould, mid 1970s to 1980s; **3.** Charles Robnett, Sheridan, 1960s; **4.** O.W. Clowers, Grapevine, 1960s to 1980s; **5.** Don and Brenda Cahill, Pine Bluff, mid 1970s to 1990s; **6.** Bobby Watson, Sheridan, early 1990s.

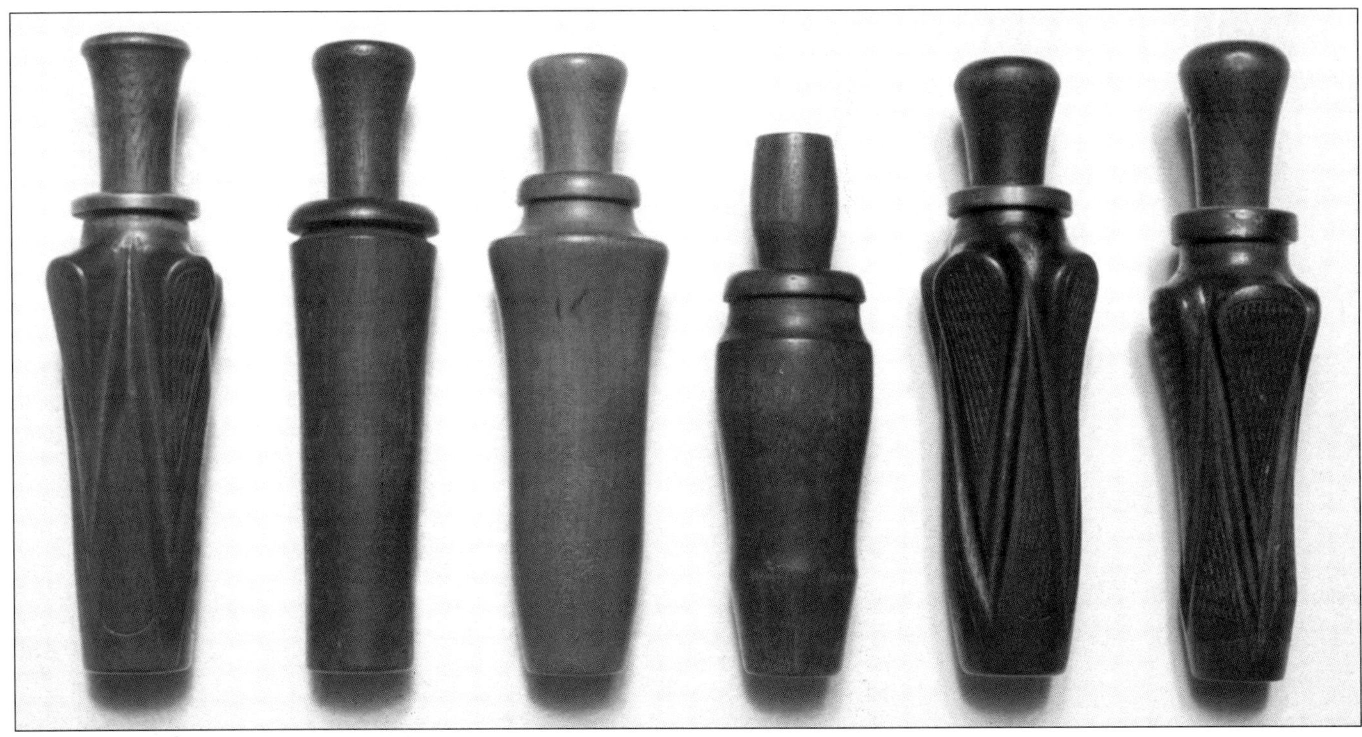

LITTLE ROCK AREA — 1. Andy Bowles, Little Rock, late 1930s to 1970s; **2.** Bowles; **3.** Bowles; **4.** Bowles; **5.** Bowles; **6.** Bowles.

LITTLE ROCK AREA — 1. Andy Bowles, Little Rock, late 1930s to 1970s; **2.** Bowles; **3.** Bowles; **4.** Bowles; **5.** Bowles; **6.** Bowles.

LITTLE ROCK AREA — 1. Pete Caldwell, North Little Rock, 1930s to 1940s; **2.** Caldwell; **3.** Mark D. Weedman, Little Rock, 1930s to 1980s, "Bicentennial," 1976; **4.** Weedman; **5.** Buddy Jones, North Little Rock, 1950s; **6.** LeRoy Elliott, Little Rock, 1974 to 1979, "Ring Neck."

LITTLE ROCK AREA — 1. Pete Jaworski, North Little Rock, mid 1970s; **2.** John Rather, Little Rock, mid 1970s; **3.** Bill Tedford, Little Rock, mid 1970s to early 1980s; **4.** Tedford; **5.** Tedford; **6.** Dick Stewart, North Little Rock, 1974 to 1990s, pear style.

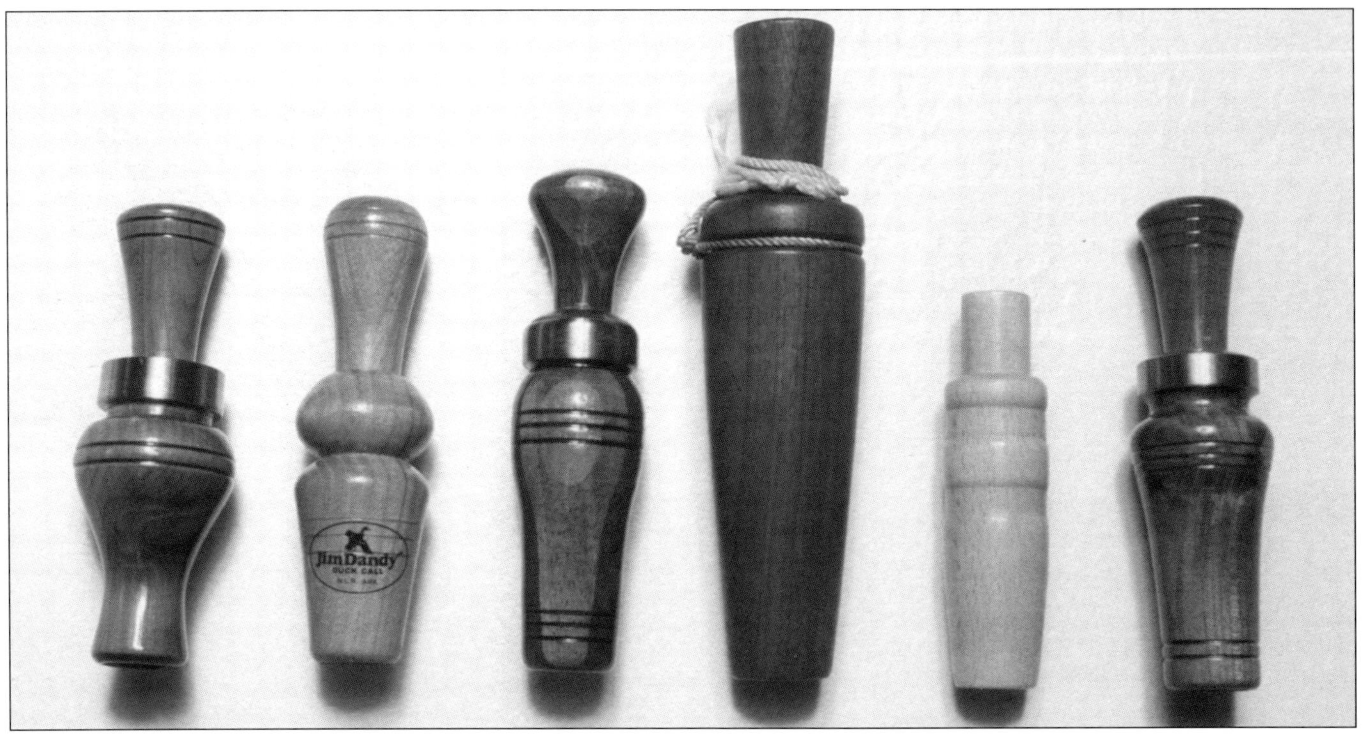

LITTLE ROCK AREA — 1. Rick Dunn, Jacksonville, mid 1970s to 1990s; **2.** Jim Allen Pearson, North Little Rock, mid 1980s, "Jim Dandy"; **3.** Ken Gathright, North Little Rock, mid 1980s to 1990s; **4.** Paul Dickenson, Little Rock, early to mid 1980s; **5.** William Lloyd Duncan, Little Rock, 1985 to 1987; **6.** Ben Rinke, Little Rock, late 1980s to 1994.

LITTLE ROCK AREA — 1. Jim Newell, Little Rock, 1988 to 1994; **2.** William P. "Billy" Selby, Little Rock, 1990s; **3.** Kenny Cartwright, North Little Rock, 1990s; **4.** Jerry Campbell, Stuttgart and Little Rock, mid 1980s to 1990s; **5.** Stan Martin, North Little Rock, 1990s; **6.** Murray Hunt, Little Rock, 1990s.

LITTLE ROCK AREA — 1. F.B. Withers, Lonoke, late 1940s to mid 1950s; **2.** Withers; **3.** W.J. Berry, Lonoke, 1950s; **4.** Rex Capps, England, early 1980s, early style; **5.** Capps, 1987; **6.** Capps, late 1980s to 1990s.

LITTLE ROCK AREA — 1. Howard Amaden, Lonoke, late 1940s to early 1950s, red and gold label; **2.** Amaden, late 1940s to early 1950s, red and gold label; **3.** Amaden, early 1950s to 1963, blue and white label; **4.** Amaden, 1963 to early 1970s, red label; **5.** Amaden, early 1970s to late 1970s, dark green label; **6.** Amaden, early 1970s to late 1970s, light green label.

LITTLE ROCK AREA — 1. Howard Amaden, Lonoke, late 1970s to early 1980s, silver label; **2.** Amaden, late 1970s to early 1980s, silver label; **3.** Amaden, late 1970s, "Ace Call" made for Babe Dabbs in Humphrey; **4.** Amaden, 1980s, gold label; **5.** Amaden, 1980s, gold and black label; **6.** Amaden, 1987, "Signature Series" - #19 of 50.

VARIOUS AREAS — 1. Ira Green Ferguson, Hamburg, 1920s to 1940s; **2.** Ferguson; **3.** Jack Smith, El Dorado, 1950s; **4.** Dan Whiddon, El Dorado, 1948 to late 1980s; **5.** E.J. Tweedle, El Dorado, 1960s to 1980s; **6.** Mike and Roger Morton, El Dorado, mid 1980s to 1990s.

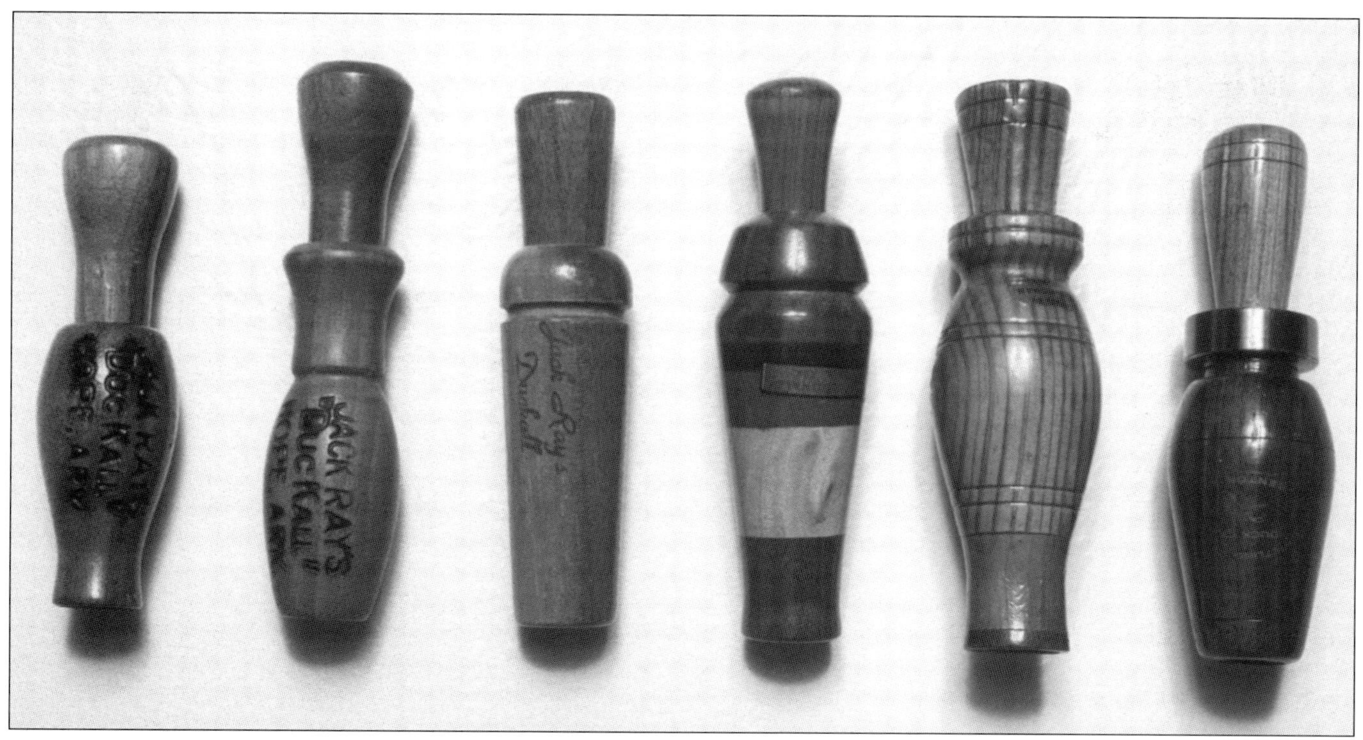

VARIOUS AREAS — 1. Jack Ray, Hope, 1950s; **2.** Ray; **3.** Ray; **4.** K.W. "Keety" McDonald, Benton, 1950s; **5.** Robert B. "Uncle Bob" Homan, Benton, 1950s to early 1960s; **6.** Delaney Kinchen, Benton, early 1980s to 1990s, early style.

VARIOUS AREAS — 1. Delaney Kinchen, Benton, early 1980s to 1990s, later style; **2.** William Thornsberry, Hot Springs, "Hawkshaw," 1980s; **3.** Lohmans, 1980s, "Hog Call"; **4.** Weems Wild Call, Fort Smith, 1980s; **5.** Jeff Earhart, Fayetteville, 1990s; **6.** Mark Badgwell, Malvern, 1990s.

World's Championship Duck Calling Contest, 1936-97

Since 1936, Stuttgart has hosted the Wings Over the Prairie Festival and World's Championship Duck Calling Contest. The following is a list of champions in all sanctioned events held over the years:

Champion of Champions

1955: Art Beauchamp
Flint, Michigan
1960: Pat Johnston
Stuttgart, Arkansas
1965: John Liston,
Knoxville, Illinois
1970: Edward L. Holt
N. Little Rock, Arkansas
1975: Butch Richenback
Stuttgart, Arkansas
1980: Mike McLemore
Hendersonville, Tenn.
1985: David Starks
Stuttgart, Arkansas
1990: Johnny Mahfouz
Stuttgart, Arkansas

World's Champions

1936: Thomas E. Walsh
Greenville, Mississippi
1937: Harry R. Wieman
Stuttgart, Arkansas
1938: Harry R. Wieman
Stuttgart, Arkansas
1939: Kenneth McCollum
Stuttgart, Arkansas
1940: W.H. Claypool
Memphis, Tennessee
1941: M.T. McCollum
Stuttgart, Arkansas
1942: Herman Callouet
Greenville, Mississippi
1943: Clyde Hancock
Stuttgart, Arkansas
1944: Howard T. Conrey
Stuttgart, Arkansas
1945: D.M. (Chick) Major
Stuttgart, Arkansas
1946: Louis (Red) Wilhelm
Stuttgart, Arkansas
1947: J.E. (Jake) Gartner
Stuttgart, Arkansas
1948: J.E. (Jake) Gartner
Stuttgart, Arkansas
1949: J.E. (Jake) Gartner
Stuttgart, Arkansas
1950: Herb Parsons
Sommerville, Tenn.
1951: Herb Parsons,
Sommerville, Tennessee
1952: W. C. Cowaan
Memphis, Tennessee
1953: Fred Parnell
Baton Rouge, Louisiana
1954: Art Beauchamp
Flint, Michigan
1955: Pat Johnston
Stuttgart, Arkansas
1956: Pat Johnston
Stuttgart, Arkansas
1957: W.C. Cross
Greenwood, Mississippi
1958: W.C. Cross
Greenwood, Mississippi
1959: James Fernandez
Port Arthur, Texas
1960: Ed Landreth
Joplin, Missouri
1961: Pete Claett
Kansas City, Missouri
1962: Charles Stepan
Port Arthur, Texas
1963: Mel DeLang
Burlington, Iowa
1964: Mick Lacy
Knoxville, Illinois
1965: John Liston
Knoxville, Illinois
1966: John Liston
Knoxville, Illinois
1967: Fred Harvey
Galesburg, Illinois
1968: Edward L. Holt
N. Little Rock, Arkansas
1969: Edward L. Holt
N. Little Rock, Arkansas
1970: Edward L. Holt
N. Little Rock, Arkansas
1971: Larry Largent
Shelton, Nebraska
1972: Butch Richenback
Stuttgart, Arkansas
1973: Mike McLemore
Hendersonville, Tenn.

1974: Mike McLemore
Hendersonville, Tenn.
1975: Mike Starks
Little Rock, Arkansas
1976: Trey Crawford
N. Little Rock, Arkansas
1977: Mike McLemore
Hallsville, Texas
1978: Richard Schultz
Cedar Rapids, Iowa
1979: Vernard Solomon
Marshall, Texas
1980: Dan Sprague
Buffalo, Iowa
1981: David Starks
Stuttgart, Arkansas
1982: Sam Hoeper
Grandview, Missouri
1983: Don Ansley
Nashville, Tennessee
1984: David Starks
Stuttgart, Arkansas
1985: Mike Keller
Kansas City, Missouri
1986: Trey Crawford
Mayflower, Arkansas
1987: David Jayne
Clovis, California
1988: Johnny Mahfouz
Stuttgart, Arkansas
1989: Barnie Calef
Cedar Rapids, Iowa
1990: Roy Rhodes
Germantown, Tenn.
1991: Tim Gesch
Woodruff, Wisconsin
1992: Blake Haynes
Pine Bluff, Arkansas
1993: Trey Crawford
N. Little Rock, Ark.
1994: Buck Gardner
Collierville, Tennessee
1995: John Stephens
Stuttgart, Arkansas
1996: Jim James
Omaha, Nebraska
1997: Rick Dunn
Beebe, Arkansas

Women's World's Champions

1948: Patsy Fricke
Stuttgart, Arkansas
1949: Mrs. John Kruesi
Signal Mountain, Tenn.
1950: Sophie Major
Stuttgart, Arkansas
1951: Pat Johnston
Stuttgart, Arkansas
1952: Pat Johnston
Stuttgart, Arkansas
1953: Pat Johnston
Stuttgart, Arkansas
1954: Pat Johnston
Stuttgart, Arkansas
1955: Pat Johnston
Stuttgart, Arkansas
1956: Mrs. Nelle Young
Pine Bluff, Arkansas
1957: Brenda Peacock
Stuttgart, Arkansas
1958: Brenda Peacock
Stuttgart, Arkansas
1959: Mrs. Frank Camp
Memphis, Tennessee
1960: Mrs. Frank Camp
Memphis, Tennessee
1961: Billie Domingue
Port Arthur, Texas
1962: Billie Domingue
Port Arthur, Texas
1963: Mrs. Ruby Abel
Stuttgart, Arkansas
1964: Sophie Major
Stuttgart, Arkansas
1965: Dixie Major
Stuttgart, Arkansas
1966: Billie Domingue
Port Arthur, Texas
1967: Mrs. Ruby Abel
Stuttgart, Arkansas
1968: Billie Domingue
Port Arthur, Texas
1969: Dixie Holt
Stuttgart, Arkansas
1970: Patti Dabbs
Humphrey, Arkansas
1971: Dixie Holt
Stuttgart, Arkansas
1972: Patti Thompson
Alexander, Arkansas
1973: Patti Thompson
Alexander, Arkansas
1974: Lee Tackett
Stuttgart, Arkansas
1975: Malu Hammans
Stuttgart, Arkansas
1976: Malu Hammans
Stuttgart, Arkansas
1977: Lee Tackett
Stuttgart, Arkansas
1978: Malu Hammans
Stuttgart, Arkansas
1979: Lee Tackett
Stuttgart, Arkansas
1980: Michelle Maier
Stuttgart, Arkansas
1981: Michelle Maier
Stuttgart, Arkansas
1982: Michelle Maier
Stuttgart, Arkansas
1983: Natalie McCollum
Stuttgart, Arkansas
1984: Natalie McCollum
Stuttgart, Arkansas
1985: Jennifer Gill
Stuttgart, Arkansas
1986: Jennifer Gill
Stuttgart, Arkansas
1987: Tammy Whitcombe
Stuttgart, Arkansas
1988: Jennifer Gill
Stuttgart, Arkansas
1989: Cindy Brewer
Stuttgart, Arkansas
1990: Cindy Brewer
Stuttgart, Arkansas
1991: Cindy Brewer
Stuttgart, Arkansas
1992: Pollyanna Ford
N. Little Rock, Arkansas
1993: Amanda Dierks
Stuttgart, Arkansas
1994: Lucy McClain
Clarksdale, Mississippi
1995: Lucy McClain
Clarksdale, Mississippi
1996: Amanda Dierks
Stuttgart, Arkansas
1997: Charlotte Merritt
Searcy, Arkansas

Intermediate World Champions

1983: Bryan Hancock
Stuttgart, Arkansas
1984: Bryan Hancock
Stuttgart, Arkansas
1985: Bryan Hancock
Stuttgart, Arkansas
1986: Troy Broussard
Port Arthur, Texas
1987: Brandon Bauman
Stuttgart, Arkansas
1988: Lee Ward
Stuttgart, Arkansas
1989: Brandon Bauman
Stuttgart, Arkansas
1990: John R. Logsdon
Stuttgart, Arkansas
1991: Tracy Henley
Stuttgart, Arkansas
1992: Dean Watson, St.
Charles, Arkansas
1993: Richard Schnoor
Camanche, Iowa
1994: Brandon Sinkey
N. Little Rock, Arkansas
1995: Brandon Sinkey
N. Little Rock, Arkansas
1996: Drake Butler
Hope, Arkansas
1997: Drake Butler
Hope, Arkansas

Junior World's Champions

1948: Don R. (Corky) Owens
Hometown not known
1949: Donald Diamont, Jr.
Cabot, Arkansas
1950: Pat Johnston
Stuttgart, Arkansas
1951: (tie) Tommy Toll
Hazen, Arkansas, and
1951: (tie) Johnny Huntsman
Monroe, Louisiana
1952: Blanchard Causey, Jr.
N. Little Rock, Arkansas
1953: Blanchard Causey, Jr.
N. Little Rock, Arkansas
1954: Blanchard Causey, Jr.
N. Little Rock, Arkansas
1955: Brenda Peacock
Stuttgart, Arkansas
1956: Darvin Purdy
DeWitt, Arkansas
1957: Butch Richenback
Stuttgart, Arkansas
1958: Ronald Stepan
Port Arthur, Texas
1959: Mike Cheney
Groves, Texas
1960: Mike Cheney
Port Arthur, Texas
1961: Terry Freeman
Stuttgart, Arkansas
1962: Terry Freeman
Stuttgart, Arkansas
1963: Vicki Stepan
Port Arthur, Texas
1964: Steve Higginbotham
Marianna, Arkansas
1965: Steve Higginbotham
Marianna, Arkansas
1966: Dennis Hogan
Stuttgart, Arkansas

Junior World's Champions (cont.)

1967: David Starks
Stuttgart, Arkansas
1968: Jeff Williams
Bridge City, Texas
1969: Jon Mark Erstine
Stuttgart, Arkansas
1970: Doug Hartz
Stuttgart, Arkansas
1971: Tim Erstine
Stuttgart, Arkansas
1972: Sterling J. Sloan
Stuttgart, Arkansas
1973: Sterling J. Sloan
Stuttgart, Arkansas
1974: Todd Hartley
Stuttgart, Arkansas
1975: Tommy Bogard
Stuttgart, Arkansas
1976: Steve Murray
Stuttgart, Arkansas
1977: Kenneth Starks
Stuttgart, Arkansas
1978: Kenneth Starks
Stuttgart, Arkansas
1979: Cliff Haydel
Bossier City, Louisiana
1980: Rob Seidenschwarz
Stuttgart, Arkansas
1981: Bryan Hancock
Stuttgart, Arkansas
1982: Clint Wood
Summer, Mississippi
1983: Troy Broussard
Port Arthur, Texas
1984: Joseph Lee Ward
Stuttgart, Arkansas
1985: John Stephens
Stuttgart, Arkansas
1986: Brandon Bauman
Stuttgart, Arkansas
1987: Tracy Henley
Stuttgart, Arkansas
1988: Heath Stephens
Stuttgart, Arkansas
1989: Dean Watson
St. Charles, Arkansas
1990: Dustin Cutrell
Goodlettsville, Tenn.
1991: Amanda Dierks
Stuttgart, Arkansas
1992: Justin Worley
Memphis, Tennessee
1993: Justin Worley
Memphis, Tennessee
1994: Drake Butler
Hope, Arkansas
1995: Jonathan Murley
Castalian Springs, Tenn.
1996: Bailey Dickson
Stuttgart, Arkansas
1997: Sean Meadows
Christopher, Illinois

Arkansas State Champions

1948: David Young
Pine Bluff, Arkansas
1949: Marian Griffin
DeValls Bluff, Ark.
1950: Roland Getchell
Pine Bluff, Arkansas
1951: Bobo Hair
Stuttgart, Arkansas
1952: Jerry Hancock
Stuttgart, Arkansas
1953: Jerry Folsom
Stuttgart, Arkansas
1954: Homer Taylor
Jacksonville, Arkansas
1955: Pat Johnston
Stuttgart, Arkansas
1956: Jerry Hancock
Stuttgart, Arkansas
1957: E.R. Dabbs
Humphrey, Arkansas
1958: Charles Jackson
Gillett, Arkansas
1959: Charles Jackson
Gillett, Arkansas
1960: Roland Getchell
Pine Bluff, Arkansas
1961: Willis Eddins
Des Arc, Arkansas
1962: Dick Stewart
Little Rock, Arkansas
1963: Roland Getchell
Pine Bluff, Arkansas
1964: Leavell Smith, Jr.
Stuttgart, Arkansas
1965: Homer Taylor
N. Little Rock, Arkansas
1966: Homer Taylor
N. Little Rock, Arkansas
1967: Richard Martin
Stuttgart, Arkansas
1968: Edward L. Holt
Crossett, Arkansas
1969: E.R. Dabbs
Humphrey, Arkansas
1970: Jon Mark Erstine
Stuttgart, Arkansas
1971: Bill Cheek
Stuttgart, Arkansas
1972: Harry Richenback
Stuttgart, Arkansas
1973: John W. Jaco
Little Rock, Arkansas
1974: David Bisbee
Stuttgart, Arkansas
1975: David Starks
Stuttgart, Arkansas
1976: Trey Crawford
N. Little Rock, Arkansas
1977: Dr. John Hatley
Little Rock, Arkansas
1978: Charles Holt
Stuttgart, Arkansas
1979: Trey Crawford
Mayflower, Arkansas
1980: Mike Starks
Little Rock, Arkansas
1981: Allen Cheek
Humnoke, Arkansas
1982: Trey Crawford
Mayflower, Arkansas
1983: Todd Hartley
Stuttgart, Arkansas
1984: Bryan Hancock
Stuttgart, Arkansas
1985: Johnny Mahfouz
Stuttgart, Arkansas
1986: Robbie Hindman
Newport, Arkansas
1987: Bill Bobo
Pine Bluff, Arkansas
1988: Lee Ward
Stuttgart, Arkansas
1989: Bryan Hancock
Stuttgart, Arkansas
1990: Terry Horton
DeWitt, Arkansas
1991: Scott Stovall
Little Rock, Arkansas
1992: Virgil Sinkey
N. Little Rock, Ark.
1993: Rick Dunn
Jacksonville, Arkansas
1994: John D. Stephens
Stuttgart, Arkansas
1995: Dean Watson
St. Charles, Arkansas
1996: John F. Rogers
Little Rock, Arkansas
1997: Jason Coleman
Holly Grove, Arkansas

Chick & Sophie Major Memorial

1974: Scott Galloway
Stuttgart, Arkansas
1975: David Bisbee
Stuttgart, Arkansas
1976: Trey Crawford
N. Little Rock, Ark.
1977: Sterling Sloan
Stuttgart, Arkansas
1978: No Contest Held
1979: Jim Simpson
Stuttgart, Arkansas
1980: David Hohn
Diaz, Arkansas
1981: Wade Mock
Stuttgart, Arkansas
1982: David Cahill
Pine Bluff, Arkansas
1983: Freddie Ibbotson
Stuttgart, Arkansas
1984: Buddy Owen
Pine Bluff, Arkansas
1985: Dean Pappas
Pine Bluff, Arkansas
1986: Bryan Hancock,
Stuttgart, Arkansas
1987: Bobby Dunn
Jacksonville, Arkansas
1988: Kirk Coker
Stuttgart, Arkansas
1989: Lee Ward
Stuttgart, Arkansas
1990: John Stephens
Stuttgart, Arkansas
1991: William Reichenback
Stuttgart, Arkansas
1992: Jason Coleman
Clarendon, Arkansas
1993: Bret Prine
Stuttgart, Arkansas
1994: Dean Watson,
St. Charles, Arkansas
1995: Brian Smith
Stuttgart, Arkansas
1996: Amanda Dierks
Stuttgart, Arkansas
1997: Jeremy Spellmeyer
Stuttgart, Arkansas

ARKANSAS PUBLIC LAND

IN THE NORTH AMERICAN WATERFOWL MANAGEMENT PLAN

MISSISSIPPI RIVER ALLUVIAL PLAIN

ST. FRANCIS RIVER

State Areas	Total acres
Big Lake WMA	11,447
St. Francis Sunken Lands WMA	25,425
Federal Areas	**Total acres**
Big Lake NWR (USFWS)	11,038
Wapanocca NWR (USFWS)	5,485
St. Francis National Forest (USFWS)	3,000

Management Unit Subtotal — 56,395

CACHE RIVER / LOWER WHITE RIVER

State Areas	Total acres
Earl Buss / Bayou DeView WMA	4,435
Rex Hancock / Black Swamp WMA	6,284
Dagmar WMA	7,920
Trusten Holder WMA	4,406
Federal Areas	**Total acres**
Cache River NWR (USFWS)	39,000
Cache River Mitigation Lands (COE)	7,950
White River NWR (USFWS)	154,000
Trusten Holder WMA (USFWS)	1,490
Arkansas River (COE)*	10,500

Management Unit Subtotal — 235,985

BLACK RIVER / MIDDLE WHITE RIVER

State Areas	Total acres
Dave Donaldson / Black River WMA	22,798
Shirey Bay-Rainey Brake WMA	10,711
Henry Gray / Hurricane Lake WMA	17,524
Wattensaw WMA	4,500
Federal Areas	**Total acres**
Bald Knob NWR (USFWS)	14,900

Management Unit Subtotal — 70,433

BAYOU METO / LOWER ARKANSAS RIVER

State Areas	Total acres
Bayou Meto WMA	33,832
Holland Bottoms WMA	5,625

Management Unit Subtotal — 39,457

BAYOU BARTHOLOMEW / BOEUF RIVER / BAYOU MACON

State Areas	Total acres
Cut Off Creek WMA	8,937
Seven Devils WMA	512
Federal Areas	**Total acres**
Overflow NWR	12,247

Management Unit Subtotal — 21,696

WESTERN ARKANSAS RIVER VALLEY

State Areas	Total acres
Ozark Lake WMA*	37,861
Dardanelle WMA*	58,117
Johnson County Rest Area*	500
Petit Jean WMA	15,000
Galla Creek WMA	3,358
Ed Gordon / Point Remove WMA	8,400
Nimrod WMA*	3,550
Harris Brake WMA	2,866
Camp Robinson WMA	2,040

*AGFC and COE

Federal Areas	Total acres
Rockefeller Lake (COE)	8,224
Toad Suck Lake (COE)	11,966
Murray Lake (COE)	14,258
Holla Bend NWR (USFWS)	6,367

Management Unit Subtotal — 172,507

OUACHITA & SALINE RIVERS

State Areas	Total acres
Beryl Anthony / Lower Ouachita WMA	7,069
Federal Areas	**Total acres**
Felsenthal NWR (USFWS)	65,000

Management Unit Subtotal — 72,069

RED, SULPHUR & LITTLE RIVERS

State Areas	Total acres
Sulphur River WMA	16,520
Bois D'Arc WMA	5,883
Millwood Lake WMA#	29,200
Federal Areas	**Total acres**
Pond Creek NWR (USFWS)	27,300

Management Unit Subtotal — 78,903

(**Notes:** No waterfowl hunting is allowed at the following areas: Wapanoca NWR, Big Lake NWR, Holla Bend NWR, Johnson County Rest Area.)

*Lands associated with navigation system

AGFC and COE

TOTAL ACREAGE — 747,445

Selected Bibliography

Andrews, William F. *Nash Buckingham: Beaver Dam and Other Hunting Tales*. Germantown, Tenn.: Chubby Andrews & Co., 1993.

Baskett, Tom Jr. *The Arkansas Delta: A Landscape of Change*. Helena, Ark.: Delta Cultural Center, 1990.

Bellrose, Frank C. *Ducks, Geese and Swans of North America*. Harrisburg, Pa.: Stackpole Books, 1942.

Buckingham, Nash. *Blood Lines: Tales of Shooting & Fishing*. New York: The Derrydale Press, 1938.

—. *De Shootinest Gent'man*. New York: The Derrydale Press, 1934.

—. *Game Bag*. New York: G.P. Putnam's Sons, 1943.

—. *Hallowed Years*. Harrisburg, Pa.: The Stackpole Company, 1953.

—. *Ole Miss'*. New York: G. P. Putnam's Sons, 1937.

Carter, Jimmy. *An Outdoor Journal*. Fayetteville, Ark.: University of Arkansas Press, 1994.

Christensen, Robert D. *Duck Calls of Illinois 1863-1963*. DeKalb, Ill.: Northern Illinois University Press, 1994.

Day, Albert M. *North American Waterfowl*. New York: Stackpole and Heck, Inc., 1949.

Evans, George Bird. *The Best of Nash Buckingham*. Selected, edited and annotated by George Bird Evans. New York: Winchester Press, 1973.

Gerstacker, Friedrich. *Wild Sports in the Far West*. Edited by E. L. Steeves and H. R. Steeves. Durham, N.C.: Duke University Press, 1968.

—. *In the Arkansas Backwoods: Tales and Sketches by Friedrich Gerstacker*. Edited and translated by James William Miller. Columbia, Mo.: University of Missouri Press, 1991.

Grinnell, George Bird. *American Duck Shooting*. Harrisburg, Pa.: Stackpole Books, 1901.

Harlan, Howard L. and W. Crew Anderson. *Duck Calls: An Enduring American Folk Art*. Nashville, Tenn.: Harlan Anderson Press, 1988.

Hazelton, William C. *Days Among the Ducks: Adventures Hunting the Winged Pilgrims of the Air*. Chicago: William C. Hazelton, 1938.

Holder, Trusten H. *Disappearing Wetlands in Eastern Arkansas*. Little Rock, Ark.: Arkansas Planning Commission, 1970.

Hunter, Carl G. *Trees, Shrubs, & Vines of Arkansas*. Little Rock, Ark.: The Ozark Society Foundation, 1989.

James, Douglas A., and Joseph C. Neal. *Arkansas Birds: Their Distribution and Abundance*. Fayetteville, Ark.: University of Arkansas Press, 1986.

Linduska, Joseph P. (Ed.) *Waterfowl Tomorrow*. Washington, D.C.: U.S. Department of the Interior, 1964.

Mayor, Archer H. *Southern Timberman: The Legacy of William Buchanan*. Athens, Ga.: University of Georgia Press, 1988.

Queeny, Edgar M. *Prairie Wings*. Exton, Pa.: Schiffer Publishing Ltd., 1946.

Reiger, George. *The Wings of Dawn: The Complete Book of North American Waterfowling*. New York: Nick Lyons Books, 1980.

Smith, Loren M., Roger L. Pederson, and Richard M. Kaminski (Eds.). *Habitat Management for Migrating and Wintering Waterfowl in North America*. Lubbock, Texas: Texas Tech University Press, 1989.

Snowden, Deanna (Ed.). *Mississippi County, Arkansas*. Little Rock, Ark.: August House, 1986.

Sutherlin, Diann. *The Arkansas Handbook*. Little Rock, Ark.: Fly-By-Night Press, 1996.

Newspapers, Periodicals

Arkansas Democrat

Arkansas Democrat-Gazette

Arkansas Game & Fish

Arkansas Gazette

Arkansas Historical Quarterly

Ducks Unlimited

Field & Stream

Forest and Stream

Memphis *Commercial Appeal*

Outdoor Life

Sports Afield

St. Louis *Post-Dispatch*

Stuttgart *Daily Leader*

Resources

Arkansas Game and Fish Commission
2 Natural Resources Drive
501-223-6300
Licenses: 1-800-364-GAME
Web site — www.agfc.state.ar.us

Arkansas Department of Parks and Tourism
One Capitol Mall
Little Rock, AR 72201
501-682-7777
1-800-NATURAL
Web site — http://www.1800natural.com.

Arkansas Geological Commission
3815 West Roosevelt Road
Little Rock, AR 72204
501-296-1877
(Topographical maps)

The Nature Conservancy — Arkansas Field Office
300 Spring Building, Suite 717
Little Rock, AR 72201
501-372-2750
Web site — http://www.tnc.org

Arkansas Wildlife Federation
7509 Cantrell Road, Suite 104
Little Rock, AR 72207
501-663-7255

Ducks Unlimited Inc.
One Waterfowl Way
Memphis, TN 38120
901-758-3825

U.S. Army Corps of Engineers
P.O. Box 867
Little Rock, AR 72203-0867
501-324-5673

U.S. Army Corps of Engineers
2101 N. Frontage Rd.
Vicksburg, MS 39180-5191
601-631-5300

Richard E. Bishop, LTD.
P.O. Box 362
Ambler, PA 19002
215-628-2963

DU Tape Project
c/o Roy Hunter
P.O. Box 1002
Pine Bluff, AR 71613
(Edgar Queeny's *Prairie Wings* videotape)
Grisham's Art
2808 E. Matthews
Jonesboro, AR 72401
870-972-6050
(Arkansas duck stamps and prints)

Derrydale Press
P.O. Box 411
Lyon, MS 38645
601-624-5514
(Some editions of Nash Buckingham books remain in print.)

Ozark Delta Press
P.O. Box 4653
Fayetteville, AR 72702-4653
501-582-4696
(Arkansas Duck Hunter's Almanac)

Wildlife Management Institute
1101 14th St., N.W., Suite 801
Washington, D.C. 20005
202-371-1808

Acklen, Joseph H., 46
Aikman, Bill, 198
Aikman, Crutch, 198
Akers, Don, 144
Alexander, Bill, 102
Allen, Garner, 121
Anderson, Keith, 78
Apple, Bob, 103, 104, 105
Apple, W.M., 175
Arkansas Irrigation Company, 132
"Arkansas style" duck call, 228
Atwell, Randy, 207

Baker, Claude, 186
Baker, Drew, 213
Bald cypress, 106, 107
    Knees, function of, 107
Bald Knob NWR, 144
Ballistic Specialties, 78
Barnett, Jim, 63, 77
Barre, Tom, 96
Bayou DeView WMA, 93
Bayou Meto WMA, 173, 175, 176, 178
Beale, Mikey, 176
Beckhart, James T., 42, 43, 49, 51
Beery, Wallace, 117
Bell, David, 146
Bellrose, Frank, 18, 21, 104
Bell Slough WMA, 201
Bennett, Wendell, 144
Benson, Frank, 134
Big Lake, 39
Big Lake WMA, 53, 54, 55
Big Lake Shooting Club, 43, 44, 45, 46, 47
Bishop, Richard, 28, 130, 132, 134
Bois D'Arc WMA, 217, 218
Bowman, Melissa, 176
Black River WMA, 68, 69
Blankenship, Koehler, 55
Borecky, Joe, 32
Boyle, Bayard, 86, 87
Boyle, Snowden, 86, 87
Brewer, Bill, 71
Bridgforth, Bill, 179, 180
Brown, Toof, 86, 87
Bryant, Juanita, 179, 180
Bryant, Walter Will, 120, 178, 179, 180
Buchanan, William, 221
Buckingham, Nash, 39, 58, 59, 78, 130, 135, 186, 187
Buckingham Flats, 176
Buerkle, Adam, 113, 114
Buffalo Island Club, 57
Bullington, Randall, 202
Bumpers, Dale, 102, 103, 104
Burnley, Tim, 109
Bush, George 36
Butler, Drake, 217
Butler, Phil, 217
Byrd, Sam, 30

Cache River-Bayou DeView
    Channelization Project, 102
Cache River NWR, 111
Cahill, Brenda, 121
Cahill, Don, 121
Cannon Brake, 178, 179
Carpenter, Warren, 145, 146, 159
Carter, Jimmy, 36, 81, 83
Cassinelli, David, 100, 101
Chancey, Hubert, 32
Christine, Lynn, 153, 154, 155
Clark, Roland, 135
Claypool's Reservoir, 81, 153
Claypool, Sally, 86
Claypool, Wallace H., 34, 81, 84, 85, 86, 87, 89, 90, 117
Cleaveland, Malcolm, 106
Clinton, Bill, 37
Clouse, John, 78
Clouse, Von, 78
Cochran, George, 109, 155, 157, 158, 159, 160, 161
Coleman, Donald, 66
Coleman, Ewell Ray, 66, 67
Connolly, Matt, 138
Cook, John Ed, 33
Cook, Leonard, 32
Craft, Darrell, 83
Craft, W. L., 83
Craig, Robert A. "Lit", 75
Crawford, Trey, 110, 125
Crowe, Roger, 132
Cut-Off Creek, 211, 212

Daggett, Jimason, 60, 61
Dagmar WMA, 108, 109
Darling, Jay "Ding," 134
Davis, Herman, 17, 50
DeLamar, Nancy, 105
Denniston, Tom, 101
DeRosier, Elmer, 30
DeVazier, Jeff, 34
Dickey, Bill, 30
Dickey, Gus, 30
Diekhoff, Dick, 116, 117
Disney, Walt, 130, 131
Dixie Mallard duck call, 121, 124
Donaldson, Dave, 70
Drennan, Dr. S.A., 116
Ducks, red legged, 161
Duck bands, 204, 205
Ducks Unlimited, 132, 138, 139, 181, 202
Dunn, Rick, 119
Dyer Lake, 202, 203

Eason, Maurice, 133
Eddy, Edward Lee, 199
Evans, Bud, 207

Farmer, Brent, 54
Faubus, Gov. Orval, 116
Felsenthal NWR, 214, 215, 216
Fisher, George, 104
Fish Lake Club, 199
France, Vincent, 176
Freudenberg, Frank, 126, 136, 137
Freudenberg's Reservoir, 136, 137
Fuller, W.H., 24, 114

Galla Creek WMA, 192
Gallagher, John, 202
Gardner, Buck, 119, 123, 161
Gartner, Jake, 117
Gerstacker, Friederich, 17, 39, 81, 90
    Wild Sports in the Far West, 39
Gillett Hunting Club, 183, 185
Gleabes, Walter, 46
Glenn, Dr. H.V., 115, 116
Godwin, John, 173
Government Cypress, 176
Grammer, Lilly Mae, 75
Grammer, Norman, 75, 76, 77
Grant, Elmer, 137
Grassy Lake, 207, 221, 222
Gray, Henry, 143
Gray, Stan, 203
Green-tree reservoirs, 128
Grisham, Larry, 94, 95
Gulledge, Danny, 207, 213

Halowell Reservoir, 181
Hammerschmidt, John Paul, 21
Hancock, Clyde, 117, 124
Hancock, Rex, 18, 89, 99, 102, 103, 105
Harris, James, 220
Harris, Mike, 220
Harris Brake WMA, 195
Hartz, Doug, 37
Hartz, Jake Jr., 116
Hartz, Marion, 37
Harville, David, 148
Hempstead Co. Hunting Club, 207, 221
Higginbotham, West, 60
Hillman, Tommy, 18, 29, 139
Hi-Tech Redneck Club, 145
Hodges, Kaneaster Jr., 36, 83, 99, 110
Holder, Trusten, 26, 89, 174, 177
Holt, Eddie, 120
Hoolihan, E.J., 14
Horner, Jess, 51
Hornersville, Mo., 42, 43
Hunnicutt, Hal, 200
Hunter, Carl, 70, 86, 130, 131, 132, 134, 135, 188
Hunter, Mary Ann, 132, 133
Hunter, Roy, 132
Hurricane Lake WMA, 77, 143-46

Jackson, Andy, 182, 183
Jackson, Ewing, 182, 184, 186
Jackson, Vernon Jr., 182, 184, 185, 186
Jackson, Vernon Sr., 182, 183, 184, 186
Jarrett, Morris, 53, 54, 55
Jerk strings, 160
Jerry, Terry, 18, 208
Jeter, Billy, 173
Jones, Jerry, 17
Jones, Jeryl, 34
Johnson, Jim, 146
Johnson County WRA, 202
Johnston, Pat, 115, 116, 120, 122

KWAK, 115
Keyes, J.C., 32
Kilby, Rob, 157
Kliner, A.L. "Arnie," 32

Kyler, Hugh, 30

LaCotts, Clarence Elmer "Tippy" Jr., 132, 187, 188
LaCotts, Clarence Elmer Sr., 187
LaGrue Bayou, 130, 132
Lake Millwood, 219
Lancaster, W.J., 30
Leach, George, 91
LeBlanc, Lee, 94, 139
Leggett, Russell, 53, 54, 55
Lewis, Lake, 207, 208, 215, 216
Lindsey, Bruce, 37
Little River Drainage District, 49
Long Bell, 176
Lower and Upper Vallier School, 176
Lower Ouachita WMA, 216
Lyle, Albert, 33
Lyon, Frank Jr., 133
Lyon, Frank Sr., 133
Lyons, Tracy, 173

Maass, David, 94, 135
Mack's Sport Shop, 129
Madison, Phil, 34
Mahfouz, Johnny, 113, 125
Major, Brenda, 120
Major, Dixie, 120
Major, D.M. "Chick," 117, 120-22, 124
Major, Sophie, 120, 121, 122
Mathis, Greg, 219, 220
Matthews, John, 30
Matthews, Justin III, 184
Matthews, Somers, 184
McAnally, Bob, 193, 194, 195, 202, 203
McCall, Larry, 145, 159
McClellan, John, 102
McCollum, Dick, 127
McCollum, Earnest, 127
McCollum, Gilbert, 127
McCollum, J.W., 126, 127, 128, 129
McCollum, Johnny, 127
McCollum, Kenneth "Slick," 117, 126-277
McCollum, Lloyd, 89, 117, 126, 127
McCollum, Marion, 89, 125, 127, 129
McCollum, Marion III, 127
McCollum, M.T. "Mack," 117, 127, 129
McCollum, M.T. Sr., 127
McCollum, Maurice, 126
McCollum, Otis, 89, 126, 127, 129
McCollum, Robert, 127
McCollum, Roy Jr., 126, 127, 129
McCollum, Roy III "Bud," 127
McCollum, Russell, 127
McCollum, Thad, 89, 115, 116, 127, 129
McCune, J.B., 32
McDaniels, John, 148
McFarland, Barry, 49
Meacham, Wiley, 148, 149
Mercer Bayou, 220
Missouri Pacific Railway, 39, 163
Moist soil management, 181
Monsanto Chemical Company, 130, 131
Moore, Frank, 36
Morgan, "Biff," 228
Morgan, Randy, 211, 212
Morrilton Hunting and Fishing Club, 199
Morris, Mark, 208, 213

New Madrid earthquakes, 41
North American Waterfowl Plan, 29, 64, 82, 142, 191
Nimrod WMA, 194

Olt, P.S., duck call, 137, 180, 187
Overflow NWR, 213, 214

Paleo-Indians, 39
Peckerwood Lake, 128, 132, 133, 153
Peel, John, 36
Perdue, David, 105
Perry, Jason, 208
Perry, Scott, 208
Petit Jean WMA, 198, 199
Pickle, Leonard, 97
Pickle, O.K. "Pop," 96, 97
Pin oak acorns, 188
Pin oak flat, 188
Pleistocene Period, 39
Point Remove WMA, 201
Pond Creek NWR, 219, 220
Powell, Ben, 32
Prairie Wings, 132, 134, 135, 188
Pruet, Chesley, 37
Pulitzer, Herbert, 114, 136
Pulitzer, Joseph, 114, 136, 154
Purvis, George, 84, 85, 86, 87, 88

Queeny, Edgar, 58, 89, 128, 130, 131, 132, 133, 135, 187
Queeny, Ethel, 132, 133, 135

Railey, Herbert, 221
Ramsar Convention, 105
Rand, Art, 145
Ratcliff, Russell, 200
Red River, 217, 219
Reece, Maynard, 94, 135
Reel, Jimmy, 90, 91
"Reelfoot style" duck call, 228
Remmel, Rollie, 89, 137, 138, 148
Remmel, Ruth, 138
Reynolds, Bobby, 145, 159
Reynolds, Henry, 86
Riceland Hotel, 137
Richenback, Butch, 115, 121, 123-25
Rich-N-Tone, 121, 123, 124, 125
Ridout, Wayne, 145
Riley, Johnny, 32, 20, 87
Robbins, Harold, 30
Robinson, Bobby, 37
Roe, Charles "Preacher," 32
Rockefeller, Winthrop Paul, 139
Rollie Stick, 139
Roth, Roland R., 117
Routon, Bill, 222
Routon, Ralph, 222
Ruesewald, Fritz, 87, 90, 91, 92
Ruesewald, Rosalie, 92
Ruff, David, 118
Rusher, Buck, 36
Schilling, Henry, 30
Schneider, Jon, 181, 204
Seay, J.I., 30
Seven Devils WMA, 209, 210
Shirey Bay-Rainey Brake WMA, 73, 74
Simpson, J.D. III, 182, 183, 185, 186
Simpson, Jimmie, 186
Singleton, Dale, 157
Sitzer, Katherine, 83
Sitzer, Leonard, 83
Slivka, Judd, 177
Smith, Ed, 33
Smith, Steve, 148
Snead, Sam, 200
Spann, Melvin, 115
Stahle, Dave, 106, 107
Stansberry, Steve, 143
St. Francis Sunken Lands, 59
St. Mary, Ed, 51
Stone, Claude, 43, 49
Strebek, Tommy, 214
Sullivan, Jim, 109
Sulphur River WMA, 220

Tarver, Vernon, 180
Tent Camp, 182, 183, 184
Tindall, Verne L., 114, 115, 116, 128
Thomas, Frank, 139
Thompson, Don, 148
Tram, 176
Tucker, Gov. Jim Guy, 122, 178
Turner, Allen, 36
Turner, Hal, 36
Turner, Norfleet, 87

Urtle, Brian, 143

Visart, E. V., 45
Von Braun, Werner, 86

Wabbaseka Scatters, 176, 178
Walker, Charlie, 222
Walsh, Thomas E., 116
Ward, John, 211
Washington, Thurman "Tadpole," 204
Webb, Keith, 145, 159
White, Larry, 205
Whiting, John, 118
White River NWR, 141, 142, 155, 157
"Wide Wide World," 84
Widner, Dennis, 111, 144
Williams, Jerry, 193, 196, 197
Willie, Bobby Joe, 68
Wilcox, Albert, 152, 153, 154
Wilcox, George, 152, 153, 154, 155
Wilcox Lake, 152, 153, 155
Wilson, Jess, 133, 188
Wilson, Steve N., 71, 105, 148
Wingmead Farms, 130, 133-34, 187-88
Wings Over the Prairie Festival, 118, 122
World's Championship Duck Calling Contest, 117-118, 121-122, 125-28
Wright, Earl, 30
Yaich, Scott, 23, 26, 177, 193
Yellow Creek Club, 222
Zebree archeological site, 39

MERRY CHRISTMAS
ETHEL AND EDGAR QUEENY ~ 1956
RICHARD E. BISHOP